Clinical Handbook of Obsessive-Compulsive Disorder and Related Problems

Clinical Handbook of Obsessive-Compulsive Disorder and Related Problems

Edited by
Jonathan S. Abramowitz
Associate Professor
Department of Psychology
University of North Carolina at Chapel Hill
Chapel Hill, North Carolina

Dean McKay
Associate Professor
Department of Psychology
Fordham University
Bronx, New York

and

Steven Taylor
Professor
Department of Psychiatry
University of British Columbia
Vancouver, British Columbia

The Johns Hopkins University Press
Baltimore

© 2008 The Johns Hopkins University Press
All rights reserved. Published 2008
Printed in the United States of America on acid-free paper
9 8 7 6 5 4 3 2 1

The Johns Hopkins University Press
2715 North Charles Street
Baltimore, Maryland 21218-4363
www.press.jhu.edu

Library of Congress Cataloging-in-Publication Data
Clinical handbook of obsessive-compulsive disorder and related problems /
edited by Jonathan S. Abramowitz, Dean McKay, and Steven Taylor.
    p. ; cm.
    Includes bibliographical references and index.
    ISBN-13: 978-0-8018-8697-3 (hardcover : alk. paper)
    ISBN-10: 0-8018-8697-X (hardcover : alk. paper)
    1. Obsessive-compulsive disorder—Handbooks, manuals, etc.
2. Compulsive behavior—Handbooks, manuals, etc. I. Abramowitz,
Jonathan S. II. McKay, Dean, 1966– III. Taylor, Steven, 1960–
    [DNLM: 1. Obsessive-Compulsive Disorder—psychology. 2. Obsessive-
Compulsive Disorder—therapy. 3. Mental Disorders—complications.
4. Obsessive Behavior—psychology. 5. Obsessive Behavior—therapy.
WM 176 C6405 2007]
    RC533.C633 2007
    616.85'227—dc22   2007023652

A catalog record for this book is available from the British Library.

Special discounts are available for bulk purchases of this book.
For more information, please contact Special Sales at 410-516-6936
or specialsales@press.jhu.edu.

To Stacy, Emily, and Miriam with love
J.S.A.

To Rebecca and Dawn with love
D.M.

To Amy and Alex with love
S.T.

Contents

	Foreword, by Gail Steketee	ix
	Preface	xi
	List of Contributors	xv

PART I: Subtyping Obsessive-Compulsive Disorder 1

1. Making Sense of Obsessive-Compulsive Disorder: Do Subtypes Exist? 5
   Steven Taylor, Dean McKay, and Jonathan S. Abramowitz
2. Fears of Contamination 18
   Dean McKay and Reuben Robbins
3. Compulsive Checking 30
   Johan Rosqvist and Darcy C. Norling
4. Ordering, Incompleteness, and Arranging 44
   Laura J. Summerfeldt
5. Unacceptable Obsessional Thoughts and Covert Rituals 61
   Christine Purdon
6. Compulsive Hoarding 76
   Randy O. Frost and David F. Tolin
7. The PANDAS Subgroup of Obsessive-Compulsive Disorder 95
   Kyle Allen Williams, Jon E. Grant, and Suck Won Kim
8. Obsessive-Compulsive Disorder with Poor Insight 109
   Cheryl Carmin, Pamela S. Wiegartz, and Kevin Wu
9. Obsessive-Compulsive Disorder and Schizotypy 126
   Dean McKay and Patricia Gruner
10. Postpartum Obsessive-Compulsive Disorder 139
    Jonathan S. Abramowitz and Nichole Fairbrother

11	Scrupulosity Jonathan S. Abramowitz	156

PART II: Problems Related to Obsessive-Compulsive Disorder — 173

12	The Empirical Basis of the Obsessive-Compulsive Spectrum Dan J. Stein and Christine Lochner	177
13	Eating Disorders Randi E. McCabe and Michele Boivin	188
14	Trichotillomania Douglas W. Woods, Amanda C. Adcock, and Christine A. Conelea	205
15	Impulse-Control Disorders Jon E. Grant and Patrick Marsh	222
16	Autistic Syndromes Christopher J. McDougle, Leslie A. Hulvershorn, Craig A. Erickson, Kimberly A. Stigler, and David J. Posey	238
17	Nonparaphilic Sexual Disorders Elias Aboujaoude and Lorrin M. Koran	257
18	Tourette Syndrome and Chronic Tic Disorders Kieron P. O'Connor and Julie Leclerc	270
19	Body Dysmorphic Disorder David H. Gleaves and Suman Ambwani	288
20	Hypochondriasis Steven Taylor and Gordon J. G. Asmundson	304
21	Obsessive-Compulsive Personality Disorder Jane L. Eisen, Maria C. Mancebo, Kimberley L. Chiappone, Anthony Pinto, and Steven A. Rasmussen	316

Index — 335

Foreword

I am more than a little pleased to see a volume of this nature make it into print. As clinicians and researchers, we can only benefit from reading the level of detail requested by my thoughtful colleagues Jonathan Abramowitz, Dean McKay, and Steven Taylor, who envisioned this work and have put it together so well. The question of how to classify the many variants of obsessive-compulsive disorder (OCD) has fascinated scholars from the beginning of efforts to formulate systematic treatments. Here, we get to explore the topic in depth with astute clinical insights.

I am biased—treating OCD and its related conditions has been my life's work—but I consider OCD a fascinating problem in no small part because of its many and varied manifestations. As a clinician, I have never felt bored by working out the strategies for treating patients' problems. Each person presents with symptoms I have never before seen in quite this fashion. The challenge is to understand how each patient's obsessions operate in real time, so it becomes clearer what I should do to interrupt the vicious cycle because a vicious cycle is always propelled by compulsive rituals.

Like most clinicians with behavioral training, I always felt I had a good set of tools to ply my trade, using exposure and blocking rituals and avoidance (i.e., response prevention). The advent of cognitive therapy for OCD, with the pioneering work of Paul Salkovskis, Paul Emmelkamp, Patricia Van Oppen, Mark Freeston, Jean Cottraux, and now many others, added new tools to my clinical arsenal. I also relied on my psychiatric colleagues for the latest advancements in medications that might be needed to jump-start treatment or supplement my cognitive-behavioral therapy (CBT) skills. It is especially interesting to consider how patients with differing symptoms of OCD respond to these treatments and how those with the so-called OCD spectrum disorders require special treatment variations, even different interventions. My recent work with compulsive hoarding and body dysmorphic disorder has presented special challenges. Standard CBT methods seem helpful but insufficient to resolve these problems. We are only beginning to understand these conditions and we have much to learn. This book is a fine start toward advancing our understanding and improving our patients' lives.

Gail Steketee, Ph.D.
Professor, Department of Clinical Practice, and Dean ad interim
Boston University School of Social Work

Preface

The current edition of the *Diagnostic and Statistical Manual of Mental Disorders* (DSM-IV-TR; American Psychiatric Association, 2000) offers a general definition of obsessive-compulsive disorder (OCD) that includes obsessions and compulsions, although the specific manifestation of these symptoms varies widely from patient to patient. For example, obsessions about contamination, harm, morality, exactness, sexual behavior, or religion are common among those with the disorder. Compulsive rituals such as washing, checking, arranging, or mental rituals, as well as avoidance of situations that provoke the obsessions, are also present.

A scientific understanding of OCD and other psychiatric conditions entails an attempt, in Plato's words, to "carve nature at its joints" (Hackforth, 1952). As research on the nature and treatment of OCD has accrued, it has become increasingly apparent that this disorder is heterogeneous and possibly composed of many different subtypes. Although the subtypes may share overlapping etiologic mechanisms and may respond to similar treatments, there appear to be some important differences. Advances in understanding and treating OCD may arise from a better understanding of the essential similarities and differences among these subtypes.

Research and clinical observations have increasingly suggested that OCD shares many similarities with other disorders. As we will see later in this volume, some experts have proposed a "spectrum" of obsessive-compulsive disorders encompassing between 10 and 20 such conditions. Examples include trichotillomania, body dysmorphic disorder, and Tourette syndrome. Such disorders seem not only to have symptoms similar to obsessions and compulsions but also respond to treatments similar to those used for OCD. The concept of spectrum disorders is not without controversy. Nevertheless, advances in understanding and treating the so-called spectrum disorders may arise from a more critical examination of how they are similar to and different from OCD.

Spectrum conditions are defined by some similarities to OCD, whereas subtypes are defined by differences among patterns of obsessive-compulsive symptoms. Although the concepts of subtypes and spectrum disorders might appear mutually exclusive at first glance, they are complementary. Indeed, clinicians and researchers often consider them together. To illustrate, we conducted a search of the Psychinfo database (October 19, 2006) using the keywords "subtype" and "spectrum." This yielded 270 articles discussing both concepts. The articles covered a range of disorders, including OCD. Given that the concepts of subtype and spectrum condition are commonly considered together in the scientific community, it is important to consider them both within the covers of a single volume.

Another reason for considering subtypes and spectrum conditions together is that there may not be a firm boundary between subtypes and spectrum conditions. A spectrum condition may actually be a subtype. An example from the classification of species makes this point clear. Evolutionary and genetic research on hominids had shed a great deal of light on the evolution of *Homo sapiens* by comparing our species with extinct hominid subtypes such as *Australopithecus, Homo erectus,* and *Homo habilis.* Research on hominid "spectrum" species—such as the great apes (orangutans, gorillas, chimpanzees, and bonobos)—has also shed much light on the place of human beings in the natural order. Although it was initially thought that the great apes fell outside the class of hominids, genetic research has demonstrated that great apes actually should be classified as subtype hominids (Wilson & Reeder, 2005). This illustrates the close conceptual and classificatory relationships among subtypes and spectra.

With these points in mind, this volume offers a series of reviews of clinical observations, theoretical and research work, and treatment data on putative OCD subtypes and spectrum conditions. Researchers and clinicians do not agree about the value of the concepts of OCD subtypes and spectra. The chapters in this volume, however, attempt to explore these controversies to arrive at a deeper understanding of the causes and treatments for the many different clinical presentations covered in the book.

The issues discussed in this volume also have important implications for the classification of mental disorders in general. As the mental health field begins to consider the next iteration of the diagnostic manual (DSM-V is planned for release in 2012), an entire research agenda is being implemented to elucidate issues such as how best to understand and classify OCD. The questions of subtypes and spectrum disorders are central to this issue and will guide how OCD is conceptualized in DSM-V.

The chapters in this volume have been contributed by experts representing a range of different specializations in the mental health field. All contributors are scientist-practitioners, which is appropriate for a book concerned with theory and treatment. The book is divided into two parts. Part I addresses the vast heterogeneity of OCD symptoms. The opening chapter examines the empirical rationale for considering different presentations of OCD as "subtypes." Each of the remaining chapters in Part I examines a particular clinical presentation of OCD that is often encountered in clinical practice. These chapters address the following aspects of each presentation: (a) symptomatology, (b) a review of the empirical support for the subtype(s), (c) a review of the etiological theories, and (d) treatment issues.

Part II addresses problems often related to OCD (i.e., the proposed OCD spectrum disorders). As in Part I, the opening chapter of Part II critically examines the rationale for the spectrum approach. Additional chapters in Part II address specific disorders. These chapters cover the following aspects of each putative spectrum condition: (a) clinical presentation and important features, (b) a brief review of empirical support for inclusion as a spectrum disorder (e.g., its similarity and relationship to OCD), (c) a brief review of etiological theories, and (d) treatment issues. We think that readers will find particularly enlightening each contributor's conclusion about the relationship of these conditions to OCD.

As the chapters throughout this volume show, the task of identifying subtypes of OCD requires investigators to grapple with many of the same issues that are involved in the task of identifying OCD spectrum conditions. One such issue concerns defining the primary and secondary features of OCD. Indeed, both types of features might serve as bases for defining subtypes and spectrum conditions. Another issue concerns the clinical or scientific value of classifying symptom patterns in terms of their relationship to OCD. That is, what is the value of classifying particular symptoms as noteworthy variants of OCD? This is important because it can help us move from a classification system based entirely on symptoms (as in the DSM) to one based on etiologic mechanisms. The contributors in this volume emphasize clinical applications throughout their chapters; yet, they also ensure that the continuity between clinical practice and clinical science is well represented. Because of its broad scope and relevance to clinical and research activity, the audience for this book includes practitioners, researchers, as well as students.

REFERENCES

American Psychiatric Association. (2000). *Diagnostic and statistical manual of mental disorders* (4th ed., text revision). Washington, DC: Author.

Hackforth, R. (1952). *Plato's Phaedrus.* Cambridge: Cambridge University Press.

Wilson, D. E., & Reeder, D. M. (2005). *Mammal species of the world* (3rd ed., pp. 181–184). Baltimore: Johns Hopkins University Press.

Contributors

Elias Aboujaoude, M.D., Clinical Instructor, Department of Psychiatry and Behavioral Sciences, Stanford University Medical Center, Stanford, California

Amanda C. Adcock, M.A., Graduate Student, Department of Psychology, University of Wisconsin–Milwaukee, Milwaukee, Wisconsin

Suman Ambwani, M.A., Graduate Student, Department of Psychology, Texas A&M University, College Station, Texas

Gordon J. G. Asmundson, Ph.D., Professor, Faculty of Kinesiology and Health Studies, University of Regina, Regina, Saskatchewan, Canada

Michele Boivin, Ph.D., Postdoctoral Fellow, Department of Psychiatry and Behavioral Neurosciences, St. Joseph's Healthcare and McMaster University, Hamilton, Ontario, Canada

Cheryl Carmin, Ph.D., Professor, Department of Psychiatry, University of Illinois at Chicago, Chicago, Illinois

Kimberley L. Chiappone, M.D., Resident, Department of Psychiatry and Human Behavior, Brown Medical School, Providence, Rhode Island

Christine A. Conelea, M.A., Graduate Student, Department of Psychology, University of Wisconsin–Milwaukee, Milwaukee, Wisconsin

Jane L. Eisen, M.D., Associate Professor, Department of Psychiatry and Human Behavior, Brown Medical School, Providence, Rhode Island

Craig A. Erickson, M.D., Resident, Department of Psychiatry, Indiana University School of Medicine and Christian Sarkine Autism Treatment Center, James Whitcomb Riley Hospital for Children, Indianapolis, Indiana

Nichole Fairbrother, Ph.D., Postdoctoral Fellow, Department of Psychology, University of British Columbia, Vancouver, British Columbia, Canada

Randy O. Frost, Ph.D., Professor, Department of Psychology, Smith College, Northampton, Massachusetts

David H. Gleaves, Ph.D., Associate Professor, Department of Psychology, University of Canterbury, Christchurch, New Zealand

Jon E. Grant, J.D., M.D., M.P.H., Associate Professor, Department of Psychiatry, University of Minnesota School of Medicine, Minneapolis, Minnesota

Patricia Gruner, M.A., Graduate Student, Department of Psychology, Fordham University, Bronx, New York

Leslie A. Hulvershorn, M.D., Resident, Department of Psychiatry, Indiana University School of Medicine and Christian Sarkine Autism Treatment Center, James Whitcomb Riley Hospital for Children, Indianapolis, Indiana

Suck Won Kim, M.D., Professor, Department of Psychiatry, University of Minnesota, Minneapolis, Minnesota

Lorrin M. Koran, M.D., Professor, Department of Psychiatry and Behavioral Sciences, Stanford University Medical Center, Stanford, California

Julie Leclerc, Graduate Student, Department of Psychology, Fernand-Seguin Research Centre, Louis-H. Lafontaine Hospital, Montreal, Quebec, Canada

Christine Lochner, Ph.D., Assistant Professor, Department of Psychiatry, University of Stellenbosch and MRC Unit on Anxiety Disorders, South Africa

Maria C. Mancebo, Ph.D., Instructor, Department of Psychiatry and Human Behavior, Brown Medical School, Providence, Rhode Island

Patrick Marsh, M.D., Resident, Department of Psychiatry and Behavioral Medicine, University of South Florida, Tampa, Florida

Randi E. McCabe, Ph.D., Assistant Professor, Department of Psychiatry and Behavioral Neurosciences, St. Joseph's Healthcare and McMaster University, Hamilton, Ontario, Canada

Christopher J. McDougle, M.D., Professor, Department of Psychiatry, Indiana University School of Medicine and Christian Sarkine Autism Treatment Center, James Whitcomb Riley Hospital for Children, Indianapolis, Indiana

Darcy C. Norling, M.S., Assistant Professor, School of Professional Psychology, Pacific University, Portland, Oregon

Kieron P. O'Connor, Ph.D., Associate Professor, Department of Psychology, Fernand-Seguin Research Centre, Louis-H. Lafontaine Hospital, Montreal, Quebec, Canada

Anthony Pinto, Ph.D., Instructor, Department of Psychiatry and Human Behavior, Brown Medical School, Providence, Rhode Island

David J. Posey, M.D., Department of Psychiatry, Indiana University School of Medicine and Christian Sarkine Autism Treatment Center, James Whitcomb Riley Hospital for Children, Indianapolis, Indiana

Christine Purdon, Ph.D., Associate Professor, Department of Psychology, University of Waterloo, Waterloo, Ontario, Canada

Steven A. Rasmussen, M.D., Professor, Department of Psychiatry and Human Behavior, Brown Medical School, Providence, Rhode Island

Reuben Robbins, M.A., Graduate Student, Department of Psychology, Fordham University, Bronx, New York

Johan Rosqvist, Psy.D., Assistant Professor, Department of Psychology, Pacific University, Portland, Oregon

Dan J. Stein, M.D., Professor, Department of Psychiatry, University of Cape Town and MRC Unit on Anxiety Disorders, Cape Town, South Africa

Kimberly A. Stigler, M.D., Assistant Professor, Department of Psychiatry, Indiana University School of Medicine and Christian Sarkine Autism Treatment Center, James Whitcomb Riley Hospital for Children, Indianapolis, Indiana

Laura J. Summerfeldt, Ph.D., Associate Professor, Department of Psychology, Trent University, Peterborough, Ontario, Canada

David F. Tolin, Ph.D., Director, Anxiety Disorders Center, The Institute of Living, and Assistant Professor, Department of Psychiatry, University of Connecticut School of Medicine, Hartford, Connecticut

Pamela S. Wiegartz, Ph.D., Assistant Professor, Department of Psychiatry, University of Illinois at Chicago, Chicago, Illinois

Kyle Allen Williams, M.D., Resident, Department of Psychiatry, University of Minnesota, Minneapolis, Minnesota

Douglas W. Woods, Ph.D., Associate Professor, Department of Psychology, University of Wisconsin–Milwaukee, Milwaukee, Wisconsin

Kevin Wu, Ph.D., Assistant Professor, Department of Psychology, Northern Illinois University, Dekalb, Illinois

Part I / Subtyping Obsessive-Compulsive Disorder

Obsessive-compulsive disorder (OCD) is a uniquely complex and heterogeneous condition that usually involves a combination of related (at least for the patient) mental and behavioral symptoms. *Obsessions* are unwanted intrusive thoughts, ideas, doubts, impulses, or images that evoke distress (e.g., anxiety) and the urge to resist. *Compulsions,* which can be overt (i.e., behavioral) or covert (i.e., unobtrusive behavioral acts or purely mental rituals), are deliberate and prescribed responses to obsessions that serve to reduce obsessional distress. For example, many patients experience obsessional doubts regarding whether they locked the door when leaving the house. To alleviate the anxiety associated with such doubts, these patients might engage in checking compulsions (e.g., locking and unlocking the door seven times to ensure that it is secure, or returning home to see if the door is locked, or calling a neighbor to check on the door).

The clinical landscape of OCD is so varied that it is difficult to refer to any particular patient with this condition as "typical." If one approaches this heterogeneity with observations of overt symptoms (as is the tendency among many clinicians and researchers), several broad themes of obsessions and compulsions can be identified, including (a) aggressive, sexual, religious, or somatic obsessions and checking compulsions; (b) obsessions concerned with symmetry and ordering and counting and repeating rituals; (c) obsessions with contamination and compulsions to clean; and (d) hoarding (Taylor, 2005). Research aimed at delimiting distinct dimensions and subtypes of symptoms has generally supported the validity of these content areas. However, an individual with OCD can present with more than one "subtype" (McKay et al., 2004), and some patients' symptoms do not adhere to the patterns mentioned previously, such as a patient with sexual obsessions and cleaning compulsions.

Subtypes characterize the diversity of OCD symptoms best characterized when symptoms are considered from the perspective of treatment planning (Sookman, Abramowitz, Calamari, Wilhelm, & McKay, 2005). To illustrate, from a psychological perspective, developing a treatment plan for contamination fear with associated cleaning compulsions is substantially different from developing a treatment plan for aggressive obsessions and checking or compulsive hoarding. Further, research has shown that there are different responses to both psychological and pharmacologic treatments for different types of OCD symptoms (e.g., Ball, Baer, & Otto, 1996), lending additional credence to the heuristic value of symptom subtypes of the disorder. Accordingly, the chapters in part 1 of this volume provide comprehensive coverage of the major symptom-based presentations associated with OCD.

Other ways in which OCD is heterogeneous include how its onset can be associated with different biological stressors, such as pediatric autoimmune neuropsychiatric disorders associated with streptococcal infection (PANDAS) (Snider & Swedo, 2004) and the perinatal period (Abramowitz, Schwartz, Moore, & Luenzmann, 2003). PANDAS and postpartum OCD possess some unique phenomena that distinguish them from other presentations of OCD and that require special treatment considerations, as is described in the chapters of part 1. Additional presentational complexities of OCD include the presence of poor insight into the senselessness of obsessions and compulsions, sometimes also referred to as *overvalued ideation* (Kozak & Foa, 1994). Poor insight is considered a poor prognostic indicator because it is associated with attenuated response to pharmacologic and psychological treatments that are generally effective for other patients with OCD. Equally challenging for clinicians are symptoms of obsessional scrupulosity, which involve recurrent senseless thoughts and doubts about religious or moral issues and compulsive behaviors that are typically aimed at averting religious sin or punishment from God (e.g., praying or confessing). Poor insight and scrupulosity are addressed in chapters in part 1.

One goal of assembling the chapters in part 1 is to help clinicians and researchers critically examine the similarities and differences between the major presentations of OCD. A second, and equally important, goal relates to the well-known challenges that these complexities pose for conceptual models and treatment algorithms. The authors in part 1 tackle these important clinical issues and offer evidence-based recommendations about the best ways of understanding and treating the multifarious manifestations of OCD.

The varied phenomenologies of OCD symptom presentations, some of which reliably emerge in the literature as bona fide subtypes, are the focus of the chapters in part 1. Beyond the descriptive psychopathology, emerging evidence suggests that, to achieve optimal efficacy, treatment techniques must be adjusted to address the specific manifestations of symptoms of OCD. As the reader will note, clinicians have begun to modify treatments to address the unique characteristics of these subgroups, and initial results are promising.

Theoretical and experimental work investigating particular symptom categories is also in progress. The reader will note the absence of a grand comprehensive theoretical model that adequately accounts for all of the symptom variations of OCD. Instead, authors of each chapter describe highly specific "minimodels" that can account for only specific sorts of clinical phenomena (e.g., checking, contamination). Although there is some overlap across many of these symptom-specific models, the absence of a general model—despite decades of research on OCD—challenges the implicit assumption that a comprehensive conceptual or etiologic model of OCD exists. We hope that, as we move to more robust classifications within OCD, it will become possible to validate theories and treatments empirically for these specific symptom presentations and better match each OCD patient to the most appropriate intervention.

REFERENCES

Abramowitz, J. S. (2001). Treatment of scrupulous obsessions and compulsions using exposure and response prevention: A case report. *Cognitive and Behavioral Practice, 8,* 79–85.

Abramowitz, J. S., Schwartz, S., Moore, K., & Luenzmann, K. (2003). Obsessive-compulsive symptoms in pregnancy and the puerperium: A review of the literature. *Journal of Anxiety Disorders, 17,* 461–478.

Ball, S. G., Baer, L., & Otto, M. W. (1996). Symptom subtypes of obsessive-compulsive disorder in behavioral treatment studies: A quantitative review. *Behaviour Research and Therapy, 34,* 47–51.

Kozak, M. J., & Foa, E. B. (1994). Obsessions, overvalued ideas, and delusions in obsessive-compulsive disorder. *Behaviour Research and Therapy, 32,* 343–353.

McKay, D., Abramowitz, J., Calamari, J., Kyrios, M., Radomsky, A., Sookman, D., et al. (2004). A critical evaluation of obsessive-compulsive disorder subtypes: Symptoms versus mechanisms. *Clinical Psychology Review, 24,* 283–313.

Snider, L. A., & Swedo, S. E. (2004). PANDAS: Current status and directions for research. *Molecular Psychiatry, 9,* 900–907.

Sookman, D., Abramowitz, J. S., Calamari, J. E., Wilhelm, S., & McKay, D. (2005). Subtypes of obsessive-compulsive disorder: Implications for specialized cognitive behavior therapy. *Behavior Therapy, 36,* 393–400.

Taylor, S. (2005). Dimensional and subtype models of OCD. In J. S. Abramowitz & A. C. Houts (Eds.), *Concepts and Controversies in Obsessive-Compulsive Disorder* (pp. 27–41). New York: Springer.

CHAPTER ONE

Making Sense of Obsessive-Compulsive Disorder

Do Subtypes Exist?

Steven Taylor, Ph.D., Dean McKay, Ph.D., and Jonathan S. Abramowitz, Ph.D.

Obsessive-compulsive disorder (OCD) is classified as an anxiety disorder that involves two main symptoms: *obsessions,* which are intrusive, unwanted thoughts, ideas, images, or impulses that are experienced as senseless yet anxiety evoking; and *compulsions,* which are urges to perform behavioral or mental rituals according to specified "rules" or in response to obsessions (i.e., to reduce obsessional anxiety; American Psychiatric Association [APA], 2000). Although the *Diagnostic and Statistical Manual of Mental Disorders* (DSM-IV; APA, 2000) describes OCD as a homogeneous condition, the specific manifestation of obsessions and compulsions varies widely from patient to patient. For example, obsessions about contamination, illness, sex, harming, morality, exactness, and intrusive unwanted, disturbing images are all common presentations (Rachman & Hodgson, 1980). If the individual cannot avoid situations that provoke these obsessions, he or she may perform various compulsions and other types of responses aimed at neutralizing the obsession, such as washing, checking, arranging, or mental rituals.

Although the DSM-IV definition of OCD captures a broad array of symptoms, clinicians and researchers have observed that patients with some types of symptoms (e.g., hoarding) are less responsive to available treatments than are other patients (e.g., those with contamination). This differential treatment response has led researchers and clinicians to propose that clinically important subtypes of OCD exist. In turn, these proposals have prompted the development of methods for identifying subtypes of OCD and for evaluating possible differences in response to treatment or etiology of the disorder.

Why Subtypes?

Why the field has become interested in identifying subtypes of OCD can be answered by considering why we delineate psychiatric syndromes in the first place. Blashfield and Livesley (1999) observed that psychiatric syndromes are delineated to facilitate communication among mental health professionals, develop a basis for theories of psychopathology, predict clinical course, and identify which treatments are most likely to be effective for which patients. Numerous schemes for classifying psychiatric disorders have been proposed and researched. Like DSM-V, the research on subtypes of OCD is couched in the idea that psychiatric disorders can be usefully classified into categories. The categorical approach works best "when all members of a diagnostic class are homogeneous, when there are clear boundaries between classes, and when the different classes are mutually exclusive" (APA, 2000, p. xxxi). As with the DSM-IV approach to defining psychiatric disorders, efforts to subtype OCD have been based on, to a greater or lesser extent, the framework laid out by Robins and Guze (1970), who proposed that advances in understanding and treating psychiatric disorders are most likely to occur if we study homogeneous groups: "Homogeneous diagnostic grouping provides the soundest base for studies of etiology, pathogenesis, and treatment. The roles of heredity, family interactions, intelligence, education, and sociological factors are most simply, directly, and reliably studied when the group studied is as homogeneous as possible" (p. 984).

To identify such groups, Robins and Guze (1970) outlined five phases that interact with one another so that new findings in any one phase may lead to modifications in one or more of the other phases. The process has as its aim ongoing self-rectification and increasing refinement, which may lead to more homogeneous grouping. The five phases are as follows:

1. *Clinical description.* The clinical description of a proposed diagnostic syndrome (or subtype) may be based on a striking clinical feature or combi-

nation of descriptive features that are thought to be associated with one another (e.g., signs and symptoms, demographic features).

2. *Laboratory studies.* These include chemical, physiologic, radiologic (e.g., neuroimaging), anatomical, and psychological (e.g., tests of cognitive functioning) findings. When laboratory tests are consistent with the defined clinical picture, they permit a more refined classification.

3. *Exclusion of other disorders.* Exclusionary criteria (including criteria for discriminating subtypes) are developed on the basis of clinical descriptions and laboratory findings. The criteria should permit exclusion of borderline or doubtful cases so that the index group may be as homogeneous as possible.

4. *Follow-up studies.* These studies can be used to determine whether the diagnostic category or subtype is stable over time. Do patients with one subtype of OCD, for example, tend to switch to another subtype over time? Follow-up studies can also investigate whether members from a putative subtype differ in their course of disorder or treatment response. A putative subtype may not be entirely homogenous if it can be further divided into patients with good versus poor prognosis.

5. *Family studies.* The validity of a proposed type or subtype of psychiatric disorder would be supported by showing that it runs in families or is of increased prevalence in first-degree relatives, reflecting the effects of genetic or shared environmental factors.

Researchers interested in identifying subtypes of OCD have used a number of the approaches outlined. Some have focused primarily on clinical descriptions, while others have focused on family studies or laboratory tests. As a result of these efforts, proposed subtyping schemes have included: (a) early- versus later-onset OCD; (b) presence versus absence of tics; (c) presence versus absence of childhood diseases, such as streptococci-related autoimmune disorders; (d) presence versus absence of psychotic or neurologic features; and (e) overt symptom theme (e.g., "washers" vs. "checkers"; e.g., Albert, Maina, Ravizza, & Bogetto, 2002; Allen, Leonard, & Swedo, 1995; Calamari, Wiegartz, & Janeck, 1999; Eichstedt & Arnold, 2001; Geller et al. 1998; Sobin et al., 2000). The merits of various subtyping schemes depend on a number of factors, including the empirical support for each subtype and whether some subtypes have advantages over others.

Identification of Subtypes Based on Symptom Theme

The most prevalent basis for deriving subtypes of OCD has been the overt symptom theme. While some authors have attempted to delineate the latent structure of OCD symptom measures via factor analysis, others have aimed to classify patients into distinct symptom-based subgroups using cluster analysis. This section summarizes the important contributions this work has made in understanding OCD.

Early approaches to subtyping OCD characterized patients by their principal compulsive behavior (e.g., "washers" and "checkers"; Lewis, 1936). For example, Hoehn-Saric and Barksdale (1983), who aimed to distinguish OCD patients with tics from those without tics, proposed an "impulsive" versus "nonimpulsive" taxonomy. Taking a more functional approach, Rasmussen and Eisen (1991) suggested that symptoms of OCD fall into three subgroups: (1) abnormal risk assessment, (2) pathological doubt, and (3) incompleteness. Although conceptually appealing, these rational approaches for deriving subtypes were not subjected to empirical study.

Hodgson and Rachman (1977) first reported using a psychometrically validated instrument—the Maudsley Obsessional Compulsive Inventory (MOCI)—to identify OCD symptom subtypes. Factor analysis of the MOCI revealed three major symptom dimensions: washing, checking, and doubting-conscientiousness. A decade later, Freund, Steketee, and Foa (1987) conducted a factor analysis of the Compulsive Activity Checklist (CAC; Philpott, 1975) and identified two symptom dimensions: (1) washing and cleanliness, and (2) checking. Factor analysis of another self-report measure, the Padua Inventory (PI; Sanavio, 1988), revealed four main symptom dimensions, including three that corresponded to MOCI and CAC factors: (1) becoming contaminated, (2) checking behavior, and (3) impaired control over mental activities (which corresponded to the MOCI doubting-conscientiousness subscale). The fourth PI factor, "urges and loss of control over motor behavior," had not been identified in previous subtype schemes and included items assessing unwanted urges to commit violent or harmful acts (e.g., murdering one's child). Using a revised version of the PI, van Oppen, Hoekstra, and Emmelkamp (1995) identified five symptom dimensions: (1) washing, (2) checking, (3) rumination, (4) impulses, and (5) precision.

Although several replicable OCD symptom domains emerged from these early studies (i.e., washing, doubting/checking, and obsessional phenomena), the following limitations must be considered. First, the measures employed in these investigations were developed to assess the quintessential presentations of OCD symptoms; thus, these measures focused on contamination, doubting, checking, and other frequently identified themes. As a result, the emergence of corresponding dimensions across studies is not surprising. Few (if any) items on these early self-report measures addressed the less-studied (at the time) symptoms of OCD such as mental rituals, symmetry, or hoarding (Baer, 1994; Summerfeldt, Richter, Antony, & Swinson, 1999). Consequently, there are a priori limitations on the potential OCD symptom subtypes that can be derived with these instruments.

Symptom-Based Subtypes Identified with the Y-BOCS Checklist

Compared with early self-report measures, the symptom checklist of the Yale-Brown Obsessive Compulsive Scale (YBOCS-SC; Goodman et al., 1989) assesses a more comprehensive array of OCD symptoms. Consequently, this instrument has been used widely to study OCD subtypes. The YBOCS-SC is a semistructured interview that contains a checklist of more than 60 specific symptoms of OCD (e.g., concerns with contamination from insects or animals) organized into eight obsession categories (aggressive, contamination, sexual, hoarding, symmetry, religious, somatic, and miscellaneous) and seven compulsion categories (washing, checking, counting, ordering/arranging, hoarding, repeating, and miscellaneous).

Latent Dimensions of the Y-BOCS Checklist

Baer (1994) was the first to use the YBOCS-SC to derive symptom subtypes. He identified three factors. A *symmetry and hoarding* factor included symmetry and hoarding obsessions and hoarding, ordering, repeating, and counting compulsions. Baer suggested that the common theme of this factor was a sense of imperfection and incompleteness, symptoms also experienced in disorders thought to be in some way associated with OCD, such as Tourette syndrome and trichotillomania. The second factor, *contamination and cleaning*, included contamination, somatic, and hoarding obsessions with cleaning and checking compulsions. The finding that checking and washing symptoms loaded together on a single factor was incongruent with previous studies based on self-report OCD measures. The third factor included religious, sexual, and aggressive obsessions and was termed *pure obsessions* because no compulsion categories loaded with these obsessional symptoms. Baer (1994) noted that the subtypes derived in this study did not refer to mutually exclusive groups of *patients* but rather to groups of *symptoms* that a given individual might evidence to varying degrees.

Leckman et al. (1997) later identified four symptom dimensions with the YBOCS-SC: (1) *cleanliness and washing,* (2) *hoarding,* (3) *symmetry and ordering,* and (4) *obsessions and checking.* These results suggested a strong correlation between aggressive, sexual, and religious obsessions and checking compulsions, a finding not previously reported. Moreover, whereas hoarding obsessions and compulsions were linked with symmetry and ordering in Baer's (1994) study, Leckman et al. identified a more homogeneous hoarding factor.

Summerfeldt et al. (1999) conducted a confirmatory factor analysis with the YBOCS-SC items and obtained support for a latent structure similar to Leckman et al.'s (1997) model. However, Summerfeldt et al. also found that the discrete symptoms listed on the YBOCS-SC did not load well on the specific YBOCS-SC dimensions they were supposed to measure. This suggests that the within-category symptoms listed on the YBOCS-SC may not be the best examples of the obsessional concerns or compulsive behavior categories listed on the measure.

Mataix-Cols et al. (1999) factor analyzed YBOCS-SC data from 354 OCD patients and identified five factors, which were quite similar to the four-factor model proposed by Leckman et al. (1997). Mataix-Cols et al.'s (1999) fifth factor, which included sexual and religious obsessions, was separate from aggressive obsessions and checking compulsions. Otherwise, the symmetry and ordering, contamination/cleaning, and hoarding, factors were identical to those found by Leckman et al. (1997). In a further factor analytic study of 153 patients, Mataix-Cols and colleagues (2002) found a factor structure similar to their earlier work. Religious obsessions loaded with aggressive obsessions and checking rituals as in Leckman et al's (1997) study. Sexual and somatic obsessions formed a singular factor that included no compulsions.

Patient Subgroups Identified with the Y-BOCS Checklist

Calamari et al. (1999) used cluster analysis to identify subgroups of individuals with OCD based on their most prominent obsessions and compulsions. These authors identified five symptom-based clusters: (1) *harming,* (2) *hoarding,*

(3) *contamination,* (4) *certainty,* and (5) *obsessionals.* The hoarding, contamination, and obsessionals clusters have obvious overlap with previously identified dimensions, and the certainty and harming clusters had similarities with Leckman et al.'s (1997) obsessions and checking factor. The certainty and harming clusters differed from each other in that the harming subgroup's main symptoms were largely aggressive obsessions and checking compulsions, whereas patients in the certainty subgroup endorsed multiple YBOCS-SC obsession and compulsion categories. Calamari et al. (1999) characterized their certainty subgroup as needing absolute certainty regarding many issues, sometimes to prevent harmful outcomes, but suggested that an overriding theme was the need to create a "just right" feeling. One difference between Calamari et al.'s (1999) study and previous research is the absence of a symmetry subtype. Calamari et al. (1999) found that symmetry obsessions were prevalent among the harming cluster and certainty cluster, and substantial levels of compulsive ordering rituals were observed in the certainty subgroup.

In another study, Calamari et al. (2004) found support for a seven-subgroup taxonomy: (1) *contamination,* (2) *harming,* (3) *hoarding,* (4) *obsessionals,* (5) *symmetry,* (6) *certainty,* and (7) *contamination/harming.* The contamination, harming, hoarding, symmetry, and obsessional groups had characteristics congruent with previously identified dimensions or subgroups. The identification of a symmetry subgroup, which was not found in their previous investigation, may have resulted from the significantly higher levels of symmetry obsessions in their new sample. High levels of contamination and aggressive obsessions and washing and checking compulsions characterized the contamination/harming subgroup. Some patients in this subgroup were concerned with contamination by evil or harm and washed or avoided contamination in order to prevent harm.

Subgroups Identified with an Updated Y-BOCS Checklist

Recognition that many individuals with OCD display mental compulsive rituals (e.g., Foa & Kozak, 1995) did not occur until after the YBOCS-SC was introduced. As a result, a limitation of the YBOCS-SC (and subtyping research based on this instrument) is that it does not adequately assess such symptoms. In fact, only one item on the scale assesses mental rituals, and this item is contained within the Miscellaneous Compulsions category, which was typically left out in the studies reviewed. Consequently, mental rituals have not been adequately accounted for in OCD subtype taxonomies.

To address this problem, Abramowitz, Franklin, Schwartz, and Furr (2003) derived subtypes of OCD patients using a revised form of the YBOCS-SC that was more sensitive than the original version to the presence of mental rituals (i.e., it contained a separate category for assessing various types of mental rituals such as neutralizing, praying, counting, list making, and reviewing events or conversations in one's mind). Abramowitz et al. (2003) identified five subgroups, four of which (harming, contamination, hoarding, and symmetry) were identical to those described by previous authors. Similar to Baer's (1994) *pure obsessions* factor and Leckman et al.'s (1997) *obsessions and checking* factor, Abramowitz et al. (2003) found that aggressive, religious, and sexual obsessions clustered together. However, mental rituals were also part of this cluster, which was named *unacceptable thoughts* because patients in this group tended to use mental and checking rituals to neutralize or reassure themselves about their unwanted thoughts.

The Clinical Utility of Subtypes of OCD

Each of the remaining chapters in Part I addresses clinical and research findings that focus on the validation of individual symptom subtypes. A number of studies, however, have evaluated the utility of OCD symptom subtype schemes, mostly focused on how different subtypes respond to treatment. In general, the identification of reliable predictors of response to pharmacologic interventions for OCD has been difficult. Mataix-Cols et al. (1999) found that higher scores on their factor analytically derived hoarding dimension predicted poorer outcome with serotonergic medications. Hoarding symptoms were also associated with dropout and attenuated response to cognitive-behavior therapy in two studies (Abramowitz et al., 2003; Mataix-Cols et al., 2002). Scoring on the sexual/religious obsessions dimension predicted poor treatment response to serotonergic medication in the Mataix-Cols et al. (2002) study, whereas Abramowitz et al. (2003) found that patients in their unacceptable thoughts subgroup, a group with high levels of mental compulsions, responded quite well to cognitive-behavior therapy. Jenike, Baer, Minichiello, Rauch, and Buttolph (1997) found that a subgroup of OCD patients with symmetry obsessions responded to treatment with phenelzine while other subgroups did not.

Neuropsychiatric Correlates of Subtypes of OCD

A growing number of studies use functional neuroimaging techniques to study neural correlates of OCD (for a review, see Whiteside, Port, & Abramowitz, 2005). Whereas most studies have combined patients with different symptom presentations, four investigations addressed the issue of symptom subtypes. Using positron emission tomography (PET), Cottraux, Gerard, Cinotti, and Froment (1996) found that OCD patients with primarily checking rituals evidenced greater orbitofrontal and temporal lobe activity and lesser basal ganglia activity, relative to nonpatient controls when the urge to check was evoked. In a small study of 14 patients, Rauch, Whalen, Dougherty, and Jenike (1998) also used PET and had patients carry out a continuous performance task during imaging. They identified positive relationships between (a) the obsessions and checking subtype and activation in bilateral striatum and (b) the contamination and washing subtype and activation in the bilateral anterior cingulate, left orbitofrontal, and other cortical areas. In contrast, symmetry and ordering symptoms tended to be negatively related to regional cerebral blood flow in the right striatum.

In another imagining study, Phillips et al. (2000) used functional magnetic resonance imaging (fMRI) to compare OCD patients with primarily washing and checking symptoms and healthy controls while they viewed pictures of normally disgusting or washing-relevant scenes. While viewing washing-related pictures, patients with OCD washing symptoms evidenced activations in visual regions and the anterior insula, brain regions previously implicated in the experience of disgust (Phillips et al., 1997, 1998). Patients with primarily checking rituals showed activation in frontostriatal regions and the thalamus.

Finally, using a symptom-provocation paradigm, Mataix-Cols et al. (2003) used fMRI to examine 10 healthy individuals as they viewed pictures and imagined confrontation with a variety of neutral, universally distressing, and OCD-relevant stimuli associated with the different subtypes (e.g., contamination/washing [public toilet], checking [light switch], hoarding [old toys]). Anxiety associated with different OCD symptom dimensions was implemented within different patterns of activation. Mataix-Cols et al. (2003) concluded that their findings supported a dimensional model of OCD in which (a) brain systems that become activated by anxiety are similar in OCD patients and nonpatients and (b) anxiety associated with different OCD symptoms is implemented within different patterns of neural activation.

Although functional neuroimaging studies of OCD and OCD subtypes have resulted in interesting findings, the results are based on small samples, and those studies that have included individuals with OCD have reported discrepant findings. More research is needed before any firm conclusions can be drawn regarding differential neural correlates of OCD symptom-based subtypes.

Conclusion

Although clinical observations and numerous studies suggest the presence of symptom-based subtypes of OCD, how subtypes are to be conceptualized has not yet been resolved. Research on the structure of obsessions and compulsions has consistently identified the following subtypes: contamination/washing, checking, hoarding, and symmetry/ordering. Given that these symptom themes have been repeatedly identified, across various statistical methodologies with self-report and interview assessment measures, we propose that these represent reliable and valid symptom OCD subtypes. However, the following proposed subtypes have had mixed empirical support: pure obsessionals, sexual/religious obsessions, and harming obsessions. A caveat to this assertion, however, is that the available research is limited by the reliance on symptom measures (e.g., the YBOCS-SC) that limit our conceptualization of latent subtypes to the manifest items available. An excellent example is the failure to include mental compulsions in most subtyping schemes based on the YBOCS-SC since mental rituals are not adequately assessed by this measure.

Several lines of investigation have emerged that, when combined with the symptom-based subtyping approach, may clarify the presence of distinct OCD subtypes. For example, research investigating typical comorbidities in OCD (i.e., tic disorders; Leckman et al., 2000) has shown that individuals with OCD who also have other conditions are distinguishable from those without such comorbidities. Another possibility exists with neuropsychiatric data reviewed earlier. These investigations, while designed principally to determine the differences between those with OCD and those without, have revealed differences between patients with OCD based on symptom manifestation. In light of the diversity of literature available that endeavors to distinguish different forms of OCD, it is timely that these diverse approaches unify in an effort to determine with greater certainty whether subtypes of OCD exist.

REFERENCES

Abramowitz, J., Franklin, M., Schwartz, S., & Furr, J. (2003). Symptom presentation and outcome of cognitive-behavior therapy for obsessive-compulsive disorder. *Journal of Consulting and Clinical Psychology, 71,* 1049–1057.

Albert, U., Maina, G., Ravizza, L., & Bogetto, F. (2002). An exploratory study on obsessive-compulsive disorder with and without a familial component: Are there any phenomenological differences? *Psychopathology, 35,* 8–16.

Allen, A. J., Leonard, H. L., & Swedo, S. E. (1995). Case study: A new infection-triggered, autoimmune subtype of pediatric OCD and Tourette's syndrome. *Journal of the American Academy of Child and Adolescent Psychiatry, 34,* 307–311.

American Psychiatric Association. (2000). *Diagnostic and statistical manual of mental disorders (4th ed., text revision).* Washington, DC: Author.

Baer, L. (1994). Factor analysis of symptom subtypes of obsessive compulsive disorder and their relation to personality and tic disorders. *Journal of Clinical Psychiatry, 55* (Suppl. 3), 18–23.

Blashfield, R. K., & Livesley, W. J. (1999). Classification. In T. Millon, P. H. Blaney, & R. D. Davis (Eds.), *Oxford textbook of psychopathology* (pp. 3–28). New York: Oxford University Press.

Calamari, J. E., Wiegartz, P. S., & Janeck, A. S. (1999). Obsessive-compulsive disorder subgroups: A symptom-based clustering approach. *Behaviour Research and Therapy, 37,* 113–125.

Calamari, J. E., Wiegartz, P. S., Riemann, B. C., Cohen, R. J., Greer, A., Jacobi, D. M., et al. (2004). Obsessive-compulsive disorder subtypes: an attempted replication and extension of a symptom-based taxonomy. *Behaviour Research and Therapy, 42,* 647–670.

Cottraux, J., Gerard, D., Cinotti, L., & Froment, J. C. (1996). A controlled positron emission tomography study of obsessive and neutral auditory stimulation in obsessive-compulsive disorder with checking rituals. *Psychiatry Research, 60,* 101–112.

Eichstedt, J. A., & Arnold, S. L. (2001). Childhood-onset obsessive-compulsive disorder: A tic-related subtype of OCD? *Clinical Psychology Review, 21,* 137–158.

Foa, E. B., & Kozak, M. J. (1995). DSM-IV field trial: Obsessive compulsive disorder. *American Journal of Psychiatry, 152,* 90–96.

Freund, B., Steketee, G. S., and Foa, E. B. (1987). Compulsive activity checklist (CAC): Psychometric analysis with obsessive-compulsive disorder. *Behavioral Assessment, 9,* 67–79.

Geller, D., Biederman, J., Jones, J., Park, K., Schwartz, S., Shapiro, S., & Coffey, B. (1998). Is juvenile obsessive-compulsive disorder a developmental subtype of the disorder? A review of the pediatric literature. *Journal of the American Academy of Child and Adolescent Psychiatry, 37,* 420–427.

Goodman, W. K., Price, L. H., Rasmussen, S. A., Mazure, C., Delgado, P., Heninger, G. R., et al. (1989). The Yale-Brown Obsessive-Compulsive Scale: Development, use, reliability, and validity. *Archives of General Psychiatry, 46,* 1006–1016.

Hodgson, R. J., & Rachman, S. (1977). Obsessional-compulsive complaints. *Behaviour Research and Therapy, 15,* 389–395.

Hoehn-Saric, R., & Barksdale, V. C. (1983). Impulsiveness in obsessive compulsive patients. *British Journal of Psychiatry, 143,* 177–182.

Jenike, M. A., Baer, L., Minichiello, W. E., Rauch, S. L., & Buttolph, M. L. (1997). Placebo-controlled trial of fluoxetine and phenelzine for obsessive-compulsive disorder. *American Journal of Psychiatry, 154,* 1261–1264.

Leckman, J., Grice, D. E., Boardman, J., Zhang, H., Vitale, A., Bondi, C., et al. (1997). Symptoms of obsessive-compulsive disorder. *American Journal of Psychiatry, 154,* 911–917.

Leckman, J. F., McDougle, C. J., Pauls, D. L., Peterson, B. S., Grice, D. E., King, R. A., et al. (2000). Tic-related versus non-tic-related obsessive-compulsive disorder. In W. K. Goodman, M. V. Rudorfer, & J. D. Maser (Eds.), *Obsessive-compulsive disorder: Contemporary issues in treatment* (pp. 43–68). Mahwah, NJ: Erlbaum.

Mataix-Cols, D., Cullen, S., Lange, K., Zelaya, F., Andrew, C., Amaro, E., et al. (2003). Neural correlates of anxiety associated with obsessive-compulsive symptom dimensions in normal volunteers. *Biological Psychiatry, 53,* 482–493.

Mataix-Cols, D., Junque, C., Sanchez-Turet, M., Vallejo, J., Verger, K., & Barrios, M. (1999). Neuropsychological functioning in a subclinical obsessive-compulsive sample. *Biological Psychiatry, 45,* 898–904.

Mataix-Cols, D., Rauch, S. L., Baer, L., Eisen, J. L., Shera, D. M., Goodman, W. K., et al. (2002). Symptom stability in adult obsessive-compulsive disorder: Data from a naturalistic two-year follow-up study. *American Journal of Psychiatry, 159,* 263–268.

Phillips, M. L., Bullmore, E. T., Howard, R., Woodruff, P. W. R., Wright, I. C., Williams, S. C. R., et al. (1998). Investigation of facial recognition memory and happy and sad facial expression perception: An fMRI study. *Psychiatry Research, 83,* 127–138.

Phillips, M. L., Marks, I. M., Senior, C., Lythgoe, D., O'Dwyer, A.-M., Meehan, O., et al. (2000). A differential neural response in obsessive-compulsive disorder patients with washing compared with checking symptoms to disgust. *Psychological Medicine, 30,* 1037–1050.

Phillips, M. L., Young, A. W., Senior, C., Brammer, M., Andrews, C., Calder, A. J., et al. (1997). A specific neural substrate for perceiving facial expressions of disgust. *Nature, 389,* 495–498.

Philpott, R. (1975). Recent advances in the behavioural assessment of obsessional illness: Difficulties common to these and other measures. *Scottish Medical Journal, 20* (Suppl.), 33–40.

Rachman, S., & Hodgson, R. J. (1980). *Obsessions and compulsions.* Englewood Cliffs, NJ: Prentice-Hall.

Rasmussen, S. A., & Eisen, J. L. (1991). Epidemiology, clinical features and genetics of obsessive-compulsive disorder. In M. A. Jenike & M. Asberg (Eds.), *Understanding obsessive-compulsive disorder (OCD)* (pp. 17–23). Kirkland, WA: Hogrefe & Huber.

Rauch, S. L., Whalen, P. J., Dougherty, D., & Jenike, M. A. (1998). Neurobiologic models of obsessive-compulsive disorder. In M. A. Jenike, L. Baer, & W. E. Minichiello (Eds.), *Obsessive-compulsive disorders: Practical management* (pp. 222–253). St. Louis: Mosby.

Robins, E., & Guze, S. B. (1970). Establishment of diagnostic validity in psychiatric illness: Its application to schizophrenia. *American Journal of Psychiatry, 126,* 983–987.

Sanavio, E. (1988). Obsessions and compulsions: The Padua Inventory. *Behaviour Research and Therapy, 26,* 169–177.

Sobin, C., Blundell, M. L., Weiller, F., Gavigan, C., Haiman, C., & Karayiorgou, M. (2000). Evidence of a schizotypy subtype in OCD. *Psychiatry Research, 34*, 15–24.

Summerfeldt, L. J., Richter, M. A., Antony, M. M., & Swinson, R. P. (1999). Symptom structure in obsessive-compulsive disorder: A confirmatory factor-analytic study. *Behaviour Research and Therapy, 37*, 297–311.

Van Oppen, P., Hoekstra, R. J., & Emmelkamp, P.M.G. (1995). The structure of obsessive-compulsive symptoms. *Behaviour Research and Therapy, 33*, 379–390.

Whiteside, S. P., Port, J. D., & Abramowitz, J. S. (2004). A review and meta-analysis of functional neuroimaging in obsessive-compulsive disorder. *Psychiatry Research: Neuroimaging, 132*, 69–79.

CHAPTER TWO

Fears of Contamination

Dean McKay, Ph.D., and Reuben Robbins, M.A.

The Nature of Contamination Fears in OCD

Fear of contamination is one of the most prevalent obsessive concerns among individuals with obsessive-compulsive disorder (OCD) (Foa & Kozak, 1995; Steketee, Grayson, & Foa, 1984), particularly so for patients with compulsive washing and cleaning rituals (Hodgson & Rachman, 1977; Leckman, Broadman, Zhang, & Grace, 1997). In fact, contamination fear has been estimated to account for 55–58 percent of obsessional worries among patients with OCD (Rasmussen & Eisen, 1998; Rasmussen & Tsuang, 1986). Contamination fears generally center on germs and illness (e.g., viruses), although some also involve concerns about being tainted with evil or negative ideas.

Behavioral components of contamination fears serve to protect the individual from the feared object or objects. Most patients with such obsessions seek to avoid situations and stimuli that are associated with feared contaminants (e.g., avoiding public washrooms, trash cans, or places frequented by people considered "contaminated"—such as gay bars). However, if such stimuli cannot be avoided, hand-washing and cleaning rituals are performed to "decontaminate" after contact (or imagined contact) with the feared object. Checking rituals might also act as a pre-emptive behavior to avoid the possibility of coming into contact with the feared contaminant.

Cognitive features of contamination fears also serve to protect the individual from feared contaminants. Foa and Kozak (1986) describe the process of "freezing," whereby an individual observes a contaminant and imagines that it is contained and no longer spreading. Other strategies are commonly used. For example, if an individual believes that thinking a bad thought about his or her parent leads to contamination by evil forces, then some type of cognitive compensation can be used to neutralize the contaminant. Such a compensatory thought may consist of a prayer or an intentionally contrived *positive* idea about the person. This is sometimes referred to as *undoing*. Mental strategies for dealing with obsessional thoughts have been collectively referred to as *covert neutralization* (Freeston & Ladouceur, 1997).

Although not a contamination fear per se, *sympathetic magic* is also a cognitive element of contamination fear (Rozin & Fallon, 1987). Sympathetic magic is defined as implausible beliefs about how contamination may be transmitted (McKay & Tsao, 2005). It is often observed in contamination-related fears and likely plays a role in how individuals respond to potentially contaminated items. To illustrate, consider a patient who finds floors to be a source of contamination. The floor appears clean, but the patient knows that others have stepped on it recently; thus, if this patient drops a shirt on the floor, the shirt would assume the same contaminated properties because it *came in contact* with the floor, which previously had contact with other contaminants (i.e., shoes or feet). It was not necessary for shoes or feet to come in direct contact with the shirt. Contact with the floor is the equivalent to contact with primary sources of contamination due to sympathetic magic.

Sympathetic magic offers an explanation for the mechanisms underlying contamination-based fears. Originally, conceptualized by Frazer (1890/1959) and Mauss (1902/1972), sympathetic magic, has two *components,* or laws. The first law of sympathetic magic, *contagion,* refers to the process by which things influence one another through contact. The influence remains even after the contact has ended. The second law of sympathetic magic is known as *similarity.* This law posits that things resembling one another have similar core properties. Like contagion, the image of something is thought to have the "essence" of the original. Thus, action taken on the image can cause comparable results in the original. In the case of contamination fear, things that resemble contaminants, or provoke the idea, can be just cause for concern.

The following experimental task used in our lab provides an example of the law of *similarity* (Tsao & McKay, 2004). A clean Styrofoam cup is placed in front of the participant. An unopened bottle of spring water is presented and opened before the participant and poured into the cup. Then the experimenter affixes a label to the cup with the words "urine sample." This labeling is consistent with the law of similarity in that cups often serve the stated purpose of providing urine samples, and despite the clear presentation of clean and unused cups and water, the label provokes strong contamination reactions. An example of the law of *contagion* from our lab is as follows. The participant is shown a clean, unused rattrap with the spring mechanism disarmed. The experimenter then opens a fresh package of miniature chocolate chip cookies, and three cookies are placed on the rattrap. The participant is then asked to eat the cookies. Individuals with elevated contamination fear take longer to initiate consumption and have a higher rate of refusal for these tasks than individuals with high trait anxiety or nonanxious individuals.

Recent research also suggests that disgust is a critical element of contamination fear (Olatunji, Sawchuk, Lohr, & de Jong, 2004; Tsao & McKay, 2004). The tendency to experience disgust is likely related to the etiology and maintenance of contamination-based obsessions and washing compulsions (Power & Dalgiesh, 1997; Woody & Tolin, 2002). Because disgust is considered a basic and highly adaptive emotion (Ekman & Freisen, 1986) that protects organisms from contact with contaminants, it is important to examine its function in contamination fears. Better understanding of the role that disgust plays in contamination may lead to better treatment of contamination fears in OCD.

Rozin, Haidt, and McCauley (1993) conceptualized two categories of disgust elicitors: *core* and *animal reminder*. Core disgust refers to the offensive feeling (and threat of contamination) evoked by items such as rotting food, waste products, and small animals associated with dirt and disease (e.g., maggots). Animal reminder disgust refers to elicitors that remind individuals of their animal origins through sight stimuli such as blood, veins, tissue, and death. Violations of hygienic norms have been conceptualized as animal reminder disgust because they are related to animalistic behavior (Haidt, McCauley, & Rozin 1994; Rozin et al., 1993).

Several recent studies have examined the relationship between disgust and contamination fears (see Olatunji & Sawchuk [2005] for a review). This work has yielded the following conclusions. First, individuals with heightened contamination fear also experience greater levels of disgust, even for unrelated, noncontamination stimuli (Olatunji et al., 2004; Tsao & McKay, 2004). Second, relative to fear, disgust is more difficult to ameliorate through cognitive-behavioral therapy, particularly via exposure methods (McKay, 2006). This is attributed to the manner that individuals develop disgust reactions. Disgust is learned through a process called *evaluative conditioning* (for a review, see McKay & Tsao, 2005). This form of conditioning has been shown to be resistant to extinction in general (de Houwer, Thomas, & Baeyens, 2001). Third, disgust, unlike fear, involves the parasympathetic nervous system (Tsao & McKay, 2005). This finding may also contribute to the difficulty in eliminating disgust reactions among individuals with contamination fear. Recent investigations have suggested that habituation, measured by self-report, occurs with prolonged exposure to disgust (Smits, Telch, & Randall, 2002). However, when habituation has been examined using psychophysiologic assessments, habituation occurred for areas associated with tensing muscles (nostrils). Habituation occurred to a lesser extent for areas associated with parasympathetic activation such as heart rate, respiration, and body temperature (Tsao & McKay, 2005). This suggests that although respondents describe habituation the physical experience associated with the stimuli remains. Further, the effects of exposure tend to generalize poorly to other ostensibly disgusting stimuli (Tsao & McKay, 2005).

Behavioral and Cognitive Features

Fear of contamination is associated with widespread avoidance of stimuli deemed contaminated as well as objects that may have come in incidental contact with the contaminant. In a functional analysis of the scope of contamination fear, one would examine both the core contaminant as well as the extent to which the contaminant can be "spread." For example, Dave, a 45-year-old man seen by one of the authors (D.M.), reported that contaminants associated with the presence of particular people led to avoidance of specific towns near his home. Because of his fear, Dave would drive out of his way by as much as 45 minutes to avoid contact with the town where "contaminated" individuals resided.

Avoidance is typical of contamination fear, perhaps at a higher level than for other symptoms of OCD (Clark, 2004). This may be accounted for by the ability of patients to identify specific stimuli associated with contamination, akin to phobias (Rachman & Hodgson, 1980; Rasmussen & Eisen, 1998). Recent findings have shown that contamination reactions may be provoked by images or ideas of dirt (Fairbrother, Newth, & Rachman, 2005). Referred to as "mental pollution" (Rachman, 2004), these reactions do not respond as well to washing, may not have a specific body region associated with the contaminated reaction, and may be more difficult to avoid (Fairbrother et al., 2005).

Contamination fear can result in a range of severe symptoms, such as washing, often with abrasive agents rather than simply soap and water. For example, one patient seen by the senior author washed her hands with granulated dishwashing detergent and had begun using steel wool when she was referred for treatment. Other examples include the use of bleach or granulated laundry detergent. In addition to these symptoms, it is common for individuals who fear contamination to develop ritualized approaches to washing, including counting the number of times washed before terminating the count. For example, the aforementioned client who washed with dishwashing detergent washed her hand 12 times before determining they were "clean." If this cycle was broken (i.e., she was interrupted), she would start over. This type of avoidance behavior is maintained by negative reinforcement, whereby the behavior is more likely to recur because it results in the alleviation of a negative state (e.g., anxiety).

In some instances, the degree of ritualized washing can become so severe that patients stop washing altogether and rely exclusively on avoidance to cope with their fear. For example, a client seen by the senior author had not showered or left her home for eight months before seeking treatment. The client spent each day on her couch and walked only on designated paths through her home (i.e., route to bathroom, kitchen, bedroom) that were regarded as "clean." She reasoned that because her last shower was "complete" (it took more than eight hours), and that she had not been in contact with any contaminants, there was no need to shower again. She recognized that this was not reasonable, but the difficulty of engaging in the washing ritual was simply too great to withstand and so avoidance was deemed a better option.

Although this type of behavior is well documented, other cognitive biases must be considered in evaluating individuals with contamination fear. Many individuals with contamination fear show cognitive errors typical of other types of OCD, including thought-action fusion (thinking of contaminants makes one contaminated), inflated responsibility, overestimation of threat, and perfectionistic concerns. These beliefs have been found to predict symp-

Table 2.1. Cognitive Distortions Common to Contamination Fear

Belief Domain	Cognitive Distortion Associated with Contamination
Thought-action fusion	"I just thought of all the germs in my pharmacy from the sick patrons, so I better wash."
Inflated responsibility	"I had better wash thoroughly so I do not get other people sick."
Overestimation of threat	"I shook hands with someone who 'looks sick,' so I will have to take a shower right away."
Perfectionism	"It is essential to completely clean all the dirt off."
Intolerance of uncertainty	"The smallest amount of contaminant might lead to harm."

toms of OCD generally (Taylor, McKay, & Abramowitz, 2005). Examples of cognitive distortions associated with each of these themes, in relation to contamination fears, are presented in Table 2.1.

Treatment

Pharmacotherapy

Contamination fears, as noted earlier, are a frequently occurring concern among persons with OCD. As such, most medication trials for OCD have included individuals with contamination fears. Recent research has shown that changes in regional cerebral blood flow in the orbitofrontal cortex predicts treatment response for OCD patients with contamination fear when fluvoxamine is prescribed (Rauch et al., 2002). Other research has shown that, collectively, serotonin reuptake inhibitor medications perform well for contamination fear (Mataix-Cols et al., 1999). The only symptom dimension that responds poorly is hoarding (see Chapter 6).

Psychological Treatment

Early treatment for contamination fear involved deliberate exposure to dirt and contaminants, followed by therapist-guided delays of cleaning rituals (e.g., Rachman, Hodgson, & Marks, 1971). This was also among the earliest interventions for OCD. Contamination fear was an ideal symptom for establishing the efficacy of exposure and response prevention (ERP) for OCD. It has clearly observable symptoms and readily identifiable stimuli for exposure. Given that compulsions typically accompanying contamination fear are also readily observed, response prevention is also more easily conducted. Because of these characteristics, the treatment of contamination fear laid the groundwork for ERP as applied to other major symptoms of OCD. Recent research has shown that contamination fear has particularly good response to this treatment (Abramowitz, Franklin, Schwartz, & Furr, 2003).

Recent modifications to ERP have included cognitive interventions. One modification, in a treatment package referred to as Danger Ideation Reduction Therapy (DIRT; Jones & Menzies, 1997, 1998) involves training in specific reappraisals regarding the dangerousness of contaminants. In one trial (Jones & Menzies, 1998), DIRT was shown to be effective in alleviating symptoms without conducting ERP. Although the research is still preliminary, it holds promise when used in conjunction with ERP, particularly for cases where clients express hesitancy regarding the specific demands of exposure-based treatment.

Case Vignette

Avoidance due to concerns with contaminants is motivated by disgust as well as by fear. Recent work has shown that disgust habituates in ways similar to fear with prolonged exposure (McKay, 2006). Habituation refers to a specific behavioral process thought to occur because of exposure-based treatments; prolonged and repeated exposure to stimuli that evoke emotional states such as fear and disgust results in the eventual diminution of the emotional state (Foa & Kozak, 1986). Because contamination fear closely resembles phobia, these distress-evoking stimuli may be readily identified. Further, given that recent findings have shown that contamination concerns may be provoked by imagery, stimuli that are inaccessible during a session (i.e., particular body fluids) may be confronted in imagery (imaginal exposure). In comparison with fear reactions, however, more time is required for disgust to habituate due in part to the aforementioned evaluative conditioning. Patients essentially label the stimuli as "disgusting," which interferes with habituation. This is not necessarily the case for fear reactions.

Peter presented for treatment with a 17-year history of contamination fear. At the time of treatment, he was 36 years old, unmarried, and living alone in an apartment in an industrial area of town. He was fully employed at the time of treatment. He traced his primary symptom onset to an occasion when his sink faucet was turned on and the water was an "unusual color." Peter grew very concerned that this water, and all that it contacted, would cause a variety of physical ailments, including loss of intellectual functioning, stomach and intestinal distress, and permanent physical disfiguration.

At the time of treatment, Peter's primary rituals included extensive washing, usually requiring more than an hour for showering in the morning, and constantly checking the water to be sure it was not discolored. If he suspected that the water was "contaminated," he would avoid showering and, instead, wash himself in the sink at his workplace. Peter also avoided certain places in his apartment where he suspected that the contaminated water had spilled or been transferred. For example, if guests to his apartment walked into the bathroom, washed, and spilled water on the floor (even a few drops), then returned to the living room and placed their feet on the couch, Peter would avoid the couch. There were numerous places in the apartment that were deemed contaminated due to this process. Likewise, areas at his workplace could also become contaminated in this manner.

While this anxiety component of Peter's contamination fear was prominent, he also went to great lengths to avoid other contaminants due to their disgusting nature. For example, he avoided garbage receptacles, large trash containers ("dumpsters") and smaller trash cans whenever possible. When he discarded food items or took his garbage out for pickup, he would wear surgical gloves to avoid direct contact. Peter reported disgust during this activity, and made facial expressions to support his assertion. This problem contributed significantly to his other contamination problems. For example, he reported that while he worried that the *contaminants* would cause physical harm, he also found it "disturbing" that such contaminants could exist, that the idea of the dirt and contaminants were "gross," and that he struggled with the possibility of contact with these toxins because he could not tolerate the "disgusting feeling" the items provoked.

Peter had never participated in cognitive-behavior therapy (CBT) before the current trial. He had been treated only with fluvoxamine, which he had taken for a period of four years before initiating CBT. Peter reported that his symptoms remitted because of the medication, but he felt that he struggled to cope with keeping track of places and objects that were clean and those that were not.

Peter agreed to begin exposure with response prevention to target his fears of stimuli that provoked fear and that caused disgust reactions. Over the course of five 90-minute exposure sessions, his anxiety regarding fear-evoking stimuli (such as objects around his home) diminished significantly. Specific treatment instructions included washing using soap and water from the contaminated sink and refraining from washing again for the remainder of the day. Following the fourth session, Peter kept the "contaminated" water with him in a bottle, and rinsed his hands with it two to three times per day, thus "recontaminating" himself. During the same five-session period, his disgust reactions diminished at a much slower rate and even *increased* after one session. During an additional five sessions, he was able to experience lower disgust reactions. Figure 2.1 shows Peter's habituation rate for both anxiety and disgust over the ten-session period.

At the start of treatment, Peter exhibited a number of cognitive distortions, notably an overestimation of threat. For example, he believed that his risk of contracting illness increased significantly if he stood outside a medical lab, even without direct contact with the door or other patients. He also described thought-action fusion for thoughts involving the following items: garbage, hospitals and doctor's offices, pharmacies, and the sink in his home. For example, when he thought of the prospect of having a blood test, which he expected when he began his medication trial, he felt as though he were in contact with a lab technician and felt contaminated at the mere thought. Although cognitive therapy was conducted briefly following the period of intensive exposure treatment, his cognitive distortions had diminished greatly by that point. This is consistent with the recent report that exposure-based exercises, even in the context of cognitive therapy, may have the greatest therapeutic benefit (Abramowitz, Taylor, & McKay, 2005).

Conclusion

Fear of contamination is one of the most common concerns among persons with OCD. While its treatment has been well documented, the literature has, until recently, focused largely on *anxiety* components of contamination fear and less on other types of psychological experiences that motivate active and passive avoidance. One area that has received attention recently is the degree that disgust plays a role in contamination fear and associated avoidance. This area has shown promise in predicting avoidance and may serve as an important area for future treatment intervention. Preliminary findings suggest that, like anxiety, disgust reactions habituate with exposure but after a longer duration than that required for anxiety (McKay, 2006). Additional work is required in this area to determine the degree that disgust contributes to treatment nonresponse or maintains avoidance following successful treatment for fear asso-

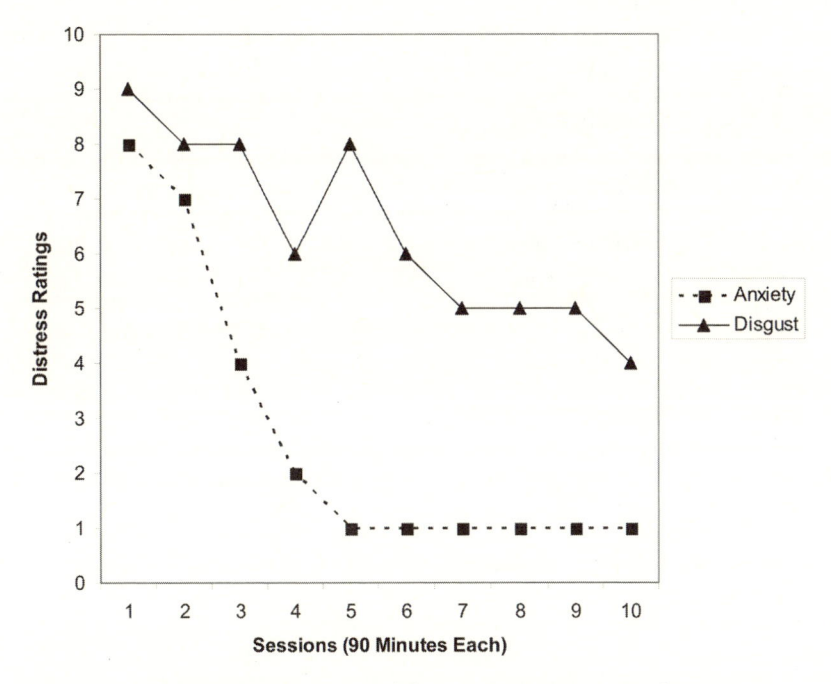

Figure 2.1. Habituation to anxiety and disgust across 10 sessions for Peter.

ciated with contamination. Similar work has been conducted in spider fear, for example (Mulkens, de Jong, & Merckelbach, 1996). The early findings suggest a similar association may exist for contamination fear.

REFERENCES

Abramowitz, J. S., Franklin, M. E., Schwartz, S. A., & Furr, J. M. (2003). Symptom presentation and outcome of cognitive-behavioral therapy for obsessive-compulsive disorder. *Journal of Consulting and Clinical Psychology, 71,* 1049–1057.

Abramowitz, J., Taylor, S., & McKay, D. (2005). Potentials and limitations of cognitive treatments for obsessive-compulsive disorder. *Cognitive Behaviour Therapy, 34,* 140–147.

Clark, D. A. (2004). *Cognitive-behavioral therapy for OCD.* New York: Guilford.

De Houwer, J., Thomas, S., & Baeyens, F. (2001). Associative learning of likes and dislikes: 25 years of research on human evaluative conditioning. *Psychological Bulletin, 127,* 853–869.

Ekman, P., & Friesen, W. V. (1986). A new pan-cultural facial expression of emotion. *Motivation and Emotion, 10,* 159–168.

Fairbrother, N., Newth, S. J., & Rachman, S. (2005). Mental pollution: Feelings of dirtiness without physical contact. *Behaviour Research and Therapy, 43,* 121–130.

Foa, E. B., & Kozak, M. J. (1986). Emotional processing of fear: Exposure to corrective information. *Psychological Bulletin, 99,* 20–35.

Foa, E. B., & Kozak, M. J. (1995). DSM-IV field trial: Obsessive-compulsive disorder. *American Journal of Psychiatry, 152,* 90–96.

Frazer, J. G. (1959). *The golden bough: A study in magic and religion,* New York.

Freeston, M. H., & Ladouceur, R. (1997). What do patients do with their obsessive thoughts? *Behaviour Research and Therapy, 35,* 335–348.

Haidt, J., McCauley, C., & Rozin, P. (1994). Individual differences in sensitivity to disgust: A scale sampling seven domains of disgust elicitors. *Personality and Individual Differences, 16,* 701–713.

Hodgson, R. J., & Rachman, S. (1977). Obsessive-compulsive complaints. *Behaviour Research and Therapy, 15,* 389–395.

Jones, M. K., & Menzies, R. G. (1997). Danger Ideation Reduction Therapy: Preliminary findings with three obsessive-compulsive washers. *Behaviour Research and Therapy, 35,* 955–960.

Jones, M. K., & Menzies, R. G. (1998). Danger Ideation Reduction Therapy for obsessive-compulsive washers: A controlled trial. *Behaviour Research and Therapy, 36,* 959–970.

Leckman, J. F., Boardman, J., Zhang, H., & Grice, D. (1997). Symptoms of obsessive-compulsive disorder. *American Journal of Psychiatry, 154,* 911–917.

Mataix-Cols, D., Rauch, S. L., Manzo, P. A., Jenike, M. A., & Baer, L. (1999). Use of factor analyzed symptom dimensions to predict outcome with serotonin reuptake inhibitors and placebo in the treatment of obsessive-compulsive disorder. *American Journal of Psychiatry, 156,* 1409–1416.

Mauss, M. (1972). *A general theory of magic* (R. Brain, Trans.). New York: W. W. Norton.

McKay, D. (2006). Treating disgust reactions in contamination-based obsessive-compulsive disorder. *Journal of Behavior Therapy and Experimental Psychiatry, 37,* 53–59.

McKay, D., & Tsao, S. (2005). A treatment most foul: Handling disgust in cognitive-behavior therapy. *Journal of Cognitive Psychotherapy: An International Quarterly, 19,* 355–367.

Mulkens, S. A. N., de Jong, P. J., & Merckelbach, H. (1996). Disgust in spider phobia. *Journal of Abnormal Psychology, 105,* 464–468.

Olatunji, B. O., & Sawchuk, C. N. (2005). Disgust: Characteristic features, social manifestations, and clinical implications. *Journal of Social and Clinical Psychology, 24,* 934–962.

Olatunji, B. O., Sawchuk, C. N., Lohr, J. M., & de Jong, P. J. (2004). Disgust domains in the prediction of contamination fear. *Behaviour Research and Therapy, 42,* 93–104.

Power, M., & Dalgleish, T. (1997). *Cognition and emotion: Form order to disorder.* East Sussex, UK: Psychology Press.

Rachman, S. (2004). Fear of contamination. *Behaviour Research and Therapy, 42,* 1227–1255.

Rachman, S., & Hodgson, R. (1980). *Obsessions and compulsions.* Englewood Cliffs, NJ: Prentice Hall.

Rachman, S., Hodgson, R., & Marks, I. M. (1971). The treatment of chronic obsessive-compulsive neurosis. *Behaviour Research and Therapy, 9,* 237–247.

Rasmussen, S. A., & Eisen, J. L. (1998). The epidemiology and clinical features of obsessive-compulsive disorder. In M. A. Jenike, L. Baer, & W. E. Minichiello (Eds.), *Obsessive-compulsive disorders: Practical management* (pp. 12–43). St. Louis: Mosby.

Rasmussen, S. A., & Tsuang, M. T. (1986). Clinical characteristics and family history in DSM-III obsessive-compulsive disorder. *American Journal of Psychiatry, 143,* 317–322.

Rauch, S. L., Shin, L. M., Dougherty, D. D., Alpert, N. M., Fischman, A. J., & Jenike, M. A. (2002). Predictors of fluvoxamine response in contamination related obsessive-compulsive disorder: A PET symptom provocation study. *Neuropsychopharmacology, 27,* 782–791.

Rozin, P., & Fallon, A. E. (1987). A perspective on disgust. *Psychological Review, 94,* 23–41.

Rozin, P., Haidt, J., & McCauley, C. (1993). Disgust. In J. M. Haviland (Ed.), *Handbook of emotions.* New York: Guilford Press.

Smits, J. A. J., Telch, M. J., & Randall, P. K. (2002). An examination of the decline in fear and disgust during exposure-based treatment. *Behaviour Research and Therapy, 40,* 1243–1253.

Steketee, G. S., Grayson, J. B., & Foa, E. B. (1985). Obsessive-compulsive disorder: Differences between washers and checkers. *Behaviour Research and Therapy, 23,* 197–201.

Taylor, S., McKay, D., & Abramowitz, J. (2005). Hierarchical structure of dysfunctional beliefs in obsessive-compulsive disorder. *Cognitive Behaviour Therapy, 34,* 216–228.

Tsao, S. D., & McKay, D. (2004). Behavioral avoidance tests and disgust in contamination fear: Distinctions from trait anxiety. *Behaviour Research and Therapy, 42,* 207–216.

Tsao, S. D., & McKay, D. (2005). *Generalizability of the effects of exposure in disgust.* Unpublished manuscript.

Woody, S. R., & Tolin, D. F. (2002). The relationship between disgust sensitivity and avoidant behavior: Studies of clinical and nonclinical samples. *Journal of Anxiety Disorders, 16,* 543–559.

CHAPTER THREE

Compulsive Checking

Johan Rosqvist, Psy.D., and Darcy C. Norling, M.S.

Repetitive checking of things such as on-off switches, windows and locks, parking brakes, and even checking with other people (asking questions over and over) in the absence of any obvious threat of responsibility for harm or mistakes is a puzzling phenomenon. How can a person keep on checking, ad nauseam, as if stuck in an endless loop, for some perceived or imagined problem or danger? Although most people would view such irrational behavior as senseless and excessive, many individuals with obsessive-compulsive disorder (OCD; American Psychiatric Association, 2000) engage in ritualized checking to the point of physical, emotional, and, at times, financial exhaustion. In this chapter we describe the clinical characteristics of OCD checking symptoms, review theoretical explanations for this problem, and focus on the assessment and treatment of this presentation of OCD. We use case examples to illustrate the clinical severity and treatment methods described.

Clinical Presentation

Rachman (2003) referred to the confusing nature of compulsive checking, one of the more common presentations of OCD, as "bewildering and self-defeating" (p. 139). Pathological doubt, indecisiveness, perfectionism, and intolerance for uncertainty, which many obsessive-compulsive patients experience at often excessive, irrational, and unreasonable levels and frequencies, virtually define and explain the backbone to this distressing, but all-too-common symptom subtype (e.g., Shafran, Cooper, & Fairburn, 2002; Tolin, Abramowitz, Brigidi, & Foa, 2003) of OCD.

The motivation behind compulsive checking appears to be related to preventing future calamities. This type of preventative behavior is commonly engaged in to protect people from harm. This desire for protection can also be directed toward property and toward the patient him or herself. To prevent harm, patients with OCD often use faulty reasoning, relying on checking and other ineffectual or even magically protective measures (Rachman & Hodgson, 1980). For example, OCD patients commonly appraise "crimes of commission" (e.g., a driver intentionally hitting a pedestrian with his or her automobile) and "crimes of omission" (e.g., a driver failing to see the pedestrian, or another car, and thereby accidentally causing "harm") as equally "bad." Thus, accidental harm is viewed, in this morally overreaching and flawed reasoning, as indistinct from intentional harm because it has any influence over outcome. This belief structure is often associated with rigid beliefs about right and wrong, good and bad, and morality, in which any influence becomes equated with absolute responsibility. This phenomenon is often referred to as *moral-action-fusion* (Shafran, Thordarson, & Rachman, 1996), which has obvious similarities to *thought-action-fusion*, the belief that thoughts are the moral equivalent of, and can influence, actions (Smari & Holmsteinsson, 2001).

Compulsions are perhaps the single most common recognizable form of OCD, as many rituals are overtly viewable and veritably odd appearing to casual and trained observers alike. Indeed, compulsions may even be the best-defining feature of OCD, and its two most typical forms are checking and cleaning compulsions, although checking appears more common than cleaning (Rachman, 2003).

By definition, compulsions are senseless and excessive repetitive purposeful acts, which can be either (overt) behavioral or cognitive (covert behavioral) and often governed by rules and stereotypes. Although *compulsions* are "voluntary" (i.e., operative rather than reflexive) behaviors, it is important to understand and appreciate the inherently coercive nature of what it means to be compelled to act. Just because a compulsion is performed to alleviate distress does not imply the patient willingly engages in such action(s). Instead, he or she often reports feeling a building pressure to relieve some unpleasant, if not outright intolerable, affective state. Conceptually, this is similar in irresistibility to premonitory urges that occur with Tourette syndrome and trichotillomania, except compulsive checking does not appear to have quite the same organic flavor as tics.

Rosqvist (2005) referred to this basic human behavioral tendency as "Hedonism 101," when he suggested, "through eons of evolution, this basic modus operandi increased sheer odds of survival" (p. 182). This basic modus operandi refers to that innately self-preserving human quality to have a natural, normal evolutionarily programmed drive to increase what feels good and decrease or eliminate what feels bad. Put differently, checking has saved people's lives over eons, and it continues into modern life to prevent disasters. Evolutionarily, this *safety behavior* follows people worldwide, through time and circumstance. Aristotle even said, "We are what we repeatedly do." Indeed, most people do check but not to pathological levels. Nonetheless, people are checkers by design and we remain so by continuing, not straying far from Aristotle's early observation.

There is a difference between ordinary checking, such as looking left-right-left or right-left-right (depending on where in the world you reside) before crossing the street, presumably sparked by the normal disinclination to be run over, and pathological checking. Pathological checking is not just about those natural inclinations but is often focused on all of the permutations for what could perhaps go wrong or possibly be bad in the world (and in oneself), absent evidence that indicates anything horrific will occur now or in the future. In *compulsive checking*, what is monitored has also never actually happened, nor would it be likely to. Yet, this pressure to check becomes too strong to resist, even when patients are otherwise completely rational and reasonable when it comes to thinking about unrelated topics and circumstances. Unfortunately, this lack of evidence (i.e., the "bad thing" did not occur, nor has it ever occurred) is in itself a compelling and powerful agent in preserving the odd behavioral presence of persistent and compulsive checking.

Case Vignette

Bill, a 34-year-old software programmer, experienced checking driven by fears he would harm others. At the beginning of treatment, he refused to drive his car, fearing he would hit someone or cause an accident. When he drove, he would engage in such extensive checking and other odd maneuvering that he ironically represented a genuine threat to others (e.g., he would unexpectedly and unpredictably speed up, slow down, switch lanes, and look behind him for long periods of time [while driving!]). He insisted that his wife ride along to assure him he had not missed some disaster he believed he must have created, and after such outings, he would voraciously check various media for information about recent car accidents. Not surprisingly, Bill had great difficulty accomplishing such tasks as traveling to and from work and driving to the grocery store without tremendous suffering. Although he had never been in a car accident, he pursued knowledge about accidents to "be prepared for what to do, if one occurred." In addition, he often had to change car insurance, after being labeled *persona non grata* on numerous occasions for calling his agent daily to check whether anyone had reported a hit-and-run accident involving him.

According to Rachman (1976), there are several predominant and notable features of compulsive checking: most checking occurs in the patient's home; it is usually done when the person is alone; it typically intensifies with depression; behaviors are worst whenever the patient feels responsible for the safety or well-being of others. Rachman also suggested that maladaptive misinterpretations of significance of one's out-of-control, repetitive checking, and poor memory often produce a conviction that more checking is needed (Rachman, 2002).

Basis for Considering Compulsive Checking a Subtype of OCD

The impetus for considering OCD as an umbrella phenomenon under which several subtypes prevail came from Marks (1969). He distinguished between contamination/washer and harm/checker types of OCD patients, and in this differentiation, he suggested there were different (sub)types of the phenomenon. A plethora of subtyping research has since been conducted (e.g., Leckman et al., 1997; Van Oppen, Hoekstra, & Emmelkamp, 1995). Although some gender-based subtype differences exist (e.g., more women compulsively wash than men), OCD occurs about equally among men and women, with lifetime prevalence rates in North America estimated at 2.3 percent (Taylor, Thordarson, & Söchting, 2002).

While evidence suggests that compulsive checking and compulsive washing are the two most common and distinct subtypes, there is less overall agreement about other subtypes (e.g., symmetry/precision, hoarding, primary slowness). In addition, patients exhibit symptoms that cut across types and symptoms, and symptoms might change over time (Skoog & Skoog, 1999). Thus, dimensional analysis of symptom clustering may have limited utility in understanding symptom processes and etiology.

Theoretical Models and Etiologic Issues

While a number of theoretical explanations exist for compulsive checking, a distinct movement in the field toward more scientific rationales has overshadowed earlier, primarily psychoanalytic and psychodynamic, ways of thinking about this issue. In particular, behavioral approaches centering around Mowrer's (1960) two-stage model offer learning-theory-based reasons for the phenomenon and especially for its maintenance. Rosqvist (2005) argued that Mowrer's two-stage theory "provides the strongest argument for why anxiety and fear do not naturally or easily extinguish when people learn to escape from, or successfully avoid, feared stimuli" (p. 28). This holds true for compulsive checking as well.

According to Mowrer's anxiety reduction hypothesis, people are motivated to avoid fear, and when feared stimuli are unavoidable, this same motivation drives people to escape. This makes sense for species survival, so with successful escape, the behavior is more likely to be repeated in the future. In the specific case of compulsive checking, such behavior reduces, if only briefly, obsessional doubts and uncertainty, leading to a corresponding temporary reduction in distress.

Rachman and Hodgson (1980) conceptualized compulsive checking as *active avoidance*, and by this line of reasoning, it persists because it is successful, however temporary, in reducing anxiety and fear that is produced by aversive obsessions. Because relief is negatively reinforcing, it increases odds the patient will re-engage the same behavior the next time the unpleasant state is experienced.

Paradoxically, compulsively checking, which is meant to alleviate distress, in effect ensures that conditioned noxious stimuli (i.e., obsessions), retain their capacity to elicit future distress and discomfort, keeping the patient continually crippled and trapped through the associative process to prior distress (Steketee, 1993). Indeed, the avoidance response of compulsive checking persists because it allows escape from a fear state, where fear has been described as a motivational system that organizes an organism's responding at many different levels (e.g., overt behavioral, autonomic functioning) so that it is best prepared to protect itself from danger. In OCD, compulsive checking functions to protect against such "threats" as guilt and criticism/fault, but such escape/relief is fleeting, and the conditioned cycle of anxiety elicitation and relief only repeats. Metaphorically, pain thusly continues veritably unchecked.

A more contemporary theoretical model of OCD is based on Salkovskis's (1985) argument that unwanted (yet normal) intrusive thoughts (e.g., those pertaining to personal responsibility) produce subjective distress when they are misinterpreted as having implications for harm or its prevention (e.g., "Having this thought implies I am responsible for making sure a bad outcome does not transpire"), which then leads to compensatory/protective behaviors. This cognitive-behavioral approach represents an increasing focus on how patients with OCD think and reason, considering pathological cognitive processes rather than the content or theme of obsessions and compulsions.

Central to this appraisal-based theory of how distress is caused are people's subjective meaning-making and personal significance-assigning to situations, objects, and events; in other words, patients with OCD generate inflated threat estimates because of, for example, flawed probability and cost estimations (Söchting, Whittal, & McLean, 1997). Combine this formula for fear with additional components, such as intolerance for uncertainty and importance of thought (e.g., Overton & Menzies, 2002), perfectionism/control, and responsibility (e.g., Salkovskis, 1985, 1989), and it appears likely that maladaptive cognition is the pathogenic culprit in maintaining in OCD. Clark (2004) reported that "in the long term, the faulty appraisals and control strategies will both heighten the salience of the mental intrusion and cause an increase in its frequency" (p. 90). Significant implications for etiologic, maintenance, and treatment issues are obvious if one accepts the ever-better supported theoretical premise that cognition is important and/or meaningful to persons with OCD and that, therefore, patients feel compelled to act on them.

Assessment

OCD is typically assessed both on broad-band and narrow-band bases, for a host of validity/reliability and empirical change-measurement reasons. To ameliorate human suffering, practitioners need to assess accurately and gauge the significance of patients' problems. They must also understand how patients suffer in order to offer meaningful, individually tailored solutions. There are now well-established instruments to facilitate accurately accessing the presence or absence of the diagnosis, as well as the breadth and severity of the disorder.

Evidence-based practice appropriately retains a foundation of relying on scientific findings, a range of tested and valid treatment regiments, and sound, consistent empirical measurement of conditions treated. This reliance on empirical standards serves as the strongest foundation for the construction of broad- and narrow-band instruments described next.

To diagnose OCD, the Anxiety Disorders Interview Schedule for DSM-IV (ADIS-IV; Di Nardo, Brown, & Barlow, 1994) supplies information required for both validly/reliably exacting not only the diagnosis but also for assessing its approximate severity and functional impact. The Structured Clinical Interview for DSM-IV (SCID-IV; First, Spitzer, Gibbon, & Williams, 1996) is diagnostically similar, and if practitioners suspect comorbid diagnosis the SCID offers the added benefit of covering a broader range of disorders.

Once the diagnosis has been confirmed, the next step is to assess thoroughly various aspects about individual patients' symptom presentation, and this has traditionally been best derived through reliance on the Yale-Brown Obsessive Compulsive Scale (Y-BOCS; Goodman et al., 1989). This instrument, like the ADIS-IV and SCID-IV, is user friendly, and can be administered by practitioners with basic comprehension of semistructured interviews; the Y-BOCS is also available in a self-administered version.

Treatment

Before the mid-1960s, OCD was not seen as being amenable to treatment, but with the advent of Meyer's (1966) exposure and response prevention (ERP), the otherwise bleak prognosis for OCD changed to strong outcomes, especially when practitioners provided CBT with an ERP focus. CBT/ERP effects are often augmented with pharmacologic agents (e.g., antidepressants). Patients improved by ERP are also typically able to maintain their gains at follow-ups of at least one to five years (Baer & Minichiello, 1998).

CBT can also be delivered without ERP because some patients indicate refusal to engage in exposure therapy (which can be highly anxiety-provoking), and some discontinue this form of treatment after having begun. When CBT is provided without ERP, the aim is to help patients accurately gauge probability, expect more reasonable outcomes, see themselves as more capable, and, if need be, access various support networks during challenging times. Although such versions of CBT do not include frequent and prolonged exposure in which repeated habituation and extinction are goals, they do emphasize "behavioral experiments." These exercises have similarities with ERP in that patients are often instructed to face certain feared circumstances, but only to the point that sufficient information has been gathered to dispute maladaptive beliefs about probability, the importance of intrusive thoughts, or responsibility. Rarely do such behavioral experiments require that the patient remain exposed to the fear-evoking stimulus for a prolonged period (i.e., until the habituation of anxiety occurs).

Evidence for the Effectiveness of Treatment

CBT with an ERP emphasis is well established as the most potent treatment for OCD symptoms, including checking rituals (Baer & Minichiello, 1998). Foa, Franklin, and Kozak (1998) reported that 70 to 83 percent of ERP patients are labeled "much improved" at termination, suggesting most patients treated with ERP techniques move from clinical to nonclinical ranges in OCD symptoms. Whittal and McLean (1999) suggested that ERP alone merely changes patients' thoughts and beliefs about dangerous situations through learning what is dangerous; and that ERP does not really change a cognitive style of erroneous reasoning.

However, careful studies illustrate that ERP produces change in irrational beliefs (Marks, 1997). When McLean and colleagues (2001) directly compared CBT and ERP, they found both approaches produced significant reductions, but that ERP was more effective than CBT by the end of treatment and again at the three-month follow-up. They also found the extent of cognitive change was similar between CBT and ERP groups. Findings such as these support the importance of ERP in efficacious, effective, and efficient treatment of OCD (cf. Rosqvist, 2005). Abramowitz (2002) recently illustrated that ERP remains the treatment of choice for extinguishing obsessive thought and cognitive rituals. Franklin, Riggs, and Pai (2005) also showed ERP as the psychosocial treatment of choice for OCD. Although EPR is not a panacea, it is an important treatment option.

Case Vignette

Martha, a 42-year-old middle school teacher, sought help for intrusive thoughts of brutally killing her two sons with kitchen knives. She avoided her sons, fearing that she might hurt them in other ways, too. She stayed out of the kitchen whenever her sons were home. Reassurance from her sons and her husband had not diminished these fears but had instead made her doubt whether she had any self-control. She had never hurt anyone. Nevertheless, she would not leave knives or other sharp implements in plain sight for fear that she would injure, or even worse, kill someone. Her suffering was almost incomprehensible because her obsessions attacked what mattered most in her life.

Like most patients with OCD, Martha demonstrated good insight into the illogical nature of her thoughts but was sufficiently disturbed when she experienced them. She was unable to rely on data that she had never harmed anyone and that she did not want to or that she was not an impulsive person and that, indeed, she loved her sons dearly.

In short, she was trapped by the need to be certain she would not harm them, and she had even come to believe having these thoughts and aversive images meant she was an evil and sinful person (i.e., she exhibited significance / importance / morality of thought). Consequently, to no surprise, she engaged in extensive checking rituals (e.g., was she [unbeknownst to her] carrying a knife in her pocket? How close was she to her sons, and where were they when she was preparing food?). She also exhibited common avoidance behaviors (e.g., she would not hug her sons, generally would not get within arm's reach of them, would never prepare food in their presence, or would frequently order pizza that came presliced).

Although Martha understood OCD somewhat, complete psychoeducation was provided at the start of treatment to help her comprehend the vicious cycle by which the obsessive fears and checking rituals were maintained. This educational module provided some relief to Martha, as she came to recognize that she was not "going crazy" and that unusual and nasty thoughts/intrusions occur among most people. Nevertheless, her fears of acting on her obsessions, and her checking rituals, were not diminished.

The therapist next explained the principles of ERP to Martha, who at first was somewhat skeptical. After collaborative exploration of learning theory principles and everyday examples, however, she agreed to give this form of treatment an earnest and honest effort. A graded hierarchy of feared circumstances was developed, focusing primarily on being around sharp implements and other people at the same time, to varying degrees. Her most feared item was using knives during food preparation with her sons present. Other items included whittling (with pocketknives) together with her sons, to carrying a knife in her pocket in their presence, and so on. At the lower end of her hierarchy was being in the presence of scissors, when around nonfamily. This is where exposure treatment started.

Early treatment sessions took place in the first author's office, with Martha sitting close to a pair of scissors without touching them, while 10 feet away was her prospective "next kill" (the therapist). This exercise was not stopped until habituation occurred. In this fashion, Martha gradually progressed toward sitting right next to Dr. Rosqvist on a sofa while holding scissors. All along, subjective units of distress were monitored on 5–10-minute intervals, gauging habituation within session. When this exercise began to fail to elicit trepidation, she was next asked to hold the scissors to Dr. Rosqvist's exposed wrist. Martha's anxiety initially peaked at the idea of cutting Dr. Rosqvist, yet after a few minutes, this distress declined and in Martha's words, the fear of acting on the unwanted thoughts seemed "ridiculous." At this point, still focusing on scissors, Martha was asked to hold the scissors to Dr. Rosqvist's exposed neck. This task again made her concerned, very uncomfortable, and quite upset, to such a degree that she would initially not agree to perform the exercise. With patience and support, and after thoroughly again exploring learning theories and the best predictors of behaviors (i.e., the past), she finally agreed and did hold the scissors to his neck. Habituation did not occur for an extended period during the first scissors-to-neck exposure, but eventually and predictably anxiety subsided. This exercise was therefore repeated several times, again until Martha began to feel a little silly sitting in Dr. Rosqvist's office with scissors to his throat.

At that point, exposures switched from using scissors to a penknife, still with Dr. Rosqvist as the "victim." The same procedures were used, but Martha was able to start this part of the hierarchy already holding the small penknife. All of the same exercises were repeated. The same results followed. When the penknife failed to produce distress, a significantly larger and much sharper kitchen knife was used. The same procedures were followed. It may be worth mentioning that Dr. Rosqvist was never so much as nicked; nor did he feel as if he was ever in any danger. When holding a kitchen knife to Dr. Rosqvist's throat repeatedly no longer produced arousal, her husband was brought into the session. She sat next to him with scissors and then knives of various sorts and types. She even brought her own knives. The next step was the hardest, as that brought in her sons and she had to repeat this process with each and both of them, as that represented the absolute core and most threatening content of her fear structure. Such exercises were also prescribed to be carried out in Martha's home, always with a focus on achieving habituation.

Following her successful trial of CBT, Martha regularly cooked with family, she did not hide anything sharp in her house, and she began carrying a pocketknife as a perpetual reminder (a relapse prevention measure) that many fears are unfounded and that unreasonable, irrational, and excessive ones are undone and conquered by eliminating unnecessary arousal and inaccurate anxiety. Toward the latter part of treatment, Martha spontaneously reported several times having few, if any, violent or aggressive thoughts. In fact, she reported that she had come to see herself as a kind, gentle, caring, and compassionate person. She had always been one, but she had just not seen it through the fear, anxiety, shame, guilt, and depression that OCD so often inflicts.

Troubleshooting

Central in preventing unreasonable treatment expectations, premature dropouts, and poor homework adherence (poor prognostic indicators) is helping patients completely and accurately understand the rationale for exposure-based treatment. Commonly, this is addressed through "consent to treatment" and "transparency." It is common to find patients working astoundingly hard at their own recoveries if they comprehend and appreciate just how what they are being asked to do will effect symptom change. Educated patients often make collaborative scientists.

That stated, sometimes particular issues may be especially pertinent to treating compulsive checking. Some issues may be more pragmatic, but some are also related to the phenomenon itself. Because compulsive checkers often do experience an inflated sense of responsibility, such basics as child care for patients' children and transportation to and from treatment may be an issue. Involving significant others, especially in the early parts of treatment, may prevent poor attendance and early dropouts.

Sometimes perfectionism can make patients feel inadequate and even stupid, which are risk factors that contribute to patients leaving treatment. To protect against such problems, clinicians should ensure that clearly defined assignments are paced for and tailored to patients' developing skill and increasing comfort with exposure therapy. This can also connect to expectations about treatment, so the more complete an informed consent can be about responsibilities and expectations (i.e., transparency), the better it may protect against such misguided beliefs that patients will, for example, feel no anxiety or completely lose the capacity for certain thoughts when treatment is completed.

Depression, common to many patients with OCD, has been hypothesized to interfere with habituation to anxiety producing ERP exercises because it is an emotion-dysregulation process; at least theoretically, depression could inhibit emotional processing, which is required for habituation, so treating it should be an overall consideration when comorbid with OCD. Poor insight and overvalued ideation are two additional phenomena that present potentially serious outcome obstacles. Without an appreciation, or recognition of sources of problems, it is, for obvious reasons, difficult to work on something that is hard for patients to either see or understand. The topic of poor insight in OCD is covered elsewhere in this volume.

REFERENCES

Abramowitz, J. S. (2002). Treatment of obsessive thoughts and cognitive rituals using exposure and response prevention. *Clinical Case Studies, 1,* 6–24.

American Psychiatric Association. (2000). *Diagnostic and statistical manual of mental disorders* (4th ed., text revision). Washington, DC: Author.

Arntz, A., Rauner, M., & Van den Hout, M. (1995). "If I feel anxious, there must be danger": Ex-consequentia reasoning in inferring danger in anxiety disorders. *Behaviour Research and Therapy, 33,* 917–925.

Baer, L., & Minichiello, W. E. (1998). Behavior therapy for obsessive-compulsive disorder. In M. A. Jenike, L. Baer, & W. E. Minichiello (Eds.), *Obsessive-compulsive disorders: Practical management* (3rd ed., pp. 337–367). Boston: Mosby.

Clark, D. A. (2004). *Cognitive-behavioral therapy for OCD.* New York: Guilford.

Di Nardo, P., Brown, T. A., & Barlow, D.H. (1994). *Anxiety disorders interview schedule for DSM-IV.* San Antonio, TX: Psychological Corporation.

First, M. B., Spitzer, R. L., Gibbon, M., & Williams, J. B. W. (1996). *Structured clinical interview for DSM-IV Axis I-patient edition.* New York: Biometrics Research Department: New York State Psychiatric Institute.

Foa, E. B., Franklin, M. E., & Kozak, M. J. (1998). Psychosocial treatments for obsessive-compulsive disorder: Literature review. In R. P. Swinson, M. M. Antony, S. Rachman, & M. A. Richter (Eds.), *Obsessive-compulsive disorder: Theory, research, and treatment* (pp. 258–276). New York: Guilford.

Franklin, M. E., Riggs, D. S., & Pai, A. (2005). Obsessive-compulsive disorder. In M. M. Antony, D. R. Ledley, & R. G. Heimberg (Eds.), *Improving outcomes and preventing relapse in cognitive-behavioral therapy* (pp. 128–173). New York: Guilford.

Freeston, M. H., Rhéaume, J., & Ladouceur, R. (1996). Correcting faulty appraisals of obsessional thoughts. *Behaviour Research and Therapy, 34,* 433–446.

Goodman, W. K., Price, L. H., Rasmussen, S. A., Mazure, C., Fleishmann, R. L., Hill, C. L., et al. (1989). The Yale-Brown obsessive-compulsive scale: I. Development, use, and reliability. *Archives of General Psychiatry, 46,* 1006–1011.

Leckman, J. F., Grice, D. E., Boardman, J., Zhang, H., Vitale, A., Bondi, C., et al. (1997). Symptoms of obsessive-compulsive disorder. *American Journal of Psychiatry, 154,* 911–917.

Marks, I. M. (1969). *Fears and phobias.* London: Heineman.

Marks, I. M. (1997). Behaviour therapy for obsessive-compulsive disorder: A decade of progress. *Canadian Journal of Psychiatry, 42,* 1021–1027.

McLean, P. D., Whittal, M. L., Thordarson, D. S., Taylor, S., Söchting, I., Koch, W. J., et al. (2001). Cognitive versus behavior therapy in the group treatment of obsessive-compulsive disorder. *Journal of Consulting and Clinical Psychology, 69,* 205–214.

Meyer, V. (1966). Modification of expectations in cases with obsessional rituals. *Behaviour Research and Therapy, 4,* 273–280.

Mowrer, O. H. (1960). *Learning theory and behavior.* New York: Wiley.

Obsessive Compulsive Cognitions Working Group. (1997).Cognitive assessment of obsessive-compulsive disorder. *Behaviour Research and Therapy, 35,* 667–681.

Overton, S. M., & Menzies, R. G. (2002). A comparison of checking-related beliefs in individuals with obsessive compulsive disorder and normal controls. *Behaviour Change, 19,* 67–74.

Rachman, S. (1976). Obsessional-compulsive checking. *Behaviour Research and Therapy, 14,* 269–277.

Rachman, S. (2002). A cognitive theory of compulsive checking. *Behaviour Research and Therapy, 40,* 625–639.

Rachman, S. (2003). Compulsive checking. In R.G. Menzies & P. de Silva (Eds.), *Obsessive-compulsive disorder: Theory, research, and treatment* (pp. 139–162). Hoboken, NJ: Wiley.

Rachman, S. J., & Hodgson, R. J. (1980). *Obsessions and compulsions.* Englewood Cliffs, NJ: Prentice-Hall.

Rosqvist, J. (2005). *Exposure treatments for anxiety disorders: A practitioner's guide to concepts, methods, and evidence-based practice.* New York: Routledge.

Salkovskis, P. M. (1985). Obsessional-compulsive problems: A cognitive-behavioural analysis. *Behaviour Research and Therapy, 23,* 571–583.

Salkovskis, P. M. (1989). Cognitive-behavioral factors and the persistence of intrusive thoughts in obsessional problems. *Behaviour Research and Therapy, 27,* 677–682.

Shafran, R., Cooper, Z., & Fairburn, C. G. (2002). Clinical perfectionism: A cognitive-behavioral analysis. *Behaviour Research and Therapy, 40,* 773–791.

Shafran, R., Thordarson, D. S., & Rachman, S. J. (1996). Thought-action fusion in obsessive compulsive disorder. *Journal of Anxiety Disorders, 10,* 379–391.

Skoog, G., & Skoog, I. (1999). A 40-year follow-up of patients with obsessive-compulsive disorder. *Archives of General Psychiatry, 56,* 121–127.

Smari, J., & Holmsteinsson, H. E. (2001). Intrusive thoughts, responsibility attitudes, thought-action fusion, and chronic thought suppression in relation to obsessive-compulsive symptoms. *Behavioural and Cognitive Psychotherapy, 29,* 13–20.

Söchting, I., Whittal, M., & McLean, P. (1997). *Group cognitive-behavioral therapy (GCBT) treatment manual for obsessive-compulsive disorder (OCD).* Unpublished manual, University of British Columbia.

Steketee, G. S. (1993). *Treatment of obsessive compulsive disorder.* New York: Guilford.

Taylor, S., Thordarson, D. S., & Söchting, I. (2002). Obsessive-compulsive disorder. In

M. M. Antony & D. H. Barlow (Eds.), *Handbook of assessment and treatment planning for psychological disorders* (pp. 182–214). New York: Guilford.

Tolin, D. F., Abramowitz, J. S., Brigidi, B. D., & Foa, E. B. (2003). Intolerance of uncertainty in obsessive-compulsive disorder. *Journal of Anxiety Disorders, 17,* 233–242.

Van Oppen, P., Hoekstra, R. J., & Emmelkamp, P. M. G. (1995). The structure of obsessive-compulsive symptoms. *Behaviour Research and Therapy, 33,* 379–390.

Whittal, M. L., & McLean, P. D. (1999). CBT for OCD: The rationale, protocol, and challenges. *Cognitive and Behavioral Practice, 6,* 383–396.

CHAPTER FOUR

Ordering, Incompleteness, and Arranging

Laura J. Summerfeldt, Ph.D.

The Nature of Incompleteness Symptoms

The pairing of symmetry obsessions with ordering and arranging compulsions is one of the most reliable findings in the empirical literature on obsessive-compulsive disorder (OCD) symptom subtypes. A recent review indicated that this pairing, which is commonly associated with counting and repeating compulsions, was identified in all of the 12 factor-analytic studies considered (Mataix-Cols, do Rosario-Campos, & Leckman, 2005). Clinical observation and empirical evidence, however, suggest that symmetry-related symptoms can take two different forms, which, although topographically identical, have different underlying functional properties (e.g., Summerfeldt, Richter, Antony, & Swinson, 1999). In particular, some symmetry obsessions involve magical thinking in which personally significant outcomes can only be prevented by arranging items in a set way (e.g., If my clothes are not arranged properly, mother will die). Functionally, this harm-avoidant symptom configuration does not differ from that of cases described in traditional accounts of OCD. In contrast, the other presentation of symmetry obsessions involves feeling driven to order and arrange solely to maintain perfection in one's environment. Whereas the former presentation is usually accompanied by a state of anxious apprehension, the latter involves a feeling of dissatisfaction, "incompleteness," or the sense of things being "not just right." This second manifestation of symmetry, exactness, and ordering symptoms is the focus of this chapter.

As noted elsewhere (Summerfeldt, 2004), the sense of things being "not just right" can manifest through any sensory modality, including the visual (e.g., appearance of documents or items in the home), auditory (e.g., preference for sameness in ambient noise), tactile (e.g., checking textures by touching or tapping), and proprioceptive (e.g., having to "even up" or perform movements symmetrically). It may also apply to more complex experiences that do not easily fall under the sensory category, such as cognition (e.g., achieving absolute understanding of a concept). Such diversity of presentation means that "ordering and arranging" may be literal or figurative.

This aspect of OCD has been historically disregarded in North America in favor of more anxiety-based approaches to understanding, diagnosis, and treatment. However, it was documented more than a century ago by Pierre Janet in his writings on OCD (see Pitman, 1987b, for a translated précis). Janet described *les sentiments d'incomplétude*—incompleteness—an inner sense of imperfection, connected with the perception that actions or intentions have been incompletely achieved. This form of sensory-affective dysregulation in OCD has been increasingly acknowledged in recent years, in different terms and theoretical contexts. Rasmussen and Eisen (1992a) described this phenomenon as *incompleteness*. Rapoport (1991) captured it in her writings on deficits in the *feeling of knowing* in OCD. More recent examples include *not just right* experiences (Coles, Frost, Heimberg, & Rhéaume, 2003; Leckman, Walker, Goodman, Pauls, & Cohen, 1994), *sensory phenomena* (Miguel et al., 2000), *sensitivity of perception* (Veale et al., 1996), and *yedasentience* (Szechtman & Woody, 2004). These are not uncommon experiences in OCD. In studies with clinical samples, Leckman et al. (1995) and Miguel et al. (2000) found that well over half of participants endorsed the need to perform compulsions to quell feelings of things being subjectively imperfect or not just right.

Case Vignette

Anne was a single, 34-year-old woman on disability leave from a position in a law firm. Her main presenting symptom was avoidance. For example, Anne had not filed a tax return or renewed her professional registration for three years because this required the completion of forms. She had long enjoyed crafts but was now unable to initiate or complete even one of her many projects because of tormenting indecision over how best to do them, how they should look, and when to consider them "done." During the assessment, Anne described being plagued by the chronic sense that actions and decisions had not been completed adequately, most notably in situations involving the weighing of open-ended alternatives and particularly when documentation was involved. For example, when writing, Anne described dissatisfaction with both the content (e.g., choice of words, how much material to include) and physical appearance (e.g., layout, font) of documents. These difficulties coalesced in three obsessional themes: (a) the need for exactness and precision in terms of both appearance and expression of written words and behavior, (b) the need to know or remember unimportant details, and (c) the need for symmetry and correctness in the physical environment.

Although avoidance was the main strategy that Anne used to manage discomfort arising from these preoccupations, she also performed compulsive rituals. These included (a) ritualization (e.g., sequencing) and slowing of daily activities, (b) overt checking for mistakes or flaws, (c) rereading and rewriting of documents, and (d) mental re-reviewing, focusing on the "best way" to do things. Anne had used time-consuming rituals, often involving arbitrary rules, for how to terminate activities. For example, to complete a short legal brief, Anne would engage in an excessive multistep review of progressively smaller subsets of all reports produced in the past six months in her office. She described often becoming "stuck" (overwhelmed by feelings of incompleteness) to the point that she could not even proceed with tasks that had deadlines. Similar feelings were now attached to almost any activity "with an end point." Consequently, Anne had withdrawn from work and other such activities and described spending her days watching television, running errands for her family, and searching the Internet for self-help resources.

Etiology

Despite a dearth of empirical research to date, there are two theoretical approaches to incompleteness: cognitive-behavioral and general-deficit perspectives. Prevailing cognitive-behavioral models of OCD, although differing in important ways, derive from the core premise that emotional responses arise from threat-related interpretations (appraisals) of objectively innocuous experiences (i.e., intrusive thoughts) (e.g., Rachman, 1997, 1998; Salkovskis, 1985). Such appraisals (e.g., "I might act on my intrusive thoughts to harm loved ones") are thought to occur because of dysfunctional core beliefs, or schemata (e.g., "thinking of something can make it come true"), acquired through experience. According to the models' behavioral component, distress that arises from threat-related appraisals fails to extinguish because of avoidance behavior or its functional equivalents: compulsive rituals. Because these passive and active avoidance strategies are successful in immediately relieving anxiety, they are negatively reinforced and thus self-perpetuating. Whereas the behavioral component is useful in explaining the perpetuation of OCD symptoms, the cognitive component is useful in explaining how obsessional anxiety arises in the first place.

In one of the only explicit attempts to apply this perspective to incompleteness symptoms, Salkovskis and Forrester (2002) suggested that "not just right" experiences arise directly from distorted appraisals of the gravity of one's thoughts and acts. Salkovskis and Forrester argued that these experiences represent an internal criterion state, or elevated evidence requirement, set by the individual in the effort to ensure that decisions having negative consequences have been correctly made. In OCD, even the most prosaic of decisions can be appraised by the individual as having negative consequences that he or she is responsible for preventing. This explains the ritualization of experiences with little objective threat value (e.g., tying ones shoes, hanging up clothes).

To date, no published research using clinical samples has evaluated the cognitive-behavioral model of incompleteness. Nonetheless, clinical accounts and research using nonclinical participants pose some problems for this model. First, patient accounts consistently exclude fears of specific negative outcomes other than that negative affect will persist (Rasmussen & Eisen, 1992b; Summerfeldt, 2004, 2007; Tallis, 1996). Second, research with analogue samples—unclouded by severe affect, poor insight, or comorbidity—has found symmetry behaviors as well as "not just right experiences" to be relatively unassociated with feared consequences (Coles, Heimberg, Frost, & Steketee, 2005; Radomsky & Rachman, 2004). The emotional correlate of feared outcomes—anticipatory anxiety—is also missing from patients' accounts. Preliminary data from our site indicate that compared with individuals with OCD low in incompleteness, those high in incompleteness endorsed significantly lower levels of anxiety irrespective of how it was operationalized:

as a symptom-specific state, a trait, or as temperamental harm avoidance. Moreover, harm-related obsessional content was notably absent from their lifetime symptom history. Although further research is needed, it appears that in incompleteness symptoms there is little evidence of three key components of the cognitive-behavioral model: (a) a trigger stimulus, (b) anxious affect, and (c) threatening appraisals from which this affect is thought to originate.

In contrast to appraisal models, deficit models assume the presence of inherent pathological processes. As applied to incompleteness symptoms, such approaches propose that the affective disturbance is intrinsic and may serve as an antecedent for problematic interpretations and behaviors. There is converging evidence of dysfunction in OCD in orbitofrontal-subcortical circuitry, particularly involving the basal ganglia (see Whiteside, Port, & Abramowitz, 2004). This circuitry is thought to be central in selecting behavioral responses, producing subsequences of goal-oriented actions, and switching priorities in response to feedback (Graybiel, 1998; Rauch & Savage, 1997). It is conceivable that these connections may contain the self-quenching circuit that provides humans with a subjective sense of completeness. Malfunctions may manifest as groundless yet persistent "error signals" (Pitman, 1987a; Schwartz, 1999), ceaselessly prompting the individual to corrective action. On these grounds, it could be proposed that the core of incompleteness is a deficit in the ability to use emotional experience and sensory feedback to guide behavior. This seems to reflect malfunction in some internal signal that terminates behaviors by producing a "feeling of knowing"—an emotional indicator that lets one know when a state has been satisfactorily achieved. Incompleteness OCD may exemplify the (often compensatory) effects of lifelong deficits in this function.

Treatment

There has been no direct investigation of treatments for incompleteness symptoms. Existing empirical and theoretical work, however, suggest that the excellent outcomes of conventional psychological interventions (e.g., exposure and response prevention; ERP) do not generalize to this particular manifestation of OCD. In a review of the representation of various OCD symptom subtypes in outcome trials of behavioral therapy, Ball, Baer, and Otto (1996) found that checking, hoarding, symmetry, and counting rituals (plausibly those most associated with incompleteness) were underrepresented. Perhaps this reflects a higher refusal or dropout rate for patients with these symptoms, or the difficulty of designing behavioral interventions for these presentations of OCD. The absence of clear obsessionally feared consequences, as is seen in incompleteness symptoms, likely contributes to these treatment obstacles. Foa, Abramowitz, Franklin, and Kozak (1999), for example, found that patients who did not articulate specific feared consequences benefited less from ERP than did those who did articulate specific obsessional fears, perhaps because ERP works by disconfirming specific obsessional fears. Foa and Kozak (1986) suggested that reductions in OCD symptoms are mediated by reductions in estimates of the probability of feared consequences and resultant modifications of fear-related schemas, achieved through the repeated disconfirmations of feared outcome that ERP provides. By these accounts, CBT may not only be difficult to apply for individuals with incompleteness OCD, but when applied will likely be less effective.

Two recent studies were conducted specifically to investigate the link between empirically derived symptom subtypes and treatment outcomes. In both, symptom presentation was assessed using the symptom checklist of the Yale-Brown Obsessive Compulsive Scale (Y-BOCS; Goodman et al., 1989), which in its current form places significant limitations on how symptom dimensions can be calculated (Summerfeldt et al., 2004). In a randomized controlled trial of computer versus clinician-guided behavior therapy for OCD, Mataix-Cols, Marks, Greist, Kobak, and Baer (2002) reported that symmetry and ordering was not among the symptom factors found to predict either compliance or response to treatment. In another study, Abramowitz, Franklin, Schwartz, and Furr (2003) found that although hoarding symptoms alone predicted poorer response to ERP, of the remaining symptom domains (contamination, harming, unacceptable obsessions, symmetry), the one most similar in response rates to hoarding was symmetry related. Of all patient groups, those in the symmetry cluster had the highest (albeit not statistically significantly so) discontinuation rate, which was most similar to the hoarding cluster.

Reports relying on descriptive features rather than symptom subtypes also suggest that incompleteness predicts modest response to treatment. In a case series of individuals with cleaning rituals driven not by contamination fears but by extreme perfectionism, Tallis (1996) reported that all showed negligible long-term therapeutic response to ERP although this response was better than that to cognitive therapy or medication with a serotonin reuptake inhibitor. OCD patients unable to articulate feared consequences have been found to show a trend toward less post-treatment improvement (45% compared with 69%) than those with clear feared consequences (Foa et al., 1999). In short, the overt symptoms and underlying characteristics most associated with incompleteness are often those identified as being least responsive to CBT and particularly to cognitive interventions. Some adaptations to conventional cognitive models and techniques may help with this (Summerfeldt, 2004), but as yet they have not received any systematic investigation.

Although complications, including attenuated outcome, may be expected in the treatment of individuals with incompleteness OCD symptoms, the existing literature suggests that ERP remains the best option available. The premise behind the effectiveness of ERP is the principle of extinction—the gradual loss of a conditioned response, such as anxiety, when it is no longer reinforced (e.g., when feared consequences do not occur). Although this model is most commonly applied to anxiety, its basic principles should apply to other emotional experiences, such as incompleteness, even though it appears to be an internally generated, rather than conditioned, emotional state. Indeed, the term *habituation* is typically used to describe this process as applied to unlearned or reflexive, rather than acquired, behaviors. When familiarizing a patient with the treatment model, the clinician can liken this to the familiar experience of becoming accustomed to a persistent situation, such as what happens over time when one is exposed to annoying background noise.

Illustration of the Treatment Strategies

Anne was diagnosed with OCD. Her obsessions concerned feelings of incompleteness. She applied rigid rules and devoted considerable time to performing even mundane activities in the futile attempt to get things "just right." Despite this, feelings of incompleteness persisted, with increased ritualizing, escalating affect, procrastination, and ultimately complete avoidance. A standard time-limited course of ERP was planned, aimed at both desensitizing Anne to the incompleteness experiences associated with her obsessions and weakening the pattern of using compulsive strategies in response to feelings of incompleteness. The plan was to progress through a hierarchy of exposure tasks designed to provoke incompleteness, with instructions to refrain from rituals and avoidance used to alleviate the associated discomfort. In Anne's case, the pervasiveness of symptoms meant that circumscribed exposure tasks might be less useful than daylong exposures to perpetual states of change in her environment.

Treatment consisted of 16 sessions of ERP modeled after the programs described by Steketee (1999) and Kozak and Foa (1997). Twice-weekly, 60–90-minute sessions were used for the first five weeks, followed by four weekly, then two biweekly sessions. This course of therapy included the following components: (a) psychoeducation to familiarize Anne with the behavioral model of OCD, especially as it applies to incompleteness; (b) information gathering and treatment planning to develop a list of cues, avoidance, and rituals and to develop an exposure hierarchy; and (c) graduated ERP involving in-session exposure tasks and daily homework tasks with self-monitoring of discomfort levels during self-administered exposure.

The first three sessions were devoted to information gathering, treatment planning, and providing Anne with a rationale for using ERP techniques. Helping Anne to internalize the conceptual model by applying each of its components to her own symptoms was emphasized. Anne was taught that the aim of ERP was to help her habituate to feelings of sensory-affective discomfort (i.e., incompleteness). The goal is to weaken the connections between feelings of incompleteness and the use of compulsive rituals, or in the words of one patient, "to build up an immunity to the feeling."

Self-monitoring clearly revealed Anne's need for exactness. Her six-page record of triggers for obsessions and rituals had to be pruned to make a workable exposure hierarchy. By week 4, however, this was done (see Tables 4.1 and 4.2),

Table 4.1. *Anne's Exposure Hierarchy: Writing-Related*

Item	SUDs
Write a legal brief to be read by colleague	100
Respond to 1 item of professional mail	90
Draft a legal brief in paragraph form (with time constraints)	85
Draft a legal brief in point form (with time constraints)	80
"Research and draft point-form opinion letter" on legal issue	75
Write final copy of letter to close friend, to be sent	70
Draft résumé update in point form	65
Draft point-form summary of brief magazine article	55
Draft point-form note to close friend	45
Draft point-form summary of paragraph from magazine article	35
Write point-form summary of the last hour's activities	30
Draft point-form summary of paragraph from professional article	50
Research and draft point-form summary of brief professional article	60

Note: SUDS, subjective units of discomfort.

Table 4.2. Anne's Exposure Hierarchy: Daily Activities

Item	SUDs
Sort stored documents: file vs. discard	100
Work on refinishing project: stain and varnish	90
Sort 1 box of books: keep vs. discard vs. donate	80
Organize shelf of craft area	75
Purchase birthday gift for family member	70
Work on refinishing project: sanding	65
Sort 1 bag of clothes: keep vs. discard vs. donate	55
Choose a library book within 5 minutes	45
Select birthday card for friend or family member	50
Make bed within 3 minutes	30
Leave house for 1 block walk, maximum preparation time 5 minutes	60
Select clothing for day's wear (within 5 minutes, before breakfast)	35

and Anne was ready to engage in her first session of therapist-assisted exposure. Incompleteness-related symptom themes, although similar in form, can have widely different content. To minimize confusion for the patient, particularly when he or she is still becoming familiar with ERP principles, it is often useful to have parallel exposure hierarchies. For Anne, separate hierarchies were generated for activities of daily living (e.g., leaving the house, shopping, crafts) and for difficulties with documentation. For in-session exposures, the maxim "use whatever has the power to prompt the sense of incompleteness" was used to decide on exposure tasks. Where incompleteness was expressed in prolonged and meticulous performance, writing (e.g., text summaries, income tax forms, greeting cards), organizing (e.g., files), and small craft projects were incorporated as exposures.

Exposure therapy began with Anne confronting the second task in her writing hierarchy: drafting a point form summary of a paragraph from a newspaper article. Anne described her desire to take excessive time and to check and recheck the document's content and appearance. We then brainstormed discomfort-inducing alternatives, focusing on randomness, time constraint, and sensory change. Anne proceeded with exposure while monitoring her subjective units of discomfort (SUDS) on a scale from 0 (no distress) to 100 (extreme distress) at five-minute intervals. During this, the therapist acted as coach, keeping Anne focused, eliciting discomfort ratings, and making encouraging statements while also prompting exploration, as SUDS decreased, of how the task could be made most discomforting. The goal was to keep exposure active and continuous until SUDS levels decreased considerably.

Anne voiced a sense of absurdity about the need for exposure to such an objectively trivial experience. Despite this, when exposure was initiated, her SUDS increased from a baseline of 30 to 60. During the session, Anne was surprised to see that her SUDS declined even when she tried to make the task increasingly uncomfortable. Within half an hour, SUDs had returned to baseline. This provided an opportunity to discuss how giving in to the compulsive urge had prevented Anne from seeing that this urge would spontaneously decline even if she resisted; Anne quickly applied this to other, more difficult, situations. She left the session with homework instructions to conduct self-administered exposure to the newspaper articles, as well as to an item lower in the hierarchy and a corresponding item in her daily living hierarchy.

A commonly observed consequence of incompleteness symptoms is the ritualized and inflexible quality of nearly all daily activities—"It's not the time, it's the manner," in the words of one individual. Thus, in planning ritual prevention, it is useful to generate methods for reducing not only the duration of behaviors but also their inflexible configuration. Anne spent long periods of time completing relatively simple behaviors because these often had to be repeated and performed meticulously. Both creativity and a thorough grasp of Anne's symptoms were needed to design an effective plan to deritualize these activities. To illustrate, the following instructions were provided to help her initiate and efficiently complete daily tasks with greater flexibility:

> Unpack boxes of belongings to set up work-table for at least 5 minutes, then walk away and engage in a writing task. Return to do another 5 minutes of unpacking, walk away, then return and do another 5 minutes of unpacking (i.e., 3 episodes of unpacking at 5 minutes each, broken up by other activities).

Anne's exposures continued to progress with clear evidence of habituation at each stage. For all hierarchy items, satisfactory reduction of SUDS took place within 60–90 minutes. However, this was only accomplished with frequent adjustments to ERP strategies, as well as ritual prevention methods. Following a few initial exposures, Anne reported that simply refraining from compulsions was less distressing than actually doing the behaviors in a way deliberately contrary to the ritual, which prompted maximal levels of incompleteness feelings, obsessions, and discomfort. At the outset of each hierarchy step, ideas for ritual interference were generated. In her homework, Anne began to modify these guidelines using her judgment about how to maximize SUDS, with the ultimate goal of introducing spontaneity and choice, rather than discomfort reduction, as a basis for behavioral choices.

By session 8, Anne was applying ERP principles to most domains of her home life—she had adopted an "exposure philosophy." By session 11, Anne had tackled the most difficult items in both exposure hierarchies. In the last two (biweekly) sessions, attention was turned to maintaining treatment gains. For Anne, and others with incompleteness-related symptoms, two issues warrant particular attention. First is the return to "normal" behavior: At the end of treatment, the patient is reminded of his or her learned ability to distinguish between freely chosen versus compulsive behaviors. The second issue is management of new symptoms and preventing relapse. It is useful to remind the patient of his or her newly acquired abilities to (a) recognize emerging obsessions and compulsions (whatever their content), and (b) apply ERP techniques learned in therapy to counter any such symptoms.

After therapy ended, Anne was seen for a few follow-up sessions. She reported that although incompleteness experiences were still "always there," they had much less influence over her behavior. This was supported by post-treatment assessment data: Six months after therapy had ended, Anne showed a 60 percent reduction in symptom severity from baseline. She had also returned to work. Her continued success with symptoms likely reflected her exceptional motivation and regular practice of response prevention in day-to-day activities. Unfortunately, in many instances, patients do not continue to resist their urges to perform rituals after therapy has ended, and this often leads to poorer outcome at follow-up (Summerfeldt, 2004, 2007).

Important Clinical Issues

Unique features of incompleteness have implications for treatment. Age of onset and (relatedly) the experience of symptoms as ego-syntonic, or consistent to some extent with one's sense of self, warrant particular mention. High rates of ordering, arranging, and symmetry symptoms are often observed in childhood OCD (Masi et al., 2005), and earlier age of onset of OCD is associated with symmetry-related symptoms in adulthood (Denys, de Geus, van Megen, & Westenberg, 2004; Hasler et al., 2005). Preliminary data from our site indicate that individuals with this presentation of OCD have an earlier age of onset of the clinical syndrome, as well as of prodromal behaviors such as perfectionism and a preference for "sameness." Many individuals report having had these tendencies for as long as they can remember. In such cases, the distinction between personality traits and OCD symptoms is often difficult to make, as symptoms may become a stable part of the person's experience and behavioral repertoire. Indeed, our research and clinical observation suggest that patients often find incompleteness experiences to be quite ego-syntonic. As is discussed in the next section, these features have implications for treatment.

Troubleshooting

Psychoeducation, Monitoring, and Planning

Because of the early onset and longstanding nature of incompleteness experiences, patients like Anne often grow accustomed to their obsessive-compulsive tendencies, with little reflection on their uncontrollability or problematic motivations. As such, careful reframing of these difficulties as OCD is needed. The assessment itself (particularly self-monitoring) is useful to this end, as the individual acquires a language to apply to her perplexing experiences. In addition, recognition of these experiences as OCD can be encouraged with strategies similar to those described by Schwartz (1996) as relabeling and reattributing.

One consequence of the long duration and ego-syntonicity of incompleteness experiences can be ambivalence about treatment (and reduced motivation to change). This may be addressed by identifying such ambivalence as understandable given the duration and strength of OCD. The clinician can then correct the individual's perception that treatment aims to end all habitual ways of doing things by pointing out that there's a difference between having to do, versus choosing to do, a behavior. Another valuable technique is to increase the patient's awareness of the cost of his or her OCD symptoms (e.g., their negative impact on relationships, employment, and plans for the future). This can be accomplished in discussion form or using a written exercise as described in Antony and Swinson (1998)'s self-help book, *When Perfect Isn't Good Enough*.

Self-monitoring of obsessional triggers, avoidance behaviors, and rituals provides the patient and clinician with a detailed picture of the functional components of OCD. Given the pervasiveness of incompleteness symptoms, however, self-monitoring for cues can become overwhelming. Patients like Anne often report that they have difficulty distinguishing obsessions and compulsions from other experiences. A useful strategy is to strengthen the patient's ability to identify accurately obsessions and compulsions by teaching him or her how these symptoms differ from other experiences; for example, if resisting the behavior would evoke a strong emotional response, this behavior is probably a compulsive ritual. We encourage patients to take the approach "if it feels like OCD, it probably is." Because of the typical pervasiveness of incompleteness symptoms, a complete cataloguing of all environmental triggers and rituals might be impossible. Instead, a core cluster of symptoms should be identified and targeted for self-monitoring based on the similarity of their subjective flavor.

Exposure and Ritual Prevention

At our center we encourage patients to move "laterally" within exposure stages, or to do self-exposure to unplanned situations of equivalent discomfort to those targeted in the hierarchy. We also encourage patients to regard ERP as a lifestyle, rather than as a situation-specific strategy. For many patients with incompleteness symptoms, self-monitoring and writing down progress with exposure tasks can themselves present obstacles to treatment. This can be addressed by purposefully introducing randomness and spontaneity into these exercises. For example, when Anne began to complete her self-monitoring (and other treatment-relevant) forms in ritualized ways, she was encouraged to change recording methods randomly, to use abbreviated (e.g., word-count restricted, timed) notation and plot progress on hand-drawn forms. Other tactics might include skipping these exercises on random days and randomly switching between planned versus unplanned exposures.

In planning treatment, decisions must be made regarding the specific aspects of compulsions that require prevention. Aspects of rituals can include: (a) time spent on specific behavior (e.g., in reading over a document, making a bed), (b) context control (e.g., no interruptions or distractions), (c) time spent on a sequence of behaviors; here, further analysis is needed of the source of the slowness (e.g., checking, mental review, repeating, or meticulous performance of each component), and (d) ritualization of single behaviors or ritualized sequencing of multiple behaviors. Other functionally equivalent behaviors to be resisted include difficulty delegating, general inflexibility, primary obsessional slowness, and indecisiveness and procrastination.

The form of ritual prevention must also be considered. If most daily activities are ritualized, several ritual prevention variants can be considered (see Steketee [1999] for a discussion). Two types of partial ritual prevention—*rit-*

ual restriction or *abbreviation*—may be particularly useful. Prompting, shaping, and pacing, for example, are effective methods for modifying slowness related to hyperperfectionism about actions (Rachman, 1974). For individuals with high discomfort, a stepwise approach to ritual prevention using *response delay* may be another option (Schwartz, 1996). *Ritual interruption* and *interference* may also be essential. The ultimate goal is for the patient to use spontaneity and choice, rather than discomfort reduction, as a basis for behavioral choices. It is particularly important with this patient population to be attuned to the possibility of inadvertent rigidity and rule-driven ritualizing of the exposure.

Ending Treatment and Preventing Relapse

Efforts to improve long-term outcomes of treatment can focus on two interrelated issues: (a) the ability to recognize symptoms, and (b) efforts spent in resistance. An important task early in treatment is to help the individual correctly identify his or her symptoms as such; when regular contact with a therapist ceases, patients may lose this ability to some degree. Several tactics may help revitalize the individual's ability to maintain perspective on symptoms, as well as the practical skills acquired in therapy. One strategy, if feasible, is to schedule monthly "booster" sessions. It may also be useful for the patient to join a local OCD support group (e.g., one affiliated with the Obsessive-Compulsive Foundation; www.ocfoundation.org). Self-help books can also be a helpful post-treatment tool, although patients with incompleteness symptoms often report that the "classic" OCD profiles usually described in them seem irrelevant. Such individuals often find the book *Brain Lock* (Schwartz, 1996) to be helpful, as are OCD-related readings from *When Perfect Isn't Good Enough* (Antony & Swinson, 1998).

Even if compulsions are correctly labeled as such, another juncture where treatment gains can be lost may be in the effort spent on resisting compulsions. Enhancing motivation to change may be particularly important for this group of patients. Discussing these issues at the outset of treatment, rather than discussing them after difficulties arise, is a sound proactive strategy.

Conclusion

Incompleteness symptoms in OCD occur often and pose challenges to clinicians hoping to apply empirically based psychological treatments. Contrary to conventional cognitive appraisal models, which maintain that affect originates from core beliefs and appraisals, in incompleteness, sensory/affective disturbance appears to be primary and intrinsic. The behavioral component of CBT, aimed at facilitating habituation to the disturbing sensory/affective experience, appears to be key. Although the case described herein ended in success, the longstanding, ego-syntonic nature of symptoms, and their association with a baseline internal state rather than an acquired aversion to specific triggers, has the potential not only to complicate treatment design and implementation but also to lead to loss of gains once therapy ends. The strategies presented are intended to help clinicians manage these potential barriers to effective treatment.

REFERENCES

Abramowitz, J. S., Franklin, M. E., Schwartz, S. A., & Furr, J. M. (2003). Symptom presentation and outcome of cognitive-behavioral therapy for obsessive-compulsive disorder. *Journal of Clinical and Consulting Psychology, 71,* 1049–1057.

Antony, M. M., & Swinson, R. P. (1998). *When perfect isn't good enough: Strategies for coping with perfectionism.* Oakland, CA: New Harbinger.

Ball, S. G., Baer, L., & Otto, M. W. (1996). Symptom subtypes of obsessive-compulsive disorder in behavioral treatment studies: A quantitative review. *Behaviour Research and Therapy, 47,* 47–51.

Coles, M. E., Frost, R. O., Heimberg, R. G., & Rhéaume, J. (2003). "Not just right experiences": Perfectionism, obsessive-compulsive features and general psychopathology. *Behaviour Research and Therapy, 41,* 681–700.

Coles, M. E., Heimberg, R. G., Frost, R. O., & Steketee, G. (2005). Not just right experiences and obsessive compulsive features: Experimental and self-monitoring perspectives. *Behaviour Research and Therapy, 43,* 153–167

Denys, D., de Geus, F., van Megen, H. J. G. M., & Westenberg, H. G. M. (2004). Use of factor analysis to detect potential phenotypes in obsessive-compulsive disorder. *Psychiatry Research, 128,* 273–280.

Foa, E. B., Abramowitz, J. S., Franklin, M. E., & Kozak, M. J. (1999). Feared consequences, fixity of belief, and treatment outcome in patients with obsessive-compulsive disorder. *Behavior Therapy, 30,* 717–724.

Foa, E. B., & Kozak, M. J. (1986). Emotional processing of fear: Exposure to corrective information, *Psychological Bulletin, 99,* 20–35.

Goodman, W. K., Price, L. H., Rasmussen, S. A., Mazure, C., Fleischmann, R. L., Hill, C. L., et al. (1989). Yale-Brown Obsessive Compulsive Scale: Part I. Development, use, and reliability. *Archives of General Psychiatry, 46,* 1006–1011.

Graybiel, A. M. (1998). The basal ganglia and chunking of action repertoires. *Neurobiology of Learning and Memory, 70,* 119–136.

Hasler, G., LaSalle-Ricci, V. H., Ronquillo, J. G., Crawley, S. A., Cochran, L. W., Kazuba, D., et al. (2005). Obsessive-compulsive disorder symptom dimensions show specific relationships to psychiatric comorbidity. *Psychiatry Research, 135,* 121–132.

Kozak, M. J., & Foa, E. B. (1997). *Mastery of obsessive-compulsive disorder: A cognitive-behavioral approach, therapist guide.* Toronto, ON: The Psychological Corporation.

Leckman, J. F., Grice, D. E., Barr, L. C., de Vries, A. L. C., Martin, C., Cohen, D. J., et al. (1995). Tic-related vs. non-tic-related obsessive compulsive disorder. *Anxiety, 1,* 208–215.

Leckman, J. F., Walker, D. E. Goodman, W. K., Pauls, D. L., & Cohen, D. J. (1994). "Just right" perceptions associated with compulsive behavior in Tourette's syndrome. *American Journal of Psychiatry, 151,* 675–680.

Masi, G., Millepiedi, S., Mucci, M., Bertini, N., Milantoni, L., & Arcangeli, F. (2005). A naturalistic study of referred children and adolescents with obsessive-compulsive disorder. *Journal of the American Academy of Child and Adolescent Psychiatry, 44,* 673–681.

Mataix-Cols, D., do Rosario-Campos, M. C., & Leckman, J. F. (2005). A multidimensional model of obsessive-compulsive disorder. *American Journal of Psychiatry, 162,* 228–238.

Mataix-Cols, D., Marks, I. M., Greist, J. H., Kobak, K. A., & Baer, L. (2002). Obsessive-compulsive symptom dimensions as predictors of compliance with and response to behaviour therapy: Results from a controlled trial. *Psychotherapy & Psychosomatics, 71,* 255–262.

Miguel, E. C., do Rosario-Campos, M.C., da Silva, P. H., do Valle, R., Rauch, S. L., Coffey, B. J., et al. (2000). Sensory phenomena in obsessive-compulsive disorder and Tourette's disorder. *Journal of Clinical Psychiatry, 61,* 150–156.

Pitman, R. K. (1987a). A cybernetic model of obsessive-compulsive psychopathology. *Comprehensive Psychiatry, 28,* 334–343.

Pitman, R. K. (1987b). Pierre Janet on obsessive-compulsive disorder (1903). *Archives of General Psychiatry, 44,* 226–232.

Rachman, S. (1974). Primary obsessional slowness. *Behaviour Research and Therapy, 12,* 9–18.

Rachman, S. (1997). A cognitive theory of obsessions. *Behaviour Research and Therapy, 35,* 793–802.

Rachman, S. (1998). A cognitive theory of obsessions: Elaborations. *Behaviour Research and Therapy, 36,* 385–401.

Radomsky, A. S., & Rachman, S. (2004). Symmetry, ordering and arranging compulsive behaviour. *Behaviour Research and Therapy, 4,* 893–913.

Rapoport, J. L. (1991). Basal ganglia dysfunction as a proposed cause of obsessive-compulsive disorder. In B. J. Carroll & J. E. Barrett (Eds.), *Psychopathology and the brain* (pp. 77–95). New York: Raven Press.

Rasmussen, S. A., & Eisen, J. L. (1992a). The epidemiology and clinical features of obsessive compulsive disorder. *The Psychiatric Clinics of North America, 15,* 743–758.

Rasmussen, S. A., & Eisen, J. L. (1992b). The epidemiology and differential diagnosis of obsessive compulsive disorder. *Journal of Clinical Psychology, 55* (suppl. 4), 4–10.

Rauch, S. L., & Savage, C. R. (1997). Neuroimaging and neuropsychology of the striatum: Bridging basic science and clinical practice. *Psychiatric Clinics of North America, 20,* 741–768.

Salkovskis, P. M. (1985). Obsessional-compulsive problems: A cognitive-behavioural analysis. *Behaviour Research and Therapy, 23,* 571–583.
Salkovskis, P. M., & Forrester, E. (2002). Responsibility. In R.O. Frost and G. Steketee (Eds.), *Cognitive approaches to obsessions and compulsions: Theory, assessment, and treatment* (pp. 45–61). New York: Pergamon.
Schwartz, J. M. (1996). *Brain lock: Free yourself from obsessive-compulsive behavior.* New York: HarperCollins.
Schwartz, J. M. (1999). A role for volition and attention in the generation of new brain circuitry: Toward a neurobiology of mental force. *Journal of Consciousness Studies, 6,* 115–142.
Steketee, G. (1999). *Overcoming obsessive-compulsive disorder: A behavioral and cognitive protocol for the treatment of OCD, therapist protocol.* Oakland, CA: New Harbinger.
Summerfeldt, L. J. (2004). Understanding and treating incompleteness in obsessive-compulsive disorder. *Journal of Clinical Psychology, 60,* 1155–1168.
Summerfeldt, L. J. (2007). Treating incompleteness, ordering, and arranging concerns. In M. Antony, C., Purdon, & L. J. Summerfeldt (Eds.). *Psychological Treatment of OCD: Beyond the Basics (pp. 197–208).* Washington, DC: American Psychological Association Press.
Summerfeldt, L. J., Kloosterman, P. H., Antony, M. M., Richter, M. A., & Swinson, R. P. (2004). The relationship between miscellaneous symptoms and major symptom factors in obsessive-compulsive disorder. *Behaviour Research and Therapy, 42,* 1453–1467.
Summerfeldt, L. J., Richter, M. A., Antony, M. M., & Swinson, R. P. (1999). Symptom structure in obsessive-compulsive disorder: A confirmatory factor-analytic study. *Behaviour Research and Therapy, 37,* 297–311.
Szechtman, H., & Woody, E. (2004). Obsessive-compulsive disorder as a disturbance of security motivation. *Psychological Review, 111,* 111–127.
Tallis, F. (1996). Compulsive washing in the absence of phobic and illness anxiety. *Behaviour Research and Therapy, 34,* 361–362.
Veale, D., Gournay, K., Dryden, W., Boocock, A., Shah, F., Willson, R., et al. (1996). Body dysmorphic disorder: A cognitive behavioral model and pilot randomised controlled trial. *Behaviour Research and Therapy, 34,* 717–279.
Whiteside, S. P., Port, J. D., & Abramowitz, J. S. (2004). A meta-analysis of functional neuroimaging in obsessive-compulsive disorder. *Psychiatry Research: Neuroimaging, 132,* 69–79.

CHAPTER FIVE

Unacceptable Obsessional Thoughts and Covert Rituals

Christine Purdon, Ph.D.

The Nature of Unacceptable Obsessions and Covert Rituals

Obsessions often take the form of repugnant thoughts that are a profound violation of the individual's morality and values. Examples of repugnant obsessions include (a) thoughts, images, or impulses of harming an innocent or helpless loved one (e.g., throwing a baby from a balcony, kicking an elderly person, swerving into the next lane while driving); (b) sexual obsessions (e.g., thoughts of touching someone sexually against his or her will, images of sexually molesting one's baby); and (c) obsessions that violate religious beliefs (e.g., images of having sex with Jesus, swearing in synagogue, committing sinful acts). Repugnant obsessions can also take the form of doubts involving harm (e.g., "Did I run over someone without realizing it?" "What if the pot I used was not clean and I have poisoned everyone?"), doubts involving sexuality ("Did seeing that [repugnant] image arouse me sexually?" "What if I molested my baby!"), and religious doubts ("Have I offended God?" "Did I contaminate that prayer with an impure thought?").

Repugnant obsessions tend to give rise to compulsive rituals of thinking a "good" or "safe" thought, engaging in ritualized and excessive prayer, and, most frequently, some form of checking (e.g., Abramowitz, Franklin, Schwartz, & Furr, 2003). Checking can take various forms, including checking whether harm has occurred (e.g., scouring the newspaper for reports of hit-and-run accidents); checking whether one has or does not have not repugnant qualities (e.g., monitoring one's body for signs of inappropriate sexual arousal, checking the Internet, and other resources for signs that one is a psychopath); checking that harm is not imminent (e.g., checking that the knives are safely in the knife block, that the car is to the right of the yellow line); and seeking reassurance, a form of checking-by-proxy (e.g., asking one's spouse if he or she thinks one is dangerous; Rachman & Shafran, 1998). Often the goal of reassurance is to obtain 100 percent certainty that the obsession is false.

Repugnant obsessions also give rise to avoidance of thought (e.g., Rachman, 2007). Examples of avoidance include avoiding places where there are knives, avoiding food preparation, avoiding taking primary care of a child, avoiding driving, avoiding certain colors (e.g., red because it is associated with blood), avoiding contact with members of the same sex, avoiding religious ceremonies and avoiding any temptations of sin. Individuals with obsessive-compulsive disorder (OCD) engage in strenuous attempts at internal avoidance of the thought, or, in attempts to suppress the thought.

Case Vignette

Roger was a 64-year-old loving grandfather who presented with obsessions that involved harming his grandchildren. These began about one year before his assessment. He was preparing a salad for his grandchildren and suddenly felt an urge to stab the youngest in the neck with the paring knife. To ameliorate the distress associated with the thought, and his concern that the thought meant he had emergent psychopathic traits, Roger would think a "good" thought about his grandchildren. He would spend hours each day tallying evidence that he was a psychopath and evidence that he was not a psychopath. He repeatedly asked his wife whether she thought he was dangerous. Roger rated the probability that he might harm his grandchildren as about zero. However, he believed that "bad things" were more likely to happen to him, so a negative occurrence with even 0.0000001 percent probability was more likely to occur to him than to someone else. To be absolutely sure his grandchildren were safe from him, he avoided their company altogether. As time went on, he began to have difficulty looking at the color red as it reminded him of blood. He could not watch television because he might see a depiction of violence that might "give him ideas," and he would not handle any sharp objects. He presented with OCD of moderate severity.

Repugnant Obsessions as a Legitimate Subtype of OCD

Repugnant obsessions and checking compulsions have long been identified as a symptom subtype of OCD. In a sample of 560 individuals, Rasmussen and Eisen (1992) found that 31 percent reported aggressive or religious obsessions and 24 percent reported sexual obsessions. Baer (1994) conducted a factor analysis of the main symptoms of the Yale-Brown Obsessive Compulsive Scale (Y-BOCS), a symptom severity measure that inventories the range of obsessions and compulsions seen in OCD. Three factors were identified, including religious, sexual, and aggressive obsessions, not associated with any particular compulsions. This latter category was labeled *pure obsessions*. Similar results have since been obtained (Leckman et al., 1997; Mataix-Cols, Rauch, Manzo, Jenike, & Baer, 1999).

However, Summerfeldt, Kloosterman, Antony, Richter, and Swinson (2004) reexamined the factor structure of the Y-BOCS, this time including miscellaneous obsessions and compulsions. Most of the miscellaneous compulsions loaded with the "aggressive/sexual obsessions with checking compulsions" factor, indicating that aggressive and sexual thoughts are associated with covert compulsions, and hence should not be referred to as "pure obsessions." Other studies have since validated that conclusion (e.g., Abramowitz et al., 2003; Calamari, Wiegartz, & Janeck, 1999; Calamari et al., 2004). Taken together, these studies provide solid evidence for the phenomenologic distinctiveness of a subtype that consists of aggression/sexual/religious obsessions with checking compulsions.

Theoretical Models and Etiologic Issues

According to contemporary cognitive-behavioral models of OCD, normal thoughts develop into obsessions when they give rise to negative automatic thoughts; that the thought is dangerous, unnatural, or harmful; and that action must be taken to prevent the feared outcome. This "catastrophic misinterpretation" of the obsession leads to anxiety, guilt, shame, disgust, fear, and discomfort (Rachman, 1997, 1998; Salkovskis, 1985, 1989, 1999). Compulsive rituals are then enacted to reduce this distress. The reduction in distress, or the perceived prevention of a further escalation in distress, serves as negative reinforcement for the compulsive act, so it will be repeated when the obsession occurs again (e.g., Foa & Tillmans, 1980; Rachman & Hodgson, 1980; Salkovskis, 1999). The nonoccurrence of the event the obsession portends is taken as evidence that the compulsion is successful (Salkovskis, 1999). Thus, no new learning about the thought's actual meaning is possible.

Strategies of overt avoidance (avoiding people, places, and situations) and covert avoidance (suppressing thoughts) are also used to prevent the thought from occurring or to dismiss the thought when it does occur. The compulsions and avoidance terminate exposure to the obsession, preventing the extinction of the aversive emotional response (Rachman & Hodgson, 1980). Meanwhile, thought suppression may result in a paradoxical increase in thought frequency (Rachman, 1997, 1998; Salkovskis, 1999), or, at the very least, failures in thought control may intensify appraisals about the thought's meaning (Purdon, Rowa, & Antony, 2005). Finally, thought suppression requires hypervigilance to thought occurrences, increasing the salience of thought-relevant cues and therefore thought occurrences (e.g., Salkovskis, 1999).

Types of Appraisal Relevant to Repugnant Obsessions

Five types of appraisal are considered relevant to the development and persistence of OCD (Obsessive-Compulsive Cognitions Working Group [OCCWG], 1997, 2001), four of which are of particular importance to understanding repugnant, or unacceptable, obsessions.

Overestimation of Threat and Intolerance of Uncertainty

Overestimation of threat refers to a tendency to overestimate the severity and the likelihood of imagined negative consequences of an obsession (OCCWG, 1997). Examples of such beliefs are "I believe that the world is a dangerous place" and "Bad things are more likely to happen to me than to other people." For example, Roger believed that bad things were more likely to happen to him. "Intolerance of uncertainty" is the belief that perfect certainty can and should be achieved before one can safely proceed. Examples of such beliefs are "If I am uncertain, there is something wrong with me" and "It is essential for me to consider all the possible outcomes of a situation" (OCCWG, 2001). Roger strived for 100 percent certainty that he was not a child murderer; any probability of being a murderer, even 0.00000001 percent, was unacceptable.

Responsibility

Salkovskis (1985, 1989, 1999) identified a number of beliefs involving responsibility, which he views as key factors in the development and persistence of OCD. They are as follows: (a) "Having a thought about an action is like performing an action." (b) "Failing to prevent (or failing to try to prevent) harm to self or others is the same as having caused the harm in the first place." (c) "Responsibility is not attenuated by other factors (e.g., low probability of occurrence)." (d) "Not neutralizing when an intrusion has occurred is similar or equivalent to seeking or wanting the harm involved in that intrusion to happen." (e) "One can and should control one's thoughts" (Salkovskis, 1985, p. 579). For example, Roger believed that as long as the probability he was a murderer was not zero, he had to behave as if he were a murderer and ensure that children were protected from him. His concern over his grandchildren's safety is not irrational or overvalued; the irrational or overvalued idea is that one is honor-bound to do everything in one's power to protect against an event whose objective probability is close to zero.

Overimportance of Thoughts

Rachman (1998) introduced the idea of "thought action fusion" to describe the beliefs that having an unacceptable thought increases the likelihood of the negative event represented in the thought coming true and that having a morally repugnant thought is the moral equivalent to committing a morally repugnant deed. Emphasizing the meaning of a thought's occurrence can also manifest itself in beliefs that "obsessional thoughts indicate something significant about oneself" (e.g., that one is terrible, weird, abnormal), and "negative intrusive thoughts must be important merely because they have occurred" (Thordarson & Shafran, 2002, p. 15). Rachman (1997) provides a number of examples of these kinds of thoughts: "This thought reflects my true evil nature," "having this thought means I am a bad person," "if I think this, I must really want it to happen," and "thinking this can make the event more likely to happen" (p. 793). Roger believed that the recurrence of his thoughts about harming his grandchildren must reflect something about his personality, or the thoughts were a prophetic warning sign that he was going to lose control and harm them.

Mental Control

Mental control refers to "overevaluation of the importance of exerting complete control over intrusive thoughts, images or impulses, and the belief that this is both possible and desirable" (OCCWG, as cited by Purdon & Clark, 2002, p. 37). Examples of such beliefs are "I would be a better person if I gained more control over my thoughts," and "If I exercise enough willpower, I should be able to gain complete control over my mind." Roger believed that he could and should be able to control his thoughts fully and that failing to do so was a sign of mental weakness.

Treatment

It is important to get a comprehensive inventory of the obsession content all ameliorative strategies used to cope with the distress it evokes, and the situations, people, and places that are avoided because of it. Clients with OCD are often reluctant to admit the content of their obsessions, especially repugnant ones (Rachman, 2007). Nonjudgmental inquiry about the basic content of the obsessions is important, along with normalizing the thought content. This can be accomplished by presenting clients with a list of repugnant thoughts reported by nonclinical samples (e.g., Rachman, 2003).

It is helpful to have clients monitor their obsessions, compulsions, and avoidance every day for a week, recording the occurrence of each on a form. Examples are provided of each, drawing from the diagnostic assessment (e.g., the target obsessions and compulsions on the Y-BOCS or the client's verbal report). It is also important to assess thought appraisal. Two self-report measures of obsessional beliefs and appraisals used widely are the Obsessional Beliefs Questionnaire (OBQ) and the Interpretation of Intrusions Inventory (III). The measures have been validated in clinical and nonclinical samples and have demonstrated good psychometric properties (OCCWG, 2001). For the purposes of treatment, the III is probably more useful because it assesses situational appraisal.

When assessing violent and sexual obsessions, it is important to ensure, to the extent one is able, that the "obsession" is truly an obsession and not a thought characteristic of a paraphilia or a precursor to violent or exploitative behavior. Currently, there are no established guidelines for doing so. Given that low victim empathy and psychopathy are two factors associated with sexual offending, my recommendation is to assess the extent to which the thought goes against the person's morals, values, past behavior, and fantasy, as well as the extent to which the concern over having the thought reflects self-interest or concern for the victim. When in doubt, and when possible, forensic assessments can be helpful in making differential diagnoses.

Educating the Client to the Model

Treatment begins with educating the client to the cognitive-behavioral model of OCD, using the data the client has collected to piece together the role appraisal, compulsive rituals, avoidance, and thought suppression play in the persistence of the disorder. This elucidates the internal logic of the problem and its solution, and it enhances therapeutic rapport by instilling confidence that the therapist truly understands the fears. It is often helpful to have family members attend this session.

Cognitive Restructuring

Cognitive therapy relies on cognitive restructuring and behavioral experiments to change the personal meaning of the obsessional thought. As Salkovskis observes, the goal of cognitive restructuring is for the "patient and therapist to work together to construct and test a new, less threatening explanation of the patient's experience, and then to explicitly examine the validity of the contrasting accounts" (Salkovskis, 1999, p. S36). Cognitive restructuring techniques are integrated with exposure a case by case. Typically, exposure to repugnant obsessions is more palatable when the client's appraisal about the nature and meaning of the thought has been decatastrophized to some extent.

When planning the cognitive component, several caveats are in order. First, individuals with OCD often overestimate the probability of a threat, and it can be helpful to develop a realistic view of its likelihood, especially if probability estimates are based on erroneous information and perceptions. However, many individuals with OCD will continue to experience distress over the obsession as long as the chance of the feared event is not absolutely and certainly 0 percent, particularly if the perceived awfulness of the threat is high (Salkovskis, 1999). Once the probabilities have been established, further discussion is likely to serve as reassurance. Cognitive restructuring instead must focus on overvalued beliefs about responsibility, about the meaning and importance of thoughts, about intolerance of uncertainty and of the meaning of thought control.

Second, cognitive restructuring around the "truth" of the obsessional thought (e.g., trying to prove that someone is not a child molester) is likely to be quite unproductive, as it is not possible to prove the null hypothesis. Furthermore, the problem here is not that the individual erroneously thinks he or she is a child molester but rather that he or she thinks he or she could be a child molester and that he or she must behave cautiously until 100 percent certainty that he or she is not a danger to children is achieved. Thus, cognitive restructuring aimed at establishing the validity of the doubt is at best fruitless and at worst assists the client in the elaboration of the reassurance ritual. Salkovskis (1999) sums up the problem in OCD that needs to be addressed as follows: "Maybe you are not dangerous, but you are very *worried* about being dangerous" (p. S35).

Finally, when treating religious obsessions it is important that treatment focus on irrational and exaggerated concerns about the meaning of the thoughts, not just beliefs about religion. The client's spiritual advisor can be consulted to establish acceptable guidelines for religious practice (e.g., frequency of prayer and other religious practices), just as when treating contamination fears one might consult a medical professional to establish acceptable guidelines for maintaining good hygiene. Useful analyses of the difference between religious observance and religious obsession are found in the *Obsessive-Compulsive Foundation Newsletter* (Vol. 17, Winter 2003). The sense of certainty about whether a transgression has occurred is absent or present, and that if it is absent, one is "off the hook" for compensating for the perceived transgression.

With these caveats in mind, there are a number of specific restructuring techniques for OCD to address the kind of appraisal relevant to repugnant obsessions (see Freeston, Rheaume & Ladouceur, 1997; Purdon, 2007; Purdon & Clark, 2005; Salkovskis, 1999; Steketee, 1999; Van Oppen & Arntz, 1994).

Exposure

Exposure can be a hard sell with repugnant obsessions because the perceived "awfulness" of the potential harm is high. Salkovskis (1999) observes that, if the client takes no risks of the sort required in exposure, then it can be guaranteed that he or she will continue to have OCD. However, if a number of exceptionally small risks are taken, chances are he or she will be freer of OCD in the future.

In the treatment of repugnant obsessions, it is easy to confuse what the client should be exposed to. A general rule is that clients should be exposed to what they are afraid of. If they are afraid of a thought or image, expose them to the thought or image. This can be done by having the client write out the thought or scene in vivid detail and review it or write it repeatedly. The therapist can also have the client read a detailed description of the image into a tape recorder and play the tape repeatedly. This method, also referred to as audiotaped habituation, is especially helpful if the client uses mental compulsions or neutralization, such as rationalizing, saying ritualized prayers, or thinking a "good" thought, as the continuous repetition of the obsession prevents completion of the mental ritual.

If the client is afraid of losing control and acting on an impulse, the client should be exposed to the situation in which the impulse occurs. For example, if the urge is to swerve into the lane while driving, have the client drive and experience the urge as often as possible without engaging in compulsions or avoidance. If the obsession takes the form of a doubt, the person should be exposed to the sense of uncertainty without engaging the doubt in any way; that is, they are not to respond to the sense of uncertainty by trying to establish certainty (e.g., forming a clear memory of the knives being in the knife block) or by protecting against the worst possible outcome (e.g., thinking a "good" thought to prevent the feared event from happening).

In cases of violent or exploitative obsessions, emphasize to the client that the goal is not to desensitize individuals to the idea of a loved one being harmed. Rather, you are helping them learn that their fear that the thought itself is the vector by which harm might occur is unfounded. Finally, if the obsession is a doubt, the client needs to be exposed to the sense of uncertainty without engaging the doubt in any way (e.g., by evaluating the likelihood of the bad event happening).

There are excellent sources on conducting exposure with OCD (e.g., Purdon & Clark, 2005; Rowa, Antony, & Swinson, 2007; Steketee, 1999). Exposure should be done in a systematic way, beginning with items that cause moderate distress. If distress is too low, no salient reduction in distress will occur, and progress will be too slow. If distress is too high, the individual is likely to refuse or to terminate the exercise prematurely. A rule of thumb is to not begin an exposure exercise unless there is a good chance that the person will be able to endure long enough for their discomfort to decline significantly. If the person does terminate the exposure, they should immediately do an exercise that is a step easier. Exposure hierarchies, in which a series of exposure exercises is plotted on a hierarchy, ranging from least to most distressing, are helpful in structuring the exposure exercises. The distress ratings associated with each exercise on the hierarchy are made, assuming no use of compulsions, thought suppression, or other ameliorative strategies. Exposure should be frequent and repeated (i.e., 10 times in one week will be far more effective than once a week for 10 weeks). Compulsions and other ameliorative strategies are, obviously, prohibited during exposure.

Case Vignette

Roger underwent 16-session treatment sessions, two hours weekly for 14 weeks and then biweekly for sessions 15 and 16. They were conducted by the author and a co-therapist. A detailed description of thoughts, emotions, compulsions, neutralizing, and avoidance was obtained, and this information was used to educate Roger to the treatment model. The next session was spent offering Roger normative information about violent and repugnant thoughts, using a list of violent and repugnant thoughts reported by a nonclinical sample (Rachman, 2003). We then provided information on attentional and thought processes, noting that we all have numerous thoughts throughout the day but that we are geared to attend to thoughts most relevant to our immediate goals, such as the goal to be a loving grandfather.

Roger was asked to identify the extent to which obsessional thoughts other than his target obsessions had bothered him in the past. He reported having had a number of other repugnant thoughts in his life but said that these had not bothered him because he was not afraid of acting on them. We explored this idea with him in light of his recent knowledge about attentional processes. The point was taken that the obsessional thoughts may be perceived as significant simply because they reflect current concerns, not because they truly are significant. Roger was relieved to learn that his thoughts were not wholly aberrant and was willing to entertain the idea that it was not the thought that was the problem but rather his interpretation of it. We asked him to keep track of the intensity of the thought and his level of belief in the idea that having the thought potentiated action throughout the following week.

Roger returned the following week. His belief that the thought was harmful was more intense when his grandchildren were visiting and when he was tired or already anxious. We used this information to illustrate that the thought's meaning is not static but varies according to a number of factors. During this session, we also addressed Roger's belief that if his thought returned despite his efforts to control it, it must have an important meaning and should not be ignored or discounted. We asked Roger to try to suppress thoughts about a white bear for several minutes, which he was unable to do perfectly. We discussed current research on thought suppression in light of this experience, noting that suppression is almost never fully successful, and thought recurrences mean nothing more than that we are not good at fully suppressing thoughts. Furthermore, failures in thought control lead to a decline in mood state, which makes negative thoughts even more accessible and credible. Roger was asked to monitor all thoughts, including strange, silly, nonsensical thoughts, as well as thought appraisal and moods for the next week.

At the next session, Roger reported having experienced numerous strange, silly, and unexpected thoughts and recognized that this past week was not an exception; however, in the past, he simply ignored such thoughts because he deemed them unimportant. We discussed the differences in his obsessional thoughts and again explored the idea that the obsessional thoughts are not problematic but rather his appraisal of their meaning makes them so. We also addressed Roger's conviction that thoughts of violence made him immoral by asking whether strange, silly thoughts made him strange and silly. Finally, we discussed Roger's ability to monitor and control every unacceptable, immoral thought that might enter his mind. Roger agreed that this would be exceedingly difficult, if not impossible and that he would likely be able to concentrate on little else should he attempt it. We then discussed whether, in light of this realization, his conclusion that he was immoral for "allowing" such thoughts to enter his mind was a fair one.

We discussed Roger's readiness to begin exposure. We sketched out a hierarchy of feared thoughts and situations based on the level of anxiety he experienced if the usual ritual and avoidance strategies were prohibited. We identified situations in which experiencing the impulse would be moderately upsetting, quite upsetting, and overwhelmingly upsetting (e.g., having the impulse while in his home near knives with the children absent vs. present). Roger fleshed out the hierarchy during the next week and prepared to begin exposure at the next session.

The following week, Roger was ready to begin exposure. He wrote down all of his thoughts related to the impulse to stab his grandchild on a sheet of paper, the least anxiety-evoking thought ("pick up a knife") followed by the most ("Kill X [grandchild's name]"). Roger read the first sentence aloud over and over again. He was encouraged to attend to the meaning of every word rather than simply recite the words automatically. At first, Roger had significant difficulty doing this; he was shaking, his voice tremulous, and his brow sweating. However, after about 15 repetitions, he began to feel bored and his mind began to wander. He then read the next sentence in the list aloud over and over again, and so on until he got to the most difficult sentence. Throughout, the therapist acted as coach and facilitator, keeping him focused on the source of his anxiety, taking anxiety ratings, and making encouraging statements such as, "You're doing really well. If you can keep going, this exercise is really going to pay off for you."

At the end of the session, we reviewed his progress, discussing what had changed in these stimuli that enabled him to tolerate them with considerably less anxiety. Roger reported that he was beginning to believe that the thoughts might just be thoughts rather than prophetic warning signs or indications of character flaws. As such, he was not as afraid of them or the consequences of speaking them aloud. Roger was asked to begin exposure to the next items in his hierarchy (while continuing to practice the items tackled that day) during the next week. These included staying in the same room as his grandchildren, handling knives when his grandchildren were absent, and wearing something red without attempting to pre-empt or suppress thoughts the color triggered.

In the next session, Roger reported having had initial success with the exposure but found it more difficult if he had recently seen his grandchildren. He had also become concerned that speaking his thoughts aloud would make the act seem more palatable or attractive, given that he may have psychopathic tendencies to begin with and retreated to the more cautious strategy of avoiding the thoughts rather than risking harm to his grandchildren by speaking the thoughts aloud. Roger said that if only he were certain he was not a psychopath, he would be able to do exposure without fear. We did some cognitive restructuring to challenge Roger's perceived need for 100 percent certainty that he was not a homicidal maniac before feeling fully safe with having the thoughts. We acknowledged that we did not know for certain that the probability of his not being a homicidal maniac was zero percent, just as we did not know for certain that his wife or his neighbor was not a homicidal maniac. We pointed out that the difference between people with OCD and those without OCD is that the latter are able to live with acceptable (everyday) levels of uncertainty (i.e., the obvious balance of probabilities—whereas Roger is probably not a killer, we cannot not be absolutely certain that he will never kill anyone!) and dismiss as unimportant intrusive ideas of very low probability events. We encouraged Roger to behave as if he was not a homicidal maniac and therefore did not need to take precautions to protect others from his potential actions.

Roger brought some red items to the therapy session, which he held and gazed at while reading aloud the thoughts about harming his grandchildren. He kept track of how much he wanted to stab his grandchildren as he read aloud the thoughts. Over the course of the exposure exercise, he reported that, contrary to this fears, his desire did not increase and instead remained at zero despite having spoken aloud thoughts of doing so many times. To address Roger's concern that having the thoughts increased the likelihood he would harm his grandchild, we asked him to try an experiment in which he would spend the next week trying to win the lottery simply by thinking about winning. Finally, to address his concern that having thoughts about an inappropriate act led to loss of control over behavior, we asked him to go to a grocery store and to try to make himself lose control by thinking about yelling something inappropriate. Roger was also to continue exposing himself to the color red, reading the newspaper without avoiding articles describing violence, and reading his thoughts aloud.

At the next session, Roger revealed that despite thinking about winning, he had not won the lottery; and despite thinking about yelling inappropriate words, had not embarrassed himself in the grocery store. He was able to tolerate news stories about violence, and he was now quite bored reading his thoughts aloud. In this and the next several sessions, Roger continued with exposure to thoughts, gradually decreasing his avoidance and increasing the level of risk he was willing to take. He brought different sharp implements into the session, starting with a paring knife, and then an axe. He read aloud his thoughts about violence while handling the implements. Between sessions, he allowed himself to experience thoughts in the presence of his grandchildren. He had thoughts of stabbing his grandchild, in the child's presence, as he chopped food in the kitchen. Roger also began interacting with his grandchildren much more and would agree to stay with them even if no other adult was present.

By session 16, Roger worried far less about the thoughts and impulses involving stabbing and found that he no longer had the need to try to preempt their occurrence. This improved his ability to concentrate, and he was able to reengage in activities he previously found difficult. As Roger's range of activities increased, he noticed that the thoughts occurred far less frequently, and when they did occur, they required little or no response from him. Roger was finally able to enjoy his grandchildren again without concerns that he was a danger to them. His score on the Y-BOCS was now in the nonclinical range.

REFERENCES

Abramowitz, J., Franklin, M., Schwartz, S. A., & Furr, J. M. (2003). Symptom presentation and outcome of cognitive-behavioural therapy for obsessive-compulsive disorder. *Journal of Consulting and Clinical Psychology, 71,* 1049–1057.

Baer, L. (1994). Factor analysis of symptom subtypes of obsessive compulsive disorder and their relation to personality and tic disorders. *Journal of Clinical Psychiatry, 55,* 18–23.

Calamari, J. E., Wiegartz, P. S., & Janeck, A. (1999). Obsessive-compulsive disorder subgroups: A symptom-based clustering approach. *Behaviour Research and Therapy, 37,* 113–125.

Calamari, J. E., Wiegartz, P. S., Riemann, B. C., Cohen, R. J., Greer, A., Jacobi, D. M., et al. (2004). Obsessive-compulsive disorder subtypes: An attempted replication and extension of a symptom-based taxonomy. *Behaviour Research and Therapy, 42,* 647–670.

Foa, E. B., & Tillmans, A. (1980). The treatment of obsessive-compulsive neurosis. In A. Goldstein & E. B. Foa (Eds.), *Handbook of behavioral interventions: A clinical guide* (pp. 416–499). New York: Wiley.

Freeston, M. H., Rheaume, J., & Ladouceur, R. (1997). Correcting faulty appraisals of obsessional thoughts. *Behaviour Research and Therapy, 34,* 433–466.

Leckman, J. F., Grice, D. E., Boardman, J., Zhang, H., Vitale, A., Bondi, C., et al. (1989). Symptoms of obsessive-compulsive disorder. *American Journal of Psychiatry, 154,* 911–917.

Mataix-Cols, D., Rauch, S. L., Manzo, P. A., Jenike, M. A., & Baer, L. (1999). Use of factor-analyzed symptom dimensions to predict outcome with serotonin reuptake inhibitors and placebo in the treatment of obsessive-compulsive disorder. *American Journal of Psychiatry, 156,* 1409–1416.

Obsessive Compulsive Cognitions Working Group. (1997). Cognitive assessment of obsessive-compulsive disorder. *Behaviour Research and Therapy, 35,* 667–681.

Obsessive Compulsive Cognitions Working Group. (2001). Development and initial validation of the obsessive beliefs questionnaire and the interpretation of intrusions inventory. *Behaviour Research and Therapy, 39,* 987–1006.

Purdon, C. (2007). Cognitive therapy for obsessive-compulsive disorder. In M. M. Antony, C. Purdon, & L. J. Summerfeldt (Eds.), *Psychological treatment of OCD: Fundamentals and beyond (pp. 111–146).* Washington, DC: American Psychological Association.

Purdon, C., & Clark, D. A. (2002). The need to control thoughts. In R. Frost and G. Steketee (Eds.), *Cognitive approaches to obsessions and compulsions: Theory, assessment and treatment* (pp. 29–43). Amsterdam: Elsevier/Pergamon.

Purdon, C., & Clark, D. A. (2005). *Overcoming obsessive thoughts.* Oakland, CA: New Harbinger.

Purdon, C., Rowa, K., & Antony, M. M. (2005). Thought suppression and its effects on thought frequency, appraisal, and mood state in individuals with obsessive-compulsive disorder. *Behaviour Research and Therapy, 43,* 93–108.

Rachman, S. (1997). A cognitive theory of obsessions. *Behaviour Research and Therapy, 35,* 793–802.

Rachman, S. (1998). A cognitive theory of obsessions: Elaborations. *Behaviour Research and Therapy, 36,* 385–401.

Rachman, S. (2003). *The treatment of obsessions.* Oxford: Oxford University Press.

Rachman, S. (2007). The treatment of religious, sexual and aggressive obsessions. In M. M. Antony, C. Purdon, & L. J. Summerfeldt (Eds.), *Psychological treatment of OCD: Fundamentals and beyond (pp. 209–230).* Washington, DC: American Psychological Association.

Rachman, S. J., & Hodgson, R. J. (1980). *Obsessions and compulsions.* Englewood Cliffs, NJ: Prentice-Hall.

Rachman, S., & Shafran, R. (1998). Cognitive and behavioural features of obsessive compulsive disorder. In R. P. Swinson, M. M. Antony, S. Rachman, & M. A. Richter (Eds.), *Obsessive-compulsive disorder: Theory, research, and treatment* (pp. 51–78). New York: Guilford.

Rasmussen, S. A., & Eisen, J. L. (1992). The epidemiology and clinical features of obsessive compulsive disorder. *Psychiatric Clinics of North America, 15,* 743–758.

Rowa, K., Antony, M. M., & Swinson, R. P. (2007). Exposure and ritual prevention. In M. M. Antony, C. Purdon & L. J. Summerfeldt (Eds.), *Psychological treatment of OCD: Fundamentals and beyond (pp. 79–110).* Washington, DC: American Psychological Association.

Salkovskis, P. M. (1985). Obsessional-compulsive problems: A cognitive-behavioural analysis. *Behaviour Research and Therapy, 23,* 571–584.

Salkovskis, P. M. (1989). Cognitive-behavioural factors and the persistence of intrusive thoughts in obsessional problems. *Behaviour Research and Therapy, 27,* 677–682.

Salkovskis, P. M. (1999). Understanding and treating obsessive-compulsive disorder. *Behaviour Research and Therapy, 37,* S29–S52.

Steketee, G. (1999). *Overcoming obsessive-compulsive disorder: A behavioral and cognitive protocol for the treatment of OCD (Therapist Protocol).* Oakland, CA: New Harbinger.

Summerfeldt, L. J., Kloosterman, P. H., Antony, M. M., Richter, M. A., & Swinson, R. P. (2004). The relationship between miscellaneous symptoms and major symptom factors in obsessive-compulsive disorder. *Behaviour Research and Therapy, 42,* 1453–1467.

Thordarson, D. S., & Shafran, R. (2002). Importance of thoughts. In R. Frost & G. Steketee (Eds.), *Cognitive approaches to obsessions and compulsions: Theory, assessment and treatment* (pp. 15–28). Amsterdam: Elsevier.

Van Oppen, P., & Arntz, A. (1994). Cognitive therapy for obsessive-compulsive disorder. *Behaviour Research and Therapy, 33,* 79–87.

CHAPTER SIX

Compulsive Hoarding

Randy O. Frost, Ph.D., and David F. Tolin, Ph.D.

Clinical Presentation

Description of Symptoms

Compared with obsessive-compulsive disorder (OCD) in general and many of its purported subtypes, compulsive hoarding has received relatively little empirical study. Thus, the working model, treatment strategies, and even basic definitions of this syndrome are still under development. Frost and Hartl (1996) suggested that compulsive hoarding consists of four major elements:

1. *Acquisition of a large number of possessions that appear to be of limited or no value* Accumulating, or collecting, objects includes compulsive buying, the compulsive acquisition of free things, or (in some cases) stealing (Frost & Gross, 1993). In some respects, this behavior appears compulsive, in the sense that the person may feel compelled to acquire and that he or she has no control over the behavior. In other respects, however, the behavior appears impulsive, in the sense that it may be positively reinforced by the pleasure of acquisition, rather than negatively reinforced by anxiety reduction. Although in

many instances the possessions are of limited value, sometimes the acquisition involves new or old objects with real value, but they are accumulated in multiples and quantities too numerous for any individual to use. They are, in fact, useless to the individual because of the volume, though they may have value in other contexts or to other people.

2. *Failure to discard possessions.* People with compulsive hoarding are typically characterized by extreme difficulty discarding objects that most people would consider useless. As will be discussed later in this chapter, research has identified several possible contributors to failure to discard. Most, if not all, people who have hoarding problems have difficulty making decisions. These problems involve decisions about possessions as well as other decisions like what to order at a restaurant or what clothes to put on in the morning. People with compulsive hoarding may also show a tendency to procrastinate on tasks they find aversive, particularly those having to do with the sorting, organizing, and discarding of possessions. People who hoard also frequently display extraordinary levels of perfectionism, manifested as a fear of making mistakes in discarding possessions or in not recycling properly.

3. *Clutter precludes activities for which living spaces were designed.* Acquisition and failure to discard are not typically considered pathological unless they are accompanied by significant clutter. In most cases, extreme clutter is the most visible and striking aspect of hoarding. Clutter prevents normal use of space; for example, people with compulsive hoarding often report being unable to cook in the kitchen, eat in the dining room, sleep in the bedroom, and move through the home. In essence, these rooms no longer function as kitchens, bedrooms, and so on but, rather, function as storage areas for clutter. The clutter in living spaces reflects difficulties with the organization of possessions. In most cases, the pile of possessions includes a seemingly random assortment of items, without any apparent organization by category or importance (e.g., paychecks may be piled with old newspapers). In some cases, there may be limited clutter if other people (e.g., a spouse or other family member) take responsibility for keeping living areas uncluttered. In other cases, the clutter may be stacked floor to ceiling, with only narrow pathways for walking, or rooms may be completely blocked off by a wall of clutter.

4. *Significant distress or impairment in functioning caused by the hoarding.* In cases in which hoarding is clinically significant, clutter prevents the normal use of space for basic activities such as cooking, cleaning, moving through the house, and even sleeping. Interference with these functions can make hoard-

ing a dangerous problem, putting people at risk for fire, falling, and poor sanitation and health (Kim, Steketee, & Frost, 2001). To examine the seriousness of hoarding problems, Frost, Steketee, and Williams (2000) surveyed health department officials in cities throughout Massachusetts regarding their most recent complaints about hoarding. The data from these surveys indicated that, for most cases, clutter inhibited movement, use of furniture, and food preparation; hoarding posed a substantial risk to the person's health, and, in 6 percent of the cases, hoarding was judged to contribute directly to the individual's death in a house fire. More than other forms of OCD, hoarding carries high levels of distress and social disruption, as well as significantly compromises the living environment of the patient and those with and near them. Individuals with compulsive hoarding typically report levels of depression and functional impairment that exceed patients with OCD in general or other anxiety disorders (Frost, Steketee, Williams, & Warren, 2000).

Case Vignette

Ann is a 75-year-old woman whose son encouraged her to seek treatment for hoarding. In this respect, she is similar to many people with compulsive hoarding: Her family members initially appear more concerned about the behavior than she does, and she comes to treatment only after much prodding by her family. She works part-time cleaning houses and lives in a small, single-family home that is filled with things. The house is so full that Ann has bruises on her hips from sliding through the front door because it cannot be opened far enough for her to walk through. In some places, objects are piled to the ceiling, while in other places, they are waist high. There are no open pathways, but there are walkways covered with only six inches of debris. She must walk carefully, but she can move around the house. Most of the objects in the house are useful to Ann, or so she insists. Many of the items either been walked on or urinated on by her elderly dog.

Ann saves many things, including newspapers and magazines. They form large piles, especially in her bedroom. She likes them there because she relaxes before bed by reading. She saves newspapers and magazines for the information they contain. For instance, she saves the personal profile sections from the local newspaper in case she happens to meet the person profiled. She feels like it will provide her with enough information to carry on a conversation. She also saves the events section of the local newspaper because it illustrates the activities at that time of the year. She believes this will give her some advance warning of upcoming events of interest. She also saves any paperwork about cosmetics. She sells cosmetics as a side business and has hundreds of samples and orders filling her home. Each time she orders something from the parent company it comes in a large box with lots of packing material. She saves all of this in case she has to send something back.

Ann saves items she has purchased, such as cosmetics, magazines, and vitamins. However, many of the saved newspapers she has picked up for free. These, she feels, will give her important information about activities around town. Many possessions have at least some monetary value and would not typically be discarded. However, most have not been used and likely never will.

Besides the acquisition of large numbers of items she cannot or will not discard, Ann has great difficulty keeping her things organized. Her cosmetics, newspapers, and magazines are scattered throughout the house. Although Ann has a plan for using the things she brings into the house as well as a place for storage, she often loses track of them before she can get them to their proper location. For instance, when she comes home from the grocery store, she has to set her grocery bag down while she moves things back against the door so she can proceed down the hallway. While she is doing that, she picks up the mail and brings it in with her, forgetting about the grocery bag. The next time she has to go out, she places the grocery bag atop other things so she can get through the door. If the grocery bag is knocked over one of her cats, the cans, bottles, plastic bags, and even plastic containers will spill onto the floor, where she has to step on or over them to pass down the hallway. Her method of cleaning involves picking up these items and placing them atop a pile of assorted objects lining the narrow hallway. Eventually these items fall onto the floor again. She works like this to clean the hallway, but it never looks any different. It seems to her that she is always working at it, but it never gets better.

Ann's hoarding behavior began early in life and was a major source of conflict with her husband, who is now deceased. At one point, the Department of Social Services investigated her housekeeping to determine whether to remove her young son from the home. Now her son will not allow his children to visit because of the condition of Ann's home.

Is Hoarding a Subtype of OCD?

Whether compulsive hoarding is a subtype of OCD has not been resolved. Some research suggests that compulsive hoarding is not specifically associated with OCD but rather may be a feature of a range of psychiatric disorders. Hoarding behavior has been reported in a variety of Axis I disorders, including schizophrenia, social phobia, organic mental disorders, eating disorders, depression, and dementia (see Steketee & Frost [2003] for a review). Furthermore, the ego-syntonic nature of hoarding symptoms contrasts with the typical clinical presentation of OCD. Typically, OCD patients display some recognition that their obsessive thoughts and compulsive behaviors are irrational and maladaptive; in contrast, many patients with compulsive hoarding report little distress or recognition of the problem (Steketee & Frost, 2003). Recent research on OCD has used factor analyses and cluster analyses to identify distinct symptom subtypes. Hoarding emerged as a distinct subgroup in all of the studies using the Yale-Brown Obsessive Compulsive Scale (Y-BOCS) symptom checklist, although in two studies hoarding combined with symmetry/ordering symptoms to form a separate subgroup (see McKay et al. [2004] for a review). In addition, studies of treatment outcome by symptom subtype have consistently shown hoarding symptoms to predict poor outcome for standard OCD treatments consisting of medication or cognitive-behavior therapy (Abramowitz, Franklin, Schwartz, & Furr, 2003; Steketee & Frost, 2003). This suggests that compulsive hoarding and OCD may involve different biological, cognitive, or behavioral mechanisms.

However, other data are consistent with a link between OCD and compulsive hoarding. Several studies of OCD populations reported hoarding frequencies up to 44 percent (Samuels et al., 2002), with hoarding as the primary symptom in 11 percent of patients (Saxena et al., 2002). The correlations between hoarding and OCD symptoms, and the frequency and severity of other OCD symptoms among people with hoarding problems (e.g., Frost et al., 2000), also suggest an association with OCD. Certain features of hoarding may be related to OCD, whereas others are not. Frost, Steketee, and Grisham (2004) found that among people with compulsive hoarding, reports of difficulty discarding and excessive acquisition were significantly and positively correlated with other OCD symptoms on the Y-BOCS, although excessive clutter was not. Furthermore, hoarders' excessive doubting, checking, and reassurance seeking before discarding appear, in many respects, similar to compulsive rituals (Rasmussen & Eisen, 1992). Although some neuroimaging studies (Mataix-Cols et al., 2004; Saxena et al., 2004) found hoarding symptoms and imagery to be associated with patterns of neural activity that differed from those of other OCD patients, using an actual decision-making task,

Maltby, Worhusky, Kiehl, and Tolin (2004) found people with compulsive hoarding to be characterized by similar patterns of neural activity as those seen among nonhoarding OCD patients.

Theoretical Model

The emerging cognitive-behavioral model of compulsive hoarding (Frost & Hartl, 1996; Steketee & Frost, 2003, in press) suggests that the manifestations of hoarding (acquisition, difficulty discarding, clutter) stem from several core vulnerabilities that accompany deficits in information processing, beliefs about and attachments to possessions, and the emotional distress and avoidance behaviors that result.

Core Vulnerabilities

Vulnerabilities that form the backdrop for the development of hoarding are common to many forms of psychopathology. These involve core beliefs about the self (e.g., self-worth, vulnerability, lovability), comorbidities (e.g., mood, attention-deficit hyperactivity disorder), parental factors (i.e., modeling, values, criticism), significant loss (e.g., loss of a parent or loved one), and physical constraints (e.g., health, time, space). Some of the parental factors we have seen involve teaching overly strict values related to waste. Although there is little research on these factors, we have seen these characteristics among our hoarding clients. In addition to these vulnerabilities, hoarding appears to run in families (Frost & Gross, 1993), and some evidence suggests a genetic component to the problem (Lochner et al., 2005; Zhang et al., 2002).

Information-Processing Deficits

Information-processing deficits include those related to attention, memory, categorization, and decision making. Both anecdotal (Steketee, Frost, Wincze, Greene, & Douglass, 2000) and empirical (Hartl, Duffany, Allen, Steketee, & Frost, 2005) studies suggest that people with compulsive hoarding exhibit substantial problems focusing and sustaining attention. These difficulties are magnified when dealing with one's own possessions. There also appears to be an attentional bias, whereby individuals are drawn to and easily absorbed in the nonessential details of a stimulus (possession). This creative attentional bias makes them easily distracted, especially by objects and their meaning, and subject to extremely selective thinking in which only certain features of a possession (e.g., utility, beauty) are entertained at the expense of others (e.g., cost, space available). This bias appears to be driven by visual cues.

People with hoarding problems appear to display an underinclusive cognitive style with respect to categorization of possessions (Wincze, Steketee, & Frost, 2005). Each possession is unique and cannot be categorized with similar ones. That means each item exists in a category of its own because of its special importance and must find a unique place in the home. This complicates the process of sorting and organizing. It also requires a memory-based strategy for finding possessions. Rather than finding things by remembering the location of a category of possessions, people with hoarding problems must remember the location of each individual item. Their recall may be based on visual/special recall (i.e., remembering where they last saw the item) rather than categorical recall (i.e., where is this category of items located). Such a strategy is highly inefficient and may explain the lack of memory confidence previously described.

We suspect that the underinclusive thinking style reflects a more complex way of thinking in which there is excessive focus on (frequently unimportant) details about objects. The extra details complicate the decision-making process by introducing more variables. Each new detail that comes to mind leads to another and another, resulting in a high degree of elaborative mental processing. Elaborative processing, in turn, increases the perceived importance of these nonessential details and makes decision making more difficult because the individual can no longer tell which details are important and which are unimportant. Decision-making problems have been observed in a variety of hoarding samples (Frost & Gross, 1993; Steketee, Frost, & Kyrios, 2003). In a neuroimaging study (Maltby et al., 2004), when making decisions about whether to discard and shred paper items that belonged to them, people with compulsive hoarding took significantly longer to decide than health controls. However, when making decisions about whether to discard items that did not belong to them, people with hoarding and control participants took the same amount of time. In addition, when deciding whether to discard their own items (but not items that did not belong to them), people with hoarding problems showed hyperactivity in the anterior cingulate cortex, a brain region associated with a subjective sense of error.

Maladaptive Beliefs about and Emotional Attachment to Possessions

Following from these vulnerabilities and information-processing deficits are specific attachments to and beliefs about possessions that distinguish people with hoarding problems. These attachments and beliefs are prominent, appear to be quite rigid, and form the basis for decisions about saving and discarding. The cognitive-behavioral model assigns a central role to these beliefs and considers them key to understanding and treating hoarding. Research on beliefs about possessions suggests that these beliefs cluster into four basic subtypes: (a) emotional attachment to possessions, (b) memory-related concerns, (c) responsibility for possessions, and (d) desire for control over possessions (Steketee et al., 2003).

Emotional Attachment to Possessions

Compulsive hoarding is associated with excessive emotional attachment to possessions (Frost, Hartl, Christian, & Williams, 1995). Emotional attachments to possessions can include an overappreciation for the aesthetics of shape, color, texture, and other features of objects. Many people with hoarding problems state that they plan to use their possessions for arts and crafts. Items other people would see as trash are often viewed as containing aesthetic value.

Some objects are saved because they represent a person, place, thing, or time with some emotional importance attached. People with hoarding problems fear they will lose those associated feelings if the item is discarded. Sometimes objects are given human qualities that make discarding them more difficult. For instance, some of our patients have reported not wanting to "hurt the feelings" of a possession by throwing it in the trash; others have stated that their possessions feel like friends or family to them and that losing them would be emotionally equivalent to the death of a loved one. Emotional attachment to objects is generally conceptualized as different from interpersonal attachment, although some authors have speculated that hoarding may result from the experience of emotional deprivation and that attachments to objects have replaced attachments to people (Seedat & Stein, 2002). Consistent with this possibility, some data suggest that hoarding may be associated with a number of indices of social maladjustment such as low marriage rates, social anxiety and withdrawal, and dependent personality traits (Frost et al., 1999; Krause, White, Frost, Steketee, & Kyrios, 2000). It is not clear, however, whether such interpersonal difficulties lead to hoarding, whether hoarding causes the interpersonal difficulties, or whether both are caused by a third, unknown factor.

Also part of the emotional attachment is the phenomenon whereby the objects come to represent a part of their identity. An unimportant bank envelope comes to symbolize the day it was acquired. If it is discarded, the experience feels like losing that day and, consequently, a part of oneself. In these cases, the emotional processes involved in discarding are more akin to grief than anxiety. We have met several people whose self-perception was based on the idea that they are artists who can find beauty in trash. Or they believe they are clever entrepreneurs who are able to find valuable items at low or no cost and will then sell them at a profit or that they are master handymen who can fix anything, no matter how badly damaged it seems. Ironically, however, these people do not actually engage in the behaviors that would typically be associated with these types of people—the "artist" does not actually produce works of art, the "entrepreneur" does not actually sell things, and the "handyman" does not actually repair things. Instead, the self-perception seems to stem primarily from owning things rather than from doing things. Relatedly, possessions provide opportunities. Discarding something means giving up the opportunities it possesses. These include not only the tangible opportunities for normal uses but also more intangible ones like the dream of being something more than you are now.

Memory-Related Concerns

Many people with hoarding problems exhibit a lack of confidence in their memories. Perhaps the most striking finding from experimental studies is that the poor memory confidence reported by people with hoarding problems appears to be independent of any actual memory deficits (Hartl et al., 2004). In this sense, compulsive hoarding seems to resemble OCD, with patients perceiving their memory as being untrustworthy and therefore needing to rely on maladaptive compensatory strategies (Tolin et al., 2001). One reason frequently given by people with hoarding problems for piling things in the middle of the room rather than putting them away is that they are visible and therefore more likely to be remembered. In other cases, people with compulsive hoarding report a concern that by discarding an item, the memories associated with it will be lost.

Responsibility for Possessions

Responsibility beliefs include the belief in the utility of objects and the avoidance of waste. These beliefs are clearly not ego-dystonic, nor are they beliefs about unlikely events. Modern cultures have indeed become wasteful, discarding items that clearly have some value remaining. Many people with hoarding problems find the idea of being wasteful particularly aversive. It seems as if even imagining a use for a specific possession means that it must be saved for that use, even if the owner will never use it in that way. The emotional experience connected with responsibility beliefs may be more akin to guilt rather than anxiety or grief.

Although the homes of people with hoarding problems appear to be a model of imperfection, for many people perfectionistic beliefs interfere with discarding or organizing. We have had clients who must find all the pieces of a board game before they can get rid of it. Others feel they must collect all the information available about a topic before making a decision. Many people with compulsive hoarding report an intense fear of making mistakes that exacerbates problems with decision making and with pursuing efforts to clean a chaotic and squalid house.

Desire for Control over Possessions

Finally, people with hoarding problems display exaggerated sensitivity to other people touching, using, or even thinking about their possessions. This sense of needing to control all access to possessions extends to any efforts to convince them to get rid of things. The most common refrain when describing the efforts of family and friends to help the people with hoarding problems is, "No one has the right to touch my stuff."

These appraisals (beliefs and meanings) can lead directly to saving and acquisition, or can lead to intense emotional experiences, especially if there is the prospect of losing (i.e., discarding or not acquiring) the object. The emotional experience often involves anxiety, grief, or guilt. The intensity of these emotions leads to avoidance and escape in the form of saving (not discarding) and acquiring. In this way, acquiring and saving are negatively reinforced. In addition, however, there are often positive emotions (i.e., elation, affection) associated with the prospect of acquiring a new item or with finding a long-lost treasure. These also lead to saving and acquiring and positively reinforce these behaviors. By saving everything and not controlling acquisition, clients have little opportunity to test the beliefs and appraisals about possessions nor to develop alternative behaviors surrounding possessions.

Treatment

As described previously, compulsive hoarding does not appear to respond particularly well to treatments that were originally validated for treating OCD.

We are currently testing a new model of treatment (Steketee & Frost, in press) that is based on the cognitive-behavioral model. Specific aspects of our treatment program are detailed next.

Motivational Enhancement

People with hoarding problems have been described as having limited insight and motivation for treatment (e.g., Christensen & Greist, 2001). In our experience, people with hoarding problems often recognize that their hoarding behavior is of concern (Frost & Gross, 1993); however, their beliefs about possessions are not seen as ego-dystonic or unreasonable. They frequently approach treatment maintaining that they only need help with organizing or more time with processing their possessions so they can organize and discard. This poses a significant challenge for the therapist in trying to change the way clients interact with their possessions. If the therapist begins by challenging the hoarding-related beliefs, therapy quickly turns into an argument in which the therapist argues for change while the client argues for the status quo. For this reason, cognitive-behavior therapy for compulsive hoarding relies heavily on principles from motivational interviewing (Miller & Rollnick, 2002), which was designed to help the client explore and resolve ambivalence about change. This approach is used throughout treatment to avoid arguments with the client who objects to changing.

Collaborative Model Building

Because the beliefs and attachments to possessions are perceived to be reasonable, a major activity in treatment is developing a case formulation and functional-analytic model of the hoarding symptoms in conjunction with the client. The case formulation identifies all of the specific factors contributing to the problem (core beliefs, information processing deficits, beliefs about and attachments to possessions, distress, and avoidance) and links them together to illustrate how the problem developed and is maintained. This begins with the first session, continues throughout treatment, is done collaboratively, and becomes a road map for therapy sessions. By seeing how the features of hoarding lead to the result (clutter), clients are more likely to consider changing their beliefs about and relationship to possessions.

Sorting of Possessions

To provide a context for developing the case formulation, sorting for the purpose of organizing and evaluating possessions is undertaken at most sessions.

Sorting becomes the main platform for developing an understanding about why they save, exploring the beliefs that come out of the case formulation, and experimenting with new beliefs and behaviors. Sorting involves two basic activities: (1) organizing and (2) discarding. The tone for sorting should be one of discovery and understanding, rather than exerting pressure to discard. In our current trial, every fourth session of the 26–session treatment is done in the client's home.

Nonacquisition

Some sessions are devoted to compulsive acquisition, with more sessions allocated for this purpose for clients with more serious acquisition problems. Once the therapist and client have a clear conceptualization of the factors involved in acquisition behaviors, nonacquiring sessions can be conducted. During these sessions, the therapist and client go to a location where acquisition is a problem (e.g., store, tag sale, dumpster) and conduct behavioral experiments designed to increase the client's ability to tolerate urges to acquire without giving into them.

Therapeutic Strategies

During most sessions, the therapist uses a set of "tools" to help develop the case formulation and to engage the client in sorting, discarding, and nonacquisition tasks. The use of these tools depends on clinical judgment about which will be most useful at any given time.

Downward Arrow

The downward arrow technique (Beck, 1995) is a cognitive strategy for uncovering clients' beliefs about likely outcomes and their personal meanings related to these outcomes. The therapist typically begins by asking the client, "If you were to discard this, what would be the worst that could happen?" If the client responds with, "I might need it some day," the therapist could respond, "And what would be bad about that?" If the client then says, "If I need it and don't have it, then I'd really feel like an idiot." The therapist could respond, "How bad would it be for you to feel like an idiot?" The end goal of the downward arrow is either to help the client recognize that nothing particularly bad will happen, or to see that, although they fear a catastrophic outcome, this is quite unlikely to occur.

Behavioral Experiments

Behavioral experiments are conducted within the spirit of collaborative empiricism, in which the therapist and client view themselves as partner scientists, teaming up to develop a shared understanding of the client's hoarding problem. Thus, when a puzzling issue or question comes up that cannot be resolved through discussion alone, the therapist might suggest an experiment to test specific hypotheses. For example, if the client says, "If I don't buy this item, I won't be able to stop thinking about it," the therapist might suggest, "How about if we test that out with an experiment? Would you be willing not to buy this item, and see whether it is true that you can't stop thinking about it?" If the client agrees to the experiment, the therapist must check in with the client the following day and the next week to inquire about whether they have been consumed with thoughts about the item.

Challenging Questions

During sorting or nonacquisition tasks, the therapist facilitates critical thinking by asking the client challenging questions about the decision. The spirit of these questions is not to argue with the client but rather to make sure that the client is examining all sides of the issue and therefore is making a well-reasoned decision. The specific questions vary from client to client, according to each client's hoarding-related beliefs. However, typical questions might include "How many of these do I already have?" "How many would be enough?" "Do I have a specific plan to use this item within a reasonable timeframe?" "Have I used this in the last year?" "Is this of good quality?" "Do I really need it?" "Will discarding this help me solve my hoarding problem?" In subsequent sessions, the therapist fades his or her role in this process by writing the questions down so that the client can ask the questions to him- or herself, and then the client is asked to generate the questions from memory.

Evidence for the Effectivesness of Treatment

In a test of an early version of this treatment, Hartl and Frost (1999) reported success in treating a 53-year-old woman with a longstanding hoarding problem. The multiple baseline experimental case study design resulted in the elimination of clutter in all target rooms as well as significant reduction in self-reported hoarding symptoms. Cermele, Melendez-Pallitto, and Pandina

(2001) reported the use of a single-session cleaning following several months of preparation based on the cognitive-behavioral model. Steketee et al. (2000) reported positive but modest results using an earlier version of this treatment in a group format.

We are currently in the midst of a controlled trial of the version of the treatment described here. Findings from the pilot open trial phase of the project ($N = 9$) revealed significant reductions in hoarding severity (25–34%) and significant reductions in specific hoarding behaviors (20–33%) as well as observational measures of clutter (23–33%). In 57 percent of treatment completers, both the therapist and client rated the client as "much improved" or "very much improved" (Frost, Steketee, & Tolin, 2005).

Case Vignette

Ann displayed many of the features outlined in the cognitive-behavioral model of compulsive hoarding. Her hoarding was due to insufficient energy, time, and motivation to clean, according to Ann. She could see no problems with her beliefs about what she acquired and what needed saving, nor did she see any problems with her lack of cleaning behavior. Using behavioral experiments, she and the therapist found a number of other factors related to her hoarding problem. Her infrequent cleaning behavior, in addition to being disorganized and ineffective, appeared to be guided by a perfectionistic ideal: She could only feel a sense of accomplishment if the living space was left in a completely pristine state. Thus, she would have to spend hours cleaning a very small area for it to meet her standards. Because this was not possible for most of her house, she preferred to avoid cleaning altogether and, perhaps, as a result had trained herself to avoid noticing the clutter. Ann also reported strong beliefs in her responsibility not to waste things, especially things that had any perceived utility. She saved all bags and containers, regardless of how deteriorated, because they could be used to hold recycling or trash. Ann also believed that the only way she could remember things was by saving magazines and newspapers in which she had read important or interesting information.

A fascinating feature of Ann's relationship to objects was her beliefs about control over her things and her behavior. She would not allow the therapist to touch items in her home or even suggest that something was not worth saving. This issue first surfaced when she failed to even attempt the first homework assignment. As Ann described it, "I have a rebellious streak. If someone tells me what to do, or even if I get the feeling they want me to do something, I will do the opposite."

As the clutter grew, Ann experienced guilt and self-reproach about her inadequacies as a mother and as a person. She became increasingly estranged from others because she did not feel comfortable inviting anyone to her house. She declined invitations to dine at other people's homes for fear they would expect an invitation in return. She came to view the real Ann as a "hoarder" but maintained the public persona of a normal person. Her belief that this was not a reflection of her true self ("the hoarder") complicated her feelings of depression and further contributed to her hoarding behavior.

It was clear that one of Ann's core beliefs was that she was a bad mother and therefore a bad person. Whether this helped cause or was caused by her hoarding is not clear. However, it contributed to the ongoing problem. Perhaps as a way to cope with this, Ann developed a peculiar ability to ignore the clutter. When she would come home and slide through her front door, she failed to notice the clutter. Only when she made a conscious effort to notice it, as part of her homework, did she notice how bad things were. When she was made to focus on it, her mood deteriorated noticeably. Her attempts at controlling her depression perhaps led her to develop this extreme form of avoidance.

Efforts to change Ann's hoarding included downward-arrow techniques to identify beliefs driving her behavior and behavioral experiments to test those beliefs. One session was particularly important for Ann's treatment. In this session, she brought to the clinic a bag of items from her bedroom floor. One of the items was a free newspaper with a section on activities for elders in the community. Although the newspaper was more than two weeks old, Ann felt a strong drive to keep it. She anticipated a feeling of distress and a sense that she would lose important information and opportunities if she were to get rid of the newspaper. She also feared that these feelings would not go away. She agreed to a behavioral experiment to test these feared outcomes by discarding the newspaper. On discarding the newspaper, Ann rated her discomfort as an 85 on a scale from 0 to 100. Five minutes later, her discomfort level was at 80, and 15 minutes later it stood at 60. Six days later, at her next treatment session, her discomfort rating was 15. The therapist pointed out to Ann that her original hypothesis, that her bad feelings would not go away if she threw away the newspaper, did not seem to have come true. After this experiment, Ann discarded items more easily than she had before. She frequently commented on the effect the experiment had on her, particularly on her beliefs about how she would feel if she were to discard something and about how long discomfort about losing something would last. In her treatment, Ann's "difficulty discarding" score on the Saving Inventory-Revised (Frost et al., 2004) fell by 44 percent from pre- to post-treatment.

Troubleshooting

In our experience, some of the most troublesome aspects of cognitive-behavior therapy for compulsive hoarding have to do with homework adherence and perfectionism-related beliefs. Frequently, clients do not complete the assigned homework and do not put in the necessary amount of time to benefit from the treatment. Commonly stated reasons for homework nonadherence include fatigue, low energy, and feeling overwhelmed due to stress. We have employed a number of strategies to deal with this, including telephone checks, scheduling marathon in-home sessions or sessions with helpers, and making sure clients actively participate in case formulation and fully understand that it is one way to prevent these problems. Whenever these problems arise, we incorporate them into the case formulation so they become part of the overall understanding of how the hoarding problem is maintained.

Perfectionistic thinking in compulsive hoarding can at times be so rigid that the client will not entertain ways of doing things that violate his or her rules (e.g., the client believes that the homework assignment is "wasteful"). In these cases, the perfectionism needs to be incorporated into the case formulation and dealt with as a problem in its own right. We frequently will incorporate the downward arrow and behavioral experiments (e.g., deliberately doing something imperfectly) as a means of challenging perfectionism beliefs.

Therapists should consider evaluating hoarding clients' readiness for change before beginning therapy and for the first few sessions. Their ambivalence often does not become apparent until after the first few sessions, when the focus narrows on beliefs and possessions they do not want to abandon. Motivational interviewing strategies can be employed to help clients weigh the pros and cons of changing and to verbalize the argument for working on the problem.

REFERENCES

Abramowitz, J. S., Franklin, M. E., Schwartz, S. A., & Furr, J. M. (2003). Symptom presentation and outcome of cognitive-behavioral therapy for obsessive-compulsive disorder. *Journal of Consulting and Clinical Psychology, 71,* 1049–1057.

Beck, J. S. (1995). *Cognitive therapy: Basics and beyond.* New York: Guilford.

Cermele, J. A., Melendez-Pallitto, L., & Pandina, G. J. (2001). Intervention in compulsive hoarding. A case study. *Behavior Modification, 25,* 214–232.

Christensen, D. D., & Greist, J. H. (2001). The challenge of obsessive-compulsive disorder hoarding. *Primary Psychiatry, 8,* 79–86.

Frost, R. O., & Gross, R. (1993). The hoarding of possessions. *Behaviour Research and Therapy, 31,* 367–382.

Frost, R. O., & Hartl, T. L. (1996). A cognitive-behavioral model of compulsive hoarding. *Behaviour Research and Therapy, 34,* 341–350.

Frost, R. O., Hartl, T., Christian, R., & Williams, N. (1995). The value of possessions in compulsive hoarding: Patterns of use and attachment. *Behaviour Research and Therapy, 33,* 897–902.

Frost, R. O., Krause, E., White, L., Ax, E., Chowdry, F., Williams, L., et al. (1999). *Compulsive hoarding: Patterns of attachment to people and possessions.* Paper presented at the 33rd meeting of the Association for Advancement of Behavior Therapy, Toronto, ON.

Frost, R. O., Steketee, G., & Grisham, J. (2004). Measurement of compulsive hoarding: Saving Inventory-Revised. *Behaviour Research and Therapy, 42,* 1163–1182.

Frost, R. O., Steketee, G., & Tolin, D. F. (2005). Cognitive changes in the treatment of hoarding. In M. Kyrios (Chair), *Cognitive changes in the treatment of obsessive-compulsive disorder and related disorders.* Symposium presented to the annual meeting of the European Association of Behavioral and Cognitive Therapies, Thessaloniki, Greece.

Frost, R. O., Steketee, G., & Williams, L. (2000). Hoarding: A community health problem. *Health and Social Care in the Community, 8,* 229–234.

Frost, R. O., Steketee, G., Williams, L. F., & Warren, R. (2000). Mood, personality disorder symptoms and disability in obsessive compulsive hoarders: A comparison with clinical and nonclinical controls. *Behaviour Research and Therapy, 38,* 1071–1081.

Hartl, T. L., Duffany, S. R., Allen, G. J., Steketee, G., & Frost, R. O. (2005). Relationships among compulsive hoarding, trauma, and attention-deficit/hyperactivity disorder. *Behaviour Research and Therapy, 43,* 269–276.

Hartl, T. L., & Frost, R. O. (1999). Cognitive-behavioral treatment of compulsive hoarding: A multiple baseline experimental case study. *Behaviour Research and Therapy, 37,* 451–461.

Hartl, T. L., Frost, R. O., Allen, G. J., Deckersbach, T., Steketee, G., Duffany, S. R., et al. (2004). Actual and perceived memory deficits in individuals with compulsive hoarding. *Depression and Anxiety, 20,* 59–69.

Kim, H. J., Steketee, G., & Frost, R. O. (2001). Hoarding by elderly people. *Health and Social Work, 26,* 176–184.

Krause, E., White, L., Frost, R. O., Steketee, G., & Kyrios, M. (2000). *Attachment deficits among compulsive hoarders: Implications for theory and treatment.* Paper presented at the 34th meeting of the Association for Advancement of Behavior Therapy, New Orleans, LA.

Lochner, C., Kinnear, C. J., Hemmings, S. M., Seller, C., Niehaus, D. J., Knowles, J. A., et al. (2005). Hoarding in obsessive-compulsive disorder: Clinical and genetic correlates. *Journal of Clinical Psychiatry, 66,* 1155–1160.

Maltby, N., Worhunsky, P., Kiehl, K. A., & Tolin, D. F. (2004). Compulsive hoarding: The neurobiological perspective. In T. L. Hartl (Chair), *Compulsive hoarding: Recent advances in research and important clinical considerations.* Symposium paper presented at the 34th meeting of the Association for Advancement of Behavior Therapy, New Orleans, LA.

Mataix-Cols, D., Wooderson, S., Lawrence, N., Brammer, M. J., Speckens, A., & Phillips, M. L. (2004). Distinct neural correlates of washing, checking, and hoarding symptom dimensions in obsessive-compulsive disorder. *Archives of General Psychiatry, 61,* 564–576.

McKay, D., Abramowitz, J., Calamari, J., Kyrios, M., Radomsky, A., Sookman, D., Taylor, S., et al. (2004). A critical evaluation of obsessive-compulsive disorder subtypes: symptoms versus mechanisms. *Clinical Psychology Review, 24,* 283–313.

Miller, W., & Rollnick, S. (2002). *Motivational interviewing: Preparing people for change* (2nd ed.). New York: Guilford.

Rasmussen, S. A., & Eisen, J. L. (1992). The epidemiology and differential diagnosis of obsessive compulsive disorder. *Journal of Clinical Psychiatry, 53 (Suppl.),* 4–10.

Samuels, J., Bienvenu, O. J., III, Riddle, M. A., Cullen, B. A., Grados, M. A., Liang, K. Y., et al. (2002). Hoarding in obsessive compulsive disorder: Results from a case-control study. *Behaviour Research and Therapy, 40,* 517–528.

Saxena, S., Brody, A. L., Maidment, K. M., Smith, E. C., Zohrabi, N., Katz, E., et al. (2004). Cerebral glucose metabolism in obsessive-compulsive hoarding. *American Journal of Psychiatry, 161,* 1038–1048.

Saxena, S., Maidment, K. M., Vapnik, T., Golden, G., Rishwain, T., Rosen, R. M., et al. (2002). Obsessive-compulsive hoarding: symptom severity and response to multimodal treatment. *Journal of Clinical Psychiatry, 63,* 21–27.

Seedat, S., & Stein, D. J. (2002). Hoarding in obsessive-compulsive disorder and related disorders: A preliminary report of 15 cases. *Psychiatry and Clinical Neurosciences, 56,* 17–23.

Steketee, G., & Frost, R. O. (2003). Compulsive hoarding: Current status of the research. *Clinical Psychology Review, 23,* 905–927.

Steketee, G., & Frost, R. O. (in press). *Treatment manual for compulsive hoarding.* New York: Oxford University Press.

Steketee, G., Frost, R. O., & Kyrios, M. (2003). Beliefs about possessions among compulsive hoarders. *Cognitive Therapy and Research, 27,* 467–479.

Steketee, G., Frost, R. O., Wincze, J., Greene, K., & Douglass, H. (2000). Group and individual treatment of compulsive hoarding: A pilot study. *Behavioural and Cognitive Psychotherapy, 28,* 259–268.

Tolin, D. F., Abramowitz, J. S., Brigidi, B. D., Amir, N., Street, G. P., & Foa, E. B. (2001). Memory and memory confidence in obsessive-compulsive disorder. *Behaviour Research and Therapy, 39,* 913–927.

Wincze, J., Steketee, G., & Frost, R. O. (2005). *Categorization in compulsive hoarding.* Unpublished manuscript, Smith College, Northampton, MA.

Zhang, H., Leckman, J. F., Pauls, D. L., Tsai, C. P., Kidd, K. K., & Campos, M. R. (2002). Genomewide scan of hoarding in sib pairs in which both sibs have Gilles de la Tourette syndrome. *American Journal of Human Genetics, 70,* 896–904.

CHAPTER SEVEN

The PANDAS Subgroup of Obsessive-Compulsive Disorder

Kyle Allen Williams, M.D., Jon E. Grant, J.D., M.D., and Suck Won Kim, M.D.

With the landmark publication of the first 50 cases of pediatric autoimmune neuropsychiatric disorder associated with streptococcal infection (PANDAS) in 1998, Swedo and colleagues expanded the etiologic possibilities in pediatric psychiatry to include bacterial pathogens in the origin of neuropsychiatric disease (Swedo et al., 1998). Numerous studies have found indirect evidence for a link between group A streptococcus (GAS) infection and neuropsychiatric sequelae; yet, few investigators have identified streptococcal virulence factors or candidate genetic markers, and the PANDAS phenotype continues to evolve (Kaplan, 2000; Kurlan, 1998; Murphy et al., 1997; Shulman, 1999). For these reasons, the PANDAS concept continues to incite considerable controversy.

Streptococcus pyogenes, the pathogen responsible for GAS infection, is a diverse organism capable of initiating an array of clinical diseases. Streptococcal diseases range from acute infections, responsible for pharyngitis and upper respiratory infections, to delayed sequelae, including Sydenham chorea (SC), a component of acute rheumatic fever (Cunningham, 2000). Whereas acute infections are known to arise from the direct effect of streptococcal replication and toxin production, the delayed streptococcal sequelae are hypothesized to arise from autoimmune cells or antibodies induced in susceptible hosts by the streptococcus organism (Cunningham, 2000). Thus, PANDAS, like SC, is hypothesized to be an autoimmune, delayed, neuropsychiatric manifestation of streptococcal infection (Swedo et al., 1998).

The difficulties in elucidating the pathogenesis of PANDAS reflect the complexity of the GAS organism and the lack of etiologic knowledge of infection-related autoimmune disorders. Furthermore, PANDAS represents a significant challenge for both diagnosis and treatment. This chapter will focus on the clinical presentation of patients with PANDAS, the proposed neuropathology of PANDAS, and how knowledge of the neuropathology may influence the treatment of PANDAS-related obsessive-compulsive disorder (OCD) and tics.

Clinical Presentation

The criteria for PANDAS (Table 7.1) put forward by Swedo and colleagues (1998) closely resemble the symptoms associated with OCD, Tourette syndrome (TS), and SC. Evidence suggests that patients with PANDAS can exhibit the obsessions and compulsions of OCD and the involuntary, motoric hyperactivity of TS and SC (Murphy & Pichichero, 2002; Snider & Swedo, 2004). In addition, a documented association between the onset, or exacerbation, of symptoms concurrent with or following GAS infection is necessary to fulfill the criteria for PANDAS, an aspect that will be discussed in further detail.

The initial report of 50 patients with PANDAS described a clinically heterogeneous group, with a split (48% each) between those meeting criteria for a primary diagnosis of OCD and those with a primary tic disorder (Swedo et al., 1998). However, there was significant comorbidity between OC symptoms and tics in this sample, with 64 percent of subjects meeting criteria for OCD (or subclinical OCD), and tics. The mean score on the Yale-Brown Obsessive Compulsive Scale (YBOCS) was 19.6 (10.5 for obsessions, 9.1 for compulsions). Boys predominated in the study group with a ratio of 2.6:1, and mean ages of onset of OCD and tic symptoms were 6.3 and 7.4 years, respectively (Swedo et al., 1998). Contamination obsessions predominated in both the primary OCD and tic groups (50% of all patients), while washing compulsions predominated in the primary OCD group (63%). Compulsive symptoms were heterogeneous in the tic disorder group; repeating compulsions were the most prevalent (46%), with ordering/arranging (31%), checking (27%), and cleaning (26%) significantly represented (Swedo et al., 1998).

Table 7.1. *Criteria for Pediatric Autoimmune Neuropsychiatric Disorder Associated with Streptococcal Infection (PANDAS)*

1. Presence of obsessive-compulsive disorder and/or tic disorder
2. Pediatric onset (age 3 years to puberty)
3. Episodic course of symptom severity
4. Association with group A beta-hemolytic streptococcal infections
5. Association with neurologic abnormalities (motor hyperactivity, adventitious movements, or choreiform movements)

Although the rates of tic disorder may seem high in this patient sample, they are consistent with cohort studies of childhood OCD, which suggest that both PANDAS and childhood-onset OCD represent a unique OCD phenotype when compared with adult-onset (>age 18) OCD (Miguel et al., 2005). For example, childhood-onset OCD shows a bimodal age of onset, with peaks in early childhood (about age 6–8, similar to onset of PANDAS) and late adolescence. The early childhood onset group is more likely to be male, have tic symptoms or TS, and have a higher familial occurrence of OCD or OC behaviors (Miguel et al., 2005). Studies have also suggested that the early-onset group has a significantly worse response to clomipramine and selective serotonin reuptake inhibitor (SSRI) monotherapies and a higher frequency of compulsions not preceded by obsessions (Miguel et al., 2005).

Although these data may suggest that childhood-onset OCD and PANDAS may not be clinically distinguishable from each other, an analysis of the symptoms of PANDAS suggests that they represent a clinically distinct subset of patients with pediatric OCD and tic disorder (Snider & Swedo, 2004). Two major clinical hallmarks of PANDAS are its association with an abrupt onset of OCD or tic disorder in childhood and evidence of recent GAS infection (Swedo et al., 1998). In theory, this association is easily documented through GAS rapid-antigen tests in the clinic. However, many patients present to clinic with symptoms of OC and without clinical signs of GAS infection, necessitating a review of medical records to confirm the association of OC/tic symptoms with GAS infection.

The most salient clinical feature of the PANDAS subgroup is the sudden onset of symptoms, commonly described by parents as "explosive." Parents report that symptoms appear overnight or can be pinpointed to a particular day. In the largest cohort study of PANDAS patients, Swedo et al. (1998) reported a mean age of onset of both OCD and tic symptoms (6.3 and 7.4 years, respectively) that was approximately three years earlier than the mean childhood onset OCD (Swedo, Rapoport, Leonard, Lenane, & Cheslow, 1989; Thomsen 1995) and two years earlier than the mean onset for tic disorders (Leckman et al., 1997).

A further defining characteristic of PANDAS symptoms is the acute exacerbation of OC or tic symptoms associated with GAS infection, a phenomenon commonly referred to as a "saw-tooth" clinical course (Swedo et al., 1998). These exacerbations occur after the initial ("sentinel") onset of PANDAS symptoms, are associated with a marked increased in PANDAS symptom severity, and may persist for days to months (Murphy & Pichichero, 2002; Snider & Swedo, 2004). Following these exacerbations, patients with PANDAS may return to their baseline symptoms or their symptoms may remit, a stark contrast to the reported progressive, persistent course of childhood-onset OCD (Leonard et al., 1993).

In further contrast to childhood-onset OCD, in which contamination obsessions and washing/cleaning compulsions predominate (Piacentini & Bergman, 2000), reports from a prospective three-year study of patients with PANDAS suggests that PANDAS patients present with symptoms not typically considered in the realm of childhood OC symptoms (Murphy & Pichichero, 2002). In this study, 4 of 12 diagnosed with PANDAS initially presented with the complaint of a kidney problem (Murphy & Pichichero, 2002), often questioning the presence of a bladder infection. Daytime urinary frequency and urgency were common, but dysuria, abdominal pain, and the high fever characteristic of a urinary tract infection were not present. Symptoms peaked at times of separation before school, when bathroom facilities were not immediately available. Children repeatedly needed to use the bathroom, urinating small amounts, followed by an elaborate urinary hygiene ritual with compulsive genital wiping (Murphy & Pichichero, 2002). In some patients, this cycle was repeated up to 10 times in an hour, taking precedence over all other activities.

Finally, patients with PANDAS have also shown signs of marked deterioration of handwriting during acute exacerbation of symptoms, a symptom hypothesized to be unique in the PANDAS subgroup (Miguel et al., 2005; Swedo et al., 1998). It has been hypothesized that the etiology of handwriting deterioration is similar to the choreiform hand movements characteristic of patients with SC (Snider & Swedo, 2004). To support this, choreiform movements were found in 50 percent of the 26 patients with PANDAS tested in the initial PANDAS groups reported, although no patient exhibited the frank chorea typical of SC (Swedo et al., 1998).

Critics of the PANDAS model point to the ubiquity of childhood infection with GAS, along with the lack of genetic knowledge of childhood OCD, and regard the association of GAS with OC/tic symptoms as correlational without evidence of causation (Kaplan, 2000; Kurlan, 1998). Although there are as yet no strong molecular or neuropathologic data to refute this argument adequately, evidence from the clinical characteristics of patients with PANDAS sheds some light on this topic. For example, it has been suggested that patients with PANDAS have abnormal and chronically elevated levels of antistreptococcal antibodies—particularly antistreptolysin O (ASO) and DNAse B—at the time of onset or exacerbation of symptoms (Cardona & Orefici, 2001; Perlmutter et al., 1999). These antibodies are known to be acutely elevated in acute streptococcal infection and fall within three months after clearance of the GAS infection (Shet & Kaplan, 2002). Thus, in the absence of positive GAS culture or rapid antigen tests, an elevated ASO or DNAse B titer may be a useful tool in PANDAS diagnosis in a child with new-onset OC or tic symptoms.

Case Vignette

Michael, a 13-year-old boy, was referred to a medical clinic for evaluation of treatment-resistant OCD, TS, and ADHD. Michael had a history of GABHS culture-positive pharyngitis beginning at age 5, which led to tonsillectomy at age 7. His symptoms of OCD and TS also manifested at age 5 with obsessions about germs, tapping and touching rituals, and repetitive throat clearing. Michael's onset of symptoms occurred after a night of high fever, throat pain, and night sweats, which was later verified as GABHS pharyngitis. Over the next 48 hours, Michael experienced an onset of unbearable sexual and violent imagery, with a compulsion to vocalize these images and make sexual gestures toward people.

Michael was seen in a mental health clinic within three days of the onset of his symptoms, and he was treated with 400 mg of amoxicillin three times a day, by a psychiatrist who suspected PANDAS. Michael's symptoms of OC were noted to decrease within three days of treatment, but coughing and repetitive throat-clearing tics were still present. After an additional four days of antibiotic therapy, Michael's symptoms resolved completely.

Michael experienced multiple recurrences of GABHS pharyngitis, each coincident with an explosive exacerbation of his symptoms of OCD and TS. Michael was placed on prophylactic antibiotic therapy with Cephalexin (Keflex), during which he continued to have bouts of pharyngitis with concurrent exacerbation of the symptoms of OCD/TS. After tonsillectomy, Michael continued to have upper respiratory infections, coincident with GABHS cultured from the posterior pharynx, which again resulted in exacerbation of OCD/TS symptoms.

Michael's symptoms of OCD and TS were poorly controlled through a variety of psychoactive medications, including SSRIs, neuroleptics, atypical antipsychotics, and tricyclic antidepressants. He continued to have significant periods of exacerbated symptoms throughout treatment, yet was also recognized to have a significant level of baseline OC and TS symptoms by his early teenage years. Michael's family history was significant for OCD in his father and acute rheumatic fever in his paternal grandmother and grandfather. Because of his failure to respond to multiple trials of psychoactive medication for his symptoms, Michael was referred to a specialty center for the treatment of OCD, where he was lost to follow-up.

The Pathogenesis of PANDAS

The proposed role of a GAS-induced autoimmune etiology in PANDAS remains controversial. Investigators have isolated antibodies that react to neuronal components of the basal ganglia in an array of tic and OC groups (Hoekstra, Kallenberg, Korf, & Minderaa, 2002). However, recent studies of antineuronal antibodies (ANAs), and antibasal ganglia antibodies (ABGAs) in patients with PANDAS and OCD have met with conflicting results on their presence (Dale, Heyman, Giovannoni, & Church, 2005; Singer, Hong, Yoon, & Williams, 2005). As such, the proposed role for autoimmune involvement in PANDAS relies heavily on symptom homology with SC, temporal relationship with GAS infections, and treatment studies using immune-based therapies.

The predominant theory of streptococcal induction of autoimmune phenomena in SC and PANDAS centers on a process termed *molecular mimicry*. It is hypothesized that antibodies directed against immunogenic streptococcal proteins bind to endogenous antigens on basal ganglia neurons because of a high degree of sequence or structural homology between the streptococcal protein and basal ganglia proteins (Dale & Heyman, 2002). In particular, the M protein, a cell-surface streptococcal protein, has been implicated as the streptococcal target and promoter of molecular mimicry because of its amino acid–sequence homology with basal ganglia protein and cross-reactivity with antineuronal antibodies and basal ganglia tissue (Bronze & Dale, 1993).

Robust molecular data for autoimmune mimicry against the basal ganglia in neuropsychiatric disease come from studies of sera from patients with SC, a disorder with known temporal association with GAS infection, and significant OC and movement symptoms (Asbahr et al., 2005; Hounie et al., 2004). Although SC and PANDAS appear etiologically related, PANDAS is distinguished by a lack of additional symptoms of rheumatic fever and a lack of associated GAS-induced rheumatic carditis (Snider, Sachdev, MaCkaronis, St. Peter, & Swedo, 2004). Because SC is hypothesized to be etiologically similar to PANDAS, and molecular studies have found evidence of basal ganglia autoimmunity following GAS infection, the data from these studies will be briefly reviewed, followed by a focus on the molecular data on autoimmunity in PANDAS.

Multiple studies have identified antibasal ganglia antibodies in SC and tic disorders using a process termed *indirect immunofluoresence*. Early evidence for reactivity was discovered by Husby and colleagues (1976); antibodies directed against the caudate and subthalamic nuclei were appreciated and provided preliminary evidence for cross-reactivity between these antibodies and streptococcal M proteins. Using similar methods, Kiessling, Marcotte, and Culpepper (1993) characterized autoimmune antibodies in children with recent onset of movement disorders; 44 percent of the movement disorders group was positive for antibodies directed against postmortem human caudate. Autoimmune antibody studies employing more sensitive Western blotting and enzyme-linked immunosorbent assay (ELISA) identified autoimmune antibodies in twenty patients with acute SC and 16 patients with persistent SC; furthermore, these antibodies were detected in 95 percent of patients with acute SC, 56 percent of patients with chronic SC, and 0 percent of controls using ELISA with whole basal ganglia tissue (caudate, putamen, globus pallidus, and subthalamic nucleus; Church et al., 2003). The investigators reported antibodies directed at antigens of 40, 45, and 60 kilodaltons using Western blotting (Church et al., 2003). However, a more recent study failed to identify any difference in antibodies to caudate, putamen, and globus pallidus using similar techniques in subjects with SC (Singer et al., 2005). Finally, a recent study found that sera from patients with acute SC induced intracellular activation of a basal ganglia cell line (Kirvan, Swedo, Heuser, & Cunningham, 2003).

ELISA and Western blotting techniques recently were used to investigate autoimmune responses in patients with PANDAS, with inconsistent results. A recent study failed to demonstrate significant reactivity of sera from patients with PANDAS against a variety of neuronal proteins, including human postmortem caudate, putamen, and prefrontal cortex (Singer et al., 2005). However, a study using sera from patients with childhood-onset OCD (unscreened for PANDAS) found positive reactivity to basal ganglia proteins when compared with normal controls, controls with streptococcal infection, and controls with neurologic disorder (Dale et al., 2005). These two studies highlight the need for a standardized methodology for assessing autoimmune antibodies in neuropsychiatric patients, a topic recently addressed (Rippel, Hong, Yoon, Williams, & Singer, 2005).

Although molecular studies of PANDAS have yet to define a clear autoimmune pathogenesis, neuroimaging data support an inflammatory basal ganglia component in PANDAS. Neuroimaging studies of patients with PANDAS found increases in caudate, putamen, and globus pallidus volumes in subjects with PANDAS compared with age- and sex-matched healthy controls (Giedd, Rapoport, Garvey, Perlmutter, & Swedo, 2000). However, the increases in basal ganglia volumes did not correlate with the severity of symptoms (Giedd et al., 2000). Furthermore, it is hypothesized that this increase in basal ganglia volume is interpreted as a consequence of active inflammation of the basal ganglia, but without corroborating postmortem data, this interpretation remains unconfirmed.

Improvement in tic and OC symptoms in all patients with PANDAS treated with either plasma exchange or intravenous immunoglobulin (IVIG) lends further support to an autoimmune etiology for PANDAS (Perlmutter et al., 1999). These treatments are considered effective therapy for autoimmune disorders and thus provided a rationale for a pilot study in the treatment of PANDAS. In this study, 10 patients treated with plasma exchange demonstrated significant improvements in OC symptoms and tics compared with 10 receiving saline infusions. The IVIG group showed a 45 percent decrease in symptoms of OC (measured using YBOCS), but tic levels failed to show significant responses based on a TS rating scale. Furthermore, the decrease in OC symptoms was maintained one year post-treatment in 82 percent of the treatment groups (Perlmutter et al., 1999).

These treatments are hypothesized to represent a removal (plasma exchange) or blockade/dilution (IVIG) of autoimmune antibodies. It is hypothesized that plasma exchange may induce a return to normal immune function with the removal of the offending autoimmune antibodies. The mechanism of long-term improvement in the IVIG group, however, is difficult to interpret, and the authors caution against overanalysis of this study because of the broad possible mechanisms of action involved in both treatments (Perlmutter et al., 1999). However, the improvement in these treatment groups is highly suggestive of an autoimmune pathology, and further studies in this area are needed. Furthermore, the hypothesis that PANDAS represents a unique, autoimmune subgroup when compared with childhood-onset OCD was supported by a pilot study of therapeutic plasma exchange in a group of five patients with non-PANDAS pediatric-onset OCD (Nicolson et al., 2000). This study failed to demonstrate efficacy in reducing OC or tic symptoms based on the YBOCS or tic rating scale (Nicolson et al., 2000).

Treatment

A prospective study of PANDAS conducted by Murphy and Pichechero (2002) lent credence to the temporal association between GAS infection and the emergence of PANDAS, as well as the ability to intervene in patients with possible PANDAS after their initial presentation. The 12 subjects in this study demonstrated an abrupt (about 1 week) onset of OCD behavior, 10 were GAS culture-positive at the onset of symptoms, and six demonstrated a significant relapse in obsessive-compulsive symptoms during a six-month follow-up period. All subjects were enrolled during their "sentinel" onset of PANDAS symptoms, and no patient had a previous history of psychiatric or movement disorder. All subjects were treated with antibiotics, and all demonstrated a marked decrease in OC symptoms, with four demonstrating complete remission of OC symptoms within 5 to 21 days. However, 50 percent of the subjects in the trial experienced subsequent recurrences of GAS, with a return of OC symptoms coincident with each infection (Murphy & Pichichero, 2002).

This study highlights an important emerging concept in the treatment of PANDAS. First, it demonstrates the possible effectiveness of immediate intervention following the sentinel presentation of PANDAS. The authors of this study used a number of different antibiotics for treatment, specifically 10-day courses of penicillin/amoxicillin or a cephalosporin (Murphy & Pichichero, 2002). A recent meta-analysis of short-course (10-day) antibiotic therapy for GAS infection reported superior cure rates of cephalosporin therapy over penicillin for GAS pharyngitis (Casey & Pichichero, 2005). However, this conclusion remains controversial, and penicillin V (500 mg twice daily, orally for 10 days) is considered the first-line therapy for the treatment of GAS infections in patients without penicillin allergies (Bisno, 2004). Discriminatory antibiotic therapy trials have yet to be conducted in PANDAS (one pilot study involving penicillin therapy is discussed in this section), and future studies are needed to address which antibiotic therapy is most effective for treating GAS infections in patients with PANDAS.

A further critical question in the pathogenesis of PANDAS surrounds the number of GAS infections required for the development of PANDAS symptoms. A recent epidemiologic study screened all children between the ages of 4 and 13 years at a large West Coast health organization (Mell, Davis, & Owens, 2005). Using computerized medical records, the authors identified 318 children with new onset OCD, TS, or tic disorders within one year of a culture-positive GAS infection. Of these, 144 had enough complete information to be included in the study and were age and sex matched with multiple (between one and five) controls. Demographic information was similar to previous reports of patients with PANDAS, with an overall male preponderance, and peak age of diagnosis in ages 7–9. The age of diagnosis reported is intriguing, as reported onset of sypmtoms was highest in the ages from 4 to 6 (42%), with peak diagnosis age lagging behind. This study also found a significant risk of multiple GAS infections in the development of PANDAS symptoms, with fewer than 1 percent of controls positive for multiple GAS infections. Conversely, PANDAS subjects were three times more likely to have had two or more GAS infections in the year before the onset of symptoms, and patients positive for new-onset TS were 13 times more likely to have multiple GAS infections in the year before onset than controls (Mell et al., 2005).

Such findings of multiple GAS infections are striking when compared with a recent study of GAS infection among school-aged children, which reported that multiple GAS infections in school-aged children are rare (Martin, Green, Barbadora, & Wald, 2004). In a four-year surveillance study of nearly 300 elementary-school children surveyed every two weeks for GAS with throat cultures, the authors found that recurrent infections (defined as two symptomatic infections within one year, with at least three weeks between infections) were rare (Martin et al., 2004). However, a surprisingly high proportion (27–30%) of children who developed GAS pharyngitis were found to be GAS carriers. The "carrier state" was defined as two or more positive throat cultures obtained one week apart in the absence of any clinical signs of infection. Finally, 40 percent of the children studied were shown to be GAS negative during the entire four-year study period (Martin et al., 2004). Future studies are needed to determine whether the carrier state has any effect on PANDAS pathogenesis, but the results of the Martin et al. (2004) study suggest clear differences in GAS susceptibility and treatment response in a relatively homogeneous population.

These studies raise a further question in the physiology of PANDAS: Do repeated infections in patients with PANDAS lead to permanent OC and tic symptoms later in life or more severe exacerbations of symptoms over time? If so, the time following the sentinel onset of PANDAS may represent a crucial treatment window to prevent further PANDAS symptoms, and prophylactic antibiotic treatment may be warranted in these patients. This rationale was tested in a pilot study of penicillin prophylaxis in patients with PANDAS (Garvey et al., 1999). In a double-blind study, 37 patients with PANDAS were randomized to receive four months of either prophylactic penicillin V (250 mg, twice daily) or placebo; after four months, the treatment and placebo arms were switched for a total study time of eight months (Garvey et al., 1999). Monthly YBOCS and Yale Global Tic Severity Scale scores were recorded, as were serum levels of the streptococcal antibodies ASO and DNAse B. Interestingly, the study failed to demonstrate a significant reduction in GAS infections in the prophylactic treatment group, and thus differences in YBOCS and tic scores between groups cannot be commented on (Garvey et al., 1999). This study suggests that either patients with PANDAS are particularly susceptible to GAS infection, even in the presence of prophylactic antibiotics, or that penicillin is not an adequate choice for prophylactic therapy in patients with PANDAS.

Finally, one major question in the treatment of PANDAS symptoms remains: What is the most effective therapy for the OC and tic symptoms associated with PANDAS? Do these symptoms require additional treatment during acute exacerbations, or just antibiotic treatment of underlying GAS infections and patience until the symptoms reside? It would appear that this question depends in large part on the severity of OC and tic symptoms present in each patient between GAS-associated exacerbations. The treatments presented here that have empirical support (plasma exchange and IVIG) are unfortunately expensive, invasive, require administration of donor-blood products, and thus represent a therapy of last resort. Unfortunately, only phenomenologic reports of SSRI and cognitive-behavioral therapy in patients with PANDAS exist (Murphy & Pichichero, 2002), and larger-scale studies of OC and tic treatment in the PANDAS subgroup are needed.

Conclusion

Although a definitive mechanism for GAS infections resulting in OC and tic pathology remains elusive, the wealth of indirect evidence provides a rationale for continued studies and clinical awareness of this association. Numerous questions remain to be answered in the pathogenesis of PANDAS. The current scenario outlined for susceptibility to PANDAS includes: (1) a genetically susceptible host, (2) a GAS infection, (3) an autoimmune reaction with damage to the basal ganglia or neuronal structure, and (4) the emergence of OCD/tic pathology (Snider & Swedo, 2004). It is possible that the genetic susceptibility in PANDAS predisposes one to either repetitive streptococcal infections or autoimmunity following a streptococcal infection, which further underlies the need for controlled genetic studies in PANDAS cohorts. Finally, outcome data for interventional antibiotic and conventional psychiatric pharmacotherapies is needed to better tailor therapy for patients with PANDAS.

PANDAS remains a controversial subject in the psychiatric and infectious disease literature, but the studies outlined here, while still largely preliminary, suggest the association between GAS infection and psychiatric symptoms is more than speculation and correlation. Studies of the molecular characteristics of GAS infection and tissue damage are progressing rapidly and may lead to valuable insights into the pathogenesis of PANDAS. The PANDAS hypothesis deserves recognition by practicing clinicians, and future studies will, we hope, aid in the recognition and treatment of this psychiatric subgroup.

REFERENCES

Asbahr, F. R., Garvey, M. A., Snider, L. A., Zanetta, D. M., Elkis, H., & Swedo, S. E. (2005). Obsessive-compulsive symptoms among patients with Sydenham chorea. *Biological Psychiatry, 57,* 1073–1076.

Bisno, A. L. (2004). Are cephalosporins superior to penicillin for treatment of acute streptococcal pharyngitis? *Clinical Infectious Diseases, 38,* 1535–1538.

Bronze, M. S., & Dale, J. B. (1993). Epitopes of streptococcal M proteins that evoke antibodies that cross-react with human brain. *Journal of Immunology, 151,* 2820–2828.

Cardona, F., & Orefici, G. (2001). Group A streptococcal infections and tic disorders in an Italian pediatric population. *Pediatrics, 138,* 71–75.

Casey, J. R., & Pichichero, M. E. (2005). Meta-analysis of short course antibiotic treatment for group A streptococcal tonsillopharyngitis. *Pediatric Infectious Disease Journal, 24,* 94– 917.

Church, A. J., Dale, R. C., Cardoso, F., Candler, P. M., Chapman, M. D., Allen, M. L., et al. (2003). CSF and serum immune parameters in Sydenham's chorea: Evidence of an autoimmune syndrome? *Journal of Neuroimmunology, 136,* 149–153.

Cunningham, M. W. (2000). Pathogenesis of group A streptococcal infections. *Clinical Microbiology Reviews, 13,* 470–511.

Dale, R. C., & Heyman, I. (2002). Post-streptococcal autoimmune psychiatric and movement disorders in children. *British Journal of Psychiatry, 181,* 188–190.

Dale, R. C., Heyman, I., Giovannoni, G., & Church, A. W. (2005). Incidence of anti-brain antibodies in children with obsessive-compulsive disorder. *British Journal of Psychiatry, 187,* 314–319.

Garvey, M. A., Perlmutter, S. J., Allen, A. J., Hamburger, S., Lougee, L., Leonard, H. L., et al. (1999). A pilot study of penicillin prophylaxis for neuropsychiatric exacerbations triggered by streptococcal infections. *Biological Psychiatry, 45,* 1564–1571.

Giedd, J. N., Rapoport, J. L., Garvey, M. A., Perlmutter, S., & Swedo, S. E. (2000). MRI assessment of children with obsessive-compulsive disorder or tics associated with streptococcal infection. *American Journal of Psychiatry, 157,* 281–283.

Hoekstra, P. J., Kallenberg, C. G. M., Korf, J., & Minderaa, R. B. (2002). Is Tourette's's syndrome an autoimmune disease? *Molecular Psychiatry, 7,* 437–445.

Hounie, A. G., Pauls, D. L., Mercadante, M. T., Rosario-Campos, M. C., Shavitt, R. G., de Mathis, M. A., et al. (2004). Obsessive-compulsive spectrum disorders in rheumatic fever with and without Sydenham's chorea. *Journal of Clinical Psychiatry, 65,* 994–999.

Husby, G., van de Rijn, I., Zabriskie J. B., Abdin, Z. H., & Williams, R. C., Jr. (1976). Predominance of T cells in the lymphocytic infiltrates of synovial tissues in rheumatoid arthritis. *Arthritis and Rheumatism, 144,* 1094–110.

Kaplan, E. L. (2000). PANDAS? Or PAND? Or both? Or neither? *Contemporary Pediatrics, 17,* 81–96.

Kiessling, L. S., Marcotte, A. C., & Culpepper, L. (1993). Antineuronal antibodies in movement disorders. *Pediatrics, 92,* 39–43.

Kirvan, C. A., Swedo, S. E., Heuser, J. S., & Cunningham, M. W. (2003). Mimicry autoantibody-mediated neuronal cell signaling in Sydenham chorea. *Nature Medicine, 9,* 914–920.

Kurlan, R. (1998). Tourette's syndrome and "PANDAS": Will the relation bear out? Pediatric autoimmune neuropsychiatric disorders associated with streptococcal infection. *Neurology, 50,* 1530–1534.

Leckman, J., Grice, D. E., Boardman, J., Zhang, H., Vitale, A., Bondi, C., et al. (1997). Symptoms of obsessive-compulsive disorder. *American Journal of Psychiatry, 154,* 911–917.

Leonard, H. L., Swedo, S. E., Lenane, M. C., Rettew, D. C., Hamburger, S. D., Bartko, J. J., et al. (1993). A 2– to 7–year follow-up study of 54 obsessive compulsive children and adolescents. *Archives of General Psychiatry, 50,* 429–439.

Martin, J. M., Green, M., Barbadora, K. A., & Wald, E. R. (2004). Group A streptococci among school-aged children: Clinical characteristics and the carrier state. *Pediatrics, 114,* 1212–1219.

Mell, L. K., Davis, R. L, & Owens, D. (2005). Association between streptococcal infection and obsessive-compulsive disorder, Tourette's syndrome, and tic disorder. *Pediatrics, 116,* 56– 60.

Miguel, E. C., Leckman, J. F., Rauch, S., Rosario-Campos, M. C., Houniel, A. G., Mecrcadante, M. T., et al. (2005). Obsessive-compulsive disorder phenotypes: Implications for genetic studies. *Molecular Psychiatry, 10,* 258–275.

Murphy, M. L., & Pichichero, M. E. (2002). Prospective identification and treatment of children with pediatric autoimmune neuropsychiatric disorder associated with group A streptococcal infection (PANDAS). *Archives of Pediatric and Adolescent Medicine, 156,* 356–361.

Murphy, T. K., Goodman, W. K., Fudge, M. W., Williams, R. C., Jr., Ayoub, E. M., Dalal, M., et al. (1997). B lymphocyte antigen D8/17: A peripheral marker for childhood-onset obsessive-compulsive disorder and Tourette's's syndrome? *American Journal of Psychiatry, 154,* 402–407.

Nicolson, R., Swedo, S. E., Lenane, M., Bedwell, J., Wudarsky, M., Gochman, P., et al. (2000). An open trial of plasma exchange in childhood-onset obsessive-compulsive disorder without poststreptococcal exacerbations. *Journal of the American Academy of Child and Adolescent Psychiatry, 39,* 1313–1315.

Perlmutter, S. J., Leitman, S. F., Garvey, M. A., Hamburger, S., Feldman, E., Leonard, H. L., et al. (1999). Therapeutic plasma exchange and intravenous immunoglobulin for obsessive-compulsive disorder and tic disorders in childhood. *Lancet, 354,* 1153–1158.

Piacentini, J., & Bergman, R. L. (2000). Obsessive-compulsive disorder in children. *Psychiatric Clinics of North America, 23,* 519–533.

Rippel, C. A., Hong, J. J., Yoon, D. Y., Williams, P. N., & Singer, H. S. (2005). Methodologic factors affect the measurement of anti-basal ganglia antibodies. *Annals of Clinical Laboratory Science, 35,* 121–130.

Shet, A., & Kaplan, E. L. (2002). Clinical use and interpretation of group A streptococcal antibody tests: A practical approach for the pediatrician or primary care physician. *Pediatriatric Infectious Diseases Journal, 21,* 420–426.

Shulman, S. T. (1999). Pediatric autoimmune neuropsychiatric disorders associated with streptococci (PANDAS). *Pediatric Infectious Diseases Journal, 18,* 281–282.

Singer, H. S., Hong, J. J., Yoon, D. Y., & Williams, P. N. (2005). Serum autoantibodies do not differentiate PANDAS and Tourette's's syndrome from controls. *Neurology, 62,* 1701–1707.

Snider, L. A., Sachdev, V., MaCkaronis, J. E., St. Peter, M., & Swedo, S. E. (2004). Echocardiographic findings in the PANDAS subgroup. *Pediatrics, 114,* 748–751.

Snider, L. A., & Swedo, S. E. (2004). PANDAS: Current status and directions for research. *Molecular Psychiatry, 9,* 900–907.

Swedo, S. E., Leonard, H. L., Garvey, M., Mittleman, B., Allen, A. J., Perlmutter, S., et al. (1998). Pediatric autoimmune neuropsychiatric disorders associated with streptococcal infections: Clinical description of the first 50 cases. *American Journal of Psychiatry, 155,* 264–271.

Swedo, S. E., Rapoport, J. L., Leonard, H., Lenane, M., & Cheslow, D. (1989). Obsessive-compulsive disorder in children and adolescents: Clinical phenomenology of 70 consecutive cases. *Archives of General Psychiatry, 46,* 335–341.

Thomsen, P. H. (1995). Obsessive-compulsive disorder in children and adolescents: Predictors in childhood for long-term phenomenological course. *Acta Psychiatrica Scandinavica, 92,* 255–259.

CHAPTER EIGHT

Obsessive-Compulsive Disorder with Poor Insight

Cheryl Carmin, Ph.D., Pamela S. Wiegartz, Ph.D., and Kevin Wu, Ph.D.

Clinical Presentation

The issue of insight in obsessive-compulsive disorder (OCD) has long been the subject of debate. More than a decade ago, Kozak and Foa (1994) noted difficulties in establishing the definitions and boundaries of obsessions, overvalued ideas (OVI), and delusions. These issues have still not been completely resolved. For this discussion, we consider poor insight to be a patient's relative lack of understanding of the degree to which his or her obsessions and compulsions are unreasonable or excessive.

Historically, a defining feature of OCD, which served to distinguish obsessionality from psychosis, included the individual's insight into the unreasonable or excessive nature of obsessions and compulsions. Beginning with *Diagnostic and Statistical Manual of Mental Disorders* (third edition, revised), or DSM-III-R, however, the requirement of intact insight regarding the sensibility of OCD symptoms was removed. Instead, DSM-IV includes the specifier "with poor insight." As such, the concept of insight does not appear to facilitate differential diagnosis as clearly as it once did. These changes might appear to have muddied the already difficult boundaries around insight-related constructs. However, they reflect progress by increased recognition that clear categorical lines are unlikely to advance our understanding of this complex issue. Therefore, despite some researchers' preference for clear-cut boundaries among these domains, many now view insight as existing on a continuum from obsessions to delusions, wherein OVI spans the region between classic obsessionality and psychosis (e.g., Insel & Akiskal, 1986; Kozak & Foa, 1994).

Assessment of Insight in OCD

There is currently no gold standard for assessing insight in OCD. The traditional method of assessment in research studies is item 11 of the Yale-Brown Obsessive Compulsive Scale (YBOCS; Goodman et al., 1989). This single item is rated on a 5-point scale ranging from 0 ("I think my obsessions or compulsions are unreasonable or excessive") to 4 ("I am sure my obsessions or compulsions are reasonable, no matter what anyone says"). As there are clear reliability concerns related to the use of a single item for assessing any construct, researchers interested in a more thorough examination of insight have consequently developed more detailed measures.

Three multi-item instruments have been developed to examine the construct of insight and OVI in OCD. Foa and Kozak (1995) developed the Fixity of Beliefs Questionnaire (FBQ) for use in the DSM-IV OCD field trial. The FBQ contains seven items that measure the degree to which OCD patients recognize their obsessional fears as unreasonable. Each item is rated on a 5-point scale, ranging from 0 to 4. Foa, Abramowitz, Franklin, and Kozak (1999) reported that two items (presence of feared consequences and certainty that feared consequences will occur) predicted OCD treatment outcome. This scale has been used in a few studies that analyzed data collected as part of the field trial (e.g., Abramowitz, Brigidi, & Foa, 1999; Tolin, Abramowitz, Kozak, & Foa, 2001) but does not appear to have been adopted for widespread use.

Eisen et al. (1998) developed the Brown Assessment of Beliefs Scale (BABS) to assess the degree of poor insight and delusions in a variety of psychiatric conditions, including OCD. The BABS is a seven-item clinician-administered, semistructured interview with probe questions and five anchors for each item. Scores for each item range from 0 (nondelusional) to 4 (delusional) and assess the patient's average experience during the past week. Data from a sample of 50 patients diagnosed with either OCD, body dysmorphic disorder, or a mood disorder with psychotic features, suggested that the BABS possesses good interrater reliability, internal consistency, moderate to strong levels of convergence with measures of delusions, and acceptable discriminant correlations with general psychiatric symptom measures (Eisen et al., 1998). Much like the FBQ, the BABS has been used in only a handful of studies (e.g., Eisen, Catapano et al., 2001; Eisen, Phillips, Coles, & Rasmussen, 2004; Kishore, Samar, Janardhan, Chandrasekhar, & Thennaras, 2004).

Having suggested that the BABS was developed to address a broad range of delusions and, as a result, that it might not be sufficiently relevant for the study of OCD, Neziroglu McKay, Yaryura-Tobias, Stevens, and Todaro (1999) developed the Overvalued Ideas Scale (OVIS). The most recent version contains 11 items assessing bizarreness, belief accuracy, fixity of belief, reasonableness, perceived effectiveness of compulsions, pervasiveness of belief, reasons others do not share the belief, stability of belief (two items), degree of resistance of the belief, and duration of belief stability. Item ratings are summed into a total score, ranging from 0 to 10. Psychometric data support the internal consistency of the measure, its two-week test-retest reliability and convergence with YBOCS item 11 ($r = .67$). However, the OVIS has failed to demonstrate acceptable levels of discriminant validity. Notably, in a sample of more than 100 OCD patients, the OVIS correlated .83 with the YBOCS compulsions subscale, .52 with the Hamilton Rating Scale for Anxiety, and .58 with the Beck Anxiety Inventory (Neziroglu et al., 1999).

Overall, it appears that none of these multi-item instruments is widely used, and there are obvious limitations based on the generalizability of those few studies that do exist. Future research in this area will be required to examine the level of convergence among the available measures, to resolve issues of relatively low discriminant validity, and to provide evidence that the scales predict treatment outcome in a consistent manner. We could find no empirical study in the extant literature that administered more than one of these multi-scale measures in the same sample. It appears that these tools have evolved independently and in relative isolation of the other available measures.

Correlates of Poor Insight in OCD

Despite the common view that there is a continuum between obsessions and delusions, many studies examining clinical correlates of poor insight in OCD have approached the topic from a more categorical stance, often dividing samples into "good" versus "poor" insight, perhaps inadvertently obscuring relationships among variables. This approach may be, in part, an artifact of the lack of an agreed-upon method by which to measure insight in OCD. As a result, much of the existing research has relied on either single-item assessment or use of newly developed instruments with cutoffs that have yet to be well established. Not surprisingly, these studies have produced inconsistent findings, making it difficult to draw firm conclusions.

Studies dividing samples on the basis of scores on item 11 of the YBOCS suggest that 15 to 36 percent of OCD patients have little or no insight (Catapano, Sperandeo, Perris, Lanzaro, & Maj, 2001; Marazziti et al., 2002; Matsunaga et al., 2002). Most, but not all, studies using item 11 have found that lack of insight is positively correlated with the severity of OCD (Catapano et al., 2001; Matsunaga et al., 2002; Turksoy, Tukel, Ozdemir, & Karali et al., 2002). Studies using other measures of insight, such as the OVIS, the FBQ, and the BABS, have either found similar relationships between poor insight and greater symptom severity (Bellino Patria, Ziero, & Bogetto, 2005; Eisen et al., 2001) or found no significant correlation between the two (Eisen et al., 2004; Tolin et al., 2001).

Insight has been inconsistently related to other variables, such as age of onset of OCD, duration of the disorder, and family history of OCD. Earlier age of onset was associated with poor insight in some research (Kishore et al., 2004) but not in other studies (Catapano et al., 2001; Matsunaga et al., 2002; Turksoy et al., 2002). Similarly, duration of disorder was found to correlate with poorer insight in one study (Kishore et al., 2004) but not in others (Catapano et al., 2001; Lochner et al., 2005; Matsunaga et al., 2002; Turksoy et al., 2002). Family history of OCD was greater for patients with poor insight in the Bellino et al. (2005) study, while another study (Matsunaga et al., 2002) found no significant relationship between insight and family history of OCD. Catapano et al. (2001) found more frequent diagnoses of schizophrenic spectrum disorders among first-degree relatives of OCD patients with poor insight, compared with OCD patients with good insight. Given the inconsistencies described above, it is difficult to draw definitive conclusions about the correlates of poor insight.

Particular symptom comorbidities, especially co-occurring depression, have been found more frequently in OCD patients with poor insight compared with those with good insight (Catapano et al., 2001; Kishore et al., 2004; Matsunaga et al., 2002; Turksoy et al., 2002). Unlike its relationship with depression, the relationship between personality disorders and insight is less clear. Some studies have found increased frequency of schizotypal (Matsunaga et al., 2002) or borderline and narcissistic (Turksoy et al., 2002) personality disorders among OCD patients with poor insight. Another investigation found higher OVIS scores (indicating poorer insight) in OCD patients with paranoid or schizotypal personality disorders, whereas OCD patients with co-morbid obsessive compulsive personality disorder had lower scores on the OVIS (Bellino et al., 2005).

The relationship between insight and the presentation of obsessive-compulsive symptoms (e.g., washing, checking) has also been examined. Although some studies have not found differences in the types of obsessions and compulsions between patients with good and poor insight (Catapano et al., 2001; Matsunaga et al., 2001), other studies have found that the level of insight is related to the nature of obsessional content. For instance, Tolin and colleagues (2001) reported that OCD patients whose primary obsessions were related to either responsibility for harm or religious concerns had poorer insight than patients with other types of symptoms, such as contamination obsessions or washing rituals. Several studies have found that somatic obsessions or health concerns were associated with poorer insight (Abramowitz et al., 1999; Erzegovesi et al., 2001; Lochner et al., 2005; Marazzitti et al., 2002). These last findings are consistent with research demonstrating that patients with hypochondriasis or body dysmorphic disorder show poorer insight compared with individuals with OCD (for a review, see Neziroglu & Khemlani-Patel, 2005).

As the research findings have accumulated, it appears that poor insight in OCD is not a homogeneous clinical condition. There are conflicting findings with respect to the variables that have been examined to date, and it is unclear whether characteristics such as age of onset, duration of illness, or family history are relevant to distinguishing poor from good insight in those individuals with OCD. One might cautiously conclude that factors such as OCD symptom severity and comorbidity with depression are associated with poor insight. Even these findings, though, are inconsistent.

Several important questions remain to be addressed about the nature of poor insight in OCD. For example, does the presence of depressive symptoms *lead* to poorer insight or vice versa? Are these two characteristics simply correlates of some other causal factor? Does the association between insight and schizotypal personality disorder simply reflect the pervasive thought disturbance of the latter, such as the tendency to engage in magical thinking and to hold unusual beliefs? Poor insight in OCD appears to be associated with somatic obsessions and health concerns. Does poor insight in such cases arise from the same mechanisms as in hypochondriasis and body dysmorphic disorder? Poor insight is a common feature of the latter two disorders. Thus, the existing research on insight in OCD raises more questions than it answers.

Case Vignettes

The two cases presented here illustrate how poor insight in OCD presents in clinical practice.

Jean, a middle-aged woman, sought treatment at our clinic largely at the insistence of her family. She had excessive concerns of illness and fears of becoming pregnant through coincidental contact with sperm (e.g., on surfaces or airborne). Her obsessional fear and avoidance was initially limited to certain stores that she considered "dirty" because they had predominantly male clientele. Over time her fear generalized to entire neighborhoods and eventually to all public areas. She even feared and avoided areas of her home that had been occupied by male relatives. She was unable to leave her home without wearing "protective" clothing, such as a long coat to cover her genital area and gloves to protect her from contact with surfaces that may have been "contaminated" by germs or sperm.

At times she was able to acknowledge that her fears were unrealistic and that it was unlikely that she would become pregnant without intimate contact. Her insight deteriorated when she was confronted with feared stimuli (i.e., obsessional triggers). This fluctuating insight has been documented in the literature (Kozak & Foa, 1994). Given the pervasive nature of her obsessional triggers (i.e., any situation in which a male might have been), she perceived danger as being omnipresent, and therefore her insight was usually poor.

When avoidance was not possible, the patient became extremely anxious and engaged in a debilitating series of cleaning and reassurance rituals. These involved several activities, including purchasing new clothing; asking female family members to clean or discard contaminated items; and seeking reassurance from family, friends, and physicians about her physical health. The patient also had elaborate checking rituals related to her health status, including palpating her lymph nodes to check for swelling and examining her urine for perceived signs of pregnancy (e.g., discoloration or traces of tissue shed from the uterine lining). She knew that some medications, such as antibiotics, can reduce the effectiveness of contraceptives, and therefore refused to take psychotropic medication for fear that it too would undermine the effects of her birth control pills, thereby leading her to become pregnant from environmental contact with sperm.

Robert, another patient with OCD and poor insight, presented with fears that harm would befall loved ones if a series of mental rituals were not performed correctly. He frequently experienced intrusive thoughts of his children or other family members being killed in accidents (e.g., being struck by a car, falling down the stairs, or being stabbed). These obsessions could be triggered by any number of situations such as seeing a car, seeing stairs, and eating. At other times, the obsessions occurred with no apparent trigger. When the thoughts occurred, the patient became extremely anxious and engaged in a series of mental rituals to help "let go" of the thoughts. He would need to focus on whatever object had triggered the obsession or, if no trigger was present, he would choose a nearby object. He then would mentally rehearse the name of the loved one while simultaneously picturing his or her face on a background of that person's favorite color. This ritual would continue until it "felt right" but could easily be disrupted if the object he was focusing on moved (as was frequently the case with cars) or if the patient became too anxious to keep his complex mental images at a sufficiently vivid level. He was able, at times, to express understanding that his rituals may be unnecessary or excessive but was rarely able to delay the performance of these compulsions (even momentarily) for fear that his intrusive thoughts would come true.

Robert pointed to coincidental events as "evidence" that his rituals prevented bad things from happening. For example, his daughter once became ill with influenza after he had experienced an intrusive thought that she would be hit by a car and was unable to perform his mental rituals to completion that day. He cited this as evidence that his compulsions were vitally necessary to the well being of his family. He was unwilling to engage in any further treatment activities, including response prevention, and became more and more firmly entrenched in his belief that he was preventing harm from occurring. Thus, the patient's insight deteriorated over time. This pattern of change has also been noted to occur in some patients with OCD (Kozak & Foa, 1994).

Treatment

Two approaches have been used in treating OCD when it is associated with poor insight. As with OCD, in general, treatment strategies involve either pharmacologic interventions, primarily with serotonergic drugs, or medication combined with cognitive-behavioral approaches (typically exposure and response prevention; ERP). Although there is a substantial body of research pertaining to treatment outcomes for OCD in general, there has been a surprising paucity of data on treating OCD with poor insight. Of even greater note, given the established positive outcomes of ERP for the treatment of OCD, we were not able to find any study that specifically examined the use of ERP for addressing poor insight or OVI.

Pharmacotherapy

The pharmacotherapy literature primarily focuses on the prognostic value of insight with respect to the use of a single medication and across a variety of serotonin reuptake inhibitor (SRI) medications. Eisen et al. (2001) used the BABS to assess how well the degree of insight predicted treatment outcome using data extracted from a multicenter study investigating relapse after discontinuation of sertraline. There was a significant difference between pre- and post-treatment BABS scores. The magnitude of this difference was significantly correlated with the magnitude of changes in the YBOCS total score (which ranges from 0 to 40). When patients with good insight were compared with those with poor insight, both had a mean decrease of 47 percent in total YBOCS scores at post-treatment. While there was a significant decrease in BABS scores for treatment responders, degree of insight at pre-treatment was not predictive of response to sertraline. In contrast, a study conducted in India (Kishore et al., 2004) found that higher pre-treatment BABS scores strongly predicted poor response to medication. In a study of OVI in 38 patients who completed treatment with fluvoxamine, Neziroglu, Pinto, Yaryura-Tobias, and McKay (2004) found that those scoring high on the OVIS showed significantly less improvement in their obsessions relative to patients with lower OVIS scores. No significant difference was found in terms of improvement in compulsions.

Two studies (Catapano et al., 2001; Erzegovesi et al., 2001) compared the effects of different SRIs on insight. In both of these investigations, patients with good insight and those with poor insight showed significant improvement by the end of treatment (treatment response was defined as at least 35% improvement from pretreatment). Catapano et al. (2001) found that poor insight was significantly negatively correlated with the magnitude of change in total YBOCS score and with changes in both the obsessions and compulsions subscale scores. The poor insight group did not demonstrate a significant change in their score on the YBOCS compulsions subscale.

Erzegovesi et al. (2001) focused on differentiating treatment responders from nonresponders. Not surprisingly, the nonresponders were more likely to have poor insight. In a subsequent logistic regression model, degree of insight accounted for the greatest amount of variance in treatment response. Similarly, a naturalistic study conducted in France examined outcomes in OCD patients who had been primarily treated with one or more antidepressant medications. Using a variety of outcome measures, the authors concluded that poor insight predicted which patients were resistant to treatment (Hantouche, Bouhassira, & Lancrenon, 2000).

These studies raise several points. First, in contrast to studies reviewed earlier in this chapter, the severity of OCD, at least as measured by the YBOCS, does not always appear to be related to the degree to which poor insight is present. In addition, patients with poor insight have an equivalent response to pharmacologic treatment regardless of the SRI agent being used. However, poor insight may best predict which patients will be resistant to treatment. Some consensus exists that obsessions are more responsive to treatment in those with poor insight, whereas medication seems to have little effect on compulsions in this group (Catapano et al., 2001; Neziroglu et al., 2004).

There has been some question about whether the addition of an antipsychotic medication will improve outcomes in OCD patients who are deemed resistant to SRI treatment. Only one clinical trial (Hollander et al., 2003) links improvement, as based on clinician's judgment, to the insight item on the YBOCS. In this study, as well as in other placebo-controlled investigations, the addition of atypical antipsychotic medications, such as olanzapine or risperidol, as well as older antipsychotics, like haloperidol, appears to result in improvement in only a portion of patients who otherwise had been considered treatment refractory (e.g., Bystritsky et al., 2004; Erzegovesi, Guglielmo, Siliprandi, & Bellodi, 2005; Koran, Ringold, & Elliott, 2000). There were similar outcomes even when OCD was accompanied by comorbid conditions, such as tics or schizotypal personality (McDougle et al., 1994, 2000). One study, however, found no difference in treatment response when either olanzapine or placebo was added to the SRI regimen of fluoxamine (Shapira et al., 2004).

Psychological Treatment

The psychological treatment of choice for OCD is ERP. This treatment is highly successful, with about 75 percent of patients showing improvement that is maintained at follow-up (Franklin, Abramowitz, Kozak, Levitt, & Foa, 2000). ERP involves exposure to anxiety- or distress-evoking situations (exposure) and practice with resisting urges to perform compulsive rituals (response prevention). Foa and Kozak (1986) suggested that to reduce obsessional fear, the fear must be accessed (i.e., experienced) and the patient must be exposed to corrective information (i.e., information that the feared stimuli are harmless). Foa and Kozak further proposed that reduction of distress is mediated by changes in the threat meaning associated with obsessional stimuli and that one important change involves a reduction in the exaggerated probability associated with explicitly feared consequences. During treatment with ERP, patients confront feared situations and refrain from ritualizing to learn that the specific consequences they fear are unlikely to occur. Foa and Kozak suggested the repeated disconfirmation of the expected harm alters the estimated probabilities associated with such disasters. This explanation raises the issue of whether OCD patients with poor insight are able to respond to a treatment such as ERP, which aims to disconfirm obsessional fears.

Several investigators have examined the relationship between insight and outcome of ERP. In a retrospective case series, Foa (1979) described four OCD patients with poor insight who responded poorly to ERP. She proposed that these patients' inability to recognize that the beliefs associated with their obsessions are senseless hinders the learning process that would otherwise presume to take place as a result of prolonged and repeated exposure to feared stimuli. Treatment efficacy is thereby reduced. Similarly, Salkovskis and Warwick (1985) described a patient who, after successful ERP, experienced a relapse of OCD symptoms accompanied by highly fixed beliefs (poor insight) and was unable to tolerate additional ERP treatment. These clinical observations suggest that patients who do *not* perceive their obsessive-compulsive symptoms as senseless may show poorer response to treatment by ERP as compared with those with good insight.

The few larger studies investigating this issue have revealed somewhat inconsistent results. Lelliott, Noshirvani, Basoglulu, Marks, and Monteiro (1988) failed to find a relationship between outcome of ERP and the strength of obsessional beliefs immediately following treatment. However, a weak relationship was found at a one-year follow-up (Basoglu, Lax, Kasvikis, & Marks, 1988). More recently, changes in how strongly patients believed that feared consequences would occur were found to parallel decreases in OCD symptom severity when ERP included a combination of situational (in vivo) and imaginal exposure (Ito, Araujo, Helmsley, & Marks, 1995).

In a more comprehensive study, Foa, Abramowitz, Franklin, and Kozak (1999) examined (a) the degree to which poor insight influenced ERP outcomes and

(b) whether patients' insight into the senselessness of their obsessional fears undergoes changes during treatment. Results indicated that patients who were most strongly certain that their obsessional fears were valid (i.e., they had *extremely* poor insight as evidenced by high scores on the FBQ) showed a poorer response to ERP than did patients with moderate or mild certainty (greater insight). This finding highlights the importance of assessing the patient's degree of insight into the senselessness of their OCD symptoms when considering ERP treatment. Extremely poor insight may indicate the need for additional interventions, such as augmentation with medication. As improvement was attenuated among patients with poor insight, such patients did receive *some* symptom reduction from treatment. To explain their finding, Foa et al. (1999) suggested that individuals with poor insight are especially reluctant to confront their feared situations. Indeed, nonadherence with ERP is associated with poorer treatment response (Abramowitz, Franklin, Zoellner, & DiBernardo, 2002).

It may be especially difficult for individuals with poor insight to incorporate information that is inconsistent with their fixed beliefs. Cognitive therapy interventions may therefore be well suited to address the core beliefs underlying their obsessions. For example, Foa et al. (1999) noted that patients who, at pre-ERP treatment, believed strongly that their feared consequences would occur became less certain of such outcomes at post-treatment. These findings are consistent with research reporting changes in the fixity of obsessional beliefs following ERP (Ito et al., 1995; Lelliott et al., 1988; O'Connor et al., 2005) and may help to explain why some medication-resistant OCD patients have subsequently responded to ERP.

In contrast with Foa et al.'s (1999) suggestion that medication should augment ERP, Tolin, Maltby, Diefenbach, Hannan, and Worhunsky (2004) conducted a 15-week study of ERP with a sample of OCD subjects who had failed medication trials, who met criteria for several comorbid conditions, and who were characterized as having generally poor insight. ERP resulted in significantly reduced scores on the YBOCS in 53 percent of the subjects, and 40 percent maintained their gains over a six-month period. Thus, ERP may be a viable option for those patients who have a less than adequate response to medication.

Implications

Given the largely inconsistent results reported previously, it is difficult to make strong recommendations regarding the treatment of OCD patients with poor insight. The available data (and clinical observations) suggest that individuals with this subtype of OCD can improve because of both pharmacologic and psychological treatments (e.g., Foa et al., 1999), although their treatment response may be attenuated compared with patients with good insight (e.g., Kishore et al., 2004). It is worth noting that even the most recent expert consensus guidelines on OCD treatment from the National Institute for Health and Clinical Excellence (NICE) did not specifically address the issue of insight but, rather, discussed ERP and medication options for those patients who had a poor response to initial treatment (NICE, 2005). Clearly, additional research is needed to examine whether certain therapeutic strategies can be added to ERP to enhance the effects of treatment for patients with poor insight and how and when medication and ERP may be best sequenced or if they should be routinely used in combination. Although there is only anecdotal data to suggest that addition of cognitive therapy to ERP for such individuals, this strategy is often used in clinical practice and its use is a logical extension of the conceptual issues noted previously.

It is also pertinent to examine whether patients with poor insight have an improved response when an antipsychotic medication, such as risperidone, is used to augment SRI treatment. Only one study suggests that there is improvement in treatment outcome, based on clinicians' judgment, which was correlated with YBOCS item 11, when an atypical antipsychotic is added to SRIs (Hollander et al., 2003). Nonetheless, this strategy is employed in the pharmacologic management for those patients whose OCD did not respond adequately to SRI monotherapy.

From a cognitive-behavioral perspective, perhaps the greatest challenge in treating patients with OCD who have limited insight into the senselessness of their symptoms relates to the day-to-day continuity of treatment. Typically, we expect that progressive learning and habituation takes place, thus allowing patients to attempt exposures that are more challenging. This is not always the case in OCD patients, whose beliefs about the consequences of not performing their rituals are firmly entrenched. For example, one of our elderly patients had had OCD for decades. He not only spent hours each day performing rituals, but he also had numerous strategies that incorporated others into his ritualizing. In fact, his family had all but given in to his illness because it was far less difficult to acquiesce than to argue about doing rituals for him. In treating this man, we provided copious education about OCD and about the nature of ERP, as well as discussion about the purpose of each specific exposure assignment. He appeared to comprehend what we were doing at the time and often successfully engaged in therapist-directed exposure tasks. However, in many cases, it seemed as though we were starting again at baseline during the next session. It might have been easy to assume that this elderly man was experiencing memory deficits, but this was not the case. He did make considerable improvement while receiving intensive inpatient treatment despite the level of frustration that his treatment team experienced. Unfortunately, he did not have adequate treatment follow-up when he returned to his community, and he returned to his previous level of functioning (see Carmin & Wiegartz [2000] for further discussion).

Conclusion

The clinical issue of insight in OCD raises some important questions. Among them is whether poor insight represents a *category* (or *subtype*) of OCD or whether it is a *dimension* of the larger clinical picture. Another important question concerns whether there exists a continuum beginning with intrusive thoughts and including obsessions, overvalued ideation/poor insight, and, ultimately, delusions. At least one study suggests that in some cases, poor insight is transient, which then leads to questions regarding whether individuals with poor insight are, in fact, differentially characterized by specific neurobiological or cognitive characteristics when compared with those OCD patients with good insight. In this regard, Matsunaga et al. (2002) suggested that there are two subtypes of OCD. One subtype includes individuals who experience a transient loss of insight due to symptom severity, and another subtype is more closely related to psychotic or delusional disorders involving firmly held bizarre beliefs or odd personality traits (e.g., schizotypal) coupled with lesser degrees of anxiety.

Another issue for consideration is how insight fits into a broader framework of OCD phenomenology and, further, whether the degree of insight is synonymous with OCD symptom severity. The data regarding whether insight is synonymous with severity or resistance are contradictory. Catapano et al. (2001) found that the degree of insight was only weakly related to severity indices. In contrast, Turksoy et al. (2002) concluded that poorer insight (as determined by the DSM-IV specifier and YBOCS item 11) correlated both with greater OCD and depressive symptoms. To further complicate the picture, Ito et al. (1995) noted that OCD patients who demonstrated good insight (i.e., expressed understanding of the senselessness of their beliefs) also reported strong fears of the consequences of not ritualizing and subsequently either did not attempt to resist their compulsions or reported having little control over the urge to ritualize. Poor insight possibly worsens prognosis by limiting the patient's ability to confront and resist symptoms, although insight may not be the only factor that affects whether a patient is able to resist ritualizing effectively. Clearly, there is little consensus in the research literature about the relationship between insight, disorder severity, and resistance to urges to ritualize.

Two decades ago, Insel and Akiskal (1986) proposed that for those with limited insight, a greater congruence between the components of intellectual and emotional insight is apparent, thus making it more difficult to treat their symptoms. This interpretation still makes clinical sense in light of the few treatment studies addressing insight as an outcome predictor and the clinical observations that many patients with poor insight, when pressed, acknowledge (often grudgingly) that at some point they recognized that their OCD symptoms were irrational. Perhaps one avenue for further investigation is how to develop a cognitive therapy strategy that would result in a greater congruence between intellectual and emotional insight.

Unlike many areas in the OCD literature, there is a surprising paucity of research specifically addressing the phenomenon of poor insight as well as how best to treat those patients whose insight into their OCD is limited. For some patients, either SRIs or EBT is helpful but not as helpful as for those who have good insight. Pharmacologic management may require successive trials of SRIs and augmentation using atypical antipsychotic medication. Combined ERP and medication are also indicated when one or the other strategy is less than effective. For some patients, an experienced cognitive behavior therapist may be less accessible than a physician who can prescribe the recommended medications. However, if the patient proves to be treatment resistant, ERP with a therapist experienced in OCD treatment is strongly encouraged (NICE, 2005), and at least one study has found that ERP has positive outcomes for approximately half of the treatment refractory group (Tolin et al., 2004). Although the issue of whether insight is a subtype of OCD is still unresolved and it is difficult to draw firm conclusions regarding clinical management, this gap in the literature underscores an important opportunity for further research.

REFERENCES

Abramowitz, J. S., Brigidi, B. D., & Foa, E. B. (1999). Health concerns in patients with obsessive-compulsive disorder. *Journal of Anxiety Disorders, 13*, 529–539.

Abramowitz, J. S., Franklin, M. E., Zoellner, L. A., & DiBernardo, C. L. (2002). Treatment compliance and outcome in obsessive-compulsive disorder. *Behavior Modification, 26*, 447–463.

Basoglu, M., Lax, T., Kasvikis, Y., & Marks, I. M. (1988). Predictors of improvement in obsessive-compulsive disorder. *Journal of Anxiety Disorders, 2*, 299–317.

Bellino, S., Patria, L., Ziero, S., & Bogetto, F. (2005). Clinical picture of obsessive-compulsive disorder with poor insight: A regression model. *Psychiatry Research, 136*, 223–231.

Bystritsky, A., Ackerman, D. L., Rosen, R. M., Vapnik, T., Gorbis, E., Maidment, K. M., & Saxena, S. (2004). Augmentation of serotonin reuptake inhibitors in refractory obsessive-compulsive disorder using adjunctive olanzapine: A placebo-controlled trial. *Journal of Clinical Psychiatry, 65*, 565–568.

Carmin, C. N., & Wiegartz, P. (2000). Successful and unsuccessful treatment of obsessive-compulsive disorder in older adults. *Journal of Contemporary Psychotherapy, 30*, 181–193.

Catapano, F., Sperandeo, R., Perris, F., Lanzaro, M., & Maj, M. (2001). Insight and resistance in patients with obsessive-compulsive disorder. *Psychopathology, 34*, 62–68.

Eisen, J. L. Phillips, K. A., Baer, L., Beer, D. A., Atala, K. D., & Rasmussen, S. A. (1998). The Brown Assessment of Beliefs Scale: Reliability and validity. *American Journal of Psychiatry, 155*, 102–108.

Eisen, J. L., Phillips, K. A., Coles, M. E., & Rasmussen, S. A. (2004). Insight in obsessive-compulsive disorder and body dysmorphic disorder. *Comprehensive Psychiatry, 45*, 10–15.

Eisen, J. L., Rasmussen, S. A., Phillips, K. A., Price, L. H., Davidson, J., Lydiard, R. B., et al. (2001). Insight and treatment outcome in obsessive-compulsive disorder. *Comprehensive Psychiatry, 42*, 494–497.

Erzegovesi, S., Cavallini, M. C., Cadedini, P., Diaferia, G., Locatelli, M., & Bellodi, L. (2001). Clinical predictors of drug response in obsessive-compulsive disorder. *Journal of Clinical Psychopharmacology, 21*, 488–492.

Erzegovesi, S., Guglielmo, E., Siliprandi, F., & Bellodi, L. (2005). Low-dose risperidone augmentation of fluvoxamine treatment in obsessive-compulsive disorder: A double-blind, placebo-controlled study. *European Neuropsychopharmacology, 15*, 69–74.

Foa, E. B. (1979). Failure in treating obsessive-compulsives. *Behaviour Research and Therapy, 17*, 169–176.

Foa, E. B., Abramowitz, J. S., Franklin, M. E., & Kozak, M. J. (1999). Feared consequences, fixity of belief, and treatment outcome in patients with obsessive-compulsive disorder. *Behavior Therapy, 30*, 717–724.

Foa, E. B., & Kozak, M. J. (1986). Emotional processing of fear: Exposure to corrective information. *Psychological Bulletin, 99*, 20–35.

Foa, E. B., & Kozak, M. J. (1995). DSM-IV field trial: Obsessive-compulsive disorder. *American Journal of Psychiatry, 152*, 90–96.

Franklin, M., Abramowitz, J. S., Kozak, M. J., Levitt, J. T., & Foa, E. B. (2000). Effectiveness of exposure and ritual prevention for obsessive-compulsive disorder: Randomized compared with nonrandomized samples. *Journal of Consulting and Clinical Psychology, 68*, 594–602.

Goodman, W. K., Price, L. H., Rasmussen, S. A., Mazure, C., Fleischmann, R. L., Hill, C. L., et al. (1989). The Yale-Brown obsessive compulsive scale: I. Development, use, and reliability. *Archives of General Psychiatry, 46,* 1006–1011.

Hantouche, E. G., Bouhassira, M., & Lancrenon, S. (2000). Prospective follow-up over a 12 month period of a cohort of 155 patients with obsessive-compulsive disorder: Phase III National DRT-TOC Study. *Encephale, 26,* 73–83.

Hollander, E., Baldini, Rossi, N., Sood, E., & Pallanti, S. (2003). Risperidone augmentation in treatment-resistant obsessive-compulsive disorder: a double-blind, placebo-controlled study. *International Journal of Neuropsychopharmacology, 6,* 397–401.

Insel, T. R., & Akiskal, H. S. (1986). Obsessive-compulsive disorder with psychotic features: A phenomenological analysis. *American Journal of Psychiatry, 143,* 1527–1533.

Ito, L. M., Araujo, L. A., Helmsley, D. R., & Marks, I. M. (1995). Beliefs and resistance in obsessive-compulsive disorder: Observations from a controlled study. *Journal of Anxiety Disorders, 9,* 269–281.

Kishore, V. R., Samar, R., Janardhan, R., Chandrasekhar, C., & Thennaras, K. (2004). Clinical characteristics and treatment response in poor and good insight obsessive-compulsive disorder. *European Psychiatry, 19,* 202–208.

Koran, L. M., Ringold, A. L., & Elliott, M. A. (2000). Olanzapine augmentation for treatment-resistant obsessive-compulsive disorder. *Journal of Clinical Psychiatry, 61,* 514–517.

Kozak, M. J., & Foa, E. B. (1994). Obsessions, overvalued ideas, and delusions in obsessive-compulsive disorder. *Behaviour Research and Therapy, 32,* 343–353.

Lelliott, P. T., Noshirvani, H. F., Basoglulu, M., Marks, I. M., & Monteiro, W. O. (1988). Obsessive-compulsive beliefs and treatment outcome. *Psychological Medicine, 18,* 697–702.

Lochner, C., Hemmings, S. M., Kinnear, C. J., Niehaus, D. J., Nel, D. G., Corfield, V. A., et al. (2005). Cluster analysis of obsessive-compulsive spectrum disorders in patients with obsessive-compulsive disorder: Clinical and genetic correlates. *Comprehensive Psychiatry, 46,* 14–19.

Marazziti, D., Dell'Osso, L., DiNasso, E., Pfanner, C., Presta, S., Mungai, F., et al. (2002). Insight in obsessive compulsive disorder: A study of an Italian sample. *European Psychiatry, 17,* 407–410.

Matsunaga, H., Kiriike, N., Matsui, T. Oya, K., Iwasaki, Y., Koshimune, K., et al. (2002). Obsessive-compulsive disorder with poor insight. *Comprehensive Psychiatry, 43,* 150–157.

McDougle, C. J., Epperson, C. N., Pelton, G. H., Wasylink, S., & Price, L. H. (2000). A double-blind, placebo-controlled study of risperidone addition in serotonin reuptake inhibitor-refractory obsessive-compulsive disorder. *Archives of General Psychiatry, 57,* 794–801.

McDougle, C. J., Goodman, W. K., Leckman, J. F., Lee, N. C., Heninger, G. R., & Price, L. H. (1994). Haloperidol addition in fluvoxamine-refractory obsessive-compulsive disorder: A double-blind, placebo-controlled study in patients with and without tics. *Archives of General Psychiatry, 51,* 302–8.

National Institute for Health and Clinical Excellence (NICE). (2005). *Obsessive compulsive disorder: Clinical guideline 31.* www.nice.org.uk.

Neziroglu, F., & Khemlani-Patel, S. (2005). Overlap of body dysmorphic disorder and hypochondriasis with OCD. In J. S. Abramowitz & A. C. Houts (Eds.), *Concepts and controversies in obsessive-compulsive disorder* (pp. 163–175). New York: Springer.

Neziroglu, F., McKay, D., Yaryura-Tobias, J., Stevens, K., & Todaro, J. (1999). The overvalued ideas scale: Development, reliability and validity in obsessive-compulsive disorder. *Behaviour Research and Therapy, 37,* 881–902.

Neziroglu, F., Pinto, A., Yaryura-Tobias, J. A., & McKay, D. (2004). Overvalued ideation as a predictor of fluvoxamine response in patients with obsessive-compulsive disorder. *Psychiatry Research, 125,* 53–60.

O'Connor, K. P., Aardema, F., Bouthillier, D., Fournier, S., Guay, S., Robillard, S., et al. (2005). Evaluation of an inference-based approach to treating obsessive-compulsive disorder. *Cognitive Behavior Therapy, 34,* 148–63.

Salkovskis, P. M., & Warwick, H. (1985). Cognitive therapy of obsessive-compulsive disorder: Treating treatment failures. *Behavioural Psychotherapy, 13,* 243–255.

Shapira, N. A., Ward, H. E., Mandoki, M., Murphy, T. K., Yang, M. C., Blier, P., et al. (2004). A double-blind, placebo-controlled trial of olanzapine addition in fluoxetine-refractory obsessive-compulsive disorder. *Biological Psychiatry, 55,* 553–555.

Tolin, D. F., Abramowitz, J. S., Kozak, M. J., & Foa, E. B. (2001). Fixity of belief, perceptual aberration, and magical ideation in obsessive-compulsive disorder. *Journal of Anxiety Disorders, 15,* 501–510.

Tolin, D. F., Maltby, N., Diefenbach, G. J., Hannan, S. E., & Worhunsky, P. (2004). Cognitive-behavioral therapy for medication nonresponders with obsessive-compulsive disorder: A wait-list-controlled open trial. *Journal of Clinical Psychiatry, 65,* 922–931.

Turksoy, N., Tukel, R., Ozdemir, O., & Karali, A. (2002). Comparison of clinical characteristics in good and poor insight obsessive-compulsive disorder. *Journal of Anxiety Disorders, 17,* 233–242.

CHAPTER NINE

Obsessive-Compulsive Disorder and Schizotypy

Dean McKay, Ph.D., and Patricia Gruner, M.A.

Obsessive-compulsive disorder (OCD) is listed as an undifferentiated syndrome in the *Diagnostic and Statistical Manual of Mental Disorders* (DSM-IV-TR; American Psychiatric Association, 2000). Although the wider psychiatric community has been willing to accept this umbrella definition, research has clearly shown that OCD is a complex disorder characterized by heterogeneous clinical presentations. Most of this recent work suggests that the heterogeneity of OCD distills into valid subtypes (e.g., McKay et al., 2004). However, as discussed in other chapters in this volume, there is no current consensus on what counts as a subtype of OCD. Further complicating matters, there are comorbid presentations and other clinical characteristics that require practitioners to alter substantially the manner of conducting treatment for individuals with this disorder. One area that has received considerable attention is the presence of schizotypal traits, or co-occurring obsessive-compulsive symptoms with schizophrenia.

OCD and Schizotypy

Schizotypy, broadly defined, includes a range of cognitive, perceptual, and information-processing deficits that are related to thought-disorder symptomatology (Coleman, Levy, Lenzenweger, & Holzman, 1996; Korfine & Lenzenweger, 1995). Schizotypy has been most closely examined as a psychological risk factor for the development of schizophrenia. In extreme cases, a diagnosis of schizotypal personality disorder (SPD) is possible. Currently, questions exist as to whether SPD is truly a distinct form of schizophrenia or merely part of a continuum of severity in schizophrenia (Raine & Lencz, 1995).

Two of the most well-established measures of schizotypy are the Perceptual Aberration Scale (PAS) and Magical Ideation Scale (MIS) (Chapman, Chapman, & Miller, 1982). Recent research has examined the relation that the PAS and MIS have to symptoms associated with OCD (Einstein & Menzies, 2004a, 2004b). Using a sample of individuals diagnosed with OCD, Einstein and Menzies (2004a) found high correlations between symptom severity and magical ideation, suggesting a basic link between a correlate of schizotypy and the symptoms of OCD. This is an important finding given that many patients with OCD report symptoms that are bizarre and difficult to characterize properly in everyday language. It also suggests that the specific cognitive deficits associated with schizotypy require consideration in the context of treatment.

Finer discriminations have been made with regard to the way schizotypy is associated with OCD. For example, Tolin, Abramowitz, Kozak, and Foa (2001) found that specific symptoms were associated with greater levels of magical ideation, notably harming and religious obsessions. In this sample, there was no relationship between symptom severity and levels of magical ideation. To reconcile the differences in findings between Tolin et al. (2001) and Einstein and Menzies (2004a), there have also been recent findings of a potential schizotypal subtype of OCD (Sobin et al., 2000), which could account for, in part, the symptom presentation and symptom severity findings. Sobin et al. (2000) examined 119 individuals with a diagnosis of OCD and found that approximately half the sample had at least mild signs of schizotypy, such as magical ideation or ideas of reference. Further, counting compulsions distinguish those with schizotypy from those without.

Investigation into the way schizotypy is related to OCD symptoms and symptom severity is based on findings that suggest schizotypy is a specific liability for treatment outcome in OCD. For example, Minichiello, Baer, and Jenike (1987) found that schizotypal personality disorder predicted poorer outcome from behavior therapy using exposure with response prevention (ERP) in a small sample ($n = 29$) of individuals with OCD. Since that time, other investigators have found similar results. Moritz et al. (2004) found that elevated scores on measures of schizotypy, and especially perceptual aberrations, predicted poor response to a multimodal cognitive-behavioral treatment (CBT) approach for OCD. Schizotypy predicted poor outcome in another study involving medication (clomipramine) and CBT, particularly among those categorized as having "poor insight" using the additional qualifier from the DSM-IV (Matsunaga et al., 2002). Finally, patients with magical obsessions that were characterized as "bizarre" in clinical ratings were associated with poorer outcome in a 40-year follow-up study (Skoog & Skoog, 1999).

The literature seems to point to significant differences between OCD patients with schizotypy compared with those without. Yet, neuropsychological research does not bear this out in direct comparisons (Spitznagel & Suhr, 2002), except in the case of certain executive functioning tests involving stimulus discrimination (Harris & Dinn, 2003). All this suggests that having schizotypy in conjunction with OCD exacerbates obsessive-compulsive symptoms and likely interferes with standard treatment protocols.

Obsessive-Compulsive Symptoms and Schizophrenia

Considerable literature has accumulated on the relation between obsessive-compulsive symptoms and schizophrenia. Several broad conclusions may be drawn from these investigations. First, it appears that obsessive-compulsive symptoms are prevalent among individuals with schizophrenia (Berman, Kalinowski, Berman, Lengua, & Green, 1995; Kruger et al., 2000; Tibbo et al., 2000). Second, substantially poorer neuropsychological functioning among individuals with schizophrenia and comorbid OCD, compared with individuals with OCD alone, have been shown in a small sample study where the effect size difference for executive functioning was large ($d > 0.5$) (Hwang, Morgan, & Losconzy, 2000; Whitney, Fasteneau, Evans, & Lysaker, 2004). Third, individuals with schizophrenia and obsessive-compulsive symptoms tend to fare worse in treatment (i.e., Fenton & McGlashan, 1986; Hwang et al., 2000), yet also have fewer negative symptoms (Poyurovsky & Koran, 2005; Tibbo, Kroetsch, Chue, & Warneke, 2000) than individuals with schizophrenia who do not have OC symptoms.

One question that arises from this work is whether obsessive-compulsive symptoms in schizophrenia can be treated using the same interventions that have been shown effective in the treatment of OCD. ERP is widely considered the behavioral treatment of choice for OCD. However, in cases with co-occurring schizotypal personality, it has been suggested that exposure could worsen symptoms (e.g., Walker, Freeman, & Christensen, 1994). Recent modifications include specific cognitive therapy procedures designed to address cognitive distortions uniquely associated with OCD (Clark, 2004). Despite this, several case reports document success in the application of ERP in the treatment of obsessive-compulsive symptoms in individuals with schizophrenia (Ekers, Carman, & Schlich, 2004; Peasley-Miklus, Massie, Baslet, & Carmin, 2005). Given the disability associated with both schizophrenia and obsessive-compulsive symptoms, these results are encouraging. However, in each of these cases, the authors note that the presence of thought-disorder symptoms influenced the pacing of treatment sessions, with exposure initiated more gradually to account for difficulties in reducing arousal. Moreover, the intervention itself was specifically tailored to patients with neurocognitive deficits. This included frequent review of the rationale of treatment, even during exposure, given the difficulty in properly integrating the information processed as part of treatment. This suggests that an important component of the working model of treatment for this subgroup involves attending to information processing deficits that could interfere with effective habituation during exposure exercises. Figure 9.1 is a flowchart of a recommended treatment approach for OCD with schizotypy personality.

General Information-Processing Deficits Associated with OCD, Schizotypy, and Schizophrenia

In both schizotypy and schizophrenia, well-known general information-processing deficits are evident. For example, both groups have difficulty with sustained attention (Bergman, O'Brien, Osgood, & Cornblatt, 1995; Lencz, Raine, Benishay, Mills, & Bird, 1995), perform poorly on memory tasks—particularly those involving working memory (Barch, 2005; Holzman et al., 1995)—and exhibit executive functioning problems (Johnson-Selfridge & Zalewski, 2001; Lencz et al., 1995), which suggests that treatment based on exposure principles would require modification to account for problems in attention and memory. Going more slowly and with more frequent repetition of exposure exercises would facilitate this. Further, frequent review of the outcome associated with exposure would be required to ensure that the new information is organized correctly when the patient completes the session.

In the case of OCD, the problems in processing information are more

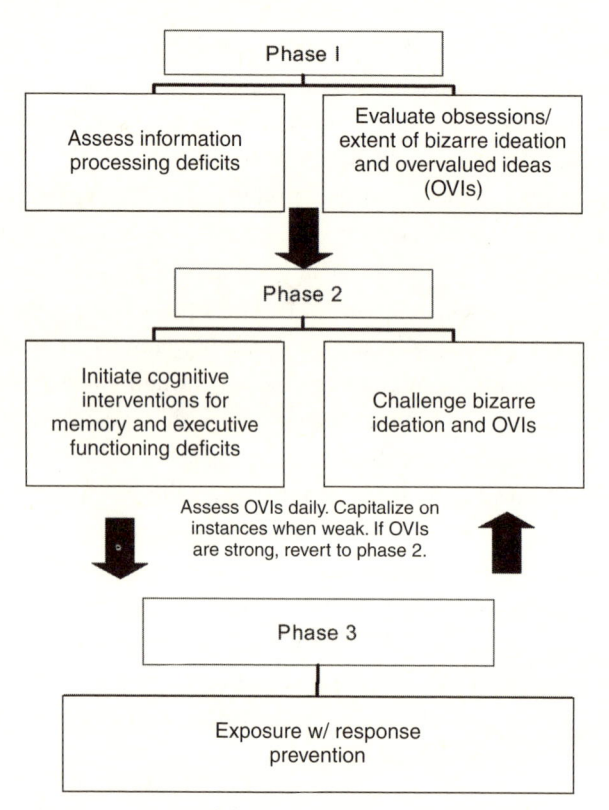

```
                    ┌─────────────┐
                    │   Phase 1   │
                    └──────┬──────┘
              ┌────────────┴────────────┐
    ┌─────────────────┐      ┌─────────────────────┐
    │ Assess information│     │ Evaluate obsessions/│
    │ processing deficits│    │ extent of bizarre   │
    │                   │     │ ideation and        │
    │                   │     │ overvalued ideas    │
    │                   │     │ (OVIs)              │
    └───────────────────┘     └──────────┬──────────┘
                                         ▼
                    ┌─────────────┐
                    │   Phase 2   │
                    └──────┬──────┘
              ┌────────────┴────────────┐
    ┌─────────────────┐      ┌─────────────────────┐
    │ Initiate cognitive│    │ Challenge bizarre   │
    │ interventions for │    │ ideation and OVIs   │
    │ memory and        │    │                     │
    │ executive         │    │                     │
    │ functioning deficits│  │                     │
    └─────────┬─────────┘    └──────────┬──────────┘
              │   Assess OVIs daily. Capitalize on
              │   instances when weak. If OVIs
              ▼   are strong, revert to phase 2.    ▲
                    ┌─────────────┐
                    │   Phase 3   │
                    └──────┬──────┘
                           │
              ┌────────────┴────────────┐
              │ Exposure w/ response    │
              │ prevention              │
              └─────────────────────────┘
```

Figure 9.1. A general framework for treating obsessive-compulsive disorder with schizotypy.

specific, centering on memory and executive functioning (Greisberg & McKay, 2003). However, when the OCD-related information-processing deficits are seen together with the aforementioned deficits involved in either schizotypy or schizophrenia, it can pose a considerable obstacle to effective treatment. For example, the presence of neurocognitive deficits could interfere with processing corrective information presented during exposure tasks. Starting with impaired attention, the ability to focus on the stimuli would be compromised, limiting the degree of habituation. Problems in working memory would lead to difficulties in establishing the essential memory structure that would serve as a counter to the prior memory of risk appraisal for specific stimuli. Finally, impaired executive functioning would prevent the necessary organization for determining how and under what conditions the stimuli serves as a risk (McKay & McKiernan, 2005).

In light of these considerations, we propose that ERP may be effectively administered in individuals with OCD and schizotypal personality or OCD with schizophrenia. However, numerous special considerations alter substantially the administration of standard treatment protocols for OCD. A case example is presented to illustrate these treatment considerations.

Treatment

Based on the literature reviewed to this point, atypical antipsychotic medication would be first-line treatment for cases of OCD with either schizotypy or schizophrenia, in light of their effect on both the serotonergic and dopaminergic systems. Few systematic investigations have examined the efficacy of atypical neuroleptics in this subgroup of OCD. One open trial examination of olanzapine in addition to fluvoxamine showed efficacy in a group of "treatment refractory" individuals with OCD (Bogetto, Bellino, Vaschetto, & Ziero, 2000). In another double-blind study, risperidone was used in conjunction with other serotonin reuptake inhibitors (SRIs), with half the sample of refractory OCD patients (9 of 18) deemed treatment responders, although this study specifically indicates that this combination may be effective for patients with comorbid schizotypal personality (McDougle, Epperson, Pelton, Wasylink, & Price, 2000). A recent review of the literature, both case and controlled trial, suggests that atypical antipsychotic medication alone may not be effective, but when used in conjunction with SRIs can be beneficial (Keuneman, Pokos, Weerasundera, & Castle, 2005).

Case Vignette

J.K., a 15-year-old male, had been diagnosed with OCD at the age of 8, but had not received CBT before his referral to our office. His mother, who complained that J.K. was spitting throughout the day, brought him in for treatment. J.K. believed that certain behaviors he was engaging in during the day were causing him to lose muscle strength and that spitting was a way to prevent this from happening. For example, he believed that the act of looking at someone whom he perceived as "weaker" than he would cause his strength to be drained from him to the weaker person. By spitting, he believed that he was protecting his strength.

Psychological assessment revealed that J.K. exhibited symptoms of both OCD and schizotypy. Schizotypal pathology included magical thinking, peculiar speech at times, some paranoid ideation, constricted affect, and general social skills deficits. J.K. also lacked close relationships outside of those he had with family members. Information-processing difficulties were also apparent. For example, he was unable to follow accurately and comprehend the storyline in a movie, demonstrating difficulties with sustained attention and executive processing. He had similar deficits in his judgments and conclusions regarding social interactions, often completely misconstruing what others were likely thinking.

J.K.'s score on the Lucky Beliefs Questionnaire (LBQ) was 65 and his score on the Magical Ideation Scale (MIS) was 9. These scores are considered high as compared with the normal population (LBQ: $M = 41.57$, $SD = 11.87$; MIS: $M = 4.85$, $SD = 3.33$) (Einstein & Menzies, 12004b) but are fairly consistent with scores found within the OCD population (LBQ: $M = 52$, $SD = 23$; MIS: $M = 6$, $SD = 4.7$) (Einstein & Menzies, 2004a). J.K.'s score on the MIS closely approaches 9.5, the optimal cutoff score for classification as schizophrenic as suggested by George and Neufeld (1987).

Although J.K.'s scores on these measures are indicative of magical thinking and the presence of many odd and superstitious beliefs, it should also be noted that his scores were attenuated by the bizarre nature of many of his beliefs. For example, J.K. endorsed as false the item on the MAS/PAS that asks about one being fearful of stepping on sidewalk cracks. He then explained to the evaluator that it is not cracks in the sidewalk that are dangerous, but names written into the concrete that are of concern. Similarly, J.K. did not endorse the idea that a person could gain or lose energy when other people look at or touch them, as he felt strongly that it was strength and not energy that could be lost. Because many of J.K.'s responses to the items on the measures fell along these same lines, his total scores were most likely an underestimate of the true extent of his magical thinking and odd beliefs.

Overall, J.K.'s complicated presentation required that various alterations be made to the standard treatment protocol for OCD. The presence of numerous schizotypal traits indicated that difficulties with sustained attention, encoding and recall, and executive processing would likely require many adjustments to standard ERP. In addition, extremely poor insight and numerous overvalued ideas (OVIs) presented additional obstacles.

J.K.'s strongly held belief that one could lose their strength by engaging in innocuous acts throughout the day is a good example of an OVI that could easily interfere with engaging in standard ERP treatment. Complicating the matter further, this particular OVI was tied to the patient's self-concept. J.K. did not believe that he had many positive attributes, but he *did* believe himself to be strong. In fact, his strength was the one aspect of his self in which he took great pride. Thus, engaging in standard ERP exercises, which would require him to do the things he believed would cause him to lose his strength, was too much of a threat to him at first. That is, because most of his self-worth was tied to his strength, exposing him to cues that he associated with the loss of strength and not allowing him to spit would have been too overwhelming for this patient. This was especially true given his lack of rational associations between behaviors and perceived outcomes; he did not recognize his beliefs to be irrational.

However, the patient's spitting was causing numerous problems for him at school and in the home and, as such, this behavior needed to be addressed as quickly as possible. Thus, J.K.'s early sessions focused on challenging his OVI regarding magical loss of strength and the protective nature of spitting and also broadening his self-concept to encompass more than just muscle strength. Using cognitive strategies to address the patient's OVI and broaden his self-concept to include other positive personal attributes, the therapist set the groundwork to begin exposure activities. Once the patient began to express some ambivalence regarding his initial OVI, the exposure work began.

As expected, J.K. exhibited several information-processing deficits during exposure work that required additional modifications to the ERP protocol. Most noteworthy, J.K. was often not able to draw accurate conclusions regarding the effects of exposure activities without the therapist's help during and after the exposure process. For example, after being exposed to a picture of a "weak" person and not spitting, J.K. could not accurately determine on his own that he had not lost strength during the process. At times, he would say that he had in fact lost strength or that he *might* have lost strength. He also misinterpreted the bodily sensations he experienced during exposure activities, stating that the numbness and tingling he felt in his extremities was his muscle strength being "sucked out." This type of perceptual aberration is consistent with those experienced by individuals with schizotypy (i.e., Korfine & Lenzenweger, 1995). The therapist, thus, needed to help the patient find ways of accurately assessing his strength after ERP exercises and to help him accurately interpret and understand the sensations associated with anxiety. It was also necessary to regularly remind him during and after exposure that he was not actually losing strength. This process of maintaining a running commentary on how the catastrophic expectation underlying the obsession has failed to occur, and helping the patient to draw appropriate conclusions, helps the patient to more effectively organize and encode his experiences during ERP (McKay & McKiernan, 2005). This process increased J.K.'s ability to face the feared stimuli, in this case the picture, with each subsequent exposure.

J.K.'s faulty reasoning skills and difficulty drawing accurate conclusions were evident throughout the treatment process. For example, many of the odd beliefs that he held so strongly had arisen from drawing inaccurate conclusions through loose, indirect associations he formed from his experiences. For example, he originally developed the belief that spitting could protect him from losing muscle strength from a show he had seen on television in which a person was sucking the venom out of a snake bite and spitting it out. From this, J.K. formed an association between spitting and expelling poison (or anything bad) from the body. He eventually concluded that he could protect bad things from happening to him, or expel any "bad" away from himself, by spitting. J.K. also showed limited capacity in his ability to reason inductively based on his memory of past experiences. For instance, on entering treatment, he believed that "the winner of a fight is always facing the same direction," although *which* direction remained unclear to him.

J.K.'s weaknesses in information processing—specifically his difficulty accurately encoding and recalling his experiences and forming logical conclusions—needed to be addressed at every step in the treatment process. For instance, the therapist needed to help the patient form accurate conclusions during and immediately following each ERP exercise, and "review segments" at the beginning and end of each session were also necessary. In addition, regular assessment of both old and new OVIs became essential to tailoring each treatment session. Finally, cognitive rehabilitation exercises were also incorporated into the treatment process.

J.K. was treated in regular weekly sessions over the course of a full year. Office sessions and home visits were conducted, because the exposure exercises practiced within the therapist's office did not always generalize well to the patient's home environment and natural surroundings. J.K.'s compulsive spitting declined substantially over the first few months of treatment and this behavior was virtually nonexistent by the end of the third month of treatment. At this point, other detrimental compulsive behaviors were targeted using the same or similar strategies. Some other compulsive behaviors J.K. exhibited included checking photographs of himself before leaving the house, again to ensure that his strength was not reduced.

Although J.K. exhibited substantial treatment gains with regard to his behavior, the OVIs continued to persist, at least to some extent, throughout his treatment. The degree to which he endorsed each of the ideas fluctuated over the course of treatment, with these ideas seemingly weakest when directly targeted regularly using cognitive treatment strategies. Capitalizing on instances when J.K.'s OVIs were weakest led to the most substantial behavioral treatment gains. However, even when J.K. stopped engaging in a specific compulsive behavior, the related OVI often persisted to some extent, intermittently appearing at different levels of intensity. Despite the persistence of some of the OVIs, J.K. maintained most of his treatment gains over the course of one year and did not revert to his old behavioral patterns even in the face of the related OVIs.

Conclusion

Longstanding clinical observations have pointed to links between schizotypy or schizophrenia with OCD. Research has examined these links from both perspectives: individuals with OCD and co-occurring schizotypal signs and individuals with schizophrenia with co-occurring obsessive-compulsive symptoms. The research in this area has suggested that, in general, obsessive-compulsive symptoms are more difficult to treat when they are in conjunction with schizotypy or when they are present in individuals with schizophrenia. Although the accepted approach to treatment for OCD in general involves ERP, questions have arisen about the applicability of this set of procedures when schizotypy is present. We illustrated a case where exposure methods were successfully applied in an individual with OCD with co-occurring schizotypy. Several important caveats are necessary in treating such cases: First, treatment sessions must be more carefully structured to address problems in information processing; second, frequent within-session reminders about the relation between exposure and outcome are necessary to ensure proper habituation; and third, opportunistic exposure based on momentary reductions in OVI are necessary to facilitate habituation to stimuli that give rise of obsessive-compulsive problems.

REFERENCES

American Psychiatric Association. (2000). *Diagnostic and statistical manual of mental diseases* (4th ed., text revision). Washington, DC: Author.

Barch, D. M. (2005). The cognitive neuroscience of schizophrenia. *Annual Review of Clinical Psychology, 1,* 321–353.

Bergman, A., O'Brien, J., Osgood, G., & Cornblatt, B. (1995). Distractibility in schizophrenia. *Psychiatry Research, 57,* 131–140.

Berman, I., Kalinowski, A., Berman, S. M., Lengua, J., & Green, A. I. (1995). Obsessive-compulsive symptoms in chronic schizophrenia. *Comprehensive Psychiatry, 36,* 6–10.

Bogetto, F., Bellino, S., Vaschetto, P., & Ziero, S. (2000). Olanzapine augmentation of fluvoxamine-refractory obsessive-compulsive disorder (OCD): A 12-week open trial. *Psychiatry Research, 96,* 91–98.

Chapman, L., Chapman, J., & Miller, E. (1982). Reliabilities and intercorrelations of eight measures of proneness to psychosis. *Journal of Consulting and Clinical Psychology, 50,* 187–195.

Clark, D. A. (2004). *Cognitive-behavioral therapy for OCD.* New York: Guilford.

Coleman, M. J., Levy, D. L., Lenzenweger, M. F., & Holzman, P. S. (1996). Thought disorder, perceptual aberrations, and schizotypy. *Journal of Abnormal Psychology, 105,* 469–473.

Einstein, D. A., & Menzies, R. G. (2004a). The presence of magical thinking in obsessive-compulsive disorder. *Behaviour Research and Therapy, 42,* 539–549.

Einstein, D. A., & Menzies, R. G. (2004b). Role of magical thinking in obsessive compulsive symptoms in an undergraduate sample. *Depression and Anxiety, 19,* 174–179.

Ekers, D., Carman, S., & Schlich, T. (2004). Successful outcome of exposure and response prevention in the treatment of obsessive compulsive disorder in a patient with schizophrenia. *Behavioural and Cognitive Psychotherapy, 32,* 375–378.

Fenton, W. S., & McGlashan, T. H. (1986). The prognostic significance of obsessive-compulsive symptoms in schizophrenia. *American Journal of Psychiatry, 143,* 437–441.

George, L., & Neufeld, R. W. (1987). Magical ideation and schizophrenia. *Journal of Consulting and Clinical Psychology, 55,* 778–779.

Greisberg, S., & McKay, D. (2003). Neuropsychology of obsessive-compulsive disorder: A review and treatment implications. *Clinical Psychology Review, 23,* 95–117.

Harris, C. L., & Dinn, W. M. (2003). Subtyping obsessive compulsive disorder: Neuropsychological correlates. *Behavioural Neurology, 14,* 75–87.

Holzman, P. S., Coleman, M., Lenzenweger, M. F., Levy, D. L., Matthysse, S., O'Driscoll, G., et al. (1995). Working memory deficits, antisaccades, and thought disorder in relation to perceptual aberration. In A. Raine, T. Lencz, & S. A. Mednick (Eds.), *Schizotypal personality* (pp. 353–381). New York: Cambridge.

Hwang, M. Y., Morgan, J. E., & Losconzcy, M. F. (2000). Clinical and neuropsychological profiles of obsessive-compulsive schizophrenia: A pilot study. *Journal of Neuropsychiatry and Clinical Neurosciences, 12,* 91–94.

Johnson-Selfridge, M., & Zalewski, C. (2001). Moderator variables of executive func-

tioning in schizophrenia: Meta-analytic findings. *Schizophrenia Bulletin, 27,* 305–316.
Keuneman, R. J., Pokos, V., Weerasundera, R., & Castle, D. (2005). Antipsychotic treatment in obsessive-compulsive disorder: A literature review. *Australian and New Zealand Journal of Psychiatry, 39,* 336–343.
Korfine, L., & Lenzenweger, M. F. (1995). The taxonicity of schizotypy: A replication. *Journal of Abnormal Psychology, 104,* 26–31.
Kruger, S., Braunig, G., Hoffler, J., Shugar, G., Borner, I., & Langkrar, J. (2000). Prevalence of obsessive compulsive disorder in schizophrenia and significance of motor symptoms. *Journal of Neuropsychiatry and Clinical Neurosciences, 12,* 16–24.
Lencz, T., Raine, A., Benishay, D. S., Mills, S., & Bird, L. (1995). Neuropsychological abnormalities associated with schizotypal personality. In A. Raine, T. Lencz, & S. A. Mednick (Eds.), *Schizotypal personality* (pp. 289–328). New York: Cambridge.
Matsunaga, H., Kiriike, N., Matsui, T., Oya, K., Iwasaki, Y., Koshimune, K., et al. (2002). Obsessive-compulsive disorder with poor insight. *Comprehensive Psychiatry, 43,* 150–157.
McDougle, C. J., Epperson, N., Pelton, G. H., Wasylink, S., & Price, L. H. (2000). A double-blind placebo controlled study of risperidone addition in serotonin reuptake inhibitor-refractory obsessive-compulsive disorder. *Archives of General Psychiatry, 57,* 794–801.
McKay, D., Abramowitz, J. S., Calamari, J. E., Kyrios, M., Radomsky, A., Sookman, D., et al. (2004). A critical evaluation of obsessive-compulsive disorder subtypes: Symptoms versus mechanisms. *Clinical Psychology Review, 24,* 283–313.
McKay, D., & McKiernan, K. (2005). Information processing and cognitive behavior therapy for obsessive-compulsive disorder: Comorbidity of delusions, overvalued ideation, and schizophrenia. *Cognitive and Behavioral Practice, 12,* 390–394.
Minichiello, W. E., Baer, L., & Jenike, M. A. (1987). Schizotypal personality disorder: A poor prognostic indicator for behavior therapy in the treatment of obsessive-compulsive disorder. *Journal of Anxiety Disorders, 1,* 273–276.
Moritz, S., Fricke, S., Jacobson, D., Kloss, M., Wien, C., Rufer, M., et al. (2004). Positive schizotypal symptoms predict treatment outcome in obsessive-compulsive disorder. *Behaviour Research and Therapy, 42,* 217–227.
Peasley-Miklus, C., Massie, E., Baslet, G., & Carmin, C. (2005). Treating comorbid obsessive compulsive disorder (OCD) and schizophrenia: The case of Sam. *Cognitive and Behavioral Practice, 12,* 379–383.
Poyurovsky, M., & Koran, L. M. (2005). Obsessive compulsive disorder with schizotypy versus schizophrenia with OCD: Diagnostic dilemmas and therapeutic implications. *Journal of Psychiatric Research, 39,* 399–408.
Raine, A., & Lencz, T. (1995). Conceptual and theoretical issues in schizotypal personality research. In A. Raine, T. Lencz, & S. A. Mednick (Eds.), *Schizotypal personality* (pp. 3–15). New York: Cambridge.
Skoog, G., & Skoog, I. (1999). A 40-year follow-up of patients with obsessive-compulsive disorder. *Archives of General Psychiatry, 56,* 121–127.
Sobin, C., Blundell, M. L., Weiller, F., Gavigan, C., Haiman, C., & Karayiorgou, M. (2000). Evidence of a schizotypal subtype of obsessive-compulsive disorder. *Journal of Psychiatric Research, 34,* 15–24.

Spitznagel, M. B., & Suhr, J. A. (2002). Executive function deficits associated with schizotypy and obsessive-compulsive disorder. *Psychiatry Research, 110,* 151–163.

Tibbo, P., Kroetsch, M., Chue, P., & Warneke, L. (2000). Obsessive compulsive disorder in schizophrenia. *Journal of Psychiatric Research, 34,* 139–146.

Tolin, D. F., Abramowitz, J. S., Kozak, M. J., & Foa, E. B. (2001). Fixity of belief, perceptual aberration, and magical ideation in obsessive-compulsive disorder. *Journal of Anxiety Disorders, 15,* 501–510.

Walker, W. R., Freeman, R. F., & Christensen, D. K. (1994). Restricting environmental stimulation (REST) to enhance cognitive behavioral treatment for obsessive-compulsive disorder with schizotypal personality disorder. *Behavior Therapy, 25,* 709–720.

Whitney, K. A., Fasteneau, P. S., Evans, J. D., & Lysaker, P. H. (2004). Comparative neuropsychological functioning in obsessive compulsive disorder and schizophrenia with and without obsessive compulsive symptoms. *Schizophrenia Research, 69,* 75–83.

CHAPTER TEN

Postpartum Obsessive-Compulsive Disorder

Jonathan S. Abramowitz, Ph.D.,
and Nichole Fairbrother, Ph.D.

For most women, the perinatal period is an exciting and joyful time. There is anticipation of the arrival of the new baby, and elation when the infant is finally born and greeted by his or her family. However, some new mothers experience the onset (or intensification) of severe emotional distress during this period. Much attention has focused on postpartum depression and psychosis, with much less attention on perinatal anxiety disorders, in particular, postpartum obsessive-compulsive disorder (ppOCD). Although early research suggested that pregnancy *protects* women from emotional disorders (Elliot, Rugg, Watson, & Brough, 1983) more recent evidence indicates that women are at an *increased* risk of developing OCD during pregnancy and the postpartum period (e.g., Buttolph & Holland, 1990; Maina et al., 1999; for a review, see Abramowitz, Schwartz, Moore, & Luenzmann, 2003). The opening section of this chapter provides an overview and description of ppOCD, including a case example to illustrate the cardinal features of this presentation or "subtype" of OCD. We then consider the relationship between ppOCD and OCD in general. Theoretical perspectives on ppOCD are presented in the second section of the chapter. The third section, which is concerned with treatment issues, includes a discussion of two interventions for ppOCD that have been shown to be effective: cognitive-behavioral therapy (CBT) and pharmacotherapy. A case vignette illustrating the treatment of a patient with ppOCD is presented, along with a discussion of relevant clinical considerations and suggestions for troubleshooting.

Clinical Presentation

Description of the Symptoms

As the chapters in this volume elucidate, OCD is a highly heterogeneous condition with a wide variation in the specific content of obsessions and compulsions. Many studies have examined the presentation of OCD symptoms occurring in the context of pregnancy and the postpartum. In many cases, ppOCD symptoms appear strongly related to meaningful circumstantial factors, such as responsibility for the care and protection of an otherwise helpless unborn or newborn child. Table 10.1 lists the characteristic signs and symptoms of this presentation of OCD. Findings from descriptive research and clinical observations are discussed below.

Buttolph and Holland (1990) provided the first report of ppOCD in the research literature. They described two women whose OCD symptoms began during pregnancy and were characterized by (a) obsessional fear of the unborn baby becoming contaminated by toxic agents and (b) compulsive washing and cleaning rituals. These authors also describe three cases in which rapid onset occurred soon *after* childbirth. Symptoms concerned unwanted obsessional thoughts of harming the child with a knife and of contaminating the baby. Sichel Cohen, Dimmock, and Rosenbaum (1993) reported a case series

Table 10.1. *Characteristic Signs and Symptoms of Perinatal Obsessive-Compulsive Disorder*

- Onset (often rapid) or worsening during pregnancy or postpartum
- Obsessional content involving contamination (particularly *during* pregnancy), illness, violence, harm, accidents, or loss
- Avoidance of obsessional cues, sometimes including avoidance of the newborn
- Compulsive rituals may be overt (washing, checking) or covert (mental rituals, neutralizing)
- Often associated with depressive symptoms
- Not associated with postpartum psychosis

of 15 women with ppOCD, all of whom reported intrusive, anxiety-evoking obsessional thoughts related to harming the infant (e.g., while the infant was sleeping). However, none of these patients evidenced overt compulsive rituals such as washing or checking. Instead, they appeared to manage their obsessions via avoidance of triggers, such as potential weapons (e.g., knives) and the infant itself. In a second report, Sichel, Cohen, Rosenbaum, and Driscoll (1993) described two ppOCD cases, each involving unwanted obsessional thoughts of stabbing the newborn. Both of these women also developed phobic avoidance of the child and of knives, and neither reported observable rituals (although mental rituals were not ruled out).

Diaz, Grush, Sichel, and Cohen (1997) described five women with perinatal onset OCD. In three of these cases, where onset coincided with pregnancy, the major symptoms were contamination obsessions and washing or cleaning compulsions. For the remaining two women, who experienced onset soon after childbirth, the main symptoms were upsetting thoughts of harming (e.g., sexually molesting or stabbing) the infant. Thus, the descriptive research indicates that women developing OCD symptoms *during* pregnancy tend to experience contamination obsessions and washing or cleaning rituals. Those with obsessional problems that begin *following* the birth of a child tend to report unwelcome, distressing intrusive obsessional thoughts of harming the infant. Phobic avoidance of situations and stimuli that trigger such obsessions is commonly observed among affected individuals. In contrast, there is little, if any, mention in the ppOCD literature of hoarding, perfectionism, or symmetry/ordering symptoms that are often present in other forms of OCD.

Consistent with research on the occurrence of intrusive thoughts in the general population (e.g., Rachman & de Silva, 1978), our own clinical observations suggest that postpartum obsessional intrusions may be either transitory or recurrent and persistent and may even elicit action to safeguard from disastrous consequences. For example, one woman spent several hours each day praying that she would not act on her violent thoughts related to her infant. Another woman never allowed herself to be alone with her infant for fear that she might, by mistake, poison the child with household items such as bleach or lye. Clinical research as well as our own observations also highlight the swift onset of postpartum obsessional symptoms, which is in contrast to the typically gradual onset of OCD symptoms that occurs *during* pregnancy or outside the context of pregnancy and childbirth altogether.

Relationship with Postpartum Depression

There is evidence of a relationship between postpartum depression and ppOCD symptoms, particularly when the obsessions involve unwanted thoughts of hurting the newborn (Jennings, Ross, & Elmore, 1999; Wisner, Peindl, Gigliotti, & Hanusa, 1999). However, it is unknown whether these OCD symptoms are a cause or an effect of the depressive symptoms. Given that depression often involves unwanted or self-destructive thoughts, it is possible that obsessional problems (e.g., unwanted aggressive thoughts) are symptoms of postpartum depression. Alternatively, it is plausible that the presence of distressing, recurrent, intrusive obsessional thoughts gives rise to depressive symptoms (e.g., hopelessness, dysphoria, social isolation). Indeed, OCD in general is typically associated with secondary depressive symptoms (Nestadt et al., 2001).

Differentiation from Postpartum Psychosis

It is important to distinguish between the symptoms of ppOCD and those of postpartum psychosis because both can involve ideation regarding harming the newborn. Table 10.2 lists key characteristics of each disorder. Despite the apparent topographical similarity in thought *content*, there are key functional distinctions between the two conditions. First, hallucinations (e.g., "I saw smoke and fire coming from the baby's nose and ears") and delusions (e.g., persecutory delusions; "The Devil is out to get the baby"), which characterize postpartum psychosis, are quite rare. Second, such symptoms usually occur along with additional stereotypically psychotic symptoms such as loose associations, labile mood, agitation, and other "bizarre" behaviors. Most important, the aggressive ideation in psychosis is experienced as consistent with the person's delusional thinking and behavior (*ego-syntonic*), is not subjectively resisted (i.e., not associated with fears or compulsive rituals), and is associated with an increased risk of aggressive behavior.

In contrast, symptoms of ppOCD (even violent and horrific obsessions; e.g., the thought to put the baby in the microwave) are *not* associated with an increased risk of committing harm. This is because obsessional thoughts are experienced as senseless, unwanted, and inconsistent with the person's typical behavior and mind-set (*ego-dystonic*). The person with OCD symptoms recognizes that the intrusive thoughts are contrary to his or her better judgment

Table 10.2. *Key Characteristics of Postpartum Obsessional Symptoms and Postpartum Psychotic Symptoms*

Characteristic	Postpartum Obsessions	Postpartum Psychosis
Thought content	Thoughts, ideas, images of harm	Thoughts, ideas, images of harm
Associated symptoms	Anxiety, avoidance, compulsion, thought suppression, depression	Delusional thinking patterns, hallucinations, negative symptoms of psychosis (lack of self-care)
Subjective experience	Thoughts are experienced as unacceptable, repulsive, and inconsistent with the person's worldview. Obsessions evoke anxiety and distress over the corresponding behavior	Thoughts are accepted as true. Objective evidence to the contrary might be distorted to confirm the person's delusion.
Resistance	Obsessions are subjectively resisted via avoidance, rituals, and thought suppression	Delusions are not resisted
Risk of harm	Very slight, if any	Increased. Requires hospitalization

and reports a fear of engaging in unacceptable behavior (including fears of even *thinking about* engaging in such behavior). Moreover, individuals with ppOCD engage in excessive resistance, avoidance, and ritualizing in an attempt to control or suppress obsessional thoughts and ensure that feared consequences do not occur. In short, women with ppOCD present with severe anxiety complaints (e.g., worry over whether they will harm), as opposed to psychotic symptoms.

Case Vignette

Jen, a 27-year-old elementary school teacher, had given birth to her son Troy two months previously. The pregnancy and delivery were uncomplicated. Although Jen had no previous psychiatric history, she informed the pediatrician that she now was feeling depressed most of the day and sometimes felt afraid of interacting with Troy. The pediatrician recognized these symptoms as a postpartum psychiatric disorder and referred Jen for further evaluation. At her initial assessment, Jen described recurrent unwanted thoughts of harming Troy, including the idea that she could suffocate him with his blanket, put him in the microwave, or stab him with a knife while her husband, who worked full time, would not be there to stop her. These intrusive thoughts were unacceptable to Jen, who considered herself a "gentle person." She reported no other signs of psychosis, no history of violent behavior, and no intent to act on these intrusions. In fact, Jen spent inordinate amounts of time praying for the thoughts to go away and was avoiding being alone with her infant. However, she admitted, whenever she tried to dismiss the terrible ideas, they seemed to recur with greater intensity. This problem also caused Jen a great deal of distress. She believed that because she could not rid herself of the thoughts even when she tried to, she was "losing her sanity" and would be more likely to do "something terrible." Jen's rituals and her avoidance of being alone with Troy for fear of "losing control" were interfering with her family functioning as well as with her relationship with Troy.

Theoretical Models

Biological Models

The temporal relationship between OCD onset or worsening and childbirth has prompted biological researchers to search for neurochemical explanations for this phenomenon. One such model derives from the "serotonin hypothesis" of OCD (Barr, Goodman, & Price, 1993), which implicates a dysregulation of the serotonin system. Specifically, fluctuations in estrogen and progesterone levels (as occur in late pregnancy) may alter serotonergic transmission, reuptake, and binding (e.g., Stockert & deRobertis, 1985). Thus, the onset or exacerbation of OCD symptoms during or immediately following pregnancy may result from the effects of rapid changes in these two hormones on serotonin functioning. Other researchers have questioned the validity of the serotonin hypothesis of OCD on the basis of largely inconsistent research findings (Rauch & Jenike, 1993).

Another biological theory implicates the hormone oxytocin, which, in late pregnancy, plays a role in uterine contractions and lactation (Leckman et al., 1994a). Leckman et al. (1994b) found correlations between OCD severity and cerebrospinal fluid oxytocin levels among untreated OCD patients. Although there is no direct evidence that hormonal imbalances play a causal role in ppOCD, these data are consistent with the idea that ppOCD is triggered by increased concentrations of oxytocin (Diaz et al., 1997). Additional research in this area is needed because much of the existing work is preliminary, and the precise neurobiological mechanisms of OCD have not been well elucidated.

Cognitive-Behavioral Models

Cognitive-behavioral models of ppOCD derive from models of obsessional problems in general (e.g., Salkovskis, 1996; see chapter 5 in this volume) and begin with the oft-replicated finding that intrusions (i.e., thoughts, images, and impulses that intrude into consciousness) are normal experiences that most people have from time to time (e.g., Rachman & de Silva, 1978). Because such intrusions usually reflect the person's current concerns, it is not surprising that obsessions about responsibility for harming a helpless infant would be observed commonly among parents of newborns. The cognitive-behavioral model proposes that such normal intrusions develop into highly distressing and time-consuming clinical obsessions when the intrusions are appraised as highly significant or as posing a threat for which the individual is personally responsible. For example, "If I even *think* about fondling my infant's genitals, it means I'm an immoral person." Such appraisals evoke distress and motivate the person to try to suppress or neutralize the unwanted thought (e.g., by praying) and to attempt to prevent any harmful events associated with the intrusion (e.g., by avoiding the baby).

Compulsive rituals and avoidance behaviors are conceptualized as maladaptive efforts to remove intrusions and prevent feared consequences (i.e., acting out the thought). There are several ways in which such responses are counterproductive. First, they are technically "effective" in temporarily providing the desired reduction in obsessional distress. Therefore, these strategies are negatively reinforced and evolve into strong patterns often consuming substantial time and effort. Second, because they reduce anxiety in the short term, rituals and avoidance prevent the natural abatement of the fear response that typically occurs when individuals stay in feared situations for longer periods of time. Third, rituals and avoidance lead to an increase in the frequency of obsessions by serving as reminders of obsessional intrusions and thereby triggering their reoccurrence. Attempts at distracting oneself from unwanted intrusions may paradoxically increase the frequency of intrusions, possibly because the distracters become reminders (retrieval cues) of the intrusions. Finally, performing rituals (e.g., praying) preserves dysfunctional beliefs and misinterpretations of obsessional thoughts. That is, when feared consequences do not occur after performance of a ritual, the person attributes this to their having ritualized.

A further strategy used by individuals with ppOCD to reduce the discomfort associated with obsessions is to conceal the thoughts from others. For example, in the Jen's case, she purposely did not divulge the contents of her obsessional thoughts to others because she was concerned that she would be labeled "crazy" or "psychotic" and be hospitalized. Concealment may be particularly important in ppOCD because the parent fears being viewed as unfit (and having the child removed from the home). However, this type of concealment insidiously maintains the obsessional problem by preventing the individual from correcting the mistaken appraisals of the essentially normal intrusive thoughts. That is, as long as Jen hides her thoughts from others, she will never have the opportunity (e.g., through social interaction) to see that others (a) probably also have unwanted intrusive thoughts and (b) do not think she is "mad" or "violent."

To summarize, when a new mother appraises an otherwise normally occurring mental intrusion about her infant as overly meaningful or significant, she becomes distressed and attempts to remove the intrusion and prevent disastrous consequences. This paradoxically increases the frequency of intrusions. Thus, the intrusions escalate into persistent and distressing clinical obsessions. Avoidance, rituals, and concealment maintain the intrusions and prevent the self-correction of the mistaken appraisals.

Treatment

The available clinical and research evidence suggests that treatments that are effective for OCD in general are similarly effective in reducing ppOCD symptoms. Thus, exposure-based CBT should be considered as the first-line treatment, with serotonergic medications as the second line. However, before treatment begins, a thorough review of the patient's medical records and a complete medical evaluation is recommended to rule out coexisting or confounding organic bases for anxiety-related symptoms. In addition, because severe depression may interfere with response to CBT or pharmacotherapy (Abramowitz, 2004), comorbid mood disorders should be assessed, and if present, appropriate treatment should be initiated. Next, we discuss effective treatment strategies for ppOCD, present a brief review of the scientific data establishing the effectiveness of these interventions, and illustrate treatment in a case example. Other important considerations in the treatment of ppOCD are also discussed.

Psychological Treatment

CBT, which is highly effective for nonpostpartum OCD, is also effective in reducing OCD symptoms during pregnancy and the postpartum. This treatment helps patients weaken their anxiety responses to intrusive obsessional thoughts so that avoidance and compulsive rituals are unnecessary (for a complete description, see Abramowitz [2006]). The initial step in CBT is a functional assessment of obsessional cues, feared consequences, avoidance, and behavioral or mental rituals. Psychoeducation focuses on teaching the patient about the cognitive-behavioral explanation for OCD. Whereas cognitive restructuring techniques might be initially used to help patients modify dysfunctional interpretations of intrusive thoughts, the primary ingredient in CBT is systematic, repeated, and prolonged exposure to situations and thoughts that cue obsessional anxiety but that are objectively low risk. Therapeutic exposure helps patients test out their predictions regarding whether, for example, they will act on their unwanted violent impulses. To modify beliefs, the situations or stimuli (e.g., thoughts) confronted during exposure must match closely with the patient's fears, as is illustrated in the case vignette.

During exposure, it is also important for patients to engage in *response prevention,* which means refraining from performing any compulsive rituals or avoidance that might bring about escape from obsessional fear before this fear would otherwise subside naturally. For example, a patient might be instructed to stop having her husband nearby "just in case" she lost control and acted on her violent thoughts. Implementing response prevention ensures that the only explanation for the nonoccurrence of feared consequences of exposure is that such consequences are unlikely.

CBT is a brief, time-limited treatment that typically involves about 12–16 sessions for ppOCD. Between treatment sessions, the patient practices exposure and response prevention exercises as assigned by the therapist. In general, a trained mental health professional, such as a behaviorally oriented psychologist, delivers CBT; however, training paraprofessionals and those involved in primary care to administer CBT has been considered.

Although CBT is associated with excellent short- and long-term response in OCD (Abramowitz, Franklin, & Foa, 2002), there are presently no data on the efficacy of this treatment for women with ppOCD. Theories on the mechanisms of exposure-based therapy for anxiety (e.g., Foa & Kozak, 1986) posit that repeated and prolonged exposure weakens connections between obsessional thoughts and anxiety by providing experiential evidence that feared catastrophes do not occur and that anxiety eventually decreases without the performance of compulsive rituals.

Pharmacotherapy

The most effective medications for OCD are the serotonin reuptake inhibitors (SRIs; e.g., fluoxetine, citalopram; Abramowitz, 1997). The decision to use SRIs during pregnancy should be approached on an individual basis, with discussion between the patient, her partner if appropriate, and her health care provider. If pharmacotherapy is considered, the relative risks and benefits associated with it must be weighed and openly and carefully discussed with the patient. Treatment should be reserved for those cases in which the risks to the mother and fetus from the disorder are felt to exceed the risk of medication usage. General guidelines for treatment include using the lowest effective dose of medication and avoiding exposure during the first trimester of pregnancy (again, considering nonpharmacologic interventions), if possible.

In a study of 15 women with ppOCD treated openly with various SRIs, Sichel, Cohen, Dimmock, and Rosenbaum (1993) reported that scores on the clinical global impression (CGI) scale improved following 12 weeks of treatment. Moreover, at post-treatment, none of these patients were rated as worse than "mildly ill." One-year follow-up data indicated that improvement was maintained as long as medication was continued. One patient was able to discontinue her medication and remain improved, whereas two others experienced a return of symptoms when they attempted to discontinue and subsequently had to be reinstated on their SRI. Indeed the return of OCD symptoms following SRI discontinuation is a well-known phenomenon (Pato, Zohar-Kadouch, Zohar, & Murphy, 1988).

Case Vignette

In this section, we describe the treatment of Jen, who was introduced at the beginning of this chapter.

Because Jen was breast-feeding her infant (Troy), she informed our evaluation team that she would prefer to try CBT rather than medication to manage her OCD. During the first therapy session, the CBT therapist assessed Jen's intrusive thoughts, inquiring about (a) the content of the thoughts and stimuli that trigger them, (b) her interpretations of the unwanted thoughts, and (c) her responses to them. Jen reported that she believed the thoughts meant that she was "evil at heart" and that their presence was a sign that she might act on them at any moment. She believed she had to take precautions, such as having others nearby to stop her if she lost control. When the thoughts came to mind, Jen repeated certain prayers in sets of three, which she believed kept her from acting out her violent thoughts. She had also been concealing the content and frequency of her obsessions from others (including her husband) for fear that they would think she was "an evil monster." Because Jen's mood symptoms began only after she had been experiencing obsessions, her depression was conceptualized as secondary to the OCD symptoms. The hypothesis was made that successful treatment of her obsessions would lead to an improvement in her mood.

Psychoeducation began after the assessment and case formulation was complete. The therapist normalized the experience of intrusive "bad" thoughts by teaching Jen that practically everyone from time to time experiences ideas, images, or impulses that are upsetting or inconsistent with how they usually think (i.e., ego-dystonic). The therapist even provided examples of his own unwanted intrusive thoughts. Jen had never considered that others also had similar kinds of intrusions and was relieved to know this. The therapist discussed how Jen's concealment of her thoughts, while understandable given Jen's interpretation of the thoughts, prevented her from finding out how common such experiences are. Jen was helped to see that her mistaken appraisals of her intrusive thoughts as very meaningful and dangerous, immoral, and needing to be controlled were the *real* problem. Normal intrusions can escalate into obsessions if they are misappraised as dangerous. By trying to suppress and control these thoughts, she was making herself even more scared and preoccupied, which accounts for their persistence and development of a "life of their own."

Jen was also helped to see that she was very unlikely to act on her unwanted thoughts if she didn't *wish* to act on them. A discussion of the relationship between thoughts and actions was followed by an experiment in which Jen was asked to hold a paperweight from the therapist's desk. The therapist turned his back and then asked Jen to imagine throwing this object at the therapist. Of course, Jen did not throw the paperweight—even after visualizing this action for several minutes and even saying "I want to hurt you" and "I'm going to throw this at you." The results of this experiment (i.e., thoughts themselves don't lead to actions) were discussed in terms of the probability that Jen would act on thoughts to harm her infant, Troy.

After a few sessions, Jen found herself feeling less distressed over her intrusive thoughts; yet, they still evoked moderate levels of anxiety. Jen also remained fearful of having the thoughts while she was with Troy. Moreover, she continued to use prayer rituals to reduce her fears of disastrous consequences. Thus, the therapist introduced exposure and response prevention as exercises for weakening Jen's patterns of (a) becoming anxious when such thoughts arose and (b) using rituals to reduce her anxiety. After providing a rationale for purposely confronting her unwanted thoughts without engaging in any prayer rituals, Jen and the therapist constructed a hierarchy of situations for Jen to practice both in-session and at home. This list is shown in Table 10.3. Jen agreed to practice the situations without saying the prayers. She realized that she needed to prove to herself that these thoughts were not indicative of danger and that her prayers were not keeping her from acting. During the first exposure session, Jen and the therapist collaboratively created a tape-recorded scenario of Jen's intrusive thought about stabbing Troy. The scenario was as follows:

> You've just started cutting the vegetables and you see little Troy lying on the floor on his blanket. He's cooing and very content. Then you have the idea that you could easily stab him to death with the knife you are using. He is so small and defenseless. He wouldn't be able to stop you. You want to push the thought away, but instead allow yourself to just 'go with it.' Then, you feel the urge to pray growing stronger and stronger. You want to say the prayers, but you know you are not supposed to because of the therapy instructions. So, you refrain from praying. But then you feel yourself going over to Troy and you begin stabbing him over and over. There is blood everywhere. What are you doing . . . this is your own son! Troy is crying, but then he goes limp as he dies on the blanket. You can't believe what you've just done. What will your husband say? If only you had said those prayers. Now, Troy is dead.

Jen practiced listening to the scenario on a loop-tape in the session. The therapist kept track of Jen's anxiety level on a scale from 0 (none) to 100 (extreme). As the exposure began, Jen's anxiety reached 75 percent, but after 15 minutes of listening to the loop-tape, it decreased to 40 percent. After another 10 minutes, the tape evoked mild anxiety (25%). Next, Troy (who had been in the waiting room with his father) was brought into the office and Jen retrieved

Table 10.3. Jen's Exposure Therapy Hierarchy

Situation	Anxiety Level
1. Thinking about stabbing Troy	40%
2. Thinking about stabbing Troy while holding a knife	50%
3. Thinking about putting Troy in the microwave	55%
4. Holding Troy in the kitchen while thinking about putting him in the microwave	65%
5. Thinking about suffocating Troy	65%
6. Watching Troy sleeping, holding a pillow, and thinking about suffocating him	75%

a large knife that she had brought from home. Troy was placed on the floor next to Jen, and Jen practiced holding the knife while listening to the tape. At first, Jen felt uncomfortable, but after about 15 minutes, her distress subsided even while she held the knife. She reported also refraining from any prayer rituals. Then, after obtaining Jen's permission, the therapist left Jen and Troy alone in the office. Again, Jen's distress level temporarily increased but soon decreased (after about 10 minutes) as she realized that she was unlikely to act on the upsetting thoughts. Jen felt very good about completing the exercise and was instructed to practice the same tasks once each day between sessions.

Over the course of the next month, Jen practiced similar exposure exercises and practiced refraining from rituals and avoidance strategies. This was extremely helpful. After only two months of treatment (eight therapy sessions), Jen was no longer avoiding being alone with Troy, and her prayer rituals had reduced substantially. Whereas Jen still experienced occasional unwanted intrusive violent thoughts, these thoughts no longer produced anxiety. Jen reported "knowing in her gut" that she didn't have to worry about these experiences. Her depressive symptoms had also abated and she reported being much happier about being a new mother. For the next three months, the therapist saw Jen monthly for follow-up sessions. Jen continued to remain improved through this time and treatment was therefore terminated.

Troubleshooting

A number of issues deserve consideration and are unique to the treatment of OCD in new parents. Given that ppOCD is typically characterized by thoughts of harming one's infant, special care needs to be taken to ensure that there are no risk factors for child harm separate from the obsessional thoughts (which in themselves are not related to an increased risk of harming one's infant). Other areas that deserve special attention include social support for the parent with OCD and the mother-infant relationship. Social support is important in the early postpartum period as this is a highly demanding time in a parent's life. Given that ppOCD can lead to avoidance of one's infant, attention should be given to the mother-infant relationship, and potentially facilitation of this relationship may be incorporated into treatment.

The clinician must weigh the pros and cons of the various treatment approaches and discuss these with the patient. The main advantages of a CBT approach include the safety, demonstrated effectiveness, and durability of this relatively brief form of treatment. Research indicates that patients often maintain their improvement up to several years after the end of formal therapy. This is likely because CBT involves learning and perfecting the use of skills. Essentially, patients learn to become their own therapists, and develop the ability to manage similar fears that might arise after the completion of treatment.

Nevertheless, CBT also has its disadvantages. First, in contrast to the ease of taking medications, CBT requires hard work from the patient (and the therapist). It demands a firm commitment to attend regular treatment sessions and complete "homework assignments" between visits. A second disadvantage of this approach is that in most cases, the patient must confront the very situations and unpleasant thought that evoke their anxiety—situations they have been taking great pains to avoid. The anxiety that is evoked during exposure is temporary, and the therapist works collaboratively with the patient to minimize any distress (e.g., by using a graded approach). However, CBT involves "investing anxiety now in a calmer future." A final disadvantage of CBT is that it can be difficult to find. That is, at present, knowledgeable treatment providers who are trained to deliver this kind of therapy are somewhat few and far between (although this is changing in many areas). Excellent resources for clinicians looking to refer patients for CBT include the Anxiety Disorders Association of America (www.adaa.org), the Obsessive Compulsive Foundation (www.ocfoundation.org), and the Association for Behavioral and Cognitive Therapies (formerly the Association for Advancement of Behavior Therapy; www.abct.org). The Web sites for each of these organizations include helpful resources for locating a trained provider.

Similarly, medications for the treatment of OCD have advantages and disadvantages. Advantages of medications include that they are easy to obtain and easy to take. There are no therapy sessions or homework involved with medication. However, along with potential side effects and the need for long-term use, disadvantages include a growing controversy over the possibility that perinatal syndromes can develop from SRI use during the third trimester of pregnancy. In the summer of 2004, based on the recommendation of the Pediatric Advisory Subcommittee of the Food and Drug Administration (FDA), the FDA opted to instruct the makers of SRIs to place warnings on the package insert describing the possible occurrence of neurobehavioral symptoms in neonates exposed to these medications late in the third trimester and through labor and delivery. Symptoms of concern have included feeding difficulties, agitation, irritability, sleep disturbance, respiratory distress, cyanosis, apnea, seizures, hypertonia, hyperflexia, and tremor. It is not clear whether these symptoms represent a type of withdrawal reaction or serotonin overstimulation. The subcommittee also recommended changes to the dosage and administration section of the drug label advising physicians to consider taper and discontinuation of these agents before labor and delivery. This has significant implications for women being treated for mood and anxiety disorders, as the postpartum period has been identified as a time of increased vulnerability to the recurrence of these problems. If a psychotropic agent is tapered around the time of labor and delivery, strong consideration should be given to reinstituting it after delivery.

Conclusion

In contrast with a number of other conditions that affect pregnant and postpartum women, such as depression and psychosis, perinatal anxiety disorders have received very little empirical attention. In the case of OCD, the perinatal period appears to be a time of increased risk for the development of this disorder. Further, available evidence suggests that ppOCD presents a distinctive clinical picture, with prenatal onset characterized most often by contamination fears, and postpartum onset, by unwanted thoughts of harm befalling one's infant.

As this is a fairly new and untapped area of study, many questions remain. First, no definitive incidence studies have been carried out. A study of this type would provide information on the relative risk of developing OCD during the perinatal period compared with other points in a woman's life. As intrusive thoughts of harm related to one's infant occur with some frequency among women with postpartum onset depression, studies that explore the relationship between perinatal OCD and perinatal depression are needed. Research aimed at furthering our understanding differences between women with ppOCD who are troubled by thoughts of accidental harm befalling their infant, and those who are plagued by thoughts of actively harming their infant. Further, studies of the impact of ppOCD on parenting behavior, infant development, and the mother-infant relationship have yet to be carried out. Finally, treatment approaches that are specifically designed to meet the needs of persons with this interesting subtype of OCD will be required to optimally meet the needs of parents of young infants.

REFERENCES

Abramowitz, J. S. (1997). Effectiveness of psychological and pharmacological treatments for obsessive-compulsive disorder: A quantitative review of the controlled treatment literature. *Journal of Consulting and Clinical Psychology, 65*, 44–52.

Abramowitz, J. S. (2004). Treatment of obsessive-compulsive disorder in patients who have comorbid major depression. *Journal of Clinical Psychology, 60*, 1133–1141.

Abramowitz, J. S. (2006). *Understanding and treating obsessive-compulsive disorder.* Mahwah, NJ: Lawrence Erlbaum Associates.

Abramowitz, J. S., Franklin, M. E., & Foa, E. B. (2002). Empirical status of cognitive-behavior therapy for obsessive-compulsive disorder: A meta-analytic review. *Romanian Journal of Cognitive and Behavioral Psychotherapies, 2*, 89–104.

Abramowitz, J. S., Schwartz, S., Moore, K., & Luenzmann, K. (2003). Obsessive-compulsive symptoms in pregnancy and the puerperium: A review of the literature. *Journal of Anxiety Disorders, 17*, 461–478.

Barr, L. C., Goodman, W. K., & Price, L. H. (1993). The serotonin hypothesis of obsessive-compulsive disorder. *International Clinical Psychopharmacology, 8* (Suppl. 2), 79–82.

Buttolph, M. L., & Holland, A. D. (1990). Obsessive-compulsive disorders in pregnancy and childbirth. In M. Jenike, L. Baer, & W. Minichiello (Eds.), *Obsessive-compulsive disorders: Theory and Management* (pp. 89–97). Chicago: Year Book Medical.

Diaz, S. F., Grush, L. R., Sichel, D. A., & Cohen, L. S. (1997). In L. J. Dickstein, M. B. Riba, & J. M. Oldham (Eds.), *Review of Psychiatry, Vol. 16,* (pp. 97–112). Washington, DC: American Psychiatric Press.

Elliot, S. A., Rugg, A. J., Watson, J. P., & Brough, D. I. (1983). Mood changes during pregnancy and after the birth of a child. *British Journal of Psychiatry, 22*, 295–308.

Foa, E. B., & Kozak, M. J. (1986). Emotional processing of fear: Exposure to corrective information. *Psychological Bulletin, 99*, 20–35.

Jennings, K. D., Ross, S., Popper, S., & Elmore, M. (1999). Thoughts of harming infants in depressed and nondepressed mothers. *Journal of Affective Disorders, 54*, 21–28.

Leckman, J., Goodman, W., North, W., Chappell, P., Price, L., Pauls, D., et al. (1994a). The role of central oxytocin in obsessive-compulsive disorder and related normal behavior. *Psychoneuroendocrinology, 19,* 723–749.

Leckman, J., Goodman, W., North, W., Chappell, P., Price, L., Pauls, D., et al. (1994b). Elevated cerebrospinal fluid levels of oxytocin in obsessive-compulsive disorder. *Archives of General Psychiatry, 51,* 782–792.

Mania, G., Albert, U., Bogetto, F., Vaschetto, P., & Ravizza, L. (1999). Recent life events and obsessive-compulsive disorder (OCD): The role of pregnancy/delivery. *Psychiatry Research, 89,* 49–58.

Nestadt, G., Samuels, J., Riddle, M. A., Liang, K.-Y., Bienvenu, O. J., Hoehn-Saric, R., et al. (2001). The relationship between obsessive-compulsive disorder and anxiety and affective disorders: Results from the Johns Hopkins OCD Family Study. *Psychological Medicine, 31,* 481–487.

Pato, T. A., Zohar-Kadouch, R., Zohar, J., & Murphy, D. L. (1988). Return of symptoms after discontinuation of clomipramine in patients with obsessive-compulsive disorder. *American Journal of Psychiatry, 145,* 1521–1525.

Rachman, S. J., & de Silva, P. (1978). Abnormal and normal obsessions. *Behaviour Research and Therapy, 16,* 233–238.

Rauch, S., & Jenike, M. (1993). Neurobiological models of obsessive-compulsive disorder. *Psychosomatics, 34,* 20–32.

Salkovskis, P. (1996). Cognitive-behavioral approaches to the understanding of obsessional problems. In R. M. Rapee (Ed.), *Current controversies in the anxiety disorders* (pp. 103–133). New York: Guilford.

Sichel, D., A., Cohen, L. S., Dimmock, J. A., & Rosenbaum, J. F. (1993). Postpartum obsessive-compulsive disorder: A case series. *Journal of Clinical Psychiatry, 54,* 156–159.

Sichel, D. A., Cohen, L. S., Rosenbaum, J. F., & Driscoll, J. D. (1993). Postpartum onset of obsessive-compulsive disorder. *Psychosomatics, 34,* 277–279.

Stockert, M., & deRobertis, E. (1985). Effect of ovariectomy and estrogen on [³H]imipramine binding on different regions of the rat brain. *European Journal of Pharmacology, 199,* 255–257.

Wisner, K. L., Peindl, K. S., Gigliotti, T., & Hanusa, B. H. (1999). Obsessions and compulsions in women with postpartum depression. *Journal of Clinical Psychiatry, 60,* 176–180.

CHAPTER ELEVEN

Scrupulosity

Jonathan S. Abramowitz, Ph.D.

Membership in a religious community is a part of life for many individuals. Religion might provide a sense of moral and spiritual guidance, foster a sense of purpose, and impart structure. Research has even identified positive relationships between involvement in religious groups and emotional well-being. However, for some people, religious beliefs and rituals undergo a transformation from comforting behaviors performed out of a sense of faith and tradition to time-consuming doubts and compulsive behaviors performed out of an intense fear of punishment. Such individuals might constantly fear that they have unwittingly committed sins, neglected to repent for the sin, and engaged in other blasphemous or unholy activities. He or she might confess for hours, seek reassurance, repeat religious phrases or prayers, or engage in various religious rituals to ensure that these have been performed "just right." Such patterns, often termed *scrupulosity*, have long been recognized as symptoms of obsessive-compulsive disorder (OCD; Greenberg & Witztum, 2001).

This chapter opens with an in-depth clinical description of scrupulosity that includes case examples. Next, the relationship between scrupulosity and other types of OCD symptoms is covered. The focus of the chapter is contemporary theoretical perspectives on scrupulosity from which effective treatment techniques have been derived. After illustrating the treatment of scrupulosity using a case example, the chapter concludes with a discussion of obstacles that are commonly encountered in the management of patients with these symptoms.

Clinical Presentation

As with OCD in general, the presentation of scrupulous obsessions and compulsions is highly heterogeneous. Examples of common religious obsessions include recurrent and groundless doubts that one has committed (or will commit) sins, intrusive sacrilegious or blasphemous thoughts and images (e.g., "Jesus with an erection on the cross"), and persistent fears of eternal damnation and punishment from God. Common religious compulsions include excessive praying, extreme perfectionism regarding minor details of religious tradition (often to the exclusion of other, more central, facets), and seeking reassurance from clergy or loved ones about religious matters. Clinical observations indicate that the specific obsessions and compulsions vary according to the individual's religion. That is, an Orthodox Jew might worry that he did not keep a particular dietary law (e.g., keeping the meat separate from milk) properly; yet, members of religious groups that do not embrace similar rules would not incorporate these concerns into OCD symptoms. Similarly, a Roman Catholic might confess the same "sin" several times, and a born-again Christian might have persistent doubts over whether he or she "really" accepts Jesus as his or her savior.

Abramowitz, Huppert, Cohen, Tolin, and Cahill (2002) developed the only psychometrically validated self-report measure of scrupulosity to date, the Penn Inventory of Scrupulosity (PIOS). These authors identified two dimensions of scrupulosity: (a) the fear of having committed a religious sin and (b) the fear of punishment from God. In most cases, the "sins" feared by individuals with scrupulosity present relatively minor religious or moral dilemmas and are not of central importance to overall religious observance. Examples include the accidental mispronunciation of a word during prayer, experiencing an unpleasant (or inappropriate) intrusive image during a church service, and swallowing one's saliva on a fast day. The individual is also usually perceived as inculpable by religious authorities (although in some instances, the person's religious community reinforces the basis for his or her fears, or at least the person's concern over breaking a rule). Nevertheless, the scrupulous patient experiences intense guilt and anxiety and may take extreme measures to reduce this distress through compulsive ritualizing and reassurance seeking. In severe cases, scrupulosity interferes substantially with social, occupational, and religious functioning. Tolin, Abramowitz, Kozak, and Foa (2001) found that independent of the severity of OCD symptoms, patients with religious obsessions had poorer insight, more perceptual distortions, and more magical ideation than did those with other types of obsessions.

Data from our clinic indicate that scrupulosity symptoms are present to some extent across the range of OCD presentations (e.g., contamination, hoarding; Nelson, Abramowitz, Whiteside, & Deacon, 2005). However, patients who primarily have severe unacceptable obsessional thoughts seem to evidence more religious symptoms than those reporting primary contamination symptoms. Scrupulosity is also associated with increased depressive and anxious symptoms (Nelson et al., 2005). Considering that scrupulosity involves the perception of sin, violation of one's moral standards, and fear of punishment (e.g., from God), it is not surprising that religious obsessions are experienced as highly distressing and anxiety evoking.

Case Vignettes

Peter was a 33-year-old Mormon who was employed as a sales representative with a pharmaceutical company. He described being tormented by one particular obsessional doubt that began following an incident four years earlier during which he had obtained an erection while embracing his girlfriend, Sue. Although both Peter and Sue were fully clothed during the embrace (and there was no ejaculation), Peter had become obsessed with the possibility that he had impregnated Sue, who may have subsequently (a) aborted the unborn child or (b) raised this child to be agnostic. Peter engaged in compulsive reassurance seeking with fertility specialists to ascertain whether a pregnancy could have taken place. He also repeatedly telephoned Sue (whom he no longer dated) to ask questions about her lifestyle and checked with Sue's work supervisor to make sure she had not missed any days for maternity leave. He had even checked local hospital admission records. Peter believed that if he ignored any opportunity to find out whether there was a pregnancy, he was acting sinfully.

Paul was a 36-year-old unmarried Catholic man who lived alone. Although he had graduated college with a degree in engineering, he reported that he was "barely getting by" in his job as an environmental engineer. Paul had been taking 20 mg/day of clomipramine for more than 10 years at the time of his evaluation; yet, this medication had not been effective in reducing his OCD symptoms. Paul's obsessions included persistent unwanted sexual thoughts that occurred whenever he saw any sort of religious icon. For example, if he saw a cross, he would think "could I insert this in my rectum?" The sight of his priest evoked unwanted explicit images of homosexual behavior between the priest and a specific young boy that attended the congregation. Other stimuli, including the church itself, bibles, and even the name "Jesus," evoked unwanted thoughts. Paul worked hard to avoid all of the external cues. He could not attend church, see the priest or certain members of the congregation, or confront any religious icons. If these stimuli were encountered, Paul engaged in prayer rituals to atone for his sinful and blasphemous thoughts. He had experienced the cognitive and affective symptoms of depression and had gained a significant amount of weight when he was referred for evaluation.

Mary, a 31-year-old wife and mother of three, was an Orthodox Jew and the daughter of an Orthodox rabbi. She worked in the home, raising her children. Mary's main OCD symptoms included recurrent, persistent doubts that she had not completed religious prayers and other rituals properly. Thus, she engaged in such behaviors repeatedly until satisfied that they had been performed correctly. For example, before eating, she felt compelled to recite (to herself) the ritual blessing 18 times (18 is a significant number in Judaism). If she experienced any stray thoughts, or if there were any distractions during the ritual, she would stop and start over from the beginning. When she was unable to finish rituals, she kept a mental note and completed them after the rest of her family had gone to bed. Frequently, Mary spent several hours each night repeating prayers and other religious rituals that she was unable to complete during the day. Mary was experiencing difficulties staying awake during the day, reported significant depressive symptoms, and expressed hopelessness and suicidal ideation.

The Basis for Considering Scrupulosity as a Subtype of OCD

Abundant clinical and research evidence supports the conceptualization of scrupulosity as a (fairly common) presentation of OCD. From a functional perspective, religious obsessions lead to increased levels of anxiety and are therefore akin to other kinds of obsessions (e.g., images of germs, aggressive thoughts) that similarly evoke anxiety. Moreover, the use of repeated praying, reassurance seeking, and excessive performance of religious behaviors serves to reduce scrupulous doubts, just as compulsive hand-washing and checking reduce fears of contamination and of responsibility for harm.

Other evidence comes from the high rate of religious symptoms among patients with OCD. Foa and Kozak (1995) identified religion as the fifth most common obsessional theme in a sample of 425 individuals with OCD (5.9% of these patients endorsed religion as central to their obsessional fears). Antony, Downie, and Swinson (1998) found that 24.2 percent of a sample of 182 adults and adolescents with OCD reported obsessions having to do with religion. As discussed, there is also evidence that the presence of religious themes in OCD is associated with membership in religious groups. That is, strictly religious patients often describe religious themes to their obsessions and rituals (Rasmussen & Tsuang, 1986), and patients with religious obsessions and compulsions tend to be more religious than those without these kinds of symptoms (Steketee, Quay, & White, 1991). On a more specific level, Khanna and Channabasavanna (1988) noted a large proportion of symptoms related to contamination and washing among Hindus with OCD, and commented that Indian culture emphasizes issues of purity and cleanliness. Others have described similar relationships between the presentation of OCD symptoms and religious practices/beliefs in orthodox Jews (Greenberg, 1987) and Muslims (Okasha et al., 1994).

In comparison to OCD patients without religious obsessions, those with scrupulosity endorse a broader range of obsessional themes but not necessarily more time spent, interference, or distress associated with such symptoms (Tek & Ulug, 2001). Consistent with this result, a growing number of factor and cluster analytic studies on the structure of obsessive-compulsive symptoms indicate that religious obsessions co-occur with sexual, violent, and somatic obsessions (e.g., Mataix-Cols, Rosario-Campos, & Leckman, 2005; McKay et al., 2004). Thus, there appears to be sufficient clinical and empirical support for conceptualizing scrupulosity as a form of OCD.

Theoretical Model

Neurobiological and psychological theories of OCD have been subjected to much empirical testing in recent years. Biological models mainly implicate abnormally functioning brain structures (e.g., the caudate) and neurotransmitter systems (i.e., serotonin) and have been elucidated elsewhere (Barr, Goodman, & Price, 1993). Although there is preliminary data suggesting that different types of OCD symptoms are associated with different neurobiological processes (Mataix-Cols et al., 2005), there is little definitive evidence of specific neuropsychiatric correlates of scrupulosity. In fact, one of the limitations of biological models of OCD is that they are largely void of content and therefore cannot account for why one patient might experience religious obsessions whereas another is obsessed with contamination.

In contrast, contemporary psychological theories of OCD view the disorder as arising from maladaptive cognitive and behavioral responses to otherwise nondangerous stimuli, including intrusive unwanted thoughts, images, and impulses. This cognitive-behavioral approach (elaborated on in Salkovskis, 1999; and in chapter 5 of this volume) can account for differences in the themes of obsessions and compulsions within and between patients and can be applied easily as a conceptual model of scrupulosity, as is described next.

To begin with, intrusive thoughts (i.e., thoughts, images, and impulses that encroach into consciousness) that are contrary to one's belief system are normal experiences for most everyone (e.g., Rachman & de Silva, 1978). Examples include doubts about having made terrible mistakes, images of loved ones being hurt or killed, impulses to harm loved ones or property, unacceptable thoughts about "impure" sexual behavior, and images of germs. Even thoughts and doubts that run contrary to religious beliefs are common experiences (e.g., "What if God doesn't exist?"; Rachman & de Silva, 1978). The cognitive-behavioral model proposes that such normal intrusions develop into clinical obsessions if the person believes that these intrusions are personally significant or threatening. For example, most people who experience a sexual intrusion while in church or synagogue would not be upset about it. Consequently, the thought might be ignored (or mentally elaborated on depending on mood state). However, if the person believes that *thinking sexual thoughts in church is a sign of immorality,* and that he or she *can and should control his or her thoughts,* this experience will evoke distress and motivate the person to suppress or neutralize the thought in an effort to prevent any harmful consequences (e.g., divine punishment).

Avoidance behavior and compulsive rituals such as excessive repetition of prayers, confessions, and religious rites that are performed in response to intrusive thoughts are therefore conceptualized as maladaptive efforts to deal with intrusions. These behaviors are counterproductive in several ways. First, because they temporarily provide a reduction in obsessional distress, such strategies are negatively reinforced and evolve into strong patterns that can consume substantial time and effort. Second, because they reduce anxiety in the short term, avoidance and rituals prevent the natural abatement of the intrusion and the associated fear response that typically occur when individuals remain exposed to feared situations for a long time. Third, avoidance and rituals lead to an increase in the frequency of obsessions by serving as reminders of obsessional intrusions and thereby triggering their reoccurrence. Attempts at distraction and suppressing unwanted intrusions may paradoxically increase the frequency of the intrusion (leading to obsessional preoccupation), possibly because the distracters become reminders (retrieval cues) of the intrusions.

To summarize, when a person appraises an otherwise normally occurring religious intrusion as overly meaningful or significant, he or she becomes distressed and attempts to remove the intrusion and prevent disastrous consequences. This paradoxically increases the frequency of intrusions. Thus, the intrusions escalate into persistent and distressing clinical obsessions. Avoidance and rituals, which are performed to escape from obsessional distress, develop into strong habits that paradoxically maintain the intrusions and prevent the self-correction of the mistaken appraisals. Essentially, scrupulosity can be conceptualized as a problem to trying too hard to thwart or control otherwise normal thoughts, doubts, images, and impulses.

Given this theoretical model, it is not surprising that some experts have speculated that religious orthodoxy plays a contributing role in the development of this form of OCD. Indeed, some religious doctrines foster beliefs about the importance of, and need to control, certain types of thoughts—a very difficult (if not impossible) task for humans (e.g., Wegner, 1994). Consider the *Sermon on the Mount,* in which Jesus cautions, "You have heard that it was said 'you shall not commit adultery'; but I say to you, that everyone who looks on a woman to lust for her has committed adultery with her already in his heart" (Matthew 5:27–28; New American Standard Version). This passage exemplifies the position that thoughts and actions are morally equivalent. Research suggests that many Christian people incorporate this doctrine into their belief system. For example, Cohen and Rozin (2001) found that Christians rated thoughts about personally unacceptable behavior as highly immoral, equivalent to the *intent* to perform such behavior, likely to be acted on, and needing to be controlled.

Empirical research indicates that certain OCD-relevant cognitive styles are related to religiosity (i.e., strength of religious devotion). For example, greater religiosity was associated with an exaggerated sense of responsibility, perfectionism, and dysfunctional beliefs about the importance of, and need to control, intrusive thoughts among Catholics (Sica, Novara, & Sanavio, 2002) and among Protestants (Abramowitz et al., 2004). Rassin and Koster (2003) found that religiosity was positively correlated with the belief that thoughts (even involuntary ones) are the moral equivalent of actions. Collectively, these findings suggest possible relationships between religiosity, scrupulosity, and maladaptive cognitive processes in OCD.

Treatment

The treatment of patients with scrupulosity should involve methods similar to those used in the treatment of other presentations of OCD. Consistent evidence suggests that cognitive-behavior therapy (CBT) using exposure and response prevention is the most effective intervention for OCD (e.g., Foa et al., 2005; for a review, see Abramowitz, 2006). Serotonergic medications (e.g., sertraline) are also helpful in many cases; yet, response to medication is somewhat more variable than with CBT. Because scrupulosity presents particular challenges to the use of exposure-based CBT, this chapter focuses on tailoring this treatment for such patients. The rationale behind the use of exposure and response prevention is that prolonged confrontation with obsessional stimuli weakens inappropriate anxiety associated with obsessional cues; and refraining from rituals reduces the urge to engage in compulsive behavior when confronted with obsessional fear.

As with other types of obsessions, exposure tasks for religious obsessions should incorporate deliberately engaging in behaviors (including thinking unacceptable thoughts) that the patient perceives as blasphemous or immoral but which are not necessarily condemned by religious authorities. For example, a patient who experiences unwanted blasphemous thoughts while reading the Bible should practice reading the Bible. One who avoids places of worship, books about atheism, and other religious icons that evoke unwanted intrusions should confront these stimuli. Unwanted, distressing ideas, such as images of Jesus masturbating on the cross, doubts about God's existence, and ideas of desecrating religious artifacts or places of worship, can be confronted in imagination. Of course, the nature of these tasks requires that the patient be familiar with, and accept, the rationale for exposure. If the reason for engaging in these *seemingly* sinful exercises is not clear to the patient, he or she may view CBT as an assault on his or her religion. Suggestions for helping scrupulous patients embrace exposure are provided in the section on troubleshooting.

With respect to response prevention, patients with scrupulosity often require assistance with differentiating between healthy religious behavior, on the one hand, and compulsive rituals (i.e., religious behaviors performed in response to obsessional fears), on the other. Whereas the former need not be targeted in response prevention, the latter should be dropped. The dialogue illustrates one method of helping the patient to identify how scrupulous behavior is counterproductive.

> *Therapist:* It sounds like you often repeat prayers to get rid of unwanted sexual thoughts.
> *Patient:* Yes. I need to call on God to save me from my immoral thoughts.
> *Therapist:* And what effect does your praying have? How well does it make the thoughts go away?
> *Patient:* It doesn't work too well. I'm *here,* aren't I?
> *Therapist:* Can you explain what you mean?
> *Patient:* I'm always praying to stop the thoughts, but I'm still having these terrible thoughts as much as ever.
> *Therapist:* So what you're saying is that, despite all your praying, the obsessions persist. What do you think that says about praying as a strategy for managing obsessional thoughts?
> *Patient:* (Thinks to himself). I never looked at it *that* way before.
> *Therapist:* I know that prayer is important for you and that it makes you feel closer to God. But because you are telling me that praying *about the obsessions* hasn't worked very well, would you consider learning a different strategy when it comes to dealing with these thoughts?
> *Patient:* Well, Father McKay did say that I pray too much about the wrong things. Maybe he was right.

Allowing the patient to take the lead in sorting out which religious behaviors are OCD symptoms and which are not is helpful. Religious behavior motivated by obsessional thoughts is not technically "religious"—such behavior is "fear based" rather than "faith based." Therefore, effective treatment will help the patient practice religion in a healthier way (without obsessive fear).

The assistance of family members and religious authorities who can reinforce the distinction between healthy and unhealthy religious practice is often necessary. Of course, such individuals must also be educated about the rationale for exposure and response prevention.

Case Vignette

Ken, a devout Catholic, was on leave from his job as a physician's assistant in a large medical center. He was unmarried and 36 when he presented for treatment, yet had been experiencing OCD symptoms since he was a teenager. These symptoms interfered with his work, as well as with his leisure and social activities. Ken entered our twice-weekly CBT program for OCD that consisted of 15 sessions (90 minutes each) over the course of eight weeks. During the first two sessions, detailed information about situations that evoked Ken's obsessional distress was gathered. Educational materials about the cognitive-behavioral conceptualization of religious OCD symptoms and the rationale for exposure and response prevention were also discussed in the context of Ken's religious background.

Ken's obsessional fear was evoked by uncertainty about whether he had committed sins and would go to hell. He viewed himself as a representative of the Catholic Church, yet often doubted whether he had indeed taken "the moral high ground" and adhered to "the requirements of Catholic law," especially in situations that presented moral ambiguity. To resolve uncertainty regarding his behavior, Ken engaged in excessive reassurance seeking by mentally reviewing his behavior, referring to the Bible, and asking others (e.g., priests, relatives) for assurances. Ken sometimes even put his own safety in jeopardy to do what he viewed as religious obligations to help others (e.g., picking up hitchhikers). He was also afraid of cursing, and avoiding using certain words such as "choice" and "molest" for fear that they would be taken out of context and result in the appearance that he was defaming God or the church. He worried a great deal about supporting "the Devil's" causes, and therefore refrained from viewing pornography (including items not typically regarded as pornography; e.g., Victoria's Secret catalogs) seeing Hollywood-made movies, and buying products made by companies that he felt had a "liberal agenda." Interestingly, Ken had good insight into the senselessness of his OCD symptoms and recognized that his fear and avoidance were excessive. He knew other Catholics that, without any concern, engaged in behaviors that he avoided. Ken, however, maintained a strong fear of punishment from God.

The intent of treatment was not to change Ken's religious orthodoxy but merely to weaken the fear response that had become associated with the various religious and moral doubts and uncertainties of everyday life. Therefore, exposure practices involved Ken deliberately behaving in ways he misunderstood to be amoral, sinful, and worthy of punishment from God, but that really were not such infractions. Response prevention entailed refraining from any behavior he previously used to escape the uncertainty (e.g., mentally reviewing events or seeking reassurances from clergy that his behavior was acceptable).

Following a discussion of the treatment, Ken wished to visit his priest once more to make sure that therapy was acceptable under Catholic law. However, because Ken had been given the all clear by this priest to proceed with exposure therapy some months ago, another visit would constitute a reassurance-seeking ritual and therefore this was discouraged. Ken agreed not to contact his priest during treatment.

Ken also became concerned that doing these exposure tasks might "corrupt" him over time and lead to his becoming an atheist. Rather than reassure Ken that this would not happen (as this would relieve him of uncertainty), the therapist pointed out this subtle attempt to gain reassurance and explained how answering questions about risk would interfere with the goal of learning to manage uncertainty. Instead, the discussion focused on the kind of person that Ken was, using Socratic dialogue to lead Ken to conclude that such a transformation was highly unlikely and therefore worth the risk in overcoming OCD.

Ken's exposure hierarchy of situations that evoked uncertainty and anxiety about sin and punishment appears in Table 11.1. Each item was ranked on a scale from 0 to 100 in terms of how much distress it would provoke. Response prevention for Ken involved refraining from reassurance seeking, mental reviewing, or clarifying his behavior with others. Ken agreed to this plan and understood its theoretical rationale.

In addition to exposure to fear cues, Ken engaged in imaginal exposure to feared consequences. For example, after he watched a Hollywood movie, Ken said that he had discussed the move with a neighbor who said that she was going to see the film herself. Ken became fearful that he was "corrupting" others by influencing them to support Hollywood (which Ken considered a liberal establishment) and that he would be punished (i.e., damned to hell). Therefore, this was incorporated into imaginal exposure as follows:

You're wondering whether or not Sarah is really going to see the movie, and the uncertainty is making you very anxious. You desperately want to explain that you don't watch Hollywood movies because the money goes to a liberal establishment that supports abortion rights and opposes school prayer. You want to discourage her from doing the same. God will send you to hell for being such a poor influence unless you stop her. As you're walking to your mailbox, you see Sarah. She's talking with several other people and you fear she may have seen the movie and recommended all of these other people to see it too. Maybe you've corrupted lots of people. You have to tell them all not to see the movie. But as you get closer, they go into Sarah's house. Now you'll never know whether other people saw the movie. The uncertainty is unbearable and you can't think about or do anything else but worry about going to hell.

Ken was tentative about completing early exposures, and he avoided doing his first home assignments. An example of subtle avoidance occurred at Session 3 when he reported that before each exposure, he was praying for God to understand that he was asked to perform sinful behavior *as part of his treatment*. Upon discussion with the therapist, Ken understood that this prayer was functioning to alleviate his uncertainty about punishment and therefore preventing him from benefiting from exposure exercises designed to evoke distress and uncertainty. He agreed to stop all prayers of this type during treatment.

Table 11.1. *Ken's Exposure Therapy Hierarchy*

Situation	Discomfort (0–100)
1. Give inaccurate negative feedback on a restaurant "comment card"	45
2. Leave shopping cart in parking lot of the grocery store	52
3. Laugh at someone else's tasteless jokes	58
4. Purposely make "wrong number" phone calls	60
5. See a Hollywood movie	65
6. Suggest, to a group of co-workers, leaving a low tip at a restaurant	70
7. Give the "middle finger" in jest to friend or co-worker	93
8. Use ambiguous language that could be mistaken as morally relevant (e.g., "Let's do it," "You have the right to choose")	94
9. Watch pornographic film	95
10. Ambiguously criticize the Catholic Church (e.g., "I feel the Catholic Church should rethink its position on some issues")	98

After a few successful exposure sessions, Ken took greater initiative in treatment. After three weeks, he could refrain from rituals 90 percent of the time as indicated by self-monitoring forms. By the fifth week, he reported taking advantage of opportunities at work to put himself in situations he once viewed as compromising his salvation (e.g., using previously avoided terms such as *molest* and *choice*).

Although considerable improvement in OCD symptoms and related impairment were evident, complete remission was not obtained. The final treatment session involved a discussion of how Ken could maintain his improvement by continuing to confront situations that he would have avoided because of fear of damnation. He was told that occasional obsessional thoughts and doubts would probably occur, but with continued practice, his conditioned fear would be extinguished. Ken reported an increase in hopefulness and was interested in meeting more people and enrolling in evening classes at a local community college. He also took more frequent bike rides and began exercising at a health club with the goal of running in a 5K race six months following treatment. At the 15th session, Ken reported that he wanted to get back to work and had initiated the process for doing so. He also felt more comfortable with practicing his Catholicism out of *faith,* as opposed to *fear.*

Troubleshooting

Conducting CBT with religious patients presents unique challenges. Differences between normal and pathological religious practice must be clarified, and patients should understand that the purpose of treatment is to restore normal religiosity. Moreover, a clear explanation of how exposure is consistent with this goal seems crucial for fostering a successful therapeutic relationship and maintaining high motivation. This section describes some strategies for sidestepping potential problems.

Patients with religious obsessions often hold catastrophic views of God and sin that are inconsistent with even their own religious doctrine. Whereas most modern religions teach that God loves all people unconditionally and that one may repent for sins and be forgiven, those with religious obsessions often view God as petulant, easily angered, and vengeful. Naturally, such beliefs lead to practicing religion out of fear of punishment. It is worth pointing this out to patients so that they can see how their extremely fearful view of God departs from what other members of their denomination (e.g., family and clergy) believe. An important message is that according to most religions, people will not lose God's love unless they (a) intentionally decide to do things they know are evil (e.g., murder someone) and (b) remain remorseless. Therefore, *unwanted* thoughts, ideas, or images do not count as violations. The therapist can also point out that if God created the human mind, then God surely understands that people sometimes have thoughts that are contrary to their true beliefs. The case should be made that doing ERP will help the patient become a more faithful follower of his or her religion because it will help him or her trust God, rather than being fearful.

People with religious obsessions often narrowly focus on trivial violations of religious doctrine, while often overlooking more important religious commandments (Greenberg, 1984). For example, Ken (introduced earlier) was fearful that he would be punished if he merely *heard* his parents discuss a disagreement they had with the Catholic Church. However, he thought nothing of cursing at his parents (a violation of the Fifth Commandment to *honor thy mother and father*) in his attempt to convince them that the church is perfect. Ken benefited from a discussion of this issue, and he learned that the purpose of CBT was to teach him how to manage his obsessional fears in a similar way.

Informing patients that for centuries theologians have prescribed strategies similar to exposure and response prevention for people with religious obsessions is another way to encourage individuals with such symptoms to undertake treatment (Ciarrocchi, 1995). From a theological perspective, scrupulosity and obsessional fear puts one in danger of sin by pride, self-will, and disobedience. The Jewish *Talmud* (Written Law) also considers religious acts performed out of the fear of punishment to be antithetical (*Sotah*, 22b). Training manuals for pastoral counselors specifically recommend suggesting to people with scrupulosity that they purposely act *contrary* to their scruples. Specific guidelines include (a) emulating conscientious people even if doing so might violate the rule in question, (b) allowing oneself to purposely evoke "impure" thoughts, and (c) disavowing oneself of repetitive confessions and redundant prayer (Jones & Adleman, 1959). Readers will note the similarities between these guidelines and the components of CBT. Ciarrocchi's (1995) self-help book on scrupulosity (*The Doubting Disease: Help for Scrupulosity and Religious Compulsions*) presents an excellent discussion of this topic and is a useful resource for helping strictly religious patients who are highly ambivalent about engaging in exposure therapy.

As a last resort, the patient may consult with a religious authority (such as a priest, rabbi, or pastor) regarding what to do for exposure. The specific exposure situations may then be chosen on the basis of this guidance. If, at all possible, the therapist should see that such advice is obtained from a more liberal authority to avoid misunderstandings and reinforcement of the patient's fears. It should also be agreed that the authority's suggestions (no matter how vague) would be followed without the pursuit of further advice or second opinions (as this would constitute reassurance seeking). If exposure can be conducted by relying on what religious authorities have *previously* told the patient (i.e., without consultation during treatment), this is ideal.

Deciding on the specific situations for exposure is also an important issue, and this process should be consistent with the goals previously described. Instructions to flagrantly violate religious laws are neither appropriate nor necessary to reduce pathological fears of sin. Patients with scrupulosity fear they *might* have sinned. Therefore, exposure should entail situations that evoke doubts and uncertainty about sin. As an analogous situation, consider an OCD patient with the obsession that that her food might be contaminated with urine. Her pathological anxiety involves uncertainty over whether her food is contaminated, not what to do when there is urine on food. Therefore, rather than actually putting urine on her food, exposure would involve taking low-level risks such as eating meals in bathrooms.

As with any presentation of OCD, therapists should be aware of scrupulous patients' overt and subtle forms of avoidance, including the use of prayers to absolve responsibility (as in Ken's case). Avoidance prohibits the evocation of anxiety during exposure, which foils the exercise and prevents the modification of fear. Persistent reassurance seeking by patients looking to avoid distress may be addressed by explaining that to get better from OCD requires taking some risks, which, in the end, will be worth the temporary anxiety. Another hurdle that often arises with exposure therapy is incomplete abstinence from ritualizing. It is important, in such instances, to discuss these lapses and provide the patient with supportive encouragement. Patients who perceive their therapist as an understanding ally, as opposed to a disciplinarian, will more likely respond favorably. Finally, for patients who fail to habituate during exposure, it may be useful to practice generalizing habituation from previous exposure before moving on to more difficult hierarchy items.

REFERENCES

Abramowitz, J. (2006). *Understanding and treating obsessive-compulsive disorder: a cognitive-behavioral approach*. Mahwah, NJ: Lawrence Erlbaum Associates.

Abramowitz, J. S., Deacon, B. J., Woods, C. M., & Tolin, D. F. (2004). Association between protestant religiosity and obsessive-compulsive symptoms and cognitions. *Depression and Anxiety, 20*, 70–76.

Abramowitz, J. S., Huppert, J. D., Cohen, A. B., Tolin, D. F., & Cahill, S. P. (2002). Religious obsessions and compulsions in a non-clinical sample: The Penn Inventory of Scrupulosity (PIOS). *Behaviour Research and Therapy, 40*, 825–838.

Antony, M. M., Downie, F., & Swinson, R. P. (1998). Diagnostic issues and epidemiology in obsessive-compulsive disorder. In R. P. Swinson & A. M. Martin (Eds.) *Obsessive-compulsive disorder: Theory, research, and treatment* (pp. 3–32). New York: Guilford Press.

Barr, L. C., Goodman, W. K., & Price, L. H. (1993). The serotonin hypothesis of obsessive-compulsive disorder. *International Clinical Psychopharmacology, 8* (Suppl. 2), 79–82.

Ciarrocchi, J. W. (1995). *The doubting disease*. New York: Paulist Press.

Cohen, A., & Rozin, P. (2001). Religion and the morality of mentality. *Journal of Personality and Social Psychology, 81*, 697–710.

Foa, E. B., & Kozak, M. J. (1995). DSM-IV field trial: Obsessive-compulsive disorder. *American Journal of Psychiatry, 152*, 90–96.

Foa, E. B., Liebowitz, M. R., Kozak, M. J., Davies, S., Campeas, R., Franklin, M. E., et al. (2005). Treatment of obsessive-compulsive disorder by exposure and ritual prevention, clomipramine, and their combination: A randomized, placebo controlled trial. *American Journal of Psychiatry, 162*, 151–161.

Greenberg, D. (1984). Are religious compulsions religious or compulsive: A phenomenological study. *American Journal of Psychotherapy, 38*, 524–532.

Greenberg, D. (1987). The behavioral treatment of religious compulsions. *Psychology and Judaism, 11*, 41–47.

Greenberg, D., & Witztum, E. (2001). Treatment of strictly religious patients. In M. T. Pato & J. Zohar (Eds.), *Current treatments of obsessive-compulsive disorder* (pp. 157–172). Washington, DC, US: American Psychiatric Association.

Jones, H., & Adleman, U. (1959). *Moral theology*. Westminster, MD: Newman Press.

Khanna, S., & Channabasavanna, S. M. (1988). Phenomenology of obsessions in obsessive-compulsive neurosis. *Psychopathology, 21*, 12–18.

Mataix-Cols, D., Rosario-Campos, M. C., & Leckman, J. F. (2005). A multidimensional model of obsessive-compulsive disorder. *American Journal of Psychiatry, 162*, 228–238.

McKay, D., Abramowtiz, J. S., Calamari, J. E., Kyrios, M., Radomsky, A., Sookman, D., et al. (2004). A critical evaluation of obsessive-compulsive disorder subtypes: Symptoms versus mechanisms. *Clinical Psychology Review, 24*, 283–313.

Nelson, E., Abramowitz, J. S., Whiteside, S. P., & Deacon, B. J. (2006). Scrupulosity in patients with obsessive-compulsive disorder: Relationship to clinical and cognitive phenomena. *Journal of Anxiety Disorders, 20*, 1071–1086.

Okasha, A., Saad, A., Khalil, A., El-Dawla, A., & Yehia, N. (1994). Phenomenology of obsessive-compulsive disorder: A transcultural study. *Comprehensive Psychiatry, 35,* 191–197.

Rasmussen, S., & Tsuang, M. 1986. Clinical characteristics and family history in DSM-III obsessive-compulsive disorder. *American Journal of Psychiatry, 143,* 317–322.

Steketee, G., Quay, S., & White, K. (1991). Religion and guilt in OCD patients. *Journal of Anxiety Disorders, 5,* 359–367.

Rachman, S. J., & de Silva, P. (1978). Abnormal and normal obsessions. *Behaviour Research and Therapy, 16,* 233–238.

Rassin, E., & Koster, E. (2003). The correlation between thought-action fusion and religiosity in a normal sample. *Behaviour Research and Therapy, 41,* 361–368.

Salkovskis, P. M. (1999). Understanding and treating obsessive-compulsive disorder. *Behaviour Research and Therapy, 37,* S29–S52.

Sica, C., Novara, C., & Sanavio, E. (2002). Religiousness and obsessive-compulsive cognitions and symptoms in an Italian population. *Behaviour Research and Therapy, 40,* 813–823.

Tek, C., & Ulug, B. (2001). Religiosity and religious obsessions in obsessive-compulsive disorder. *Psychiatry Research, 104,* 99–108.

Tolin, D., Abramowitz, J., Kozak, M., & Foa, E. (2001). Fixity of belief, perceptual aberration, and magical ideation in obsessive-compulsive disorder, *Journal of Anxiety Disorders, 15,* 501–510.

Wegner, D. (1994). *White bears and other unwanted thoughts: suppression, obsession, and the psychology of mental control.* New York: Guilford.

Part II / Problems Related to Obsessive-Compulsive Disorder

The chapters in part 1 of this volume cover various distinct but related *subtypes* or *dimensions* of obsessive-compulsive disorder (OCD). In doing so, they highlight the heterogeneity of this disorder and raise the possibility that what we currently call OCD is in fact a set of separate but closely related conditions. But in contrast to *splitting* OCD into subtypes, some authors have focused on *lumping* with OCD a number of disorders from entirely different diagnostic categories (i.e., the so-called obsessive-compulsive spectrum disorders). The chapters in part 2 consider the ways in which OCD might be grouped or associated with other disorders on the basis of shared similarities. Taken together, parts 1 and 2 reflect an essential tension in psychiatric classification concerning the merits of splitting disorders into separate entities versus grouping them together. Both approaches can be useful for understanding and treating psychopathology, depending on the way in which disorders are grouped together or split into separate entities.

The relative emphasis on *lumping* versus *splitting* represents a general theme in biological taxonomy. This distinction harkens back to the folk observation that there are two kinds of people in the world: those who believe there are two kinds of people in the world and those who do not. Like biological taxonomy, psychiatric nosology has evidenced periods of both lumping and splitting. With its emphasis on psychoanalytic theory as an organizing framework, DSM-II lumped a number of conditions under the general concept of neurosis (American Psychiatric Association, 1968). With the advent of DSM-III and the ensuing revisions, we have witnessed a general trend of splitting within official psychiatric diagnoses over the past 20 years (American Psychiatric Association, 1980, 1987, 1994, 2000). For example, the DSM-II diagnosis of anxiety neurosis was abandoned in favor of several more specific diagnoses, such as panic disorder, specific phobia, and generalized anxiety disorder. Numerous other examples of the splitting trend are noted when one compares DSM-II with DSM-IV.

Whether one prefers lumping to splitting may be a matter of mere personal preference, but at least some critics of the last three editions of the *Diagnostic and Statistical Manual of Mental Disorders* have argued that the splitting trend is problematic, with finer-grained distinctions bearing little evidence of organizing principles of classification (Houts, 2000; Kutchins & Kirk, 1997). Therefore, when lumpers come along with empirically driven proposals to aggregate existing diagnoses into larger categories, it is worth attending to their proposals. For example, two factor-analytic studies of symptom co-occurrence within the context of epidemiologic studies, one in the United States and one in the Netherlands, have reported that one needs only three underlying dimensions to describe nine different DSM-III-R diagnoses (Krueger, 1999; Vollebergh et al., 2001). These rather remarkable findings suggest that at the symptom level one needs only three broad constructs to account for the manner in which symptoms co-occur in large population-wide samples. Such empirical lumping helps explain the comorbidity of mood disorders and anxiety disorders and also raises questions about the wisdom of continuing to conduct research as if, for example, generalized anxiety disorder is uniquely different from major depression. A similar approach to lumping disorders has been proposed by those who advocate for an obsessive-compulsive spectrum.

As the chapters in this part illustrate, advocates of the obsessive-compulsive spectrum have identified a number of psychiatric conditions that, because they appear to share some characteristics with OCD, seem to belong to a family of related disorders (Hollander, Friedberg, Wasserman, Yeh, & Iyengar, 2005). Spectrum proponents point to several features that might link the obsessive-compulsive spectrum disorders, including the presence of repetitive thoughts and behaviors, high rates of comorbidity, common associated features (i.e., demographics), related neurobiological etiologies, and response to behavioral and pharmacologic treatments (Hollander et al., 2005). In their delineation of the OCD spectrum, Hollander and colleagues (2005) include a variety of disorders representing numerous forms of psychopathology. Among this list are impulse-control disorders (e.g., trichotillomania), neurologic disorders (e.g., Tourette syndrome), and disorders featuring preoccupation with one's own body or appearance (e.g., body dysmorphic disorder).

Although the idea of an OCD spectrum may have some popular appeal, experts on the nature and treatment of OCD disagree regarding the range and scope of the spectrum (and even whether such a spectrum exists). Some, for example, have pointed out critical flaws in the reasoning behind the spectrum approach, arguing that criteria for inclusion are overinclusive (e.g., Abramowitz & Deacon, 2005). Each of the chapters in part 2 of this book (with the exception of chapter 12, which presents an overview of the OCD spectrum approach) focuses on a disorder that has in one way or another been considered as related to OCD (i.e., an obsessive-compulsive spectrum disorder, or OCSD). In addition to discussing the nature and treatment of each condition, contributors have drawn conclusions—on the basis of clinical and research data—regarding each particular condition's relationship to OCD (i.e., the extent to which it represents an OCSD). The reader will note that authors have described different approaches to determining a disorder's status with regard to the putative spectrum, once again raising questions about how best to classify psychiatric disorders.

REFERENCES

Abramowitz, J. S., & Deacon, B. J. (2005). The OC spectrum: A closer look at the arguments and the data. In. J. S. Abramowitz & A. C. Houts (Eds.), *Concepts and controversies in obsessive-compulsive disorder* (pp. 141–149). New York: Springer.

American Psychiatric Association. (1968). *Diagnostic and statistical manual of mental disorders* (2nd ed.). Washington, DC: Author.

American Psychiatric Association. (1980). *Diagnostic and statistical manual of mental disorders* (3rd ed.). Washington, DC: Author.

American Psychiatric Association. (1987). *Diagnostic and statistical manual of mental disorders* (3rd ed., revised). Washington, DC: Author.

American Psychiatric Association. (1994). *Diagnostic and statistical manual of mental disorders* (4th ed.). Washington, DC: Author.

American Psychiatric Association. (2000). *Diagnostic and statistical manual of mental disorders* (4th ed., text revision). Washington, DC: Author.

Hollander, E., Friedberg, J., Wasserman, S., Yeh, C,-C., & Iyengar, R. (2005). The case for the OCD spectrum. In. J. S. Abramowitz & A. C. Houts (Eds.), *Concepts and controversies in obsessive-compulsive disorder* (pp. 95–118). New York: Springer.

Houts, A. C. (2000). Fifty years of psychiatric nomenclature: Reflections on the 1943 War Department Technical Bulletin, Medical 203. *Journal of Clinical Psychology, 56,* 935–967.

Krueger, R. F. (1999). The structure of common mental disorders. *Archives of General Psychiatry, 56,* 921–926.

Kutchins, H., & Kirk, S. A. (1997). *Making us crazy: DSM: The psychiatric bible and the creation of mental disorders.* New York: Free Press.

Vollebergh, W. A. M., Iedema, J., Bijl, R. V., deGraaf, R., Smit, F., & Ormel, J. (2001). The structure and stability of common mental disorders: The Nemesis study. *Archives of General Psychiatry, 58,* 597–603.

CHAPTER TWELVE

The Empirical Basis of the Obsessive-Compulsive Spectrum

Dan J. Stein, M.D., and Christine Lochner, Ph.D.

During the course of the twentieth century, several different conceptual approaches to understanding obsessive-compulsive disorder (OCD) and disorders thought to be related to OCD (i.e., OC spectrum disorders) were developed. Around the start of the century, psychoanalytic authors argued that obsessive-compulsive character (or personality) was characterized by specific mediating mechanisms, namely, a particular set of unconscious defense mechanisms (Stein & Stone, 1997). Under certain circumstances, the same set of dynamics could ultimately result in the development of obsessive-compulsive neurosis (that is, OCD), or even psychosis. These authors provided the field with rich descriptions of obsessive-compulsive phenomena and with a thought-provoking set of hypotheses. Nevertheless, little empirical support for these hypotheses has emerged, and treatments based on them have not been shown effective.

Somewhat later, a cognitive-behavioral approach to OCD emerged and emphasized the functional relationship between the different symptoms of this and related disorders. Thus, in OCD, obsessions are anxiety arousing, while compulsions are anxiety diminishing. An obsessive-compulsive spectrum disorder would be characterized by an analogous relationship between its characteristic symptoms. Body dysmorphic disorder and hypochondriasis, for example, are both characterized by intrusive cognitive concerns accompanied by increased anxiety, which then lead to repetitive behaviors (including mental actions) or avoidance in order to decrease anxiety. This utility of this approach is supported by data on the efficacy of exposure and response prevention strategies across these three disorders (Abramowitz & Deacon, 2005).

A third approach to the obsessive-compulsive spectrum has emphasized the underlying psychobiological mechanisms that are thought to produce these conditions. An important early idea was that OCD and Tourette disorder (TD) are closely related. A significant proportion of patients with OCD have tics or a history of tics, and many TD patients have OCD. Despite phenomenologic and functional differences between compulsions and tics, symptoms in OCD probands and relatives with TD are mediated by similar neurocircuitry (Moriarty et al., 1997). Further, family studies have suggested that TD is more likely in relatives of OCD probands, and vice versa, and that these relationships are mediated by genetic transmission (Pauls, Towbin, Leckman, Zahner, & Cohen, 1986). This set of studies has made a crucial contribution to the treatment of OCD, insofar as the dopamine receptor blockers previously known to be effective for tic disorders have since been shown to be useful as augmenting agents in treatment-refractory OCD (McDougle, Epperson, Pelton, Wasylink, & Price, 2000).

In addition to these three relatively narrowly defined approaches, a number of authors have taken more expansive approaches, emphasizing phenomenologic or psychobiological overlaps between OCD and a broad range of other conditions. OCD has been suggested to lie on a reward-related or affective spectrum of disorders (along with mood disorders such as depression; Blum et al., 1995; Hudson & Pope, 1990), on a compulsive-impulsive spectrum of disorders (ranging from compulsive to impulsive; Phillips, 2002; Stein & Hollander, 1993), or on a spectrum of stereotypic disorders (including trichotillomania and nail-biting; Ridley, 1994; Stein, Bouwer, & Neihaus, 1997). Researchers have also suggested that OCD is one of a range of developmental basal ganglia disorders (Palumbo, Maugham, & Kurlan, 1997), of serotonergically mediated conditions (Stein, 2001), or of the pediatric neuropsychiatric disorders associated with streptococcus (Swedo et al., 1998). Broader hypotheses may have heuristic value, but they also run the risk of being overly inclusive and inaccurate (Abramowitz & Deacon, 2005).

A crucial difficulty in defining the OC spectrum is that the underlying psychobiology of OCD remains to be fully delineated. At the same time, there have been significant advances in areas that may be relevant to understanding OCD and related conditions, and in this chapter, we focus on a number of these. Some of our thinking has been influenced by data on how putative obsessive-compulsive disorders cluster together in patients with OCD (Lochner et al., 2005). Insofar as these disorders are frequently comorbid with OCD, our approach is therefore not as all-inclusive as some. At the same time, the mechanisms that we consider are relevant to a broad range of psychopathology. This approach therefore allows for an exploration of relationships between disorders that too narrow an approach would exclude. Although somewhat speculative, the schema here will therefore provide an opportunity to examine empirical data relevant to the construct of an obsessive-compulsive spectrum of disorders.

Neurocircuitry and Neurotransmitters in OCD

Although much remains to be understood about the psychobiology of OCD, it seems clear that ventral cortical-striatal-thalamic-cortical (CSTC) circuits, which include neurons with serotonergic and dopaminergic receptors, play a key role. Evidence of the importance of this circuitry comes from studies of neurologic disorders with CSTC lesions and obsessive-compulsive symptoms, from data on neuropsychological deficits in OCD, from research on structural and functional brain imaging, and from reports on the therapeutic effects of neurosurgical disruption of CSTC circuits (Stein, 2002; Whiteside, Port, & Abramowitz, 2004). It is noteworthy that both specific pharmacotherapy and psychotherapy are able to normalize the functional neuroanatomy of OCD (Baxter et al., 1992).

Evidence of the importance of serotonergic and dopaminergic circuitry in OCD comes from pharmacologic challenge studies, from receptor imaging studies, from studies of patients with variants in serotonergic genes, and from treatment studies (Stein, 2002; Zohar & Insel, 1987). Despite this wealth of data, a weakness of the neurotransmitter hypotheses of OCD has been that studies have only found that monoaminergic systems play a role in mediating the symptoms of OCD and have not demonstrated a causal role. Nevertheless, recent genetics research has indicated that particular variants in the serotonergic system, even if rare, can play a causal role in the pathogenesis of OCD (Ozaki et al., 2003).

On the basis of this literature, it might be hypothesized that OC spectrum disorders are those that involve some degree of phenomenologic overlap and that are mediated by the same pathways. Body dysmorphic disorder, where there are intrusive concerns about imagined ugliness, and hypochondriasis (HYP), where there are anxiety-arousing concerns about medical illnesses, share some important phenomenologic features with OCD (Phillips, 2002). Further, a cluster analysis of putative OC spectrum disorders in patients with OCD found that these conditions cluster together (Lochner et al., 2005). Psychobiological data are relatively few, but some do provide support for the hypothesis of an overlap between OCD, BDD, and HYP. Thus, functional imaging data suggest at least some overlap with the neurocircuitry of OCD (Carey, Seedat, Warwick, van Heerden, & Stein, 2004). Similarly, patients with BDD have a selective response to serotonin reuptake inhibitors (Hollander et al., 1999), and those with HYP also respond to these agents (Fallon et al., 1996). Nevertheless, there are limited family data, and the genetic basis of BDD and HYP is not well studied.

In other cases, however, determining whether there is overlap in phenomenology and psychobiology with OCD can be more problematic. Obsessive-compulsive disorder is heterogeneous in that there are multiple kinds of possible symptoms and homogeneous insofar as the structure of symptoms is fairly invariant; so deciding whether there is phenomenologic overlap can be complex. In addition, CSTC pathways and monaminergic receptors mediate a wide range of different psychobiological processes, including affective (e.g., reward processing), motoric (e.g., chunking of actions), and cognitive (e.g., implicit learning) ones; thus, the OC spectrum is potentially very broad, including a wide range of psychiatric and neurologic disorders.

In this chapter, we will discuss two striatally mediated psychobiological processes that may be relevant to OCD and therefore to the obsessive-compulsive spectrum disorders: reward processing and action chunking. There has been progress in delineating the neurocircuitry and neurotransmitters that mediate these different processes, and there is some evidence that each may be relevant to understanding OCD. In the sections that follow, we argue that they may also be relevant to understanding obsessive-compulsive spectrum disorders.

Reward Processing in OCD and OC Spectrum Disorders

Over the past few decades, significant progress has been made toward understanding the psychobiology of reward processing. Animal models and functional imaging have allowed the neurocircuitry of reward processing to be delineated, and the ventral striatum plays a key role (Knutson, Fong, Adams, Varner, & Hommer, 2001). These investigations have also provided data about the particular neurotransmitters involved in mediating the processing of rewards, with dopamine playing a particularly important role (Fiorillo, Tobler, & Schultz, 2003). Such basic work has proved particularly relevant to understanding drug addiction in the clinic; patients with substance use show abnormalities in the neurocircuitry and neurotransmitters that mediate reward processing and may respond to treatments that act on these pathways (Bechara, Dolan, & Hindes, 2002; Volkow, Fowler, Wang, & Swanson, 2004).

At first blush, this work may not seem relevant to understanding OCD. Nevertheless, one way of conceptualizing OCD is in terms of the absence of a feeling of goal completion after an action is performed; people continue with their compulsions repetitively until there is finally the sense that things are now "just right." Furthermore, at the level of neurocircuitry, structural and functional imaging studies of OCD demonstrate that the ventral striatum plays an important role in mediating obsessive-compulsive symptoms (Whiteside, Port, & Abramowitz, 2004), perhaps disruption of this neurocircuitry underpins the failure of the signal that denotes goal completion. Finally, at a neurotransmitter level, dopamine is released in the ventral striatum under conditions of maximal uncertainty about subsequent reward and also appears to plays a key role in mediating the symptoms of OCD (Fiorillo et al., 2003), perhaps underpinning the continued sense of uncertainty about goal completion in OCD.

Apart from substance use disorders, what other psychiatric or obsessive-compulsive spectrum conditions are characterized by disturbances in reward processing? Reward processes are of course disrupted in mood disorders (Naranjo, Tremblay, & Busto, 2001). A number of conditions involve repetitive goal-seeking behaviors; pathological gambling (PG) and hypersexual disorder, for example, may be characterized by disturbances in the processing of rewards (Stein & Grant, 2005; Stein, Black, Shapira, & Spitzer, 2001). Finally, Tourette's disorder, and stereotypic disorders such as trichotillomania, have also been described in terms of reward deficiency by some authors (Blum et al., 1995). It turns out that in patients with OCD one cluster of putative comorbid OCD disorders comprises PG, hypersexual disorder, Tourette's, and trichotillomania (Lochner et al., 2005), again raising the question of whether these diverse disorders share some underlying psychobiological features.

These various disorders, even if sometimes called *compulsive*, differ from OCD in key phenomenologic and functional ways. PG, hypersexual disorder, and trichotillomania may involve a sense of pleasure at the time of the behavior. In contrast, depression involves an inability to feel pleasure, whereas OCD is typically characterized by anxiety-inducing obsessions and anxiety-relieving compulsions. Perhaps different kinds of disturbances in reward processing result in a spectrum of diverse reward-related disorders. In terms of their underlying neurocircuitry, OCD is characterized by increased corticostriatal activity, whereas PG, substance use disorders, and depression tend to be associated with reduced orbitofrontal activity (Volkow et al., 2004; Whiteside, Port, & Abramowitz, 2004). However, substance use disorders and OCD may both be characterized by low striatal D2 receptor availability (Denys, van der Wee, Janssen, de Geus, & Westenberg, 2004; Volkow et al., 2004) and by glutamate dysfunction (Carlsson, 2001).

Significant additional research is needed to consolidate the preliminary ideas outlined here. There is good family data that OCD and TD are related, but the data indicate that the relationships are much weaker for PG and TTM. In the case of TD, the relevant genes remain unknown, and some in which there is current interest may not be involved in reward processes per se. It may be that disruption in processes signaling goal completion is only a secondary phenomenon relevant to some subtypes of OCD and obsessive-compulsive spectrum disorders, with other striatally mediated psychobiological processes typically more pertinent.

Action Chunking in OCD and OC Spectrum Disorders

There is a growing understanding of the role of the striatum in the chunking of motor actions (Graybiel, 1998). This understanding has primarily emerged from basic laboratory studies, rather than from studies in clinical populations. Nevertheless, if there is dysfunction in the striatum, then there may be a disruption in control processes, with inappropriate release of various procedural strategies, ranging from simple stereotypies through to more complex behavioral programs.

There are many reasons for conceptualizing OCD in terms of a dysfunction in the control of procedural strategies, with inappropriate release of some behaviors and cognitions. At a phenomenologic level, OCD is characterized by sudden intrusive symptoms, by inappropriate behavioral sequences, and by evidence of behavioral and cognitive disinhibition on neuropsychological testing (Chamberlain, Blackwell, Fineberg, Robbins, & Sahakian, 2005). At a neurocircuitry level, it has been suggested that increased frontal activity in OCD may be a compensatory mechanism, allowing higher-order restraint over striatally mediated dyscontrol. Finally, the serotonin system not only plays a key role in impulse dyscontrol but also is a crucial system in the mediation of OCD symptoms (Stein, Hollander, & Liebowitz, 1993; Zohar & Insel, 1987).

Subtle forms of cognitive-affective dyscontrol or the inappropriate execution of motoric sequences may also characterize a range of psychiatric and obsessive-compulsive spectrum conditions. The impulse control disorders include intermittent explosive disorder and kleptomania, as well as a range of other disorders in the "not otherwise specified category," including compulsive shopping, Internet addiction, and so on. Disorders characterized by significant dyscontrol are also found in a range of other sections in *DSM-IV-TR*, including eating disorders, personality disorders, and pervasive developmental disorders. Dyscontrol may also be seen in general medical disorders, particularly those affecting the frontal lobe (Stein & Moeller, 2005). In patients with OCD, one cluster of comorbid OC spectrum disorders comprises intermittent explosive disorder, kleptomania, eating disorders, and stereotypic self-injurious behaviors (Lochner et al., 2005). However, the existence of an impulse control dimension within OCD means that compulsivity and impulsivity are not diametrically opposed but rather may lie on orthogonal planes.

The phenomenology of OCD is typically entirely different from that of conditions such as impulse-control disorders. In OCD, there is a strong attempt to regulate symptoms; for example, obsessions with aggressive content are very rarely enacted. At a neurocircuitry level, there is again the contrast between increased frontal activity in OCD (perhaps compensatory in nature) versus decreased frontal activity in patients with impulsive symptoms. Similarly, whereas there is some evidence of serotonergic hypersensitivity in OCD, in impulse control disorders there may be serotonergic hypofunction. Given that compulsivity and impulsivity may lie on orthogonal planes, any unidimensional contrast between increased compulsivity, frontal activity, and serotonergic function versus decreased impulse control, frontal activity, and serotonergic function, must however be oversimplified.

The possibility that striatally mediated control processes are disrupted in OCD and obsessive-compulsive spectrum disorders is a tentative hypothesis that requires much additional work. The lack of familial relationships between OCD and impulse control disorders suggests that even if there is overlap in some cognitive-affective processes, different molecular mechanisms are likely at play. Indeed, there has been relatively little evidence to date that genes thought important in impulse control disorders are involved in OCD. It is possible that disruption in control processes is a only a secondary phenomenon relevant to some subtypes of OCD and obsessive-compulsive spectrum disorders, with other striatally mediated psychobiological processes more important in most cases.

Conclusion

We have suggested here that perhaps there is not one obsessive-compulsive spectrum of disorder, but rather there may be a number of different dimensions along which obsessive-compulsive-related disorders lie. Phenomenologic data on obsessive-compulsive spectrum disorders in patients with OCD suggest these conditions fall into at least three clusters, and psychobiological data can be used to suggest tentatively that these involve disruption in reward processes or failures in control processes.

Reward processing and control of procedural strategies are not only likely to be influenced by genotype but also by environment. Early exposure to trauma results in disruption of striatal architecture (Martin, Spicer, Lewis, Gluck, & Cork, 1991), sensitization of the dopaminergic system (Thierry, Tassin, Blanc, & Glowinski, 1976), and increased vulnerability to subsequent psychopathology (Seedat & Stein, 2000). The role of trauma in the pathogenesis of OCD has received relatively little study (Lochner et al., 2002) and may well deserve additional attention. Similarly, stressful conditions may exacerbate some obsessive-compulsive-related conditions, including some of those discussed in this section.

One advantage of conceptualizing two disorders can be in raising the question of whether a similar treatment is effective for both conditions. However, the approach taken in this chapter is somewhat different. We have argued that although a particular process may be relevant to OCD and OC conditions, it may be disrupted in different ways in various conditions that fall on a spectrum. If this is the case, then different OC spectrum disorders may well require different treatments. Thus, while OCD and trichotillomania can be conceptualized in terms of the pathological release of motor programs, they may require rather different treatment approaches.

Furthermore, in the absence of a detailed understanding of the psychobiology of OCD and related disorders, conceptualizations of OC spectrum disorders can only remain preliminary in nature. The involvement of CTSTC circuitry in OCD suggests that OC spectrum disorders may be characterized by involvement of these paths. However, striatal circuits mediate many different functions (including reward processes) and are involved in many disorders. Similarly, the involvement of serotonergic neurotransmitters in OCD suggests that these are central to defining spectrum disorders. But again, serotonin plays a role in many functions (including impulse control), and mediates many different disorders. It is only recently that the first evidence that 5-HT may play a causal role in OCD was established (Ozaki et al., 2003).

Much work remains to be done, therefore, to delineate optimally the obsessive-compulsive spectrum of disorders. Nevertheless, significant progress has been made to date. There is empirical data demonstrating involvement of CSTC circuitry in a number of putative obsessive-compulsive spectrum disorders (Stein, 2001). Similarly there is data demonstrating that a selective response to serotonin reuptake inhibitors is seen in a range of these different spectrum disorders. As further progress is made in understanding the cognitive-affective neuroscience of OCD and related conditions, our constructs about obsessive-compulsive spectrum disorders will become increasingly sharp.

REFERENCES

Abramowitz, J. S., & Deacon, B. J. (2005). The OC spectrum: A closer look at the arguments and the data. In J. S. Abramowitz & A. C. Houts (Eds.), *Concepts and controversies in obsessive-compulsive disorder* (pp. 41–49). New York: Springer.

Baxter, L. R., Schwartz, J. M., Bergman, K. S., Szuba, M. P., Guze, B. H., Mazziotta, J.C., et al. (1992). Caudate glucose metabolic rate changes with both drug and behavior therapy for OCD. *Archives of General Psychiatry, 49,* 681–689.

Blum, K., Sheridan, P. J., Wood, R. C., Braverman E. R., Chen T. J., Comings D. E. (1995). Dopamine D2 receptor gene variants: association and linkage studies in impulsive-addictive-compulsive behavior. *Pharmacogenetics 5,* 121–141.

Carey, P., Seedat, S., Warwick, J., van Heerden, B., & Stein, D. J. (2004). SPECT imaging of body dysmorphic disorder. *Journal of Neuropsychiatry and Clinical Neurosciences, 16,* 357–359.

Carlsson, M. L. (2001). On the role of prefrontal cortex glutamate for the antithetical phenomenology of obsessive compulsive disorder and attention deficit hyperactivity disorder. *Progress in Neuropsychopharmacology and Biological Psychiatry, 25,* 5–26.

Chamberlain, S. R., Blackwell, A. D., Fineberg, N. A., Robbins, T. W., & Sahakian, B. J. (2005). The neuropsychology of obsessive compulsive disorder: The importance of failures in cognitive and behavioural inhibition as candidate endophenotypic markers. *Neuroscience and Biobehavioral Reviews, 29,* 399–419.

Denys, D., van der Wee, N., Janssen, J., de Geus, F., & Westenberg, H. G. M. (2004). Low level of dopaminergic D2 receptor binding in obsessive-compulsive disorder. *Biological Psychiatry, 55,* 1041–1045.

Fallon, B. A., Schneier, F. R., Marshall, R., Campeas, R., Vermes, D., Goetz, D., et al. (1996). The pharmacotherapy of hypochondriasis. *Psychopharmacology Bulletin, 32,* 607–611.

Fiorillo, C. D., Tobler, P. N., & Schultz, W. (2003). Discrete coding of reward probability and uncertainty by dopamine neurons. *Science 299,* 1898–1902.

Bechara, A., Dolan, S., & Hindes, A. (2002). Decision-making and addiction. II: Myopia for the future or hypersensitivity to reward? *Neuropsychologia, 40,* 1690–1705.

Graybiel, A. M. (1998). The basal ganglia and chunking of action repertoires. *Neurobiological Learning and Memory, 70,* 119–136.

Hollander, E., Allen, A., Kwon, J., Aronowitz, B., Schmeidler, J., Wong, C., et al. (1999). Clomipramine vs. desipramine crossover trial in body dysmorphic disorder: selective efficacy of a serotonin reuptake inhibitor in imagined ugliness. *Archives of General Psychiatry, 56,* 1033–1039.

Hudson, J. I., & Pope, H. G., Jr. (1990). Affective spectrum disorder: Does antidepressant response identify a family of disorders with a common pathophysiology? *American Journal of Psychiatry, 147,* 552–564.

Knutson, B., Fong, G. W., Adams, C. M., Varner, J. L., & Hommer, D. (2001). Dissociation of reward anticipation and outcome with event-related fMRI. *Neuroreport, 12,* 3683–3687.

Lochner, C., du Toit, P. L., Zungu-Dirwayi, N., Marais, A., van Kradenburg, J., Seedat, S., et al. (2002). Childhood trauma in obsessive-compulsive disorder, trichotillomania, and controls. *Depression and Anxiety, 15,* 66–68.

Lochner, C., Hemmings, S. M. J., Kinnear, C. J., Niehaus, D. J. H., Nel, D. G., Corfield, V. A., et al. (2005). Cluster analysis of obsessive-compulsive spectrum disorders in patients with obsessive-compulsive disorder: Clinical and genetic correlates. *Comprehensive Psychiatry, 46,* 14–19.

Martin, L. J., Spicer, D. M., Lewis, M. H., Gluck, J. P., & Cork, L. C. (1991). Social deprivation of infant monkeys alters the chemoarchitecture of the brain: I. Subcortical regions. *Journal of Neuroscience, 11,* 3344–3358.

McDougle, C. J., Epperson, C. N., Pelton, G. H., Wasylink, S., & Price, L. H. (2000). A double-blind, placebo-controlled study of risperidone addition in serotonin reuptake inhibitor-refractory obsessive-compulsive disorder. *Archives of General Psychiatry, 57,* 794–802.

Moriarty, J., Eapen, V., Costa, D. C., Gacinovic, S., Trimble, M., Ell, P. J., & Robertson, M. M. (1997). HMPAO SPET does not distinguish obsessive-compulsive and tic syndromes in families multiply affected with Gilles de la Tourette's syndrome. *Psychological Medicine, 27,* 737–740.

Naranjo, C. A., Tremblay, L. K., & Busto, U. E. (2001). The role of the brain reward system in depression. *Progress In NeuroPsychopharmacology & Biological Psychiatry, 25,* 781–823.

Ozaki, N., Goldman, D., Kaye, W. H., Plotnicov, K., Greenberg, B. D., Lappalainen, J., et al. (2003). Serotonin transporter missense mutation associated with a complex neuropsychiatric phenotype. *Molecular Psychiatry, 8,* 933–936.

Palumbo, D., Maugham, A., & Kurlan, A. (1997). Hypothesis III: Tourette syndrome is only one of several causes of a developmental basal ganglia syndrome. *Archives of General Psychiatry* 54, 475–483.

Pauls, D. L., Towbin, K. E., Leckman, J. F., Zahner, G. E., & D. J. Cohen. (1986). Gilles de la Tourette's syndrome and obsessive compulsive disorder: Evidence supporting a genetic relationship. *Archives of General Psychiatry, 43*, 1180–1182.

Phillips K. A. (2002). The obsessive-compulsive spectrums. *Psychiatric Clinics Of North America, 25,* 791–809.

Ridley, R. M. (1994). The psychology of perseverative and stereotyped behavior. *Progress in Neurobiology, 44,* 221–231.

Seedat, S., & Stein, D. J. (2000). Trauma and post-traumatic stress disorder in women: A review. *International Journal of Clinical Psychopharmacology, 15*(Suppl. 3), 25–34.

Stein, D. J. (2001). Neurobiology of the obsessive-compulsive spectrum of disorders. *Biological Psychiatry, 47,* 296–304.

Stein, D. J. (2002). Seminar on obsessive-compulsive disorder. *Lancet, 360,* 397–405.

Stein, D. J., Black, D. W., Shapira, N. A., & Spitzer, R. L. (2001). Hypersexual disorder and preoccupation with internet pornography. *American Journal Of Psychiatry, 158,* 1590–1594.

Stein, D. J., Bouwer, C., & Niehaus, D. J. (1997). Stereotypic movement disorder. *Journal of Clinical Psychiatry, 58,* 177–178.

Stein, D. J., & Grant, J. E. (2005). Betting on dopamine. *CNS Spectrums, 10,* 268–270.

Stein, D. J., & Hollander, E. (1993). The spectrum of obsessive-compulsive related disorders. In E. Hollander (Ed.), *Obsessive-Compulsive Related Disorders* (pp. 373–399). Washington, DC: American Psychiatric Press.

Stein, D. J., Hollander, E., & Liebowitz, M. R. (1993). Neurobiology of impulsivity and impulse control disorders. *Journal of Neuropsychiatry & Clininical Neurosciences 5,* 9–17.

Stein, D. J., & Moeller, F. G. (2005). The man who turned bad. *CNS Spectrums, 10,* 88–90.

Stein, D. J., & Stone, M. H. (1997). *Essential papers on obsessive-compulsive disorders.* New York: New York University Press.

Swedo, S. E., Leonard, H. L., Garvey, M., Mittleman, B., Allen, A. J., Perlmutter, S., et al. (1998). Pediatric autoimmune neuropsychiatric disorders associated with streptococcal infections: Clinical description of the first 50 cases. *American Journal of Psychiatry 155,* 264–271.

Thierry, A. M., Tassin, J. P., Blanc, G., & Glowinski, J. (2000). Selective activation of mesocortical DA system by stress. *Nature, 263,* 242–244.

Volkow, N. D., Fowler, J. S., Wang, G. J., & Swanson, J. M. (2004). Dopamine in drug abuse and addiction: Results from imaging studies and treatment implications. *Molecular Psychiatry, 9,* 557–569.

Whiteside, S. P., Port, J. D., & Abramowitz, J. S. (2004). A meta-analysis of functional neuroimaging in obsessive-compulsive disorder. *Psychiatry Research: Neuroimaging, 132,* 69–79.

Zohar, J., & Insel, T. R. (1987). Obsessive-compulsive disorder: Psychobiological approaches to diagnosis, treatment, and pathophysiology. *Biological Psychiatry, 22,* 667–687.

CHAPTER THIRTEEN

Eating Disorders

Randi E. McCabe, Ph.D., and Michele Boivin, Ph.D.

Two categories of eating disorder are specified in the *Diagnostic and Statistical Manual of Mental Disorders* (DSM-IV-TR; American Psychiatric Association [APA] 2000): anorexia nervosa (AN) and bulimia nervosa (BN). A third category, eating disorder not otherwise specified (ED-NOS), is reserved for capturing clinical presentations that do not meet criteria for either AN or BN. Many patients presenting with eating disorders are assigned a diagnosis of EDNOS, which unfortunately lacks descriptive specificity. Although binge-eating disorder (BED) has been proposed as a separate eating disorder, it is currently listed as an example of EDNOS. In addition, numerous individuals present with partial syndromes (subthreshold AN or BN) and are thus assigned an EDNOS diagnosis. Partial syndromes are clinically significant, given the high degree of similarity these patients have with those presenting with full AN or BN (Crow, Agras, Halmi, Mitchell, & Kraemer, 2002).

This chapter reviews eating disorders in the context of their consideration as an obsessive-compulsive (OC) spectrum disorder. Following a description of clinical features and a case vignette, the clinical and scientific basis for this perspective is presented. Theoretical and etiologic issues related to eating disorders are highlighted to aid case conceptualization. Finally, empirically supported treatment approaches are reviewed with attention to clinical issues that may arise in the treatment process.

Clinical Presentation

There is significant overlap in the core clinical features of AN and BN. For both disorders, personal worth is almost exclusively determined by body shape and weight, to the neglect of other dimensions of the self (e.g., personality, relationships, academic and occupational achievement, community service, spirituality). In addition, both disorders are characterized by intense preoccupation with body shape and weight as well as maladaptive behavioral attempts to control weight.

Central features of AN include severe caloric restriction and maintenance of a body weight less than 85 percent of that expected based on age and height, intense fear of weight gain despite being underweight, amenorrhea for at least three consecutive menstrual cycles, and distorted perception of body weight or shape (APA, 2000). Two types of AN are defined by the presence (binge eating/purging type) or absence (restricting type) of regular binge eating and purging behaviors (e.g., self-induced vomiting, misuse of laxatives, diuretics, or enemas). AN is generally experienced as ego-syntonic (i.e., consistent with one's sense of self), providing the individual with many perceived benefits (e.g., sense of identity, control). Thus, individuals with AN are often unlikely to want treatment until the medical and psychological complications of their eating disorder have become severe.

Central features of BN include recurrent episodes of binge eating followed by maladaptive compensatory behaviors to prevent weight gain. Binge eating is defined as consumption of an objectively large amount of food within a discrete period of time accompanied by a lack of control over the eating episode (APA, 2000). Two types of BN are defined by the presence (purging type) or absence (nonpurging type) of purging behaviors. Examples of nonpurging behaviors include fasting, extreme caloric restriction, and excessive exercise. Individuals with BN are typically motivated for treatment as the caloric restriction they strive for ultimately leads to lapses of binge eating that are often followed by feelings of shame and disgust and efforts to compensate by vomiting or misuse of laxatives or other substances.

A recent review of epidemiologic studies and eating disorders found average prevalence rates to be 1 percent for young females with BN, 0.1 percent for young males with BN, 0.3 percent for AN in young women, and 1 percent for BED (Hoek & van Hoeken, 2003). These prevalence rates underestimate the problem as they reflect only those meeting strict diagnostic criteria and do not take into account the considerable number of individuals presenting with partial syndromes.

Case Vignette

In addition to capturing the main clinical features of AN, the following case clearly illustrates the phenomenologic overlap between AN and obsessive-compulsive disorder (OCD).

T.J. is 21 years old and has struggled with AN for the past eight years. She was raised in a loving, middle-class family. She has an older sister who has always excelled in school and sports and is currently studying to be a doctor. T.J. described always feeling like she was in her sister's shadow. She described her parents as supportive; however, she felt like she could never live up to their expectations. Although severely underweight with a body mass index (BMI) of 17, she perceives herself as fat and has an extremely distorted perception of her body. On her first day at a day hospital program, she reported feeling as if she did not belong in the therapy group because she was "too big" despite the fact that the group was of mixed composition and consisted of patients with BN and BED as well. T.J. was fearful of her weight exceeding 100 pounds and she made sure that her weight was significantly below this number as a buffer to reduce her anxiety. When asked about the significance of the number, T.J. recalled watching a movie when she was 13 in which the handsome lead actor stated that there was nothing more perfect than a 100–pound ballerina. This idea stayed with T.J. and played a role in her conception of beauty and perfection.

T.J. had never experienced menstruation. She ate minimally except for dinner, when her parents ensured that she ate whatever the family was eating. She ate according to specific rules: ensuring that the foods did not touch on her plate, eating the different foods on her plate in a specific order, and chewing each bite of food a set number of times. T.J. engaged in two to three hours of exercise per day, primarily walking. She exercised despite illness, injury, or fatigue. If for some reason she was unable to exercise to the degree that she liked, T.J. felt anxious and distressed. T.J.'s fear of gaining weight also extended to a fear of "contamination" by fat or grease. She feared rain and snow, which she believed may be contaminated by oil and thus, she would avoid getting wet at all costs. She also feared that grease residue was on her dishes, so she washed dishes repeatedly. T.J. would repeatedly doubt whether she had eaten a forbidden food. In response to these thoughts, she would engage in further exercise to compensate. In addition, T.J. avoided crowds and public transportation because she feared that she would be "contaminated" by grease or fat from people around her (e.g., greasy fingerprints on public surfaces would lead to weight gain). When she asked what would happen to her if she became "contaminated," she responded that she would gain a "significant amount" of weight. When probed about how much weight she might gain, she stated "maybe 10 pounds." Throughout the day, T.J. repeatedly washed her hands to wash away grease contamination.

The case of T.J. illustrates the overlap of the core features of AN with OCD, specifically obsessions and compulsions related to eating and weight gain. Although the case of T.J. is unusual because of her grease contamination concerns, it is characteristic of individuals with eating disorders to display obsessions and compulsions related to food and weight control.

Eating Disorders as OC Spectrum Disorders: Clinical and Scientific Basis

Rapoport (1994, p. 677) defined OC spectrum disorders as "a broad category of disturbances whose common symptom is the inability to delay or inhibit repetitive behaviors." Although this definition highlights the centrality of compulsions or rituals in the putative OC spectrum disorders, others have noted that disorders conceptualized as spectrum disorders also appear to be characterized by repetitive intrusive thoughts (e.g., Dannon, 2002). On the basis of these descriptions, the primary difference between OC spectrum disorders and OCD lies not in the occurrence of the specific symptoms but rather in the focus of those symptoms. Recently, the OC spectrum model has been applied to understanding eating disorders. According to this formulation, the preoccupation with weight and shape, along with the drastic weight-loss efforts evident in AN and BN, can be explained with reference to the cardinal features of OCD. Several lines of evidence converge to support this assertion.

First, OCD, obsessive-compulsive spectrum disorders, and eating disorders have a higher rate of comorbidity than would be expected by chance. In one study, the lifetime prevalence of eating disorders in an OCD population was 12.9 percent, and another 17.7 percent of patients had symptoms that met criteria for a subthreshold eating disorder (Rubenstein, Pigott, L'Heureux, Hill, & Murphy, 1992). Further, the morbidity risk for OC spectrum disorders is significantly higher among relatives of eating disorder probands than among relatives of controls, even when comorbid OC spectrum diagnosis is statistically controlled (Bellodi et al., 2001). Similarly, the lifetime prevalence of OCD in patients with eating disorder is as high as 37 percent (Thiel, Broocks, Ohlmeier, Jacoby, & Schussler, 1995).

Second, research supports broad phenomenologic similarities between eating disorders and OCD (namely, the presence of obsessive thoughts, repetitive behaviors, and a motivation to avoid perceived harm; du Toit, van Kradenburg, Niehaus, & Stein, 2001). Symptoms of both AN and BN may be interpreted as obsessions and compulsions. With respect to obsessions (recurrent, intrusive thoughts), anecdotally, patients with eating disorder often describe their preoccupation with weight, shape, and eating, and their impulses to adhere to rigid rules or to binge as intrusive and disruptive to their normal thought patterns. The urge to binge is often described as senseless and experienced as disgusting.

With respect to compulsions (repetitive acts performed in response to obsessions to decrease resulting anxiety), patients with AN adhere to rigid rules and engage in strict dieting to manage the anxiety associated with the idea of potential weight gain; patients with BN, in addition to periods of restriction, engage in various purging behaviors to manage the anxiety associated with failed dietary restraint or abstinence violation. These "compulsive" behaviors are direct responses to intrusive thoughts, have the effect of temporarily reducing the anxiety associated with the thoughts, and feel at least at times to be beyond the patient's conscious control (i.e., even after patients enter treatment to attempt to change these behaviors, they are often unable to resist the urge to restrict or engage in compensatory behaviors). The cognitive preoccupation and rituals that characterize eating disorders, as with OCD, are time consuming, distressing, and interfere with functioning (Sunday, Halmi, & Einhorn, 1995).

Finally, several studies have identified specific phenomenologic overlap between eating disorders and OCD. The OCD symptom dimensions of contamination obsessions and cleaning compulsions, show specific relationships to comorbid eating disorders (Hasler et al., 2005). Further, patients with AN and

OCD appear to be equal in the frequency of symmetry and somatic obsessions, as well as ordering and arranging compulsions (Halmi et al., 2003), leading to suggestions that these disorders may share "common brain behavioral pathways" (p. 308).

One obvious implication of conceptualizing eating disorders as OC spectrum disorders is the use of the model as a clinical heuristic. For example, understanding T.J.'s fear of being contaminated by grease as an intrusive, anxiety-provoking thought that pops into her mind offers a different perspective on this symptom than the interpretation that it results from a reasoned (if erroneous) committed belief in the importance of thinness. Although such an interpretation has been debated, invoking it implies that empirically validated treatment approaches for OCD could be applied in the treatment of eating disorders. The addition of exposure with response prevention to eating disorder treatment protocols will be discussed later in this chapter.

There are also, however, some potential limitations of invoking the OC spectrum model to explain eating disorders. The key differences among obsessions and rituals in eating disorders versus OCD have been summarized in the following way: repeated phobic thoughts of food and weight happen but not necessarily against the will of the patient with eating disorder; the thoughts are distressing but not regarded as senseless; and patients with eating disorders feel compelled to perform the behaviors even though they are anxiety provoking, but the behaviors are not regarded as unwanted (Halmi et al., 2003). It is possible that eating disorders involve *both* obsessive-compulsive features as well as ego-syntonic, reasoned thoughts and behaviors.

Theoretical Models and Etiologic Issues

In addition to shared phenomenology, preliminary evidence suggests at least some degree of overlap in the etiology of eating disorders and OCD. Obsessive-compulsive behaviors have been shown to predict the onset of, and persist after recovery from, eating-disordered behaviors, suggesting that OC behaviors may be precursors or contributors to the pathogenesis of AN (Price Foundation Collaborative Group, 2001; von Ranson, Kaye, Weltzin, Rao, & Matsunaga, 1999). This relationship may be, or become, reciprocal: obsessionality may predispose individuals to eating disorders, and once restrained eating becomes entrenched, obsessions and compulsive behaviors may be maintained or amplified by a semistarvation state (Inanuma, 1994).

To eliminate the alternative hypothesis that anxiety disorders are found to be comorbid with eating disorders due to the effects of nutritional deprivation, Keel, Klump, Miller, McGue, and Iacono (2005) conducted a discordant monozygotic twin study (see article for a review of the methodology). Results showed that noneating disordered twins were twice as likely to have an anxiety disorder, even when the presence of anxiety disorders within the probands was controlled. Similarly, non-anxiety-disordered twins showed increased risk for eating disorders, relative to controls, lending support to the idea of a common biological or environmental origin for both disorders (see also Shafran, Bryant-Waugh, Lask, & Arscott, 1995).

Further research is needed to determine the relative effect of neurobiology and environment on the observed etiologic overlap in these disorders. Although preliminary evidence suggests broad neurochemical, neuroanatomical, neuroimmunological, and genetic similarities (see Stein [2000] for a review), specific mechanisms have not yet been identified.

One of the most often cited models of eating disorders is the Cognitive Behavioral Model of BN (Fairburn, Cooper, & Cooper, 1986). This model posits that overconcern with weight and shape, combined with low self-esteem, leads vulnerable individuals to follow rigid diet rules and engage in restrained eating in a misguided attempt to bolster self-esteem through weight loss. When minor violations of the rules occur (i.e., eating a small amount of a forbidden food), "all-or-nothing" thinking leads to the abandonment of restriction and the initiation of bingeing. Binge eating, in turn, is said to lead to perceived loss of control and anxiety. Purging behaviors represent an attempt to undo the damage of a binge and reestablish control over one's eating and weight. Purging perpetuates a binge-purge cycle because it relieves anxiety about weight gain in addition to predisposing the individual to overeat again.

Although this model is widely accepted and forms the basis of cognitive behavioral therapy for eating disorders, the first study to test this model as a whole (Byrne & McLean, 2002) found partial, but not complete, support for it. An OCD model may therefore lend further insight into the onset and maintenance of eating disorders. Before putting forward a new model for understanding eating disorders as OC spectrum disorders, we will first review the predominant model of OCD, its potential relationship to eating disorder symptoms, and its theoretical and clinical implications.

The principal etiologic model of OCD is Salkovskis's (1985) cognitive behavioral model, which emphasizes the way in which obsessions are interpreted in explaining the maintenance of OCD. This model posits that individuals with OCD misinterpret intrusive thoughts in a variety of ways. In addition to being precursors to obsessions (Rassin, Merkelbach, Muris, & Spaan, 1999), thought-action fusion (the belief that thinking about something makes it more likely to happen or that thinking about something is the moral equivalent of doing it; Shafran, Thordarson, & Rachman, 1996), as well as attributions of personal responsibility for harm (Salkovskis et al., 2000), are said to heighten the "perceived awfulness" of the anticipated outcomes. It is this misinterpretation, rather than the intrusive thought, that leads to anxiety and the urge to engage in compulsions. Anxiety, compulsions, attentional biases, and safety strategies maintain the OCD cycle by making subsequent intrusive thoughts, as well as threatening interpretations, more likely.

The core of the cognitive model of OCD, namely, misinterpretation of intrusive thoughts, has recently been investigated in anorexia nervosa. Shafran, Teachman, Kerry, and Rachman (1999) proposed the concept of "thought-shape fusion" as the eating disorder equivalent of thought-action fusion. Thought-shape fusion "occurs when thinking about eating certain types of food increases a person's estimate of their shape and/or weight, elicits a perception of moral wrongdoing, and/or makes the person feel fat" (Radomsky, de Silva, Todd, Treasure, & Murphy, 2002) and has been found to have significant associations with eating disorder pathology (Shafran & Robinson, 2004). T.J.'s belief that she would gain 10 pounds if she became contaminated by grease (i.e., ate from a dish that was not washed thoroughly) is an example of thought-shape fusion.

A direct application of Salkovskis' cognitive model to eating disorders would imply that weight- and shape-related obsessions ("I am fat"; "This food will contaminate me and I will gain 10 pounds") are misinterpreted (e.g., I feel fat therefore I am fat; thought-shape fusion). This misinterpretation leads to anxiety, compulsions (rigid dieting, purging behaviors, repeatedly checking body weight on the scale), attentional biases (noticing subtle body changes after eating), and safety strategies (e.g., avoiding social situations involving food, reassurance seeking around food or weight), all of which reinforce both the misinterpretation as well as the obsessions, thus creating a self-perpetuating cycle.

Evidence suggests that eating disorders also involve several changes at a chemical or biological level that in themselves contribute to the maintenance of the disorder. For example, the effects of nutritional deprivation have been shown to increase obsessive thoughts (e.g., Franklin, Schiele, Brozek, & Keys,

1948). Therefore, the addition of a physiologic feedback loop (resulting from dieting/purging) to an OC spectrum disorder model of eating disorders is necessary. In addition, although some eating disorder thoughts and behaviors appear to have obsessive-compulsive qualities, it has been argued that eating disorders involve more intentional thoughts and purposeful behaviors than OCD. Therefore, a pathway to account for these ego-syntonic thoughts and behaviors is also warranted.

Based on Salkovskis's (1985) cognitive-behavioral model of OCD, and incorporating modifications derived from the eating disorders literature and the available evidence on the overlap between eating disorders and OCD, a preliminary OC spectrum disorder model of eating disorders is presented in Figure 13.1. Examples from T.J.'s case are used to illustrate how this model may aid in clinical case conceptualization.

Treatment

The few randomized controlled trials on treatments for AN reflect the low prevalence rate, lengthy treatment course, presence of medical complications that require hospitalization, and ego-syntonic nature of the disorder. Thus, existing studies are limited by small sample size and high rates of attrition. For AN, the initial treatment focus is on weight restoration. This necessitates a more intensive treatment approach either through an inpatient or day hospital program. Unfortunately, relapse rates are high upon discharge (e.g., Carter, Blackmore, Sutander-Pinnock, & Woodside, 2004). The few available studies examining pharmacotherapy for AN indicate little utility for the use of antidepressants in the treatment of patients at low weight; however, evidence shows that the addition of fluoxetine to weight-restored individuals with AN at discharge may prevent relapse (e.g., Kaye et al., 2001). Including family members in the treatment of younger patients is beneficial (e.g., Eisler et al., 2000).

Cognitive behavioral treatment (CBT) for AN, developed by Garner and colleagues (e.g., Garner, Vitousek, & Pike, 1997), occurs in three phases. The initial phase focuses on the development of trust and establishment of treatment parameters (e.g., minimal body weight threshold). Therapy interventions focus on motivation enhancement, implementation of a meal plan with the goal of weight gain, and strategies for symptom interruption (e.g., bingeing, vomiting, exercise). The second phase focuses on modification of beliefs

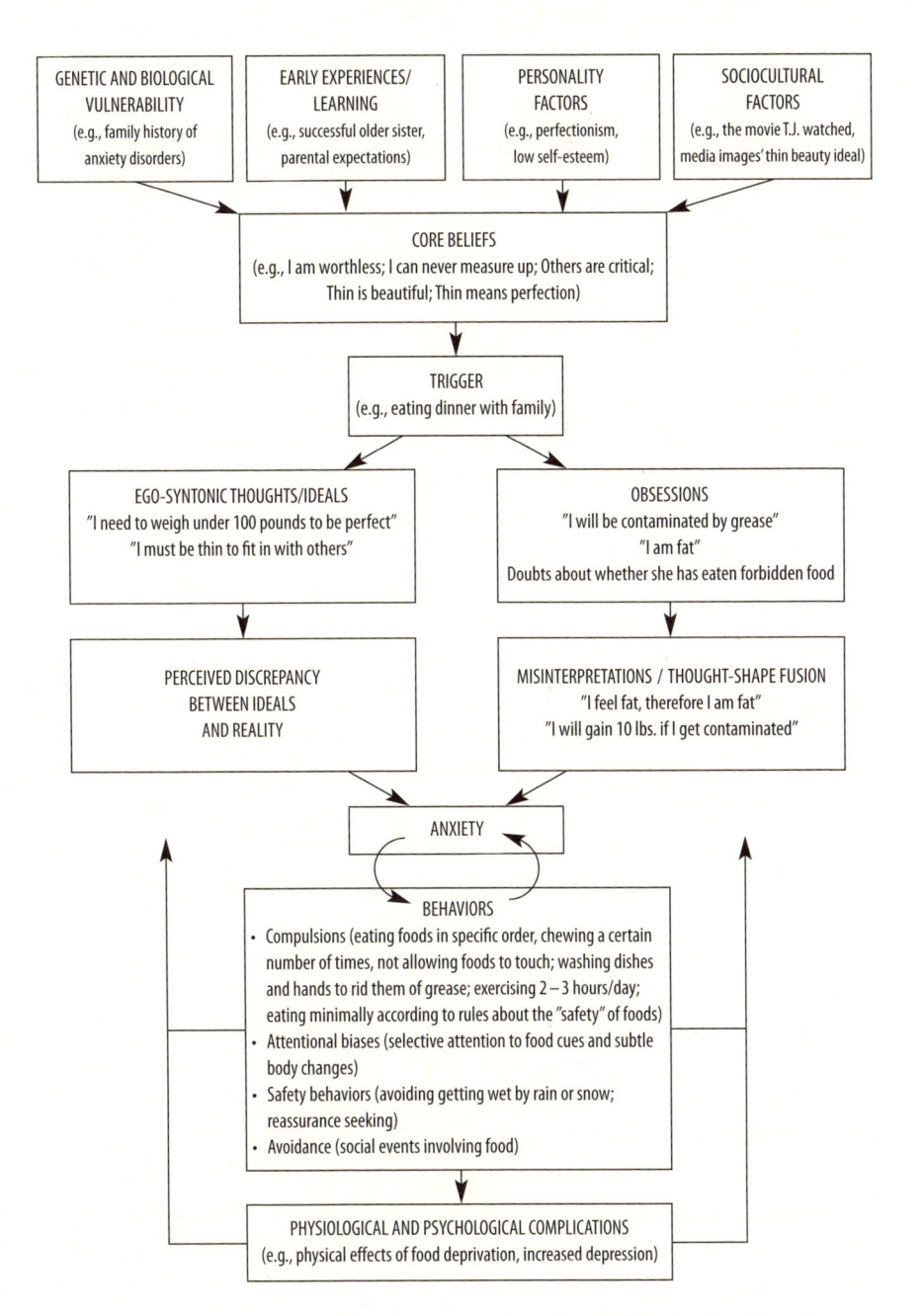

Figure 13.1. An obsessive-compulsive spectrum disorder model of eating disorders illustrated using the case of T.J.

related to food and weight and associated symptoms (e.g., behaviors aimed at weight control) as well as broader issues that play a role in the eating disorder (e.g., self-esteem, self-control, impulse regulation, interpersonal functioning, and emotional expression). The third phase focuses on relapse prevention and issues related to termination. CBT for AN typically lasts one to two years due to a number of factors that prolong the therapy process (e.g., motivational obstacles, the degree of weight gain needed to achieve a minimal healthy weight, and the necessity for occasional hospitalization or partial hospitalization). Preliminary evidence suggests that CBT has significantly improved treatment outcome and lower rates of relapse compared to nutritional counseling (Pike, Walsh, Vitousek, Wilson, & Bauer, 2003).

CBT for BN typically spans 20 weeks and is also structured in three stages (Fairburn Marcus, & Wilson, 1993). In the first stage, treatment strategies include self-monitoring, weekly weighing, psychoeducation about weight and eating, prescription of regular eating patterns, and self-control strategies. The second phase of treatment focuses on eliminating dieting, teaching problem-solving skills, and implementing cognitive and behavioral strategies. The third stage of treatment focuses on relapse prevention.

Numerous studies demonstrate the efficacy of CBT for BN such that it is considered the first-line treatment, with improvements in the core clinical features of the eating disorder as well as concurrent psychological symptoms (e.g., low self-esteem and depression) (Wilson & Fairburn, 2002) and maintenance of treatment gains in follow-up (e.g., Carter, McIntosh, Joyce, Sullivan, & Bulik, 2003). Despite the proven clinical efficacy of CBT in the treatment of BN, there is room for improvement, as approximately 50 percent of patients achieve only partial improvement or exhibit no response to treatment (Wilson, 1999). It has been suggested that CBT be improved through either expansion of clinical focus to broader issues (e.g., self-esteem, emotion regulation, interpersonal issues, etc.) or increased emphasis on the core features of BN, especially weight and shape-related cognition (Wilson, 1999).

In addition to CBT, other interventions found to be beneficial for individuals with BN include interpersonal therapy (e.g., Agras, Walsh, Fairburn, Wilson, & Kraemer, 2000), psychoeducation (e.g., Olmsted et al., 1991), and cognitive behavioral self help (e.g., Carter et al., 2003). Pharmacotherapy using selective serotonin reuptake inhibitors (SSRIs) has been shown to reduce the frequency of binge eating and purging behaviors (for review, see Mitchell, Peterson, Myers, & Wonderlich, 2001).

Given the phenomenologic overlap among the eating disorders, Fairburn and colleagues (2003) proposed a transdiagnostic theory of eating disorders that extends the focus of standard CBT to encompass additional mechanisms that serve to maintain an eating disorder, including low self-esteem, perfectionism, mood intolerance, and interpersonal difficulties. This expanded CBT for eating disorders is currently being studied.

Clinically, exposure and response prevention strategies (ERP) are an important component of CBT for eating disorders and target obsessions related to eating (e.g., exposure to a risky food such as a piece of chocolate cake combined with prevention of a purging response such as vomiting or exercise) and shape or weight (e.g., exposure to wearing a bathing suit combined with prevention of compensating responses such as mirror checking). The goal of such exposures is to reduce anxiety associated with intrusive thoughts without the use of compulsive behaviors. Unlike with OCD, ERP alone would be inadequate as a stand-alone treatment for eating disorders. Given that ERP emphasizes behavioral change and has typically excluded a cognitive focus, it may fail to address relevant longer-term goals of establishing a healthier body image and examining unrealistic standards of attractiveness. Few studies have examined the utility of ERP strategies in the context of CBT for eating disorders. For BN, preliminary evidence suggests that ERP alone is no more effective than standard CBT and the addition of ERP to CBT offers little if any enhancement in effectiveness (Wilson, Eldredge, Smith, & Niles, 1991; Leitenberg, Rosen, Gross, Nudelman, & Vara, 1988). We are not aware of any studies examining the effectiveness of ERP for anorexia.

The logical implication of the cognitive model is the addition of cognitive therapy to ERP strategies. For example, in addition to systematically exposing patients with eating disorder to forbidden foods, this model emphasizes the importance of cognitive restructuring to reframe not only inflated beliefs of the importance of shape and weight, as in traditional CBT for eating disorders, but also misinterpretations of eating disorder–related obsessions (e.g., thought-shape fusion). Given its emphasis on both the behavioral and cognitive dimensions of OCD, Salkovskis's formulation may represent a more accurate theoretical model for the explanation of eating disordered behaviors relative to purely behavioral models.

For T.J., ERP strategies were essential for reducing her anxiety. Exposure practices included putting her hand in a pail of snow, taking public transportation to trigger her intrusive thoughts about being contaminated by fat, eating from dishes that she had not washed to trigger her intrusive thoughts about weight gain, and walking by a display counter at a bakery to trigger her doubts that she might have eaten a fattening food. These exposure practices were combined with preventing her typical responses aimed to alleviate distress (e.g., using an umbrella in the rain and snow, washing her hands or dishes to eliminate any "fat residue," further restriction of her food intake, and reassurance-seeking behaviors).

Many issues specific to eating disorders often present as obstacles to the treatment process. Unlike other psychiatric disorders, eating disorders are associated with a host of medical complications (e.g., gastrointestinal problems, electrolyte disturbance, cardiovascular abnormalities, renal dysfunction) that in some cases can be fatal (e.g., Walsh, Wheat, & Freund, 2000). Many of these medical complications are reversible; however, in some cases, they may result in death. The long-term mortality rate of eating disorders is over 10 percent, with death most commonly caused by starvation, suicide, or electrolyte imbalance (APA, 2000). The clinician must coordinate treatment efforts with medical personnel such that medical complications are monitored and treated. This may require regular visits to the patient's family doctor or, in more serious cases, hospitalization.

Eating disorders are often experienced as ego-syntonic or consistent with the self. Thus, a patient may not want to give up her eating disorder because of important functions it may play in her life (e.g., control, sense of effectiveness). This translates into issues of motivation and, in some cases, treatment dropout. The clinician may use motivational enhancement strategies to boost a patient's readiness to change (e.g., Wilson & Schlam, 2004). These strategies may be helpful at various points over the course of treatment in response to fluctuating levels of motivation for recovery.

Societal emphasis on thinness as both a beauty and health ideal also presents a challenge to treatment. The abundant images of thin models in print and television media set unrealistic standards for beauty and body weight that are impossible for the average person to attain. As therapy efforts focus on shifting unrealistic expectations and beliefs regarding body weight and shape, they are met with the challenge that these expectations and beliefs are perpetuated and reinforced by the sociocultural milieu. Therapeutic strategies that may be helpful for overcoming this obstacle include psychoeducation, exploration of the personal meaning of body weight ("fat" and "thin"), and examination of the pursuit of thinness in the context of the patient's values and life goals (e.g., McCabe, McFarlane, & Olmsted, 2003).

Eating disorders are associated with a high degree of comorbidity with other disorders, most commonly depression, anxiety, or substance use (APA, 2000). The presence of comorbid disorders may complicate the treatment process. The clinician must determine whether associated symptoms are indeed a separate syndrome or secondary to the eating disorder (e.g., depression due to the effects of starvation; anxiety related to social gatherings involving food). If associated symptoms are secondary, they should improve upon recovery from the eating disorder.

Conclusion

In addition to the phenomenologic overlap between eating disorders and OCD, there are many clinical and scientific reasons for conceptualizing eating disorders as an obsessive-compulsive spectrum disorder. The application of an OCD theoretical model to eating disorders furthers our understanding of these challenging disorders as well as provides helpful directions for enhancing treatment efforts through incorporation of ERP strategies. Further research on the efficacy of ERP combined with cognitive strategies in the treatment of eating disorders is warranted.

REFERENCES

Agras, W. S., Walsh, B. T., Fairburn, C. G., Wilson, G. T., & Kraemer, H. C. (2000). A multicenter comparison of cognitive-behavioral therapy and interpersonal therapy for bulimia nervosa. *Archives of General Psychiatry, 47*, 459–466.

American Psychiatric Association. (2000). *Diagnostic and statistical manual of mental disorders* (4th ed., text revision). Washington, DC: Author.

Bellodi, L., Cavallini, M. C., Bertelli, S., Chiapparino, D., Riboldi, C., & Smeraldi, E. (2001). Morbidity risk for obsessive-compulsive spectrum disorders in first-degree relatives of patients with eating disorders. *American Journal of Psychiatry, 158*, 563–569.

Byrne, S. M., & McLean, N. J. (2002). The cognitive-behavioral model of bulimia nervosa: A direct evaluation. *International Journal of Eating Disorders, 31*, 17–31.

Carter, J. C., Blackmore, E., Sutandar-Pinnock, K., & Woodside, D. B. (2004). Relapse in anorexia nervosa: A survival analysis. *Psychological Medicine, 34*, 671–679.

Carter, F. A., McIntosh, V. V. W., Joyce, P. R., Sullivan, P. F., & Bulik, C. M. (2003). Role of exposure with response prevention in cognitive-behavioral therapy for bulimia nervosa: Three-year follow-up results. *International Journal of Eating Disorders, 33*, 127–135.

Carter, J. C., Olmsted, M. P., Kaplan, A. S., McCabe, R. E., Mills, J., & Aime, A. (2003). Self-help for bulimia nervosa: A randomized controlled trial. *American Journal of Psychiatry, 160,* 973–978.

Crow, S. J., Agras, S., Halmi, K., Mitchell, J. E., & Kraemer, H. C. (2002). Full syndromal versus subthreshold anorexia nervosa, bulimia nervosa, and binge eating disorder: A multicentre study. *International Journal of Eating Disorders, 32,* 309–318.

Dannon, P. N. (2002). Kleptomania: An impulse control disorder? *International Journal of Psychiatry in Clinical Practice, 6,* 3–7.

du Toit, P. L., van Kradenburg, J., Niehaus, D., & Stein, D. J. (2001). Comparison of obsessive-compulsive disorder patients with and without comorbid putative obsessive-compulsive spectrum disorders using a structured clinical interview. *Comprehensive Psychiatry, 42,* 291–300.

Eisler, I., Dare, C., Hodes, M., Russell, G., Dodge, E., & Le Grange, D. (2000). Family therapy for adolescent anorexia nervosa: The results of a controlled comparison of two family interventions. *Journal of Child Psychology and Psychiatry, 41,* 727–736.

Fairburn, C. G., Cooper, Z., & Cooper, P. J. (1986). The clinical features and maintenance of bulimia nervosa. In K. D. Brownell & J. P. Foreyt (Eds.), *Handbook of eating disorders: Physiology, psychology and treatment of obesity, anorexia and bulimia* (pp. 389–404). New York: Basic Books.

Fairburn, C. G., Cooper, Z., & Shafran, R. (2003). Cognitive behaviour therapy for eating disorders: A "transdiagnostic theory" and treatment. *Behaviour Research and Therapy, 41,* 509–528.

Fairburn, C. G., Marcus, M. D., & Wilson, G. T. (1993). Cognitive-behavioral therapy for binge eating and bulimia nervosa: A comprehensive treatment manual. In C. G. Fairburn & G. T. Wilson (Eds.), *Binge eating: Nature, assessment and treatment* (pp. 361–405). New York: Guilford Press.

Franklin, J. C., Schiele, B. C., Brozek, J., & Keys, A. (1948). Observations of human behavior in experimental semistarvation and rehabilitation. *Journal of Clinical Psychology, 4,* 28–45.

Garner, D. M., Vitousek, K. M., & Pike, K. M. (1997). Cognitive-behavioral therapy for anorexia nervosa. In D. M. Garner & P. E. Garfinkel (Eds.), *Handbook of Treatment for Eating Disorders* (pp. 94–144). New York: Guilford Press.

Halmi, K. A., Sunday, S. R., Klump, K. L., Strober, M., Leckman, J. F., Fichter, M., et al. (2003). Obsessions and compulsions in anorexia nervosa subtypes. *International Journal of Eating Disorders, 33,* 308–319.

Hasler, G., LaSalle-Ricci, V. H., Ronquillo, J. G., Crawley, S. A., Cochran, L. W., Kazuba, D., et al. (2005). Obsessive-compulsive disorder symptom dimensions show specific relationships to psychiatric comorbidity. *Psychiatry Research, 135,* 121–132.

Hoek, H. W., & van Hoeken, D. (2003). Review of the prevalence and incidence of eating disorders. *International Journal of Eating Disorders, 34,* 383–396.

Inanuma, K. (1994). Obsessive states in anorexia nervosa. *Japanese Journal of Child and Adolescent Psychiatry, 35,* 465–476.

Kaye, W. H., Nagata, T., Weltzin, T. E., Hsu, L. K. G., Sokol, M. S., McConaha, C., et al. (2001). Double-blind placebo-controlled administration of fluoxetine in restricting-and restricting-purging-type anorexia nervosa. *Biological Psychiatry, 49,* 644–652.

Keel, P. K., Klump, K. L., Miller, K. B., McGue, M., & Iacono, W. G. (2005). Shared

Transmission of Eating Disorders and Anxiety Disorders. *International Journal of Eating Disorders, 38,* 99–105.

Leitenberg, H., Rosen, J. C., Gross, J., Nudelman, S., & Vara, L. S. (1988). Exposure plus response-prevention treatment of bulimia nervosa. *Journal of Consulting and Clinical Psychology, 56,* 535–541.

McCabe, R. E., McFarlane, T., & Olmsted, M. P. (2003). The overcoming bulimia workbook. Oakland, CA: New Harbinger Publications.

Mitchell, J. E., Peterson, C. B., Myers, T., & Wonderlich, S. (2001). Combining pharmacotherapy and psychotherapy in the treatment of patients with eating disorders. *Psychiatric Clinics of North America, 24,* 315–323.

Olmsted, M. P., Davis, R., Rockert, W., Irvine, M. J. R., Eagle, M., & Garner, D. M. (1991). Efficacy of a brief group psychoeducation intervention for bulimia nervosa. *Behaviour Research and Therapy, 29,* 71–83.

Pike, K. M., Walsh, B. T., Vitousek, K., Wilson, G. T., & Bauer, J. (2003). Cognitive-behavioural therapy in the posthospital treatment of anorexia nervosa. *American Journal of Psychiatry, 160,* 2046–2049.

Price Foundation Collaborative Group. (2001). Deriving behavioural phenotypes in an international, multi-centre study of eating disorders. *Psychological Medicine, 31,* 635–645.

Radomsky, A. S., de Silva, P., Todd, G., Treasure, J., & Murphy, T. (2002). Thought-shape fusion in anorexia nervosa: An experimental investigation. *Behaviour Research and Therapy, 40,* 1169–1177.

Rapoport, J. L. (1994). "Obsessive compulsive spectrum disorder": A useful concept? [Special issue]. *Encéphale, 20,* 677–680.

Rassin, E., Merkelbach, H., Muris, P., & Spaan, V. (1999). Thought-action fusion as a causal factor in the development of intrusions. *Behaviour Research and Therapy, 37,* 231–237.

Rubenstein, C. S., Pigott, T. A., L'Heureux, F., Hill, J. L., & Murphy, D. L. (1992). A preliminary investigation of the lifetime prevalence of anorexia and bulimia nervosa in patients with obsessive compulsive disorder. *Journal of Clinical Psychiatry, 53,* 309–314.

Salkovskis, P. M. (1985). Obsessional-compulsive problems: A cognitive-behavioural analysis. *Behaviour Research and Therapy, 23,* 571–583.

Salkovskis, P. M., Wroe, A. L., Gledhill, A., Morrison, N., Forrester, E., Richards, C., et al. (2000). Responsibility attitudes and interpretations are characteristic of obsessive compulsive disorder. *Behaviour Research and Therapy, 38,* 347–372.

Shafran, R., Bryant-Waugh R., Lask, B., & Arscott, K. (1995). Obsessive-compulsive symptoms in children with eating disorders: A preliminary investigation. *Eating Disorders: The Journal of Treatment and Prevention, 3,* 304–310.

Shafran, R., & Robinson, P. (2004). Thought-shape fusion in eating disorders. *British Journal of Clinical Psychology, 43,* 399–407.

Shafran, R., Teachman, B. A., Kerry, S., & Rachman, S. (1999). A cognitive distortion associated with eating disorders: Thought-shape fusion. *British Journal of Clinical Psychology, 38,* 167–179.

Shafran, R., Thordarson, D. S., & Rachman, S. (1996). Thought-action fusion in obsessive compulsive disorder. *Journal of Anxiety Disorders, 10,* 379–391.

Stein, D. J. (2000). Advances in the neurobiology of obsessive-compulsive disorder:

Implications for conceptualizing putative obsessive-compulsive and spectrum disorders. *Psychiatric Clinics of North America, 23,* 545–562.

Sunday, S. R., Halmi, K. A., & Einhorn, A. (1995). The Yale-Brown-Cornell Eating Disorder Scale: A new scale to assess eating disorders symptomatology. *International Journal of Eating Disorders, 18,* 237–245.

Thiel, A., Broocks, A., Ohlmeier, M., Jacoby, G., & Schussler, G. E. (1995). Obsessive-compulsive disorder among patients with anorexia nervosa and bulimia nervosa. *American Journal of Psychiatry, 152,* 72–75.

von Ranson, K. M., Kaye, W. H., Weltzin, T. E., Rao, R., & Matsunaga, H. (1999). Obsessive-compulsive disorder symptoms before and after recovery from bulimia nervosa. *American Journal of Psychiatry, 156,* 1703–1708.

Walsh, J., Wheat, M. E., & Freund, K. (2000). Detection, evaluation, and treatment of eating disorders: The role of the primary care physician. *Journal of General Internal Medicine, 15,* 577–590.

Wilson, G. T. (1999). Cognitive behavior therapy for eating disorders: Progress and problems. *Behaviour Research and Therapy, 37*(Suppl. 1), S79–S97.

Wilson, G. T., Eldredge, K. L., Smith, D., & Niles, B. (1991). Cognitive-behavioral treatment with and without response prevention for bulimia. *Behaviour Research and Therapy, 29,* 575–583.

Wilson, G. T., & Fairburn, C. G. (2002). Treatments for eating disorders. In P. E. Nathan & J. M. Gorman (Eds.), *A guide to treatments that work* (2nd ed., pp. 559–592). New York: Oxford University Press.

Wilson, G. T., & Schlam, T. R. (2004). The transtheoretical model and motivational interviewing in the treatment of eating and weight disorders. *Clinical Psychology Review, 24,* 361–378.

CHAPTER FOURTEEN

Trichotillomania

Douglas W. Woods, Ph.D., Amanda C. Adcock, M.A., and Christine A. Conelea, M.A.

Trichotillomania (TTM) is characterized by recurrent hair pulling that results in noticeable hair loss (American Psychiatric Association [APA], 2000). Additional diagnostic criteria for TTM include (1) increased tension immediately preceding hair pulling or attempts to resist pulling; (2) feelings of gratification, pleasure, or relief that accompany pulling; (3) no alternative explanation for pulling (i.e., medical condition or mental disorder); and (4) significant impairment or distress in important areas of functioning (APA, 2000). TTM is currently classified as an impulse-control disorder (APA, 2000), but there is ongoing debate about whether it would be more appropriately classified as an obsessive-compulsive (OC) spectrum disorder (Himle, Bordnick, & Thyer, 1995; Stanley & Cohen, 1999; Swedo, 1993).

Estimates of the prevalence of TTM range between 0.6 percent (Christenson, Pyle, & Mitchell, 1991) and 3.2 percent of the population (Woods, Miltenberger, & Flach, 1996). However, some research suggests that these rates are higher if certain DSM criteria are excluded. For example, Christenson, Pyle, and Mitchell (1991) found that prevalence rates increased to 2.5 percent when they included participants who reported visible hair loss, regardless of any sensation of tension or tension relief. Similarly, Woods et al. (1996) found that 10.5 percent of their college sample endorsed hair-pulling habits. Research has shown that TTM affects more females than males, although the gender distribution appears to be equal among younger children (Christenson & Mansueto, 1999).

The onset of TTM generally occurs in middle childhood or early adolescence. Cohen et al. (1995) surveyed 123 chronic hair pullers and found the mean age of onset to be 10.7 ± 6.3 years of age. Similarly, Christenson, Mackenzie, and Mitchell (1991) found a mean age of onset of 13 ± 8 years in a sample of 60 hair pullers. There is some speculation that hair pulling in younger children (onset of 2–3 years of age) lasts for a shorter duration and is more responsive to intervention (Miltenberger, Rapp, & Long, 2001).

TTM is associated with physical, social, and psychological impairments. Hair loss is the most obvious physical effect, but chronic hair pulling can result in damage to follicles and scalp and cause regrown hair to have a changed appearance (e.g., thicker, coarser, discolored; Christenson & Mansueto, 1999). Furthermore, approximately 5–18 percent of people ingest pulled hairs, putting them at risk of developing trichobezoars (i.e., hair balls), which can cause abdominal pain, vomiting, weight loss, and anemia (Christenson & Mansueto, 1999).

Casati, Toner, and Yu (2000) interviewed seven women with TTM to identify some of the psychosocial issues faced by those with the disorder. All participants reported negative effects of embarrassment, isolation, fear, and anger, and all struggled with a negative body image and the inability to control their pulling. In another study, Diefenbach, Tolin, Hannan, Crocetto, and Worhunsky (2005) found that those with TTM reported higher levels of distress than a control group.

Hair-pulling behaviors vary from person to person, but some patterns are fairly typical. The most common bodily sites from which hair is pulled include the scalp, eyelashes, eyebrows, and pubic area (Christenson, Mackenzie, & Mitchell, 1991; Cohen et al., 1995). Hairs are generally pulled out one by one with the person's dominant hand or, less frequently, with the aid of tweezers (Christenson et al.). Hairs then either are discarded or become the focus of postpulling manipulations, such as rolling hairs between the index finger and thumb or repetitive biting and chewing of hairs (Miltenberger et al., 2001).

Several cues that trigger hair pulling have been identified. Christenson, Ristvedt, and Mackenzie (1993) identified two groups of cues: negative affect, including feelings such as sadness, tension, and anxiety, and sedentary activities, such as reading, watching television, and driving. Diefenbach, Mouton-Odum, and Stanley (2002) examined the affective correlates of TTM and found that during the hair-pulling cycle, participants experienced significant decreases in tension, boredom, and anxiety and significant increases in anger, guilt, and sadness. The authors suggest that these changes indicate that hair pulling may occur in a "tension-reduction-tension" cycle, in which pulling produces immediate relief in some unpleasant state but that the negative emotions that follow pulling eventually prompt future pulling.

TTM in the OC Spectrum

Although it is currently classified as an impulse-control disorder (APA, 2000), TTM has also been considered an OC spectrum disorder (Swedo & Leonard, 1992). Looking at the topography and phenomenology of the disorder, one can easily see how it would appear to be related to obsessive-compulsive disorder (OCD). Clients with TTM often report an unpleasant private antecedent experience (tension or urge to pull) that is then temporarily relieved by engaging in a public repetitive behavior (pulling). Despite these similarities, converging streams of evidence suggest that OCD and TTM are separate conditions. First, unlike individuals with OCD, many with TTM report the specific act of pulling to be quite enjoyable (though they often experience guilt and sadness after a pulling episode; Penzel, 2003). Second, that selective serotonin reuptake inhibitors (SSRIs) have been effective in reducing OCD (Hollander, 1998) but not in controlled trials for TTM (Christenson, Mackenzie, Mitchell, & Callies, 1991), suggesting different biological etiologies. Third, the psychological and neuropsychological profiles suggest that while both individuals with TTM and OCD have a bias toward attending to negative information, only those with OCD have a deficit inhibiting such information (Bohne, Keuthen, Tuschen-Caffier, & Wilhelm, 2005). Likewise, Bohne, Savage et al. (2005) found that while individuals with TTM appeared to have impaired response flexibility, those with OCD were impaired on the Wisconsin Card Sorting Task (a measure of ability to learn from feedback). Other studies differentiating between TTM and OCD have found that individuals with TTM have an earlier age of onset than those with OCD, while those with OCD are more likely to have comorbid symptomatology (Himle et al., 1995).

Case Vignette

The following vignette provides an idea of how a case may present in clinic:

Mary was a 30-year-old female who began pulling her hair at age 12. Upon examination, there was significant hair loss from the crown of the head, and a small bald patch above her right ear. In addition, she had removed all of her eyelashes, but her eyebrows remained intact. She disguised the hair loss by frequently wearing wigs and bandannas and by using heavy eyeliner. Throughout the course of the disorder, there had been periods of waxing and waning with the longest pull-free period (11 months) occurring during and shortly after the pregnancy with her first child. Mary reported being most likely to pull when in idle (e.g., driving, watching television) or highly stressful (e.g., difficult days at work) situations. During those times when she pulled in reaction to stress, she reported heightened states of an uncomfortable urge to pull. When these urges arose, she would go to a discrete place (e.g., the bathroom) and begin to pull her hair. While pulling, she reported searching for an appropriate hair (one that was discolored or coarse), isolating that hair, twirling it around her finger, and pulling it. After a bout of pulling, which typically lasted up to 40 minutes, Mary reported feeling much more calm but also noted that she felt guilty because she had again pulled. Mary was happily married but stated that her husband was upset because he knew the pulling bothered her. Mary reported that she rarely did outdoor activities such as bike riding or swimming because of embarrassment about her pulling. Mary had prior episodes of depression but was not currently depressed. Prior episodes of depression appeared secondary to the TTM diagnosis. Mary was on fluoxetine for her depression and TTM at the time she presented for treatment. She had no prior behavior therapy but had received counseling after she first started pulling as a child, which ended after approximately three months when her parents determined it was ineffective.

Etiology and Theoretical Models

Many etiologic models have been generated, ranging from animal to behavioral models, although empirical support for any one is limited. Some of the more common proposed etiologies are briefly described.

Animal Models

Abnormal grooming behaviors in a variety of animals caught the attention of researchers and led to the development of animal models of TTM. For example, cats and dogs sometimes continually lick their coats until there is a bald spot, a condition known as *acral lick dermatitis* (Sischo, Ihrke, & Franti, 1989). Likewise, birds have been reported to pick out their feathers with no identifiable biological etiology, a condition labeled *feather-picking disorder* (Bordnick, Thyer, & Ritchie, 1994). Mice that have mutations on the Hoxb8 gene display excessive grooming behaviors (Greer & Capecchi, 2002). They tend to groom not only themselves but also cage mates. The findings of Greer and Capecchi suggest a genetic basis to chronic hair pulling, though research has not isolated such a gene in humans. Nevertheless, the familial pattern of TTM in humans does suggest a genetic component to the disorder (Lenane et al., 1992).

Biological Model

In humans, the two primary models with existing empirical support include the biological and behavioral models. Support for the biological underpinnings of TTM come from various neuroimaging and treatment studies. Research has shown that individuals with TTM have elevated cerebral glucose metabolism in the right superior parietal lobe and cerebellum when compared with normal controls (Swedo et al., 1991). In addition, O'Sullivan et al. (1997) found that individuals with TTM have decreased left putamen volumes, and in an imaging study of twins with TTM, Vythilingum, Warwick, von Kradenburg, von Heerden, and Stein (1997) showed that both twins showed considerable abnormalities, such as decreased temporal lobe perfusion.

Stein et al. (2002) replicated and extended the results of Vythilingum et al. by studying 10 TTM clients before and after administration of the drug citalopram. TTM severity was correlated with decreased frontal and parietal lobe activity. Likewise, there was significant correlation between improvements in hair pulling and activity in the frontal lobe after citalopram treatment. Nonrandomized or non-placebo-controlled studies have suggested that SSRIs and antipsychotics may be efficacious in the treatment of TTM. As a result, the dopamine and serotonin systems have been implicated as neurologic contributors to TTM (Stein & Hollander, 1992; Swedo et al., 1989).

Behavioral Models

Most behavioral models do not focus on the variables that originally contributed to the development of TTM but rather emphasize the antecedent and consequent variables that maintain the pulling. Two primary types of pulling are believed to co-occur in many with TTM, and these different types of pulling appear to be associated with different controlling variables (Christenson & Mackenzie, 1994; Christenson & Mansueto, 1999). The first type of pulling, called *nonfocused,* or *automatic pulling,* involves pulling with little awareness that the behavior is occurring. It is viewed as an automatic response maintained by sensory consequences and is more likely to happen during periods of low arousal or when few competing activities are available. There is some evidence that these controlling variables are important in maintaining automatic pulling for some individuals. For example, a functional analysis conducted on a 38-year-old woman with mental retardation showed that pulling occurred most often when she was alone (Miltenberger Long, Rapp, Lumley, & Elliot, 1998), suggesting an automatic reinforcement function. Rapp, Miltenberger, Galensky, Ellingson, and Long (1999) replicated this analysis on a 19-year-old woman with severe mental retardation and cerebral palsy. To determine the sensory factors maintaining the pulling, the woman was alternately given access to hair that was previously pulled or cut and wore gloves that attenuated the tactile sensation. Almost no pulling occurred when the individual was given free access to the hair, and no hair pulling occurred when the individual wore gloves. This analysis determined that the pulling was maintained by the sensory stimulation produced by manipulating the pulled hair.

Nonfocused pulling appears to be quite common. Du Toit, van Krandenburg, Niehaus, and Stein (2001) determined that 61.7 percent of their sample ($n = 47$) reported pulling outside of unawareness or automatic pulling with 46.8 percent reporting that automatic pulling represented most of their pulling episodes. Christenson, Mackenzie, and Mitchell (1991) reported that 5 percent of their sample ($n = 60$) experienced only automatic pulling, and 43 percent reported pulling episodes that began without awareness. The majority of individuals reporting automatic pulling indicated that most episodes occurred during sedentary activities such as watching television, reading, or talking on the telephone (Christenson et al.).

The second type of pulling has been called *focused pulling* and appears to involve a conscious effort to reduce or eliminate an unpleasant private experience (e.g., an urge to pull, or a thought). Indeed, du Toit and colleagues (2001) report a strong positive correlation between the experience of tension before pulling and the sense of relief/gratification immediately following pulling, suggesting that pulling may produce a reduction in tension. Likewise, Christenson, Mackenzie, and Mitchell (1991) reported that 95 percent of subjects reported tension before pulling, and 88 percent reported gratification following pulling. Such results suggest that focused pulling may be negatively reinforced by the reduction of unpleasant private experiences. Additional research has further explored this negative reinforcement function by considering whether focused pulling represented a broader class of behavior in which one tends to escape from or avoid unpleasant private experiences (experiential avoidance). Early research suggests a link, such that those with more severe pulling have been found to be more experientially avoidant (Begotka, Woods, & Wetterneck, 2004). Likewise, experiential avoidance seems to be related to measures of focused pulling but not nonfocused pulling (Begotka, Woods, & Wetterneck, 2003), and experiential avoidance has been found to mediate partially the relationship between pulling severity and specific cognitions (Norberg, Woods, & Wetterneck, in press).

In addition to these two pathways maintaining pulling, it is understood that pulling can come under the control of any number of antecedent experiences that predict the aforementioned consequences. The result is a great deal of individual variability in variables that increase or decrease pulling severity (Mansueto, Townsley-Stemberger, Thomas, & Golomb, 1997).

Treatment

Multiple approaches have been used for the treatment of TTM (Elliott & Fuqua, 2000), but the two most prominent methods include pharmacotherapy and behavior therapy. Whereas pharmacotherapy typically involves SSRIs or tricyclic antidepressants, most versions of behavior therapy involve three components, including stimulus-control techniques, habit reversal training, and some type of cognitive intervention (Penzel, 2003).

Stimulus-Control Procedures

Stimulus-control procedures have three foci. First, an attempt is made to identify those situations or events that are likely to exacerbate or maintain pulling and to modify or eliminate them from the client's environment. Research shows that certain environments or cues within environments are likely to increase the risk of pulling for persons with TTM (e.g., Christenson, Mackenzie, & Mitchell, 1991; du Toit et al., 2001; Mansueto et al., 1997). Examples include idle times, the presence of tweezers or mirrors, specific rooms (e.g., bathrooms or bedrooms), being in a car, and reading a book. In conducting antecedent stimulus-control procedures, the therapist seeks to eliminate or attenuate these situations so their effect is minimized. Examples of such strategies include removing tweezers from the house or covering or removing mirrors from the bathrooms.

The second focus of stimulus-control procedures involves increasing the response effort necessary to engage in pulling, thus making the behavior more difficult. Examples include wearing gloves on hands in high-risk pulling situations, wearing shorter hair styles, manipulating objects, putting bandages on fingers used to pull, putting petroleum jelly on the eyelashes, and so on (Christenson, Mackenzie, & Mitchell, 1991; Rapp, Dozier, Carr, Patel, & Enloe, 2000).

The final focus of stimulus-control interventions involves determining the reinforcing sensory consequences produced by the pulling or subsequent manipulation of the hair and then eliminating or attenuating these stimuli. Research shows that pulling may produce a number of reinforcing sensory consequences. For example, some persons are highly reinforced by the slightly painful sensation on the scalp that is produced as the hair is pulled. Others may gaze at the hair after it is pulled and be reinforced by its sight. Still, others may be reinforced by the tactile stimulation received as the pulled hair is manipulated (Rapp et al., 1999). It is the job of the clinician to conduct a careful functional assessment to determine whether any of these sensory stimuli are functioning as reinforcers, and to attenuate them when possible. For example, assume a tactile sensation on the lips and fingers is achieved after rubbing the pulled hair between one's fingers and lips. If these sensations appear to reinforce the pulling, then a stimulus-control intervention may involve wearing rubber gloves when pulling and putting mild numbing agents on the lips in pulling-prone situations.

Habit-Reversal Training

Central to behavioral treatments for various repetitive behavior disorders (Woods & Miltenberger, 1995), habit-reversal training (HRT) includes three primary components: (1) awareness training, (2) competing response training, and (3) social support. Awareness training involves the client describing in detail the act of pulling, along with its antecedents and consequences. Antecedents, labeled "warning signs" for the client, include physical settings, early behaviors in the chain leading to pulling (e.g., stroking the hair), and private sensations such as urges, tension, specific thoughts, or anxiety. After the entire behavioral sequence is fully described, the client and therapist work together to teach the client to detect the behavior in session. Clients are asked to signal the therapist (e.g., by raising a finger) when a warning sign or an actual hair pull occurs. Warning signs or hair pulls missed by the client are pointed out by the clinician, and when the client accurately notes an occurrence, the therapist praises the client. This portion of treatment continues until the clinician is confident the client is aware of the pulling and its antecedents. Self-monitoring is assigned as homework to enhance further the client's awareness.

After awareness has been achieved, competing response (CR) training is implemented. In CR training, the participant is taught to engage in a CR, which is a behavior that is physically incompatible with the act of pulling. Clients are encouraged to engage in the CR for one minute or until the urge to pull goes away (whichever is longer) when he or she notices a warning sign, or when he or she begins to pull. Typically, the CR for TTM involves clenching one's fists, but it should be jointly determined by the client and clinician using the following criteria. First, the CR should be easy to implement. Second, it should be physically incompatible with the pulling behavior, and third, it should be socially inconspicuous.

The CR is taught in session by first having the clinician describe its implementation to the client. Next, the therapist should demonstrate proper implementation and then have the client practice doing the same. It is often useful to set up specific in-session practices in which the client role plays the initiation of pulling or a warning sign and then implements the CR for the prescribed time period. This should continue until the client is consistently able to implement the CR contingent on the pulling and warning signs. In addition to in-session practice, clients are encouraged to conduct practice sessions at home and are instructed to use the CR contingent on every warning sign or pulling episode, even if it is outside of the scheduled practice sessions.

The final component of HRT involves social support. Although some evidence suggests that social support may not be beneficial for adults with repetitive behavior problems (Flessner et al., 2005), it is still recommended for children, and we will continue to recommend it for adults until dismantling studies deem it unnecessary for adults with TTM. Social support involves finding a significant other in the client's life who can gently prompt the client to use the CR when he or she is seen pulling but not using the CR. Likewise, the support person is asked to praise the client for correctly engaging in the CR.

Social support can be implemented in a number of ways. Ideally, the client will bring the support person to the session, and the therapist can directly instruct the support person in his or her duties. Therapists should take care that the support persons' prompting does not come across as nagging or the praising as backhanded. If the client is unable to bring a support person to session, the therapist should ask the client to recruit the support person and make it a homework assignment for the client to provide accurate instructions to him or her regarding the support person's role in treatment. In addition to awareness training, CR training, and social support, relaxation training is sometimes added to HRT, if it is thought that the pulling is exacerbated by anxiety.

Cognitive Interventions

Cognitive interventions have primarily targeted specific cognitions believed to contribute to or maintain the pulling cycle. Specific cognitions targeted for modification include perfectionistic thoughts, distortions about controllability of pulling (e.g., "I can pull just one hair and then stop."), and rationalizations (e.g., "I need to pull so I can be relaxed and study."). More recently, attempts have been made to alter the function of these thoughts along with the antecedent pulling "urge," through acceptance-based strategies such as acceptance and commitment therapy (ACT; Hayes, Strosahl, & Wilson, 1999). The purpose of these strategies is to change the way the client experiences private events (e.g., urges, thoughts) from things to be controlled or eliminated to things to be experienced when present. Because the current chapter is too brief to describe these sets of techniques extensively, interested readers should consult the following resources for additional information (Hayes et al., 1999; Twohig & Woods, 2004; Woods, Wetterneck, & Flessner, 2006).

Typically, the three behavior therapy components (stimulus control, HRT, and cognitive interventions) are done in combination across various sessions. This combined treatment approach is used because it is thought the components cover the two separate pathways believed to maintain TTM (nonfocused and focused pulling).

Evidence for the Effectiveness of Treatment

Pharmacotherapy

Evidence for the efficacy of pharmacotherapy for TTM is limited and contradictory. Open trials have suggested that the atypical neuroleptic olanzapine (Stewart & Nejtek, 2003) and SSRIs fluoxetine (Koran, Ringold, & Hewlett, 1992; Winchell, Jones, Stanley, Molcho, & Stanley, 1992), fluvoxamine (Stanley, Breckenridge, Swann, Freeman, & Reich, 1997), citalopram (Stein, Bouwer, & Maud, 1997), and paroxetine (Ravindran, Lapierre, & Anisman, 1999) are effective in reducing symptoms of TTM. However, other more well-controlled trials using waitlist (van Minnen, Hoogduin, Keijsers, Hellenbrand, & Hendriks, 2003) and placebo controls, showed that fluoxetine was less effective than behavior therapy (van Minnen et al., 2003) and as effective as pill placebo (Christenson, Mackenzie, Mitchell, & Callies, 1991; Streichenwein & Thornby, 1995). Combined, these results cast serious doubt about the utility of SSRIs in treating TTM.

In addition to the aforementioned medications, one of the first pharmacotherapy studies for TTM found that the tricyclic antidepressant clomipramine was more effective than desipramine in non-placebo-controlled crossover study (Swedo et al., 1989), but again, subsequent research comparing clomipramine to behavior therapy and pill placebo found that clomipramine was no more effective than pill placebo and less effective than cognitive behavior therapy (Ninan, Rothbaum, Marsteller, Knight, & Eccard, 2000). Although the use of pharmacotherapy does not have strong empirical support, few medications have been tested, and it is not clear if medications may be an effective adjunct to a treatment that has relatively greater empirical support, behavior therapy.

Psychological Treatment

Evidence for the efficacy of the various permutations of behavioral treatment has been growing since Azrin and Nunn (1973) first introduced HRT. Early research in this area was conducted on HRT alone (i.e., without stimulus-control or cognitive procedures), and results showed that it was more effective than negative practice (Azrin, Nunn, & Frantz, 1980) and effective in a group format (Mouton & Stanley, 1996). However, given the various methodologic limitations of these early studies, their findings should be interpreted with caution. In lieu of other large-scale group trials on the original HRT procedure, a series of studies using single-subject designs were conducted, and positive results were still obtained (Elliott & Fuqua, 2000). Although HRT has a growing body of empirical support as a stand-alone treatment, it has more recently been combined with stimulus-control and cognitive procedures. As such, these studies represent a more general cognitive-behavior therapy (CBT) approach to treatment.

In an early open trial of CBT for treating TTM in a mixed-age sample, Lerner, Franklin, Meadows, Hembree, and Foa (1998) found that 12 of 14 treatment completers were classified as "responders" immediately after treatment. However, relapse was a significant concern as only 4 of 13 completers were classified as "responders" at the 3.6-year follow-up. Other studies of CBT for TTM have used stronger randomized controls and found similar results. Ninan et al. (2000) found that CBT was more effective than pill placebo and clomipramine in 16 persons, and van Minnen et al. (2003) found that CBT was more effective than fluoxetine and waitlist control in 43 persons.

In the most recent addition to the TTM literature, Twohig and Woods (2004) combined HRT with ACT. Results from this multiple-baseline study suggested that the combined treatment was effective and also demonstrated support for the purported mechanism of change (i.e., reducing one's avoidance of private experiences was highly correlated with reductions in pulling). To provide stronger empirical support for the combined treatment Woods et al. (2006) implemented ACT+HRT along with stimulus control and relapse prevention procedures to 25 participants who were randomly assigned to either a treatment or waitlist control group. After 10 sessions across 12 weeks, the treatment group demonstrated significantly less hair pulling and greater reductions in anxiety and depressive symptoms compared with the waitlist group. At post-treatment, approximately 66 percent of treatment completers were deemed clinically improved, and these results were maintained at the three-month follow-up. Similar to the findings from Twohig and Woods, treatment compliance and post-treatment reductions in experiential avoidance were strongly correlated with reductions in pulling severity.

Case Vignette

Consistent with the aforementioned approach, a three-part intervention was conducted with Mary. The intervention consisted of stimulus-control procedures, HRT, and ACT. Using the ACT+HRT manual tested by Woods et al. (2006), ACT was first implemented to address Mary's tendency to use pulling as a means of reducing her unpleasant private sensations. The first six sessions were dedicated entirely to ACT, which focused on allowing Mary to identify the emotional control mechanism involved in her pulling and using experiential exercises to undermine her verbally mediated tendency to engage in such avoidance/escape behavior. These techniques were viewed as primarily addressing her focused pulling. Nevertheless, our functional assessment suggested that Mary also engaged in habitual or "nonfocused" pulling, so to bring such behavior into awareness and break up the habitual chain (as well as force habituation to unpleasant private sensations—a treatment component that is quite consistent with ACT), we implemented HRT in sessions 7 and 8. In sessions 9 and 10, we discussed relapse prevention strategies and stimulus-control techniques. Treatment ended after 10 weeks with a 67 percent reduction in her pulling severity as measured by the Massachusetts General Hospital Hair-pulling Scale (Keuthen et al., 1995).

Issues to Consider

As this chapter reveals, research on TTM and its treatment is relatively incomplete. The existing studies generally have been small, weakly controlled, and nearly all have been conducted with adult samples. Still, given the current state of the literature, CBT appears to be the most effective intervention for the disorder. As such, it would be worthwhile to consider a number of issues when conducting clinical assessments and interventions.

First, treatment compliance and vigilance with the procedure appears to be quite important. Compliance is a significant predictor of treatment response in the TTM population (e.g., Woods et al., 2006), but it is our clinical experience that vigilance with using the treatment strategies declines as symptoms improve, and this decline often leads to relapse. As such, it may be useful to schedule periodic "booster sessions" to remind the client of the treatment techniques. The second issue to consider in assessment and treatment involves comorbidities. Clients may present with comorbid depression/anxiety or, more generally, low self-esteem. Careful attention should be given to whether TTM is a primary or secondary diagnosis, and treatment should be planned accordingly. Likewise, it is unclear whether the treatment approaches described are effective for highly comorbid individuals. A third issue clinicians should understand is that clients may be highly embarrassed about the pulling. We have treated clients in our clinic who have been married to their spouses for over a decade, but the spouses do not know about the pulling and hair loss. Given this level of secrecy in some clients, the therapist should be very sensitive when asking specific questions about the pulling and should not be surprised if the complete story regarding the client's suffering does not emerge until later in treatment.

In summary, TTM is a fascinating, but understudied, disorder. CBT approaches appear to have the greatest promise as an effective treatment, but it seems that a comprehensive CBT package may be needed along with strong compliance to manage the multiple streams of controlling variables found in the disorder.

REFERENCES

American Psychiatric Association. (2000). *Diagnostic and statistical manual of mental disorders* (4th ed., text revision). Washington, DC: Author.

Azrin, N. H., & Nunn, R. G. (1973). Habit reversal: A method of eliminating nervous habits and tics. *Behaviour Research and Therapy, 11,* 619–628.

Azrin, N. H., Nunn, R. G., & Frantz, S. E. (1980). Treatment of hairpulling (trichotillomania): A comparative study of habit reversal and negative practice training. *Journal of Behavior Therapy and Experimental Psychiatry, 11,* 13–20.

Begotka, A. M., Woods, D. W., & Wetterneck, C. T. (2003, November). The relationship between experiential avoidance and the severity of trichotillomania in a nonreferred sample. In M. E. Franklin & N. J. Keuthen (Chairs), *New Developments in Trichotillomania Research.* Symposium conducted at the meeting of the Association for the Advancement of Behavior Therapy, Boston, MA.

Begotka, A. M., Woods, D. W., & Wetterneck, C. T. (2004). The relationship between experiential avoidance and the severity of trichotillomania in a nonreferred sample. *Journal of Behavior Therapy and Experimental Psychiatry, 35,* 17–24.

Bohne, A., Keuthen, N. J., Tuschen-Caffier, B., & Wilhelm, S. (2005). Cognitive inhibition in trichotillomania and obsessive-compulsive disorder. *Behaviour Research and Therapy, 43,* 923–942.

Bohne, A., Savage, C. R., Deckersbach, T., Keuthen, N. J., Jenike, M. A., Tuschen-Caffier, B., et al. (2005). Visuospatial abilities, memory, and executive functioning in trichotillomania and obsessive-compulsive disorder. *Journal of Clinical & Experimental Neuropsychology, 27,* 385–399.

Bordnick, P. S., Thyer, B. A., & Ritchie, B. W. (1994). Feather picking disorder and trichotillomania: An avian model of human psychopathology. *Journal of Behavior Therapy and Experimental Psychiatry, 25,* 189–196.

Casati, J., Toner, B. B., & Yu, B. (2000). Psychosocial issues for women with trichotillomania. *Comprehensive Psychiatry, 41,* 344–351.

Christenson, G. A., & Mackenzie, T. B. (1994). Trichotillomania. In M. Hersen & R. T.

Ammerman (Eds.), *Handbook of Prescriptive Treatments for Adults* (pp. 217–235). New York: Plenum.

Christenson, G. A., Mackenzie, T. B., & Mitchell, J. E. (1991). Characteristics of 60 adult chronic hair pullers. *American Journal of Psychiatry, 148,* 365–370.

Christenson, G. A., Mackenzie, T. B., Mitchell, J. E., & Callies, A. L. (1991). A placebo-controlled, double-blind crossover study of fluoxetine in trichotillomania. *American Journal of Psychiatry, 148,* 1566–1571.

Christenson, G. A., & Mansueto, C. S. (1999). Trichotillomania: Descriptive characteristics and phenomenology. In D. J. Stein, G. A. Christenson, & E. Hollander (Eds.), *Trichotillomania* (pp. 1–42). Boston: Kluwer Academic Press.

Christenson, G. A., Pyle, R. L., & Mitchell, J. E. (1991). Estimated lifetime prevalence of trichotillomania in college students. *Journal of Clinical Psychology, 52,* 415–417.

Christenson, G. A., Ristvedt, S. L., & Mackenzie, T. B. (1993). Identification of trichotillomania cue profiles. *Behaviour Research and Therapy, 31,* 315–320.

Cohen, L. J., Stein, D. J., Simeon, D., Spadaccini, E., Rosen, J., Aronowitz, B., et al. (1995). Clinical profile, comorbidity, and treatment history in 123 hair pullers: A survey study. *Journal of Clinical Psychiatry, 56,* 319–326.

Diefenbach, G. J., Mouton-Odum, S., & Stanley, M. A. (2002). Affective correlates of trichotillomania. *Behaviour Research and Therapy, 40,* 1302–1315.

Diefenbach, G. J., Tolin, D. F., Hannan, S., Crocetto, J., & Worhunsky, P. (2005). Trichotillomania: Impact on psychosocial functioning and quality of life. *Behaviour Research and Therapy, 43,* 869–884.

Du Toit, P. L., van Kradenburg, J., Niehaus, D. J. H., & Stein, D. J. (2001). Characteristics and phenomenology of hair-pulling: An exploration of subtypes. *Comprehensive Psychiatry, 42,* 247–256.

Elliott, A. J., & Fuqua, R. W. (2000). Trichotillomania: Conceptualization, measurement, and treatment. *Behavior Therapy, 31,* 529–545.

Flessner, C. A., Miltenberger, R. G., Egemo, K., Kelso, P., Jostad, C., Johnson, B., et al. (2005). An evaluation of the social support component of simplified habit reversal. *Behavior Therapy, 36,* 35–42.

Greer, J. M., & Capecchi, M. R. (2002). Hoxb8 is required for normal grooming behavior in mice. *Neuron, 33,* 23–34.

Hayes, S. C., Strosahl, K. D., & Wilson, K. G. (1999). *Acceptance and commitment therapy: An experiential approach to behavior change.* New York: Guilford Press.

Himle, J. A., Bordnick, P. S., & Thyer, B. A. (1995). A comparison of trichotillomania and obsessive-compulsive disorder. *Journal of Psychopathology and Behavioral Assessment, 17,* 251–260.

Hollander, E. (1998). Treatment of obsessive-compulsive spectrum disorders with SSRIs. *British Journal of Psychiatry, 173*(Suppl. 35), 7–12.

Keuthen, N. J., O'Sullivan, R. L., Ricciardi, J. N., Shera, D., Savage, C. R., Borgmann, A. S., et al. (1995). The Massachusetts General Hospital (MGH) hairpulling scale: 1. Development and factor analysis. *Psychotherapy and Psychosomatics, 64,* 141–145.

Koran, L. M., Ringold, A., & Hewlett, W. (1992). Fluoxetine for trichotillomania: An open clinical trial. *Psychopharmacology Bulletin, 28,* 145–149.

Lenane, M. C., Swedo, S. E., Rapoport, J. L., Leonard, H., Sceery, W., & Guroff, J. J. (1992). Rates of obsessive compulsive disorder in first degree relatives of patients with trichotillomania: A research note. *Journal of Child Psychiatry, 33,* 925–933.

Lerner, J., Franklin, M. E., Meadows, E. A., Hembree, E., & Foa, E. B. (1998). Effectiveness of a cognitive behavioral treatment program for trichotillomania: An uncontrolled evaluation. *Behavior Therapy, 29,* 157–171.

Mansueto, C. S., Townsley-Stemberger, R. M., Thomas, A. M., & Golomb, R. G. (1997). Trichotillomania: A comprehensive behavioral model. *Clinical Psychology Review, 17,* 567–577.

Miltenberger, R. G., Long, E. S., Rapp, J. T., Lumley, V. A., & Elliot, A. J. (1998). Evaluating the function of hair pulling: A preliminary investigation. *Behavior Therapy, 29,* 211–219.

Miltenberger, R. G, Rapp, J. T., & Long, E. S. (2001). Characteristics of trichotillomania. In D. W. Woods & R. G. Miltenberger (Eds.), *Tic disorders, trichotillomania, and other repetitive behavior disorders: Behavioral approaches to analysis and treatment* (pp. 133–150). Boston: Kluwer Academic Press.

Mouton, S. G., & Stanley, M. A. (1996). Habit reversal training for trichotillomania: A group approach. *Cognitive and Behavioral Practice, 3,* 159–162.

Ninan, P. T., Rothbaum, B. O., Marsteller, F. A., Knight, B. T., & Eccard, M. B. (2000). A placebo-controlled trial of cognitive behavior therapy and clomipramine in trichotillomania. *Journal of Clinical Psychiatry, 61,* 47–50.

Norberg, M. M., Woods, D. W., & Wetterneck, C. T. (in press). Examination of the mediating role of psychological acceptance in relationships between cognitions and severity of chronic hairpulling. *Behavior Modification.*

O'Sullivan, R. L., Rauch, S. L., Breiter, H. C., Grachev, I. D., Baer, L., Kennedy, D. N., et al. (1997). Reduced basal ganglia volumes in trichotillomania measured via morphmetric magnetic resonance imaging. *Society of Biological Psychiatry, 42,* 39–45.

Penzel, F. (2003). *The hair pulling problem: A complete guide to trichotillomania.* New York: Oxford University Press.

Rapp, J. T., Dozier, C. L., Carr, J. E., Patel, M. R., & Enloe, K. A. (2000). Functional analysis of hair manipulation: A replication and extension. *Behavioral Interventions, 15,* 121–133.

Rapp, J. T., Miltenberger, R. G., Galensky, T. L., Ellingson, S. A., & Long, E. S. (1999). A functional analysis of hair pulling. *Journal of Applied Behavior Analysis, 32,* 329–337.

Ravindran, A. V., Lapierre, Y. D., & Anisman, H. (1999). Obsessive-compulsive spectrum disorders: Effective treatment with paroxetine. *Canadian Journal of Psychiatry, 44,* 805–807.

Sischo, W. M., Ihrke, P. J., & Franti, C. E. (1989). Regional distribution of ten common skin diseases in dogs. *Journal of American Veterinary Association, 195,* 752–756.

Stanley, M. A., Breckenridge, J. K., Swann, A. C., Freeman, E. B., & Reich, L. (1997). Fluvoxamine treatment of trichotillomania. *Journal of Clinical Psychopharmacology, 17,* 278–283.

Stanley, M. A., & Cohen, L. J. (1999). Trichotillomania and obsessive-compulsive disorder. In D. J. Stein, G. A. Christenson, & E. Hollander (Eds.), *Trichotillomania* (pp. 225–262). Washington, DC: American Psychiatric Press.

Stein, D. J., Bouwer, C., & Maud, C. M. (1997). Use of the selective serotonin reuptake inhibitor citalopram in treatment of trichotillomania. *European Archives of Psychiatry and Clinical Neuroscience, 247,* 234–236.

Stein, D. J., & Hollander, E. (1992). Low-dose pimozide augmentation of serotonin reuptake blockers in the treatment of trichotillomania. *Journal of Clinical Psychology, 53*, 123–126.

Stein, D. J., von Heerden, B., Hugo, C., von Kradenburg, J., Warwick, J., Zungu-Dirwayi, et al. (2002). Functional brain imaging and pharmacotherapy in trichotillomania single photon emission computed tomography before and after treatment with the selective serotonin reuptake inhibitor citalopram. *Progress in Neuro-Psychopharmacology and Biological Psychiatry, 26*, 885–890.

Stewart, R. S., & Nejtek, V. A. (2003). An open-label, flexible-dose study of olanzapine in the treatment of trichotillomania. *Journal of Clinical Psychiatry, 64*, 49–52.

Streichenwein, S. M., & Thornby, J. I. (1995). A long-term, double-blind, placebo-controlled crossover trial of the efficacy of fluoxetine for trichotillomania. *American Journal of Psychiatry, 152*, 1192–1196.

Swedo, S. E. (1993). Trichotillomania. *Psychiatric Annals, 23*, 402–407.

Swedo, S. E., & Leonard, H. L. (1992). Trichotillomania: An obsessive-compulsive spectrum disorder? *Psychiatric Clinics of North America, 15*, 777–790.

Swedo, S. E., Leonard, H. L., Rapoport, J. L., Lenane, M. C., Goldberger, E. L., & Cheslow, D. L. (1989). A double-blind comparison of clomipramine and desipramine in the treatment of trichotillomania (hair pulling). *New England Journal of Medicine, 24*, 497–501.

Swedo, S. E., Rapoport, J. L., Leonard, H. L., Schapiro, M. B., Rapoport, S. I., & Grady, C. L. (1991). Regional cerebral glucose metabolism of women with trichotillomania. *Archives of General Psychiatry, 48*, 828–833.

Twohig, M. P., & Woods, D. W. (2004). A preliminary investigation of acceptance and commitment therapy and habit reversal as a treatment for trichotillomania. *Behavior Therapy, 35*, 803–820.

van Minnen, A., Hoogduin, K. A., Keijsers, G. P., Hellenbrand, I., & Hendriks, G. J. (2003). Treatment of trichotillomania with behavioral therapy or fluoxetine: A randomized waiting-list controlled study. *Archives of General Psychiatry, 60*, 517–522.

Vythilingum, B., Warwick, J., von Kradenburg, J., von Heerden, B., & Stein, D. J. (2002). SPECT scans in identical twins with trichotillomania. *Journal of Neuropsychiatry and Clinical Neuroscience, 14*, 340–342.

Winchell, R. M., Jones, J. S., Stanley, B., Molcho, A., & Stanley, M. (1992). Clinical characteristics of trichotillomania and its response to fluoxetine. *Journal of Clinical Psychiatry, 53*, 35–36.

Woods, D. W., & Miltenberger, R. G. (1995). Habit reversal: A review of applications and variations. *Journal of Behavior Therapy and Experimental Psychiatry, 26*, 123–131.

Woods, D. W., Miltenberger, R. G., & Flach, A. D. (1996). Habits, tics, and stuttering: Prevalence and relation to anxiety and somatic awareness. *Behavior Modification, 20*, 216–225.

Woods, D. W., Wetterneck, C. T., & Flessner, C. A. (2006). A controlled evaluation of acceptance and commitment therapy plus habit reversal for trichotillomania. *Behaviour Research and Therapy, 44*, 639–656.

CHAPTER FIFTEEN

Impulse-Control Disorders

Jon E. Grant, J.D., M.D., M.P.H., and Patrick Marsh, M.D.

Approximately 10 years ago, researchers suggested that one way to understand impulse-control disorders (ICDs) was as part of an obsessive-compulsive spectrum (Hollander, 1993). This conceptualization of ICDs was based on what was then known about the clinical characteristics of these disorders, familial transmission, and response to both pharmacologic and psychosocial treatment interventions. Over the past five years, there has been a dramatic increase in research concerning ICDs (Grant & Potenza, 2004). What has emerged from this research is a more detailed understanding of the ICDs and a complex picture of their relationship to obsessive-compulsive disorder (OCD).

In *Diagnostic and Statistical Manual of Mental Disorders* (DSM-IV-TR), the category of Impulse Control Disorders Not Elsewhere Classified currently includes intermittent explosive disorder, kleptomania, pyromania, pathological gambling, and trichotillomania. Other disorders have been proposed for inclusion based on perceived phenomenologic, clinical, and possibly biological similarities: psychogenic excoriation (skin picking), compulsive buying, compulsive Internet use, and nonparaphilic compulsive sexual behavior. The extent to which these impulse control disorders share clinical, genetic, phenomenologic, and biological features is still of some debate.

Because rigorous research is limited on several of these disorders, this chapter reviews the available clinical characteristics, associated psychopathology, and clinical management of pathological gambling, kleptomania, and compulsive buying. The relationship of these disorders to OCD will also be examined. Trichotollomania and nonparaphilic sexual compulsions are covered in separate chapters.

Clinical Presentation

Pathological Gambling

Pathological gambling (PG), characterized by persistent and recurrent maladaptive patterns of gambling behavior, is associated with impaired functioning, reduced quality of life, and high rates of bankruptcy, divorce, and incarceration. PG usually begins in early adulthood, with males tending to start at an earlier age (Ibanez, Blanco, Moreryra, & Saiz-Ruiz, 2003). In epidemiologic studies, women represent approximately 32 percent of the pathological gamblers in the United States (Volberg, 1994). If left untreated, PG appears to be a chronic, recurring condition.

Male pathological gamblers appear more likely to report problems with strategic or "face-to-face" forms of gambling (e.g., blackjack or poker). Female pathological gamblers tend to report problems with nonstrategic, less interpersonally interactive forms of gambling (e.g., slot machines or bingo; Potenza et al., 2001). Both female and male gamblers report that advertisements are a common trigger of their urges to gamble, although females are more likely to report that feeling bored or lonely may also trigger their urges to gamble (Grant & Kim, 2001). Financial and marital problems are common (Grant & Kim, 2001). Many pathological gamblers engage in illegal behavior, such as stealing, embezzlement, and writing bad checks to fund their gambling (Potenza et al., 2001).

Kleptomania

Kleptomania is characterized by repetitive, uncontrollable stealing of items not needed for their personal use. Kleptomania begins most often in late adolescence or early adulthood (McElroy, Pope, Hudson, Keck, & White, 1991). The course of the illness is generally chronic, with waxing and waning symptoms. Women appear twice as likely to have kleptomania (Grant & Kim, 2002;

Presta et al. 2002; Sarasalo, Bergman, & Toth, 1996). Most individuals with kleptomania steal from stores. In one study, 68.2 percent of individuals reported that the value of stolen items had increased over the duration of the disorder (Grant & Kim, 2002), suggesting tolerance. Individuals with kleptomania frequently hoard, discard, or return stolen items (McElroy et al., 1991).

Most individuals with kleptomania try unsuccessfully to stop stealing. The inability to stop the behavior often leads to feelings of shame and guilt (Grant & Kim, 2002). Of married subjects, fewer than half (41.7%) had told their spouses about their behavior because of the shame and guilt (Grant & Kim, 2002). Many individuals with kleptomania (64–87%) have been apprehended at some time because of their stealing behavior (McElroy et al., 1991; Presta et al., 2002), with a smaller percentage (15–23%) having been jailed (Grant & Kim, 2002).

Compulsive Buying

Although not specifically recognized by DSM, the following diagnostic criteria have been proposed for compulsive buying: (1) maladaptive preoccupation with or engagement in buying (evidenced by frequent preoccupation with or irresistible impulses to buy; or frequent buying of items that are not needed or not affordable; or shopping for longer periods of time than intended); (2) preoccupations or the buying lead to significant distress or impairment; and (3) the buying does not occur exclusively during hypomanic or manic episodes (McElroy, Keck, Pope, Smith, & Strakowski, 1994).

The onset of compulsive buying appears to occur during late adolescence or early adulthood, although the full disorder may take several years to develop (Black, 1996). The disorder tends to be more common among females (Black, 1996; Christenson et al., 1994; McElroy et al., 1994). Individuals with compulsive buying report repetitive, intrusive urges to shop that may be triggered by being in stores and worsen during times of stress, emotional difficulties, or boredom. Compulsive buying regularly results in large amounts of financial debt, marital or family disruption, and even legal consequences (Christenson et al., 1994). Guilt, shame, and embarrassment typically follow the buying episodes. Most items are not used or even removed from the packaging. Hoarding of particular items is common (Christenson et al., 1994).

Case Vignette

Jason, a 32-year-old male, described himself as having a "compulsive personality." He reported a history, beginning in late adolescence, of uncontrollable gambling. At that time, he reports that he became "obsessed" with gambling, thinking about it "all day." He stated that his gambling began as poker games with friends and, over a period of several years, developed into casino gambling by himself. In fact, Jason reports that he currently gambles three or four times each week. He primarily plays blackjack, often gambling for six or more hours at a time. Jason describes daily preoccupation with gambling. He often leaves work early with projects unfinished so that he can get to the casino. In addition, he lies to his wife, telling her that he is working late. Financially, Jason has embezzled more than $5,000 from work to pay off gambling debts.

During the last year, Jason feels that he has also become "obsessed" with shopping. Jason describes daily preoccupation with thoughts of buying various items for the house and spending at least five hours each day on either the Internet looking for items to buy or in stores. He feels unable to limit the amount of time or energy he spends in this behavior. When he has no money or credit, Jason also reports feeling "compelled" to shoplift items.

The Clinical and Scientific Relationship of ICDs to OCD

As seen in the case vignette, the ICDs are characterized by repetitive behaviors and impaired inhibition of these behaviors. The irresistible and uncontrollable behaviors characteristic of ICDs suggest a similarity to the frequently excessive, unnecessary, and unwanted rituals of OCD. One study found that 85 percent of individuals with uncontrolled buying ($n = 20$) described recurrent intrusive and irresistible urges or impulses to buy that resemble obsessions (McElroy et al., 1994). Individuals with PG, kleptomania, and compulsive buying also report hoarding symptoms that resemble individuals with OCD (Black, 1996; Frost, Meagher, & Riskind, 2001; Grant & Kim, 2002).

There are, however, some clear differences between ICDs and OCD. For example, people with ICDs may report an urge or craving state before engaging in the problematic behavior and a hedonic quality during the performance of the behavior (Grant & Potenza, 2004). Individuals with OCD are also generally harm avoidant with a compulsive risk-aversive endpoint to their behaviors (Hollander, 1993), whereas individuals with ICDs are generally sensation seeking (Kim & Grant, 2001).

Co-occurrence of ICDs and OCD

To demonstrate that a relationship exists between ICDs and OCD, OCD should be overrepresented in patients with ICDs, or ICDs should be overrepresented in patients with OCD. Studies examining rates of OCD in subjects with ICDs have reported inconsistent results, with some ICDs showing relatively high rates of co-occurrence with OCD (trichotillomania, compulsive buying; Christenson & Mansueto, 1999; McElroy et al., 1994) and others demonstrating low rates (pathological gambling; Argo & Black, 2004). When rates of ICDs have been examined in subjects with OCD, only trichotillomania and skin picking have consistently shown elevated co-occurrence rates (Fontenelle, Mendlowicz, & Versiani, 2005; Matsunaga et al., 2005).

Family History

A relationship between ICDs and OCD may also be shown by demonstrating that OCD is common in relatives of subjects with ICDs. Family history studies of ICD subjects are, however, limited. Of the few studies that have used control groups, only trichotillomania has shown some suggestion of a familial relationship with OCD (Christenson & Mansuetto, 1999; see Chapter 14, "Trichotillomania").

Neurobiology

Although pathogenesis is arguably the most valid indicator of whether disorders are related, only a sparse amount of research on possible neurobiological correlates of ICDs has been conducted. For example, a functional magnetic resonance imaging study of gambling urges in men suggests that PG has neural features (decreased activity within cortical, basal ganglionic, and thalamic brain regions compared with control subjects) distinct from those of OCD (increased cortico-basal-ganglionic-thalamic activity; Potenza et al., 2003; Reuter et al., 2005; Saxena & Rauch, 2000).

In addition, response to pharmacologic intervention may also inform us about possible underlying biological mechanisms of the disorders. Originally, there was a suggestion that ICDs, like OCD, may demonstrate a preferential response to serotonin reuptake inhibitors (SRIs). Date from multiple pharmacotherapy trials of SRIs in the treatment of ICDs, however, have been inconclusive with some studies suggesting that ICDs respond to serotonergic medications and others failing to find a difference when compared to placebo (Grant & Potenza, 2004).

Reasons for the possible shortcomings of the obsessive-compulsive spectrum model as it pertains to ICDs may be due to the diagnostic category of ICDs. Perhaps only some ICDs share common features with OCD. Conceptualizing all ICDs as similar may be too broad. Moreover, there may be subtypes of each ICD that are more like OCD, whereas other ICD subtypes have more in common with addictive or mood disorders.

Theoretical Models and Etiologic Issues

Although the idea of an obsessive-compulsive spectrum was initially useful as a means of understanding the ICDs, other models have also been proposed.

Behavioral Addiction Model

The model of ICDs as behavioral addictions has strong support from recent research. ICDs share certain distinct features with substance use disorders (SUDs): (1) an urge to engage in a behavior with negative consequences; (2) mounting tension unless the behavior is completed; (3) rapid but temporary reduction of the urge after completion of the behavior; (4) return of the urge over hours, days, or weeks; (5) external cues unique to the behavior; (6) secondary conditioning by external and internal cues (dysphoria, boredom); and (7) hedonic feeling early in the addiction (Marks, 1990). In addition, the symptoms of escalation, tolerance, and withdrawal have analogies in the ICDs. Individuals with ICDs spend increasing amounts of time thinking about, planning, and engaging in the behaviors as the disorder progresses. When an individual is prevented from engaging in the impulsive behavior they may become irritable and restless (Grant & Potenza, 2004).

ICDs frequently co-occur with SUDs. High lifetime rates of SUDs have been found in PG (33–63%; Argo & Black, 2004), kleptomania (23–50%; Grant & Kim, 2002; McElroy et al., 1991), and compulsive buying (30–46%; Black, Repertinger, Gaffney, & Gabel, 1998; Christenson et al., 1994). It is also common for individuals with ICDs to have first-degree relatives who have SUDs (Grant & Potenza, 2004).

Although genetic studies have been performed only in PG, investigations into the possible shared genetic basis for PG and SUDs used genetic model-fitting methods to quantify the extent to which genetic and environmental risk might explain the risk for alcohol dependence in adult male twin pairs from the Vietnam Era Twin Registry. The risk for alcohol dependence accounts for a significant but modest proportion of the genetic and environmental risk for PG (Slutske et al., 2000).

Molecular genetic studies also have provided evidence for the addictive aspects of ICDs. The Taq-AI allele of the dopamine D2 receptor has been implicated in substance use disorders (Blum, 1995). A statistically significant association between the Taq-A1 allele and PG compared with controls has also been found (Comings et al., 1996).

Finally, PG, kleptomania, compulsive buying, and trichotillomania have all demonstrated response to naltrexone, an opioid antagonist that is FDA approved for opiate and alcohol use disorders (Christenson & Mansuetto, 1999; Grant & Potenza, 2004; see "Treatment" section). Naltrexone has not been shown effective in OCD. The finding that ICDs may be responsive to antiaddiction medications may support the inclusion of ICDs within an addictive spectrum.

Affective Spectrum Model

Elevated rates of mood disorders in PG (60–76%; Argo & Black, 2004), kleptomania (59–75%; Bayle, Caci, Millet, Richa, & Olie, 2003; Grant & Kim, 2002), and compulsive buying (59–75%; Black et al., 1998; Christenson et al., 1994) may suggest an association between ICDs and affective disorders. Individuals with ICDs often report that their symptoms worsen when they are depressed. The ICD behavior may have an antidepressant effect (McElroy et al., 1994).

Because of the elevated rates of co-occurring bipolar disorder found in some studies (McElroy et al., 1992), ICDs may also be a symptom of subclinical hypomania or mania. Although many individuals with ICDs may report depression driving the behavior, one must consider a mixed manic state. Also, are impulsive behaviors associated with an affective state merely symptoms of the primary mood disorder? There is currently no research describing whether ICD behaviors differ when they are secondary to mood disorder compared with being independent disorders. Although mood symptoms are common in individuals with ICDs, it is not always clear whether the mood symptoms precede the ICD or may be considered reactive.

Attention Deficit Hyperactivity Model

The attention deficit hyperactivity disorder (ADHD) model for ICDs is just beginning to generate research attention. The main symptoms of ADHD in adults are impulsiveness and inattention (American Psychiatric Association, 2000). Although an early study of PG found that 24 percent had co-occurring ADHD (Specker, Carlson, Christenson, & Marcotte, 1995), no further studies of the possible clinical relationship of ADHD to ICDs have been published.

Anecdotal reports of the use of ADHD medications in the treatment of a subset of pathologic gamblers who appear to have an inattentive, impulsive drive to gamble supports the hypothesis that a subset of individuals with ICDs may be functionally related to ADHD. A recently conducted open-label study of bupropion (a medication found to be effective in treating adults with ADHD) in PG found that subjects responded well to medication, independent of its antidepressant effects (Black, 2004).

Treatment

Pharmacotherapy

Because ICDs were originally conceptualized as forms of OCD, the initial pharmacologic studies used serotonin reuptake inhibitors (SRIs). Data from double-blind randomized pharmacotherapy trials of SRIs in the treatment of ICDs, however, have been inconclusive (Grant & Potenza, 2004). Only two antidepressants have been examined in at least two controlled trials of ICDs. Fluvoxamine, a medication approved by the FDA for OCD, has demonstrated only limited efficacy in ICDs. A double-blind, 16-week crossover study of fluvoxamine in 15 PG subjects demonstrated a statistically significant difference compared with placebo. However, improvement in subjects who received placebo then fluvoxamine was significant, but not for subjects who received fluvoxamine then placebo (Hollander et al., 2000). A six-month double-blind placebo-controlled trial of fluvoxamine in 32 gamblers, however, failed to show statistically significance compared with placebo (Blanco et al., 2002). In the case of compulsive buying, two placebo-controlled trials of fluvoxamine failed to demonstrate any advantage over placebo (Black, Gabel, Hansen, & Schlosser, 2000; Ninan et al., 2000).

Similarly, studies have failed to demonstrate the efficacy of paroxetine, another FDA-approved medication for OCD, in treating ICDs. An initial double-blind placebo-controlled study of paroxetine seemed to indicate its potential efficacy as a treatment for PG. Significant improvement was seen in subjects randomized to eight weeks of treatment with paroxetine compared with those assigned to placebo (Kim, Grant, Adson, Shin, & Zaninelli, 2002). A larger multicenter double-blind placebo-controlled trial in PG, however, failed to reproduce the results (Grant et al., 2003).

The antidepressant trials in ICDs are limited by their small size, high dropout rates, and very high placebo response rates. The two longest studies of PG (each six months) had placebo responses of 59 percent and 72 percent that persisted throughout the study. No positive, placebo-controlled study of an antidepressant in ICDs has been successfully reproduced.

Although case reports suggest that mood stabilizers may be effective in the treatment of ICDs (Grant & Potenza, 2004), only one controlled trial examining a mood stabilizer in ICDs has been published. A 10-week randomized double-blind placebo-controlled trial of lithium in PG with bipolar spectrum disorders suggests lithium may be useful in this subset of individuals with ICDs. Those taking lithium reported statistically significant improvement in gambling thoughts and urges. No difference was found, however, in amount of money lost, episodes of gambling per week, or time spent per gambling episode (Hollander et al., 2005).

Because of the possible relationship of ICDs to addictive disorders, studies of ICDs have examined the efficacy of opioid antagonists in the treatment of ICDs. Opioid antagonists are hypothesized to work indirectly on dopamine and thereby affect the subjective experience of pleasure and urges seen in ICDs (Brahen, Capone, Wiechert, & Desiderio, 1977; Berridge, 1996).

A 12-week, double-blind placebo-controlled naltrexone trial in PG demonstrated superiority to placebo, particularly for those gamblers reporting more severe urges to gamble (Kim, Grant, Adson, & Shin, 2001). Naltrexone's clinical use, however, is limited by significant side effects as well as the occurrence of liver enzyme elevations, especially in patients taking nonsteroidal anti-inflammatory drugs (Kim, Grant, Adson, & Remmel, 2001). A recently completed multicenter study further demonstrated the efficacy of another opioid antagonist, nalmefene, in the treatment of PG. In a sample of 207 subjects, nalmefene demonstrated statistically significant improvement in gambling symptoms (Grant et al., 2006).

In summary, pharmacologic research has resulted in a complex picture for clinicians treating ICDs. Antidepressants appear to be somewhat helpful, but the literature is not clear whether they are any more helpful than placebo. Opioid antagonists appear to be effective in reducing ICD behaviors, but there are serious side effects associated with naltrexone, and nalmefene is not currently available. Other medication options hold some promise, but the studies either have been only open-label designs or, in the case of lithium, have not been reproduced by a different investigator.

Psychological Treatment

Most of the ICDs have related 12-step programs—Gamblers Anonymous, Shopaholics Anonymous, and Shoplifters Anonymous. Although the structure of these groups vary, and not all follow the model of Alcoholics Anonymous, many follow a 12-step approach to recovery.

Gamblers Anonymous (GA) is reportedly the most popular intervention for problem gambling, with about 1000 chapters in the United States. Although GA may help some people achieve and maintain abstinence from gambling, only 8 percent of attendees achieve a year or more of abstinence (Petry & Armentano, 1999). One study examining a multimodal program of combined alcohol, drug, and gambling therapy, along with GA attendance, reported a 64 percent abstinence rate at 6 to 14 months (Lesieur & Blume, 1991). A similar inpatient study at a Veterans Affairs hospital, combining psychotherapy, group therapy, and GA reported a six-month abstinence rate of 55 percent (Russo, Taber, McCormick, & Ramirez, 1984). No published data exist evaluating the efficacy of either Shopaholics Anonymous or Shoplifters Anonymous.

Controlled studies support the efficacy of cognitive and behavioral therapies for PG (Hodgins & Petry, 2004). In one study, individual cognitive therapy resulted in reduced gambling frequency and increased perceived self-control over gambling when compared with a waitlist control group (Sylvain, Ladouceur, & Boisvert, 1997). Another study of cognitive therapy that included relapse prevention also produced improvement in gambling symptoms compared with a waitlist group (Ladouceur et al., 2001).

Cognitive-behavioral therapy has also been used to treat PG. One study compared four groups: (1) individual stimulus control and in vivo exposure with response prevention, (2) group cognitive restructuring, (3) a combination of 1 and 2, and (4) a waitlist control (Eucheburua, Baez, & Fernandez-Montalvo, 1996). At 12 months, rates of abstinence or minimal gambling were higher in the individual treatment (69%) compared with group cognitive restructuring (38%) and the combined treatment (38%).

Other interventions have also shown promise for PG. Brief interventions in the form of workbooks have demonstrated reductions in gambling at a six-month follow-up (the workbook included cognitive-behavioral and motivational enhancement techniques; Dickerson, Hinchy, & Legg England, 1990). A separate study assigned gamblers to a workbook, a workbook plus a telephone motivational enhancement intervention, or a waitlist. Compared with the workbook alone, those gamblers assigned to the motivational intervention and workbook reduced gambling throughout a two-year follow-up period (Hodgins, Currie, & el-Guebaly, 2001).

McConaghy reported significant reduction in gambling behaviors in a comparison of imaginal desensitization to traditional aversion therapy in the treatment of 20 compulsive gamblers (Hodgins & Petry, 2004). Imaginal desensitization therapy has also shown some promise in treating kleptomania. Undergoing fourteen 15-minute sessions over five days, two kleptomania subjects reported complete remission of symptoms for a two-year period (McConaghy & Blaszczynski, 1988).

In summary, the effectiveness of psychosocial interventions appears promising for the treatment of ICDs. Cognitive behavioral therapy or forms of cognitive and behavioral therapies are promising for PG, but large-scale studies with control groups are lacking. In addition, studies in ICDs other than PG are lacking. There also may be a lack of clinicians skilled in these therapies for ICDs, and published manualized treatments are only beginning to appear in the literature.

Case Vignette

Jason, introduced earlier in this chapter, began treatment for his ICDs. Because of his almost constant urges to gamble and buy things, he was started on naltrexone 25 mg/day after informing him of the off-label use of medication and checking his liver function tests. Jason was unable to take advantage of cognitive behavioral therapy due to his urges, and he was first started on the medication to reduce the intrusiveness of these cravings. After four days, his dose was increased to 50 mg/day and then to 100 mg/day after two weeks. With his urges reduced, Jason started cognitive behavioral therapy.

Cognitive behavioral therapy was weekly for 10 weeks. During these sessions Jason identified triggers to his gambling and shopping urges, his cognitive distortions regarding money, gambling probabilities and how to respond to his cravings were all examined, and he was trained in challenging them. In addition, Jason began exploring alternative behaviors that he could perform instead of the ICD behaviors. After 10 weeks of therapy and medication to control his urges, Jason had his behaviors well controlled. Over the next 12 months, Jason was able to control his behavior by staying on medication and receiving a one-hour therapy session per month.

Troubleshooting

The first and most important step to treating a disorder is to diagnose it properly. Many people are ashamed of the problematic behaviors associated with ICDs and therefore may not self-report. Clinicians need to screen for behaviors associated with ICDs if these disorders are to be treated properly.

Although the ICDs have some commonality with OCD, they also have important differences and these differences may necessitate different treatment strategies. Many people with ICDs have co-occurring substance use disorders and these co-occurring conditions need to be addressed as they may both influence the ICD and interfere with the treatment of the ICD.

Subtyping of the ICDs based on clinical similarities to other disorders (e.g., ADHD), existence of co-occurring conditions (e.g., bipolar disorder), or due to core features of the behavior (e.g., cravings), may all be useful ways to decide on treatment interventions. Although subtyping of ICDs needs more research, the early studies suggest that looking beyond the DSM diagnostic criteria and examining what maintains the ICD behavior may be clinically helpful.

Although both pharmacologic and psychosocial treatment interventions have shown early promise for ICDs, no comparative studies have been performed. Should an individual with an ICD start with medication, therapy, or both? Also, are there differences in individuals with ICDs that may indicate a preferential response to a particular intervention? Research addressing these issues is lacking, and therefore, no treatment algorithm can be established at this time.

Given the pleasure associated with ICDs, motivating individuals to enter and adhere to treatment is difficult. In the case of pharmacologic studies of PG, high rates of treatment discontinuation (40–66%) are consistently seen (Grant et al., in press; Kim et al., 2001). Interestingly, rates of treatment adherence appear only minimally better for psychosocial treatments. Two previous studies of CBT in PG resulted in high rates of treatment discontinuation (48–52%; Ladouceur et al., 2001; Sylvain et al., 1997). Naturalistic, longitudinal studies of ICDs are currently lacking, and whether treatment adherence is better in a clinic setting than in controlled studies needs to be examined. In addition, whether certain ICDs pose more challenging or unique problems with treatment adherence is not currently understood.

Conclusion

Impulse-control disorders have historically received relatively little attention from clinicians and researchers. As a consequence, our understanding of efficacious and well-tolerated treatment interventions for ICDs lags significantly behind those for other major neuropsychiatric disorders. Emerging data from controlled clinical trials, however, suggest that ICDs frequently respond to both pharmacologic and psychosocial interventions. More definitive treatment recommendations await completion of additional, large-scale controlled treatment studies for these disorders and comparative studies of pharmacologic agents with psychosocial interventions. Advances in these areas hold the potential for significantly improving the lives of individuals with ICDs and those directly or indirectly affected by their conditions.

REFERENCES

American Psychiatric Association. (2000). *Diagnositic and Statistical Manual of Mental Disorders* (4th ed., text revision). Washington, DC: Author.

Argo, T. R., & Black, D. W. (2004). Clinical characteristics. In J. E. Grant & M. N. Potenza (Eds.), *Pathological Gambling: A Clinical Guide to Treatment* (pp. 39–53). Washington, DC: American Psychiatric Publishing.

Bayle, F. J., Caci, H., Millet, B., Richa, S., & Olie, J. (2003). Psychopathology and comorbidity of psychiatric disorders in patients with kleptomania. *American Journal of Psychiatry, 160,* 1509–1513.

Berridge, K. C. (1996). Food reward: Brain substrates of wanting and liking. *Neuroscience and Biobehavioral Reviews, 20,* 1–25.

Black, D. W. (1996). Compulsive buying: A review. *Journal of Clinical Psychiatry, 57*(Suppl. 8), 50–54.

Black, D. W. (2004). An open-label trial of bupropion in the treatment of pathologic gambling [Letter to the editor]. *Journal of Clinical Psychopharmacology, 24,* 108–110.

Black, D. W., Repertinger, S., Gaffney, G. R., & Gabel, J. (1998). Family history and psychiatric comorbidity in persons with compulsive buying: Preliminary findings. *American Journal of Psychiatry, 155,* 960–963.

Black, D. W., Gabel, J., Hansen, J., & Schlosser, S. (2000). A double-blind comparison of fluvoxamine versus placebo in the treatment of compulsive buying disorder. *Annals of Clinical Psychiatry, 12,* 205–211.

Blanco, C., Petkova, E., Ibanez, A., & Saiz-Ruiz, J. (2002). A pilot placebo-controlled study of fluvoxamine for pathological gambling. *Annals of Clinical Psychiatry, 14,* 9–15.

Blum, K. (1995). Dopamine D2 receptor gene variants: Association and linkage studies in impulsive-addictive-compulsive behaviour. *Pharmacogenetics, 5,* 121–141.
Brahen, L. S., Capone, T., Wiechert, V., & Desiderio, D. (1977). Naltrexone and cyclazocine. A controlled treatment study. *Archives of General Psychiatry, 34,* 1181–1184.
Christenson, G. A., Faber, R. J., de Zwaan, M., Raymond, N. C., Specker, S. M., Ekern, M. D., et al. (1994). Compulsive buying: Descriptive characteristics and psychiatric comorbidity. *Journal of Clinical Psychiatry, 55,* 5–11.
Christenson, G. A., & Mansueto, C. S. (1999). Trichotillomania: Descriptive characteristics and phenomenology. In D. J. Stein, G. A. Christenson, & E. Hollander (Eds.), *Trichotillomania* (pp. 1–42). Washington, DC: American Psychiatric Publishing.
Comings, D. E., Rosenthal, R. J., Lesieur, H. R., Rugle, L. J., Muhleman, D., Chiu, C., et al. (1996). A study of the dopamine D2 receptor gene in pathological gambling. *Pharmacogenetics, 6,* 223–234.
Dickerson, M., Hinchy, J., & Legg England, S. (1990). Minimal treatments and problem gamblers: A preliminary investigation. *Journal of Gambling Studies, 6,* 87–102.
Eucheburua, E., Baez, C., & Fernandez-Montalvo, J. (1996). Comparative effectiveness of three therapeutic modalities in psychological treatment of pathological gambling: Longterm outcome. *Behavioral and Cognitive Psychotherapy, 24,* 51–72.
Fontenelle, L. F., Mendlowicz, M. V., & Versiani, M. (2005). Impulse control disorders in patients with obsessive-compulsive disorder. *Psychiatry and Clinical Neurosciences, 59,* 30–37.
Frost, R. O., Meagher, B. M., & Riskind, J. H. (2001). Obsessive-compulsive features in pathological lottery and scratch-ticket gamblers. *Journal of Gambling Studies, 17,* 5–19.
Grant, J. E., & Kim, S. W. (2001). Demographic and clinical features of 131 adult pathological gamblers. *Journal of Clinical Psychiatry, 62,* 957–962.
Grant, J. E., Kim, S. W., Potenza, M. N., Blanco, C., Ibanez, A., Stevens, L. C., et al. (2003). Paroxetine treatment of pathological gambling: A multi-center randomized controlled trial. *International Clinical Psychopharmacology, 18,* 243–249.
Grant, J. E., & Potenza, M. N. (2004). Impulse control disorders: Clinical characteristics and pharmacological management. *Annals of Clinical Psychiatry, 16,* 27–34.
Grant, J. E., Potenza, M. N., Hollander, E., Cunningham-Williams, R., Nurminen, T., Smits, G., et al. (2006). A multicenter investigation of the opioid antagonist nalmefene in the treatment of pathological gambling. *American Journal of Psychiatry, 163,* 303–312.
Grant, J. E., & Kim, S. W. (2002). Clinical characteristics and associated psychopathology in 22 patients with kleptomania. *Comprehensive Psychiatry, 43,* 378–384.
Hodgins, D. C., & Petry, N. M. (2004). Cognitive and behavioral treatments. In J. E. Grant & M. N. Potenza (Eds.), *Pathological Gambling: A Clinical Guide to Treatment* (pp. 169–187). Washington DC: American Psychiatric Press.
Hodgins, D. C., Currie, S. R., & el-Guebaly, N. (2001). Motivational enhancement and self-help treatments for problem gambling. *Journal of Consulting and Clinical Psychology, 69,* 50–57.
Hollander, E. (1993). Obsessive-compulsive spectrum disorders: An overview. *Psychiatric Annals, 23,* 355–358.
Hollander, E., DeCaria, C. M., Finkell, J. N., Begaz, T., Wong, C. M., & Cartwright, C. (2000). A randomized double-blind fluvoxamine/placebo crossover trial in pathologic gambling. *Biological Psychiatry, 47,* 813–817.

Hollander, E., Pallanti, S., Allen, A., Sood, E., & Baldini Rossi, N. (2005). Does sustained-release lithium reduce impulsive gambling and affective instability versus placebo in pathological gamblers with bipolar spectrum disorders? *American Journal of Psychiatry, 162*, 137–145.

Ibanez, A., Blanco, C., Moreryra, P., & Saiz-Ruiz, J. (2003). Gender differences in pathological gambling. *Journal of Clinical Psychiatry, 64*, 295–301.

Kim, S. W., & Grant, J. E. (2001). Personality dimensions in pathological gambling disorder and obsessive-compulsive disorder. *Psychiatry Research, 104*, 205–212.

Kim, S. W., Grant, J. E., Adson, D. E., & Remmel, R. P. (2001). A preliminary report on possible naltrexone and nonsteroidal analgesic interactions [Letter to the editor]. *Journal of Clinical Psychopharmacology, 21*, 632–634.

Kim, S. W., Grant, J. E., Adson, D. E., & Shin, Y. C. (2001). Double-blind naltrexone and placebo comparison study in the treatment of pathological gambling. *Biological Psychiatry, 49*, 914–921.

Kim, S. W., Grant, J. E., Adson, D. E., Shin, Y. C., & Zaninelli, R. (2002). A double-blind placebo-controlled study of the efficacy and safety of paroxetine in the treatment of pathological gambling. *Journal of Clinical Psychiatry, 63*, 501–507.

Ladouceur, R., Sylvain, C., Boutin, C., Lachance, S., Doucet, C., Leblond, J., et al. (2001). Cognitive treatment of pathological gambling. *Journal of Nervous and Mental Disease, 189*, 774–780.

Lesieur, H. R., & Blume, S. B. (1991). Evaluation of patients treated for pathological gambling in a combined alcohol, substance abuse and pathological gambling treatment unit using the Addiction Severity Index. *British Journal of Addiction, 86*, 1017–1028.

Marks, I. (1990). Behavioural (non-chemical) addictions. *British Journal of Addiction, 85*, 1389–1394.

Matsunaga, H., Kiriike, N., Matsui, T., Oya, K., Okino, K., & Stein, D. J. (2005). Impulsive disorders in Japanese adult patients with obsessive-compulsive disorder. *Comprehensive Psychiatry, 46*, 43–49.

McConaghy, N., & Blaszczynski, A. (1988). Imaginal desensitization: A cost-effective treatment in two shop-lifters and a binge-eater resistant to previous therapy. *Australian and New Zealand Journal of Psychiatry, 22*, 78–82.

McElroy, S. L., Hudson, J. I., Pope, H. G., Keck, P. E., & Aizley, H. G. (1992). The DSM-III-R impulse control disorders not elsewhere classified: Clinical characteristics and relationship to other psychiatric disorders. *American Journal of Psychiatry, 149*, 318–327.

McElroy, S. L., Keck, P. E., Pope, H. G., Jr., Smith, J. M., & Strakowski, S. M. (1994). Compulsive buying: A report of 20 cases. *Journal of Clinical Psychiatry, 55*, 242–248.

McElroy, S. L., Pope, H. G., Jr., Hudson, J. I., Keck, P. E., & White, K. L. (1991). Kleptomania: A report of 20 cases. *American Journal of Psychiatry, 148*, 652–657.

Ninan, P. T., McElroy, S. L., Kane, C. P., Knight, B. T., Casuto, L. S., Rose, S. E., et al. (2000). Placebo-controlled study of fluvoxamine in the treatment of patients with compulsive buying. *Journal of Clinical Psychopharmacology, 20*, 362–366.

Petry, N. M., & Armentano, C. (1999). Prevalence, assessment, and treatment of pathological gambling: a review. *Psychiatric Services, 50*, 1021–1027.

Potenza, M. N., Steinberg, M. A., McLaughlin, S. D., Wu, R., Rounsaville, B. J., & O'Malley, S. S. (2001). Gender-related differences in the characteristics of problem gamblers using a gambling helpline. *American Journal of Psychiatry, 158*, 1500–1505.

Potenza, M. N., Leung, H. C., Blumberg, H. P., Peterson, B. S., Fulbright, R. K., Lacadie, C. M., et al. (2003). An FMRI Stroop task study of ventromedial prefrontal cortical function in pathological gamblers. *American Journal of Psychiatry, 160,* 1990–1994.

Presta, S., Marazziti, D., Dell'Osso, L., Pfanner, C., Pallanti, S., & Cassano, G. B. (2002). Kleptomania: Clinical features and comorbidity in an Italian sample. *Comprehensive Psychiatry, 43,* 7–12.

Reuter, J., Raedler, T., Rose, M., Hand, I., Glascher, J., & Buchel, C. (2005). Pathological gambling is linked to reduced activation of the mesolimbic reward system. *Nature Neuroscience, 8,* 147–148.

Russo, A. M., Taber, J. I., McCormick, R. A., & Ramirez, L. F. (1984). An outcome study of an inpatient treatment program for pathological gamblers. *Hospital and Community Psychiatry, 35,* 823–827.

Saiz-Ruiz, J., Blanco, C., Ibanez, A., Masramon, X., Gomez, M. M., Madrigal, M., et al. (2005). Sertraline treatment of pathological gambling: a pilot study. *Journal of Clinical Psychiatry, 66,* 28–33.

Sarasalo, E., Bergman, B., & Toth, J. (1996). Personality traits and psychiatric and somatic morbidity among kleptomaniacs. *Acta Psychiatrica Scandinavica, 94,* 358–364.

Saxena, S., & Rauch, S. L. (2000). Functional neuroimaging and the neuroanatomy of obsessive-compulsive disorder. *Psychiatric Clinics of North America, 23,* 545–562.

Slutske, W. S., Eisen, S., True, W. R., Lyons, M. J., Goldberg, J., & Tsuang, M. (2000). Common genetic vulnerability for pathological gambling and alcohol dependence in men. *Archives of General Psychiatry, 57,* 666–673.

Specker, S. M., Carlson, G. A., Christenson, G. A., & Marcotte, M. (1995). Impulse control disorders and attention deficit disorder in pathological gamblers. *Annals of Clinical Psychiatry, 7,* 175–179.

Sylvain, C., Ladouceur, R., & Boisvert, J. M. (1997). Cognitive and behavioral treatment of pathological gambling: a controlled study. *Journal of Consulting and Clinical Psychology, 65,* 727–732.

Volberg, R. A. (1994). The prevalence and demographics of pathological gamblers: implications for public health. *American Journal of Public Health, 84,* 237–241.

CHAPTER SIXTEEN

Autistic Syndromes

Christopher J. McDougle, M.D.,
Leslie A. Hulvershorn, M.D., Craig A. Erickson, M.D.,
Kimberly A. Stigler, M.D., and David J. Posey, M.D.

Beginning with Kanner's (1943) original description of autistic disorder (autism), repetitive thoughts and behaviors have been considered common and, at times, disabling features of pervasive developmental disorders (PDDs). A review of phenomenology, etiology, and treatment will provide the rationale for considering PDDs among the obsessive-compulsive spectrum disorders.

Clinical Presentation

Among the PDDs are three diagnostic subtypes, which share impairment across development in social interaction and communication. In addition, the symptomatology of autism, Asperger disorder, and PDD not otherwise specified (NOS) typically includes restrictive, repetitive, and stereotyped behaviors (American Psychiatric Association, 2000). Several reviews of the literature have described a heterogeneous collection of repetitive phenomena in patients with these disorders, ranging from repetitive movements to circumscribed interests and insistence on sameness (for review, see Gross-Isseroff, Hermesh, & Weizman, 2001; McDougle, 1998; McDougle, Kresch, & Posey,

2000; Turner, 1999). The difficulty that many individuals with PDDs have in articulating their internal state can impair their ability to describe repetitive thoughts and behaviors, making an accurate diagnosis of concomitant obsessive-compulsive disorder (OCD) challenging (McDougle, 1998; McDougle, Epperson, Pelton, Wasylink, & Price, 2000). Although repetitive behaviors have been documented in patients with other disorders (for example, specific mental retardation syndromes), unique features seen in PDDs include the severity and character of the phenomena (Turner, 1999). In general, repetitive behavior observed in PDDs has been reported to be more severe and frequent than that seen in IQ-matched controls (Freeman et al., 1981).

Two reports have attempted to characterize differences between repetitive behaviors displayed in OCD and PDDs (McDougle, Kresch, et al., 1995a; Russell, Mataix-Cols, Anson, & Murphy, 2005). In one study, 50 patients (36 male and 14 female, age range 18–53 years) with autism and 50 age- and sex-matched controls with OCD without a lifetime history of motor or phonic tics were compared (McDougle, Fleischmann, et al., 1995). Using the Yale-Brown Obsessive Compulsive Scale Symptom Checklist (Y-BOCS SCL) (Goodman, Price, Rasmussen, Mazure, Delgado, et al., 1989; Goodman, Price, Rasmussen, Mazure, Fleischmann, et al., 1989), McDougle and colleagues (1995) determined that adults with autism and OCD can be distinguished on the basis of their type of repetitive thoughts and behavior. Compared with the OCD group, the autistic patients were less likely to have aggressive, contamination, sexual, religious, symmetry, and somatic thoughts. Autistic patients exhibited increased repetitive ordering, hoarding, telling, tapping or rubbing, and self-damaging or self-mutilating behaviors. Cleaning, checking, and counting behaviors were more common in the OCD group. Overall, significantly more autistic patients had repetitive behaviors alone, and only 8 of 50 (16%) autistic patients versus 47 of 50 (94%) of those with OCD attempted to suppress their thoughts due to an ego-dystonic nature. In general, the repetitive behavior of the autistic group was less well organized and complex. The autistic group, which included 15 nonverbal patients, had a mean full-scale IQ of 69.7 ± 27.2. The authors commented that the lower cognitive functioning in the autistic group may have, in part, accounted for the differences noted between the groups, in particular the low prevalence of obsessions given the requirement of awareness of and ability to describe intrusive thoughts.

In an attempt to further explore the role of IQ difference in the expression of repetitive behavior in autism and related disorders, Russell et al. (2005)

compared the repetitive phenomena exhibited by 40 high-functioning (IQ > 70) adults with autism or Asperger's with 45 gender-matched adults with primary OCD. Overall, the OCD patients scored significantly higher on the Y-BOCS SCL total scale with specifically more somatic obsessions and repeating and checking compulsions. Given the lack of cognitive impairment in adults with PDDs participating in this trial, it was not surprising that 10 of the patients (25%) were determined to warrant a concomitant OCD diagnosis given their insight into the ego-dystonic nature of their thoughts/behaviors.

While it is clear that IQ may play a key role in the manifestation of repetitive phenomena associated with PDDs, there is also evidence that regardless of IQ, patients with PDDs exhibit generally less severe obsessive-compulsive symptoms than their counterparts with primary OCD. Outside of severity, there is also evidence that particular differences in the content of repetitive thoughts and actions may exist between the groups, with somatic content being increased in patients with OCD.

Case Vignette

M.T. is a 12-year-old male with a diagnosis of Asperger disorder who presented with his mother at our outpatient treatment center. Neuropsychological testing revealed a full-scale IQ of 125. M.T. presented with a number of problematic behaviors. He had an intense, all-encompassing preoccupation with pheasants that interfered greatly with his attempts at reciprocal social interaction. He was knowledgeable about different types of pheasants throughout the world, including differences in size, feeding habits, vulnerability to disease, and life span. M.T. learned about pheasants through reading library books, by watching television shows, and by surfing the Internet. His mother estimated that he spent up to 8 hours per day in efforts to learn and talk about pheasants. He would often be awake until 2 or 3 a.m. using the computer in his room for these purposes. As a result, he had difficulty rising for school, resulting in tantrums and refusal to go to school. He had extreme difficulty maintaining friendships with his peers, as they would become frustrated with his need to talk solely about pheasants and because of his difficulty tolerating discussion of their interests. With the help of a behavior therapist, his mother instituted a program with the goal of limiting M.T.'s access to information related to pheasants to particular times of the day. Attempts to prevent him from watching television shows or looking at Web sites related to pheasants resulted in aggressive behavior toward his mother. These episodes consisted of hitting, kicking, and spitting, along with property destruction. At the time of presentation, these episodes had been going on for the past 18 months.

Theoretical Models and Etiologic Issues

Research into the pathophysiology and etiology of autism has been ongoing for half a century. Despite these efforts, the cause remains unknown. The heterogeneity of the PDD population makes this research difficult. Attempts to limit this heterogeneity have included looking at subsets of persons with PDDs. One such subset investigated to date includes persons exhibiting intense repetitive phenomena. This work has facilitated the comparison of research findings into the etiology of PDDs and OCD (Gross-Isseroff et al., 2001).

The history of theoretical models describing PDDs will be reviewed. Then, current etiologic theories giving emphasis to the overlap between PDDs and OCD will be discussed.

Theoretical Models

Early theoretical models describing autistic phenomenology were couched in a Freudian tradition. Out of this tradition came the idea that aloof, cold parents (in particular, mothers) were responsible for their autistic child turning inward (Bettelheim, 1967). During the last quarter century, the body of literature addressing autism has shifted away from blaming parents for the development of PDDs. The currently employed biological model of PDDs views these disorders with some yet undefined biologic etiology. This model fits better with the existence of some known causes of autistic phenomena, including congenital rubella, tuberous sclerosis, and fragile X syndrome, among others. The biological model of PDDs includes heterogeneous themes such as neurochemistry, genetics, neuroanatomy, gastrointestinal function, and autoimmunity.

Etiologic Issues

Genetics

While the search for autism susceptibility genes has been complicated by phenotypic heterogeneity, observational accounts have pointed towards a strong genetic contribution to the disorder (Wassink, Brzustowicz, Bartlett, & Szatmari, 2004). A heritable component to the etiology of autism was first supported by twin studies noting a 60 percent monozygotic twin concordance rate (Bailey et al., 1995; Folstein & Rutter, 1977). Up to 5 percent of siblings of autistic individuals have been described as developing autism (Ritvo, Freeman, Mason-Brothers, Mo, & Ritvo, 1985), a rate up to 50 times the 0.67 percent prevalence of PDDs in the general population (Bertrand et al., 2001).

Gene association and linkage studies to date have identified more than 100 candidate genes (Wassink et al., 2004). The results of studies identifying candidate genes are often in conflict. This discordance is likely, in part, to sample heterogeneity. Means of addressing the difficulties associated with phenotypic complexity have included investigating subsets of autistic patients, and looking for a genetic predisposition to certain symptoms displayed by individuals with PDDs. While a full discussion of all subset analyses to date is beyond the scope of this chapter, references to work done in the area of repetitive and obsessive-compulsive phenomena will be presented.

An assessment of parents of 16 autistic patients compared with those in control families noted no overall increase in obsessive-compulsive characteristics in the parents of affected children (Kano, Ohta, Nagai, Pauls, & Leckman, 2004). On subset analysis, Kano et al. (2004) reported that fathers of autistic patients had an increase in cleaning behaviors compared with normal controls. In addition, there was no correlation noted between the severity of repetitive phenomena in the autistic patients and obsessive-compulsive symptoms in their parents. A conflicting report on 176 patients with autism in 57 families noted a strong correlation between high scores on the repetitive domain of the Autism Diagnostic Interview-Revised (ADI-R; Lord, Rutter, & LeCouteur, 1994) and parents with obsessive-compulsive traits or OCD (Hollander, King, Delaney, Smith, & Silverman, 2003). A genetic linkage study analyzed 62 families, each that had two persons with a PDD, and more severe obsessive-compulsive behaviors as recorded on the ADI-R (Buxbaum et al., 2004). In this study, the strongest evidence for linkage was found at chromosome 1, marker D1S1656 with additional evidence for linkage on chromosomes 4, 5, 6, 10, 11, and 19. The use of obsessive-compulsive characteristics as a means to better define genetic studies of PDDs has yielded conflicting results. Interpretation will necessitate further investigation, likely using large samples, as well as standardized measures of repetitive phenomena and parental OCD symptomatology.

Genes associated with serotonin (5-HT) transport represent one area of autism etiologic research with potential overlap with OCD. Six reports have noted noncoding polymorphisms in the noncoding promoter region of the

5-HT transporter gene (Wassink et al., 2004). Other reports have found no consistent polymorphisms in this region; and even among studies with some promise of linkage to this site, different alleles for the same polymorphism or different polymorphisms altogether have been reported (Wassink et al., 2004). These findings may show some overlap with an investigation of OCD that found a polymorphism at the 5-HT transporter region (McDougle, Epperson, Price, & Gelernter, 1998).

Although emphasis on a possible overlap with OCD has been used to further delineate and potentially even guide genetic studies of autism, these attempts to limit heterogeneity and overcome some of the complexity associated with the phenotypic expression of autism have yielded limited data in support of any specific genetic defects.

Neurochemistry

Serotonin has been implicated as a possible factor in the developmental of both OCD and PDDs (Gross-Isseroff et al., 2001). Whole blood serotonin (WBS) levels have been evaluated in many studies in autism. Most, but not all, reports have pointed toward elevated WBS in autism (McDougle, Erickson, Stigler, & Posey, 2005). Although normal subjects generally experience an age-related decline in WBS, autistic patients have not generally followed this trend, leading to the hypothesis that autistic subjects may have an abnormal maturation of the 5-HT system (Anderson et al., 1987; Leboyer et al., 1999). Possible central 5-HT dysregulation has been supported by decreased prolactin response to 5-hydroxytryptophan (5-HTP) (an immediate 5-HT precursor; Hoshino, Watanabe, Tachibana, Kaneko, & Kumashiro, 1983), and worsening of symptoms in 11 of 17 adults with autism subjected to acute tryptophan depletion (McDougle, Naylor, Cohen, Aghajanian, et al., 1996). The possible interpretation of peripheral hyperserotonemia with central hypoactivity in autism may parallel findings noted in OCD. Some studies in OCD have noted elevated cerebral spinal fluid (CSF) concentration of the 5-HT metabolite 5-hydroxy indoleacetic acid (5-HIAA), whereas others have not replicated this finding (Gross-Isseroff et al., 2001). In addition, some pharmacologic challenge studies have reported central 5-HT hypoactivity in OCD (Gross-Isseroff et al., 2004).

Functional neuroimaging has further defined the role of 5-HT in PDD and OCD. Using positron emission tomography (PET) to assess tracer 5-HT precursor molecules, gross asymmetries of 5-HT synthesis were noted in frontal cortex, thalamus, and cerebellum in seven autistic boys, but not in one female autistic patient (Chugani et al., 1997). A PET study of 11 adults with OCD noted normal 5-HT transporter availability in subcortical and limbic brain regions (Simpson et al., 2003). Abnormally high 5-HT$_{2A}$ receptor binding in the caudate nucleus was noted in a PET study of 15 unmedicated OCD patients compared with controls (Adams et al., 2005). While early findings may show some consistency in 5-HT dysregulation in PDDs and OCD, more work is needed to better define the specifics of these differences, and in particular with PDDs, to evaluate the developmental course of these changes.

The beneficial effects of dopamine antagonists (DA) in the treatment of behavioral symptoms associated with PDDs led to the investigation of DA in the pathophysiology of these disorders. Neurochemical research in this area has centered on the measurement of the primary DA metabolite, homovanillic acid (HVA), in urine, plasma, and CSF (for review, see McDougle et al., 2005). No consistent differences in HVA have been noted in patients with PDDs. In general, neurochemical studies of DA in OCD have yielded no consistent evidence for a primary DA dysfunction (Denys, Zohar, & Westenberg, 2004).

Peripheral levels of glutamate and GABA, the primary excitatory and inhibitory neurotransmitters in the brain, respectively, have been measured in patients with PDDs. Studies to date have reported conflicting results of elevated or decreased glutamate and GABA levels in plasma (for review, see McDougle et al., 2005). In OCD, a recent report noted elevated CSF glutamate in 21 affected adults compared with normal controls (Chakrabarty, Bhattacharyya, Christopher, & Khanna, 2005). The future of this area of research will include attempts to better measure and understand central glutamate/GABA function in PDDs.

The implication of the nine amino acid peptides oxytocin (OT) and arginine vasopressin (AVP) in social behavior in mammals (Insel, 1997) has led to the investigation of these neurohormones in PDDs. The hypothesis that human neonatal exposure to OT (pitocin) during labor induction may lead to long-term OT receptor down-regulation has been evaluated in two studies comparing affected children and controls (Gale, Ozonoff, & Lainhart, 2003; Fein et al., 1997). Both of these reports note similar birth induction rates between children who developed PDDs and control subjects. A report on 30 autistic male children noted a decreased plasma level of OT with an increased level of the extended form precursor of OT. In OCD, one report of CSF OT levels noted no difference in the peptide level in 14 affected adults compared with control subjects (Altemus et al., 1999). An earlier report describing CSF

OT levels in 29 adults with OCD compared with patients with Tourette disorder and normal controls noted an increased level of OT in OCD patients ($n = 22$) without a personal or family history of tic disorders (Leckman et al., 1994).

In summary, heterogeneous findings in the neurochemistry of PDDs mirror the results of other investigations into the etiology of PDDs. These results, however, suggest that further research is needed to understand better the possible overlap in pathophysiology of PDDs and OCD.

Autoimmunity

Discussion of autoimmunity in the pathogenesis of PDDs may provide added insight into possible autoimmune factors in OCD. The existence of childhood-onset OCD among pediatric autoimmune neuropsychiatric disorders associated with streptococcal infections (PANDAS) points to the potential of autoimmune factors in the development of this disorder (Snider & Swedo, 2004). Heterogeneous reports in PDDs have described many signs of potential immune system dysregulation. The reports have included descriptions of elevated antibodies to numerous CNS proteins (for review, see Krause, Xiao-Song, Gershwin, & Schoenfeld, 2002), gastrointestinal associated immune hyperactivity (Murch, 2005), and increased prevalence of familial autoimmunity in patients with PDDs (Sweeten et al., 2003). Among the neuroproteins reported to be subject to autoantibodies in PDDs, myelin basic protein (MBP) is of particular interest since it contains a 5-HT binding site (Field, Caspary, & Carnegie, 1971). In theory, MBP may act as an autoantigen possibly leading to the production of autoantibodies against the 5-HT receptor (Westall & Root-Bernstein, 1983; Yuwiler et al., 1992). The existence of OCD associated with PANDAS and numerous autoimmune factors reported in PDDs provides a basis for continued research into the potential overlap in the pathogenesis of these disorders.

Treatment

Pharmacotherapy

In part, secondary to the diverse neurochemical findings involving patients with PDDs, many classes of drugs have been evaluated in this population. These drug trials have included the use of medications often found to be effective in treating OCD, in particular, serotonin reuptake inhibitors (SRIs). The overlap of pharmacotherapy between PDDs and OCD has been marked at times by decreased drug tolerance and more limited efficacy in the PDD population. While a full discussion of the pharmacotherapy of PDDs is beyond the scope of this chapter, specific reference will be made to drugs widely used to target repetitive phenomena.

Clomipramine is a tricyclic antidepressant that inhibits norepinephrine (NE), DA, and, most potently, 5-HT neuronal uptake. Clomipramine is approved by the U.S. Food and Drug Administration (FDA) for the treatment of child, adolescent, and adult OCD. Several controlled trials have evaluated the efficacy of clomipramine in targeting repetitive behavior in autistic patients. In seven children and adolescents with autism, Gordon, Rapoport, Hamburger, State, and Mannheim (1992) reported clomipramine (mean dose 129 mg/day) efficacious compared with desipramine, a more selective NE reuptake inhibitor, and placebo in a 10-week crossover trial. Patients taking clomipramine experienced decreased anger and repetitive behavior. Similar results from the same group of investigators were reported in two 10-week double-blind, placebo-controlled trials each containing 12 autistic children (Gordon, State, Nelson, Hamburger, & Rapoport, 1993). Both crossover trials, one comparing clomipramine (mean dose 152 mg/day across both trials) to placebo and one using desipramine as a comparator, noted an association between decreased stereotypies and compulsive behaviors during treatment with clomipramine. In this report, clomipramine-associated side effects included single reports of prolonged QTc interval, resting tachycardia, and a tonic-clonic seizure. Remington et al. (2001) compared clomipramine (128 mg/day), haloperidol (1.3 mg/day), and placebo in 36 patients (mean age 16.3 years) with autism. In this seven-week trial, approximately two-thirds of patients receiving clomipramine exited the study secondary to lack of efficacy or side effects (fatigue and tremor being the most common). Among patients who were able to tolerate clomipramine, the drug was as efficacious as haloperidol, but more poorly tolerated.

Clomipramine has been shown to be effective in reducing repetitive thoughts and behaviors in some individuals with autism, adverse effects have prevented it from remaining a mainstay of treatment. These side effects, including constipation, behavioral activation, irritability, and sedation, among others, have been particularly notable in children and adolescents.

Fluvoxamine is a selective serotonin reuptake inhibitor (SSRI) that is also FDA approved to treat children, adolescents, and adults with OCD. The only published double-blind, placebo-controlled study of fluvoxamine (mean dose

276.7 mg/day) in autistic adults noted a significant reduction in repetitive and maladaptive behavior in 8 of 15 (53%) participants (McDougle, Naylor, Cohen, Volkmar, et al., 1996). Adverse effects included sedation and nausea. In an unpublished double-blind, placebo-controlled study, McDougle and colleagues did not find fluvoxamine (mean dose 107 mg/day) efficacious in 34 children and adolescents with PDDs. Fluvoxamine was poorly tolerated in 14 of 18 (78%) patients who developed various side effects including hyperactivity, insomnia, aggression, and agitation. A recent 12-week double-blind, placebo-controlled crossover study looking at the impact of 5-HT transporter gene polymorphisms on response to fluvoxamine in 18 autistic children noted 10 children (55%) had at least "mild" response, with 5 (28%) showing "excellent" drug response (Sugie et al., 2005). No mention was made of medication-associated improvement in repetitive behavior.

Fluoxetine is another SSRI that is FDA approved for the treatment of OCD in children, adolescents, and adults. The only published controlled trial of fluoxetine (mean dose 9.9 mg/day) in patients with PDDs enrolled 39 children (mean age 8.2 years) who completed a 20-week, placebo-controlled crossover study (eight weeks on each treatment separated by a four-week washout period; Hollander et al., 2005). Low-dose liquid fluoxetine (mean dose 9.9 mg/day, range 2.4–20 mg/day) was significantly better than placebo in reducing repetitive behaviors on the Children's Yale-Brown Obsessive Compulsive Scale (CY-BOCS; Scahill et al., 1997). The side-effect profiles of fluoxetine and placebo were similar in this trial.

Sertraline is also an SSRI that is FDA approved to treat OCD in children, adolescents, and adults. No controlled studies of sertraline in PDDs have been published. Among several case series and open-label trials, two reports have addressed the effects of sertraline on repetitive phenomena in PDDs. McDougle, Brodkin, et al. (1998) reported improvement in repetitive behavior in 42 adults with PDDs treated with sertraline (mean dose 122.0 mg/day) over a 12-week period. Participants with autism ($n = 22$) and PDD NOS ($n = 14$) had a higher rate of response than those with Asperger disorder ($n = 6$), independent of degree of mental retardation. Three patients (7%) dropped out of this study due to increased agitation/anxiety. In a case series, 8 of 9 (88%) autistic children (ages 6 to 12 years) receiving sertraline (25–50 mg/day) showed significant improvement, including a decreased "need for sameness" (Steingard, Zimnitzky, DeMaso, Bauman, & Bucci, 1997). In this case series, two responders developed agitation when their dose was raised to 75 mg/day.

The SSRI citalopram is approved for use in adult major depressive disorder (MDD). Only retrospective data is available describing the use of citalopram in PDDs. Couturier and Nicolson (2002) reported improvement in 10 of 17 (59%) children (mean age 9.4 years) with PDDs taking citalopram (mean dose 19.7 mg/day) for an average of 7.4 months. Among the behaviors targeted were stereotypies and preoccupations. Four patients had to discontinue citalopram due to medication-induced agitation (two patients), tics (one patient), and insomnia (one patient). A second retrospective report on 15 children (mean age 11.1 years) with various PDDs receiving citalopram (mean dose 16.9 mg/day) noted improvement in 11 patients (73%; Namerow, Thomas, Bostic, Prince, & Monuteaux, 2003). Over a period of 10 weeks, in those children who responded, decreased preoccupations and repetitive behaviors were noted. Five patients (33%) had side effects from the drug that included lip movements, aggressiveness, and agitation.

Escitalopram, a single enantiomer of citalopram, is currently FDA approved for use in adult generalized anxiety disorder (GAD) and MDD. A 10-week, open-label study described the use of escitalopram (mean dose 11.1 mg/day) in 28 children (mean age 12.6 years) with PDDs (Owley et al., 2005). Over a mean treatment duration of 218.8 days, improvement in repetitive behavior was noted as measured by the Aberrant Behavior Checklist Community Version (ABC CV; Aman, Singh, Stewart, & Field, 1985) Stereotypy subscale. Adverse effects, including disinhibition and hyperactivity, occurred in 10 (36%) subjects when their dose was increased to 10 mg daily.

While atypical antipsychotics currently are the most widely studied agents used in the treatment of aggressive and maladaptive behavior in PDDs, less information is available about their use in attenuating interfering repetitive phenomena.

In addition to DA receptor blockade, the atypical antipsychotic risperidone is also a potent 5-HT_{2A} receptor antagonist (Richelson & Souder, 2000). In addition to FDA approval for use in adult bipolar and schizophrenic disorders, risperidone has shown positive effects in controlled (McDougle, Fleischmann, et al., 1995; Li et al., 2005) and open-label reports (Jacobsen, 1995; Ravizza, Barzega, Bellino, Bogetto, & Maina, 1996; Saxena, Wang, Bystritsky, & Baxter, 1996; Stein, Bouwer, Hawkridge, & Emsley, 1997) when used adjunctively with SSRIs in the treatment of adults with OCD.

Risperidone is the most widely studied atypical antipsychotic in PDDs. McDougle, Holmes, et al. (1998) conducted a 12-week double-blind, placebo-controlled study of risperidone (mean dose 2.9 ± 1.4 mg/day) in 31 adults (mean age 28.1 years) with a PDD. Eight of 14 (57%) patients receiving risperidone were considered treatment responders, and reduced repetitive behavior was reported. The largest double-blind, placebo-controlled trial to date in autism included 101 children (mean age 8.8 years) who received risperidone (dose range 0.5–3.5 mg/day) or placebo over eight weeks (Research Units on Pediatric Psychopharmacology [RUPP] Autism Network, 2002). Among the reported risperidone-associated benefits was a decrease in the stereotypy subscale score of the ABC. Weight gain (mean 2.7 ± 2.9 kg), increased appetite, fatigue, drowsiness, dizziness, and drooling were side effects associated with risperidone treatment. The RUPP Autism Network results have been replicated in 79 children with PDDs (ages 5 to 12 years) participating in a subsequent eight-week double-blind, placebo-controlled trial of risperidone (mean dose 1.17 mg/day; Shea et al., 2004). Among markers of risperidone efficacy was a decreased stereotypy subscale score on the ABC. Significant side effects included weight gain (2.7 mg vs. 1.0 kg for placebo) and increased pulse and systolic blood pressure.

Oxytocin is a neurohypophyseal peptide that plays a role in the development of social behavior, learning, and memory (for review, see Insel & Young, 2001). Reduction in repetitive behavior as measured by the Y-BOCS (Goodman, Price, Rasmussen, Mazure, Delgado, et al., 1989; Goodman, Price, Rasmussen, Mazure, Fleischmann, et al., 1989) was associated with synthetic oxytocin (pitocin) infusion in a placebo-controlled trial in 15 adults with Asperger disorder or autism (Hollander, Novotny, et al., 2003). Pitocin side effects were generally considered mild and included drowsiness, anxiety, and depression, among others.

Psychological Treatment

Ideal treatment of OCD combines both pharmacotherapy and cognitive-behavioral therapy (CBT; American Academy of Child and Adolescent Psychiatry, 1999). The use of CBT in persons with PDD is limited by the high incidence of mental retardation in this population. The only description of CBT targeting repetitive phenomena in PDD comes from individual case reports in high-functioning individuals. In one report, CBT was effectively used to target obsessions in a high-functioning male with autistic disorder (Lord, 1995). Reaven and Hepburn (2003) used a modified CBT protocol to treat obsessive-compulsive disorder in a 7-year-old girl with Asperger disorder. Effective use of CBT in PDD has been limited to the minority of patients with normal cognitive function.

In general, SSRIs and atypical antipsychotics have shown the most promise in treating repetitive behavior in PDDs. Overall, the effect of these agents on repetitive behavior in PDD has been less than that noted in OCD. This phenomenon may be in part due to decreased tolerability of SSRIs in patients with PDDs. In particular, children with PDDs appear to be more prone to SSRI side effects, including behavioral activation and agitation. The addition of CBT to pharmacotherapy may be useful in higher functioning individuals with PDD.

Case Vignette

Before visiting our clinic, M.T. had previous attempts at pharmacotherapy, including the use of methylphenidate up to a dose of 54 mg/day, over three months. This drug helped with inattention but led to increased irritability, a worsening of repetitive thoughts and behavior, and the emergence of motor tics, all of which resolved upon discontinuation of the drug. Our treatment team initially prescribed sertraline 25 mg/day, increased to 50 mg after one week. Five days after the dose increase, M.T.'s mother reported heightened agitation and hyperactivity. At this point, sertraline was discontinued, and a trial of risperidone was begun. In addition to adding risperidone, M.T. was enrolled in weekly cognitively based therapy sessions. In these sessions, M.T. learned to use phrases, including "I'll do something else, think about other things, talk to someone else," when he was exposed to television programming featuring pheasants. M.T. also wrote his own social story discussing how excessive talk about pheasants is socially inappropriate. After one month of combined treatment, including a dose titration up to 1 mg of risperidone at bedtime, M.T. showed some positive effects. These included less time looking up information about pheasants and a decreased frequency of aggressive outbursts when others interfered with his pursuit of such information. After one year, M.T.'s dose of risperidone was gradually increased to 1 mg twice daily. His body weight was monitored regularly during risperidone treatment, and it remained developmentally normal during his course of treatment. Currently, M.T. is still very interested in pheasants, but he is willing to be redirected away from his pursuit of pheasant-related material. The aggressive behavior surrounding his obsession also ceased after two months of combined treatment.

Conclusion

Evidence for inclusion of PDDs among the OCD spectrum disorders exists to some extent, at phenomenologic, etiologic, and treatment levels. A review of pathophysiology combined with results from empiric pharmacotherapy trials leads to several potential characteristics shared by OCD and PDD beyond just behavioral overlap. First among these themes is the potential role of 5-HT in the pathophysiology of both disorders. This has been evaluated at neurochemical, genetic, treatment, and even autoimmune levels. Future work investigating these disorders should be focused on comparing the neurobiology of persons with OCD, PDD, and both disorders. Such research will not only contribute to a better understanding of the etiology and pathogenesis of OCD and PDDs, but also help to define such issues as they pertain to repetitive phenomena across the entire spectrum of psychopathology.

ACKNOWLEDGMENTS

This work was supported in part by a Department of Housing and Urban Development (HUD) Grant No. B-01-SP-IN-0200 (Dr. McDougle), a Research Unit on Pediatric Psychopharmacology Grant (U10-MH66766) from the National Institute of Mental Health (NIMH) to Indiana University (Drs. McDougle, Stigler, and Posey), a Daniel X. Freedman Psychiatric Research Fellowship Award (Dr. Stigler), and a Research Career Development Award (K23-MH068627) from NIMH (Dr. Posey).

REFERENCES

Adams, K. H., Hansen, E. S., Pinborg, L. H., Hasselbalch, S. G., Svarer, C., Holm, S., et al. (2005). Patients with obsessive-compulsive disorder have increased 5-HT2A receptor binding in the caudate nuclei. *International Journal of Neuropsychopharmacology, 8,* 391–401.

Altemus, M., Jacobson, K. R., Debellis, M., Kling, M., Pigott, T., Murphy, D. L., et al. (1999). Normal CSF oxytocin and NPY levels in OCD. *Biological Psychiatry, 45,* 931–933.

Aman, M. G., Singh, N. N., Stewart, A. W., & Field, C. J. (1985). Psychometric characteristics of the aberrant behavior checklist. *American Journal of Mental Deficiency*, 89, 492–502.

American Academy of Child and Adolescent Psychiatry. (1999). Practice parameters for assessment and treatment of children and adolescents with obsessive-compulsive disorder. *Journal of the American Academy of Child and Adolescent Psychiatry*, 37(10, Suppl.), 27S–45S.

American Psychiatric Association. (2000). *Diagnostic and statistical manual of mental disorders* (4th ed., text revision). Washington, DC: Author.

Anderson, G. M., Freedman D. X., Cohen, D. J., Volkmar, F. R., Hoder, E. L., McPhedron, P., et al. (1987). Whole blood serotonin in autistic and normal subjects. *Journal of Child Psychology and Psychiatry*, 28, 885–900.

Bailey, A., Le, C. A., Gottesman, I., Bolton, P., Simonoff, E., Yuzda, E., et al. (1995). Autism as a strongly genetic disorder: Evidence from a British twin study. *Psychology and Medicine*, 25, 63–77.

Bertrand, J., Mars, A., Boyle, C., Bove, F., Yeargin-Allsopp, M., & Decoufle, P. (2001). Prevalence of autism in a United States population: the Brick Township, New Jersey investigation. *Pediatrics*, 108, 1155–1161.

Bettelheim, B. (1967). *The empty fortress*. New York: Free Press.

Buxbaum, J. D., Silverman, J., Keddache, M., Smith, C. J., Hollander, E., Ramoz, N., et al. (2004). Linkage analysis for autism in a subset of families with obsessive-compulsive behaviors: Evidence for an autism susceptibility gene on chromosome 1 and further support for susceptibility genes on chromosome 6 and 19. *Molecular Psychiatry*, 9, 144–150.

Chakrabarty, K., Bhattacharyya, S., Christopher, R., & Khanna, S. (2005). Glutamatergic dysfunction in OCD. *Neuropsychopharmacology*, 30, 1735–1740.

Chugani, D. C., Muzik, O., Rothermel, R., Behen, M., Chakraborty, P., Mangner, T., et al. (1997). Altered serotonin synthesis in the dentatothalaocortical pathway in autistic boys. *Annals of Neurology*, 42, 666–669.

Couturier, J. L., & Nicolson, R. (2002). A retrospective assessment of citalopram in children and adolescents with pervasive developmental disorders. *Journal of Child and Adolescent Psychopharmacology*, 12, 243–248.

Denys, D., Zohar, J., & Westenberg, H. G. (2004). The role of dopamine in obsessive-compulsive disorder: Preclinical and clinical evidence. *Journal of Clinical Psychiatry*, 65(Suppl. 14), 11–17.

Fein, D., Allen, D., Dunn, M., Feinstein, C., Green, L., Morris, R., et al. (1997). Pitocin induction and autism. *American Journal of Psychiatry*, 154, 438–439.

Field, E. J., Caspary, E. A., & Carnegie, P. R. (1971). Lymphocyte sensitization to basic protein of brain in malignant neoplasia: Experiments with serotonin and related compounds. *Nature*, 233, 284–286.

Folstein, S., & Rutter, M. (1977). Infantile autism: A genetic study of 21 twin pairs. *Journal of Child Psychology and Psychiatry*, 18, 297–321.

Freeman, B. J., Ritvo, E. R., Schroth, P. C., Tonick, I., Guthrie, D., & Wake, L. (1981). Behavioral characteristics of high-and low-IQ autistic children. *American Journal of Psychiatry*, 138, 25–29.

Gale, S., Ozonoff, S., & Lainhart, J. (2003). Brief report: Pitocin induction in autistic

and nonautistic individuals. *Journal of Autism and Developmental Disorders, 33*, 205–208.
Goodman, W. K., Price, L. H., Rasmussen, S. A., Mazure, C., Delgado, P., Heninger, G. R., et al. (1989). The Yale-Brown Obsessive Compulsive Scale: II. Validity. *Archives of General Psychiatry, 46*, 1012–1016.
Goodman, W. K., Price, L. H., Rasmussen, S. A., Mazure, C., Fleischmann, R. L., Hill, C. L., et al. (1989). The Yale-Brown Obsessive Compulsive Scale. I. Development, use, and reliability. *Archives of General Psychiatry, 46*, 1006–1011.
Gordon, C. T., Rapoport, J. L., Hamburger, S. D., State R. C., & Mannheim, G. B. (1992). Differential response of seven subjects with autistic disorder to clomipramine and desipramine. *American Journal of Psychiatry, 149*, 363–366.
Gordon, C. T., State, R. C., Nelson, J. E., Hamburger, S. D., & Rapoport, J. L. (1993). A double-blind comparison of clomipramine, desipramine, and placebo in the treatment of autistic disorder. *Archives of General Psychiatry, 50*, 441–447.
Gross-Isseroff, R., Hermesh, H., & Weizman, A. (2001). Obsessive compulsive behavior in autism: Towards an autistic-obsessive compulsive syndrome? *World Journal of Biological Psychiatry, 2*, 193–197.
Hollander, E., King, A., Delaney, K., Smith, C. J., & Silverman, J. M. (2003). Obsessive-compulsive behaviors in parents of multiplex autism families. *Psychiatry Research, 117*, 11–16.
Hollander, E., Novotny, S., Hanratty, M., Yaffe, R., DeCaria, C. M., Aronowitz, B. R., et al. (2003). Oxytocin infusion reduces repetitive behaviors in adults with autistic and Asperger's disorders. *Neuropsychopharmacology, 28*, 193–198.
Hollander, E., Phillips, A., Chaplin, W., Zagursky, K., Novotny, S., Wasserman, S., et al. (2005). A placebo controlled crossover trial of liquid fluoxetine on repetitive behaviors in childhood and adolescent autism. *Neuropsychopharmacology, 30*, 582–589.
Hoshino, Y., Watanabe, M., Tachibana, R., Kaneko, M., & Kumashiro, H. (1983). A study of the hypothalamic-pituitary function in autistic children by the loading test of 5HTP, TRH, and LH-RH. *Japan Journal of Brain Research, 9*, 94–95.
Insel, T. R. (1997). A neurobiological basis of social attachment. *American Journal of Psychiatry, 154*, 726–735.
Insel, T. R., & Young, L. J. (2001). The neurobiology of attachment. *Nature Reviews Neuroscience, 2*, 129–136.
Jacobsen, F. M. (1995). Risperidone in the treatment of affective illness and obsessive-compulsive disorder. *Journal of Clinical Psychiatry, 56*, 423–429.
Kanner, L. (1943). Autistic disturbances of affective contact. *Nervous Child, 2*, 217–250.
Kano, Y., Ohta, M., Nagai, Y., Pauls, D. L., & Leckman, J. F. (2004). Obsessive-compulsive symptoms in parents of Tourette syndrome probands and autism spectrum disorder probands. *Psychiatry and Clinical Neurosciences, 58*, 348–352.
Krause, I., Xiao-Song, H., Gershwin, M. E., & Shoenfeld, Y. (2002). Brief report: Immune factors in autism: a critical review. *Journal of Autism and Developmental Disorders, 32*, 337–345.
Leboyer, M., Philippe, A., Bouvard, M., Guilloud-Bataille, M., Bondoux, D., Tabuteau, F., et al. (1999). Whole blood serotonin and plasma beta endorphin in autistic probands and their first-degree relatives. *Biological Psychiatry, 45*, 158–163.
Leckman, J. F., Goodman, W. K., North, M. G., Chappell, P. B., Price, L. H., Pauls, D. L.,

et al. (1994). Elevated cerebrospinal fluid levels of oxytocin in obsessive-compulsive disorder: Comparison with Tourette's syndrome and healthy controls. *Archives of General Psychiatry, 51,* 782–792.

Li, X., May, R. S., Tolbert, L. C., Jackson, W. T., Flournoy, J. M., & Baxter, L. R. (2005). Risperidone and haloperidol augmentation of serotonin reuptake inhibitors in refractory obsessive-compulsive disorder: A crossover study. *Journal of Clinical Psychiatry, 66,* 736–743.

Lord, C. (1995). Treatment of a high-functioning adolescent with autism: A review of published cases. In M. A. Reinecke & F. M. Dattilio (Eds.), *Cognitive Therapy with Children and Adolescents: A Casebook for Clinical Practice* (pp. 394–404). New York: Guilford.

Lord, C., Rutter, M., & LeCouteur, A. (1994). Autism Diagnostic Interview-Revised: A revised version of a diagnostic interview for caregivers of individuals with possible pervasive developmental disorders. *Journal of Autism and Developmental Disorders, 24,* 659–685.

McDougle, C. J. (1998). Repetitive thoughts and behavior in pervasive developmental disorders: Phenomenology and pharmacotherapy. In E. Schopler, G. B. Mesibov, & L. J. Kunce (Eds.), *Asperger syndrome or high functioning autism?* (pp. 293–316). New York: Plenum.

McDougle, C. J., Brodkin, E. S., Naylor, S. T., Carlson, D. C., Cohen, D. J., & Price, L. H. (1998). Sertraline in adults with pervasive developmental disorders: A prospective open-label investigation. *Journal of Clinical Psychopharmacology, 18,* 62–66.

McDougle, C. J., Epperson, C. N., Pelton, G. H., Wasylink, S., & Price, L. H. (2000). A double-blind, placebo-controlled study of risperidone addition in serotonin reuptake inhibition-refractory obsessive-compulsive disorder. *Archives of General Psychiatry, 57,* 794–801.

McDougle, C. J., Epperson, C. N., Price, L. H., & Gelernter, J. (1998). Evidence for linkage disequilibrium between serotonin transporter protein gene (SLC6A4) and obsessive compulsive disorder. *Molecular Psychiatry, 3,* 270–273.

McDougle, C. J., Erickson, C. A., Stigler, K. A., & Posey, D. J. (2005). Neurochemistry in the pathophysiology of autism. *Journal of Clinical Psychiatry, 66 (suppl 10),* 9–18.

McDougle, C. J., Fleischmann, R. L. Epperson, C. N., Wasylink, S., Leckman, J. F., & Price, L. H. (1995b). Risperidone addition in fluvoxamine-refractory obsessive-compulsive disorder: Three cases. *Journal of Clinical Psychiatry, 56,* 526–528.

McDougle, C. J., Holmes, J. P., Carlson, D. C., Pelton, G. H., Cohen, D. J., & Price, L. H. (1998). A double-blind, placebo-controlled study of risperidone in adults with autistic disorder and other pervasive developmental disorders. *Archives of General Psychiatry, 55,* 633–641.

McDougle, C. J., Kresch, L. E., Goodman, W. K., Naylor, S. T., Volkmar, F. R., Cohen, D. J., et al. (1995a). A case-controlled study of repetitive thoughts and behavior in adults with autistic disorder and obsessive-compulsive disorder. *American Journal of Psychiatry, 152,* 772–776.

McDougle, C. J., Kresch, L. E., & Posey, D. J. (2000). Repetitive thoughts and behavior in pervasive developmental disorders: Treatment with serotonin reuptake inhibitors. *Journal of Autism and Developmental Disorders, 30,* 427–435.

McDougle, C. J., Naylor, S. T., Cohen, D. J., Aghajanian, G. K., Heninger, G. R., & Price,

L. H. (1996). Effects of trypophan depletion in drug-free adults with autistic disorder. *Archives of General Psychiatry, 53,* 993–1000.
McDougle, C. J., Naylor, S. T., Cohen, D. J., Volkmar, F. R., Heninger, G. R., & Price, L. H. (1996). A double-blind, placebo-controlled study of fluvoxamine in adults with autistic disorder. *Archives of General Psychiatry, 53,* 1001–1008.
Murch, S. (2005). Diet, immunity, and autistic spectrum disorders. *Journal of Pediatrics, 146,* 582–584.
Namerow, L. B., Thomas, P., Bostic, J. Q., Prince, J., & Monuteaux, M. C. (2003). Use of citalopram in pervasive developmental disorders. *Journal of Developmental and Behavioral Pediatrics, 24,* 2, 104–108.
Owley, T., Walton, L., Salt, J., Guter, S.J., Winnega, M., Leventhal, B. L., et al. (2005). An open-label trial of escitalopram in pervasive developmental disorders. *Journal of the American Academy of Child and Adolescent Psychiatry, 44,* 343–348.
Pelphrey, K., Adolphs, R., & Morris, J. P. (2004). Neuroanatomical substrates of social cognition dysfunction in autism. *Mental Retardation and Developmental Disabilities, 10,* 259–271.
Ravizza, L., Barzega, G., Bellino, S., Bogetto, F., & Maina, G. (1996). Therapeutic effect and safety of adjunctive risperidone in refractory obsessive-compulsive disorder. *Psychopharmacology Bulletin, 32,* 677–682.
Reaven, J., & Hepburn, S. (2003). Cognitive-behavioral treatment of obsessive-compulsive disorder in a child with Asperger syndrome. *Autism, 7,* 145–164.
Remington, G., Sloman, L., Konstantareas, M., Parker, K., & Gow, R. (2001). Clomipramine versus haloperidol in the treatment of autistic disorder: a double-blind, placebo-controlled, crossover study. *Journal of Clinical Psychopharmacology, 21,* 440–444.
Research Units on Pediatric Psychopharmacology Autism Network. (2002). Risperidone in children with autism and serious behavioral problems. *New England Journal of Medicine, 347,* 314–321.
Richelson, E., & Souder, T. (2000). Binding of antipsychotic drugs to human brain receptors focus on newer generation compounds. *Life Sciences, 68,* 29–39.
Ritvo, E. R., Freeman, B. J., Mason-Brothers, A., Mo, A., & Ritvo, A. M. (1985). Concordance for the syndrome of autism in 40 pairs of afflicted twins. *American Journal of Psychiatry, 142,* 74–77.
Russell, A. J., Mataix-Cols, D., Anson, M. A., & Murphy, D. G. (2005). Obsessions and compulsions in Asperger syndrome and high-functioning autism. *British Journal of Psychiatry, 186,* 525–528.
Saxena, S., Wang, D., Bystritsky, A., & Baxter L. R., Jr. (1996). Risperidone augmentation of SRI treatments for refractory obsessive-compulsive disorder. *Journal of Clinical Psychiatry, 57,* 303–306.
Scahill, L., Riddle, M. A., McSwiggin-Hardin, M., Ort, S. I., King, R. A., Goodman, W. K., et al. (1997). Children's Yale-Brown Obsessive Compulsive Scale: Reliability and validity. *Journal of the American Academy of Child and Adolescent Psychiatry, 36,* 844–852.
Shea, S., Turgay, A., Carroll, A., Schulz, M., Orlik, H., Smith, I., et al. (2004). Risperidone in the treatment of disruptive behavioral symptoms in children with autistic and other pervasive developmental disorders. *Pediatrics, 114,* 634–641.

Simpson, H. B., Lombardo, I., Slifstein, M., Huang, H. Y., Hwang, D. R., Abi-Dargham, A., et al. (2003). Serotonin transporters in obsessive-compulsive disorder: a positron emission tomography study with [(11)C]McN 5652. *Biological Psychiatry, 54,* 1414–1421.

Snider, L. A., & Swedo, S. E. (2004). PANDAS: Current status and directions for research. *Molecular Psychiatry, 9,* 900–907.

Stein, D. J., Bouwer, M. B., Hawkridge, S., & Emsley, R. A. (1997). Risperidone augmentation of serotonin reuptake inhibitors in obsessive-compulsive and related disorders. *Journal of Clinical Psychiatry, 58,* 119–122.

Steingard, R. J., Zimnitzky, B., DeMaso, D. R., Bauman, M. L., & Bucci, J. P. (1997). Sertraline treatment of transition-associated anxiety and agitation in children with autistic disorder. *Journal of Child and Adolescent Psychopharmacology, 7,* 9–15.

Sugie, Y., Sugie, H., Fukuda, T., Ito, M., Sasada, Y., Nakabayashi, M., et al. (2005). Clinical efficacy of fluvoxamine and functional polymorphism in a serotonin transporter gene. *Journal of Autism and Developmental Disorders, 35,* 377–385.

Sweeten, T. L., Bowyer, S. L., Posey, D. J., Halberstadt, G. M., & McDougle, C. J. (2003). Increased prevalence of familial autoimmunity in probands with pervasive developmental disorders. *Pediatrics, 112,* e420.

Turner, M. (1999). Annotation: Repetitive behavior in autism: A review of psychological research. *Journal of Child Psychology and Psychiatry, 40,* 839–849.

Wassink, T. H., Brzustowicz, L. M., Bartlett, C. W., & Szatmari, P. (2004). The search for autism disease genes. *Mental Retardation and Developmental Disabilities, 10,* 272–283.

Westall, F. C., & Root-Bernstein, R. S. (1983). Suggested connection between autism, serotonin, and myelin basic protein. *American Journal of Psychiatry, 140,* 1260–1261.

Velisek, L., Veliskova, J., Ravizza, T., Giorgi, F. S., & Moshe, S. L. (2005). Circling behavior and [^{14}C]2-deoxyglucose mapping in rats: Possible implications for autistic repetitive behaviors. *Neurobiology of Disease, 18,* 346–355.

Yuwiler, A., Shih, J. C., Chen, C. H., Ritvo, E. R., Hanna, G., Ellison, G. W., et al. (1992). Hyperserotoninemia and antiserotonin antibodies in autism and other disorders. *Journal of Autism and Developmental Disorders, 22,* 33–45.

CHAPTER SEVENTEEN

Nonparaphilic Sexual Disorders

Elias Aboujaoude, M.D., and Lorrin M. Koran, M.D.

Despite the cultural and media fascination with nonparaphilic sexual disorders—often referred to as "sex addiction," "hypersexuality," "compulsive sexual disorders," or "paraphilia-related disorders"—these conditions have received relatively little research attention. The role of nonparaphilic sexual disorders in the public health issues of unwanted pregnancies, the AIDS epidemic, and the recent resurgence of syphilis, have also received little attention. The advent of the Internet as a major facilitator of casual sexual encounters, with the potential to increase the risks associated with these diagnoses significantly, also remains to be explored. Among the factors contributing to the dearth of research on sexual disorders are (1) the refusal of pharmaceutical companies to fund studies in this area, (2) difficulty with recruiting volunteers to participate in clinical and epidemiologic research, and (3) the perception that nonparaphilias are rare and mostly affect individuals on the fringes of society.

This relative lack of attention to psychosexual symptoms might also be understood in the context of a backlash against psychoanalysis, which overemphasized sexual behavior and psychosexual development as keys to understanding and resolving psychopathology. Even the fourth edition of the

Diagnostic and Statistical Manual of Mental Disorders (DSM-IV; American Psychiatric Association, 1994) is remarkably silent on the subject of nonparaphilic sexual disorders, despite a mention of "sexual addiction" in DSM-III-R, and despite categorizing disorders of sexual desire, aversion, arousal, pain, orgasm, and gender identity, as well as the paraphilic sexual disorders.

Symptoms and Conceptual Models

The essential features of paraphilic sexual disorders are recurrent, intense, sexually arousing fantasies, urges, or behaviors that fall outside the culturally accepted spectrum of sexual expression. Paraphilias generally involve reliance on one or more of the following as a source of sexual gratification: nonhuman objects; the suffering or humiliation of oneself or one's partner; or children or other nonconsenting persons. These symptoms occur over a period of at least six months. In some paraphilic sexual disorders (e.g., fetishism), expressed personal distress is needed to meet the DSM-IV diagnostic criteria for the disorder, whereas in others (e.g., sexual sadism), this is not the case. Individuals with paraphilias are subject to arrest and incarceration and may find that the unusual sexual behaviors become their major sexual activity. Table 17.1 lists DSM-IV–defined paraphilic sexual disorders.

Unlike the paraphilias, *nonparaphilic* sexual disorders are neither culturally deviant nor illegal, and usually involve disinhibited forms of the normative, culturally sanctioned, heterosexual or homosexual experience. Commonly

Table 17.1. DSM-IV–Defined Paraphilic Sexual Disorders

- Exhibitionism: exposure of genitals
- Fetishism: use of nonliving objects
- Frotteurism: touching or rubbing against a nonconsenting person
- Sexual masochism: receiving suffering or humiliation
- Sexual sadism: inflicting suffering or humiliation
- Transvestic fetishism: cross-dressing
- Voyeurism: observing sexual behavior
- Paraphilia not otherwise specified: includes, but is not limited to
    Necrophilia: sexual gratification involving corpses
    Zoophilia: sexual gratification involving animals
    Coprophilia: sexual gratification involving fecal matter
    Klismaphilia: sexual gratification involving enemas
    Urophilia: sexual gratification involving urine

Note: DSM-IV, *Diagnostic and Statistical Manual of Mental Disorders* (4th ed.).

identified nonparaphilic sexual disorders are listed in Table 17.2 (Coleman, 1992; Cooper & Scherer, 1999; Kafka & Prentky, 1997).

Several organic etiologies have been associated with nonparaphilic sexual disorders. These include diencephalic, frontal lobe and septal lesions (Elliott & Biever, 1996; Gorman & Cummings, 1992); unilateral strokes involving the temporal lobe (Monga, Monga, Raina, & Hardjasudarma, 1986); bilateral damage of the temporal lobes as seen in the Kluver-Bucy syndrome (Goscinski, Kwiatkowski, Polak, Orlowiejska, & Partyk, 1997); temporal lobe epilepsy (intraictally, postictally, or as a result of medical or surgical treatment; Blumer & Walker, 1967; Savard & Walker, 1965); dementia, including Alzheimer-type (Kuhn, Greiner, & Arseneau, 1998); and the use of prodopaminergic agents in the treatment of Parkinson's disease (Uitti et al., 1989). Also, substances, including alcohol, methamphetamine, cocaine, amyl nitrite ("poppers"), and gamma hydroxybutyric acid ("date rape drug"), have all been implicated in sexual disinhibition and increased impulsivity (Colfax et al., 2005; Johnson & Stahl, 2004; Varela, Nogue, Oros, & Miro, 2004). Further, the manic phase of bipolar or schizoaffective disorder is well known to include hypersexual behavior that might be confused with a nonparaphilic sexual disorder.

Nonparaphilic sexual behaviors that are not organic or substance related in their etiology, and that are not the result of a mood episode or psychotic process, have been conceptualized as "compulsions," "addictions," or disorders of impulse control (Koran, 1999). Like compulsions in obsessive compulsive disorder (OCD), nonparaphilic sexual disorders can be characterized by repetitive, sometimes ritualized, excessive exaggerations of normal behaviors. However, in contrast to the compulsive behavior in OCD, compulsive sexual behaviors are gratifying in their consummation, whereas OCD compulsions

Table 17.2. Nonparaphilic Sexual Disorders

- Ego-dystonic, compulsive masturbation
- Persistent, ego-dystonic promiscuity
- Compulsive "cruising" for sex, including in public bathrooms, parks, bookstores
- Demanding unwanted sexual activity from a partner whose sexual drive is not hypoactive
- Fixation on an unobtainable partner
- Dependence for sexual arousal on:
  –Pornography, including Internet websites, movies, videos, and telephone sex venues such as "900 numbers"
  –Drugs (e.g., alcohol, stimulants such as methamphetamines, amyl nitrate or "poppers")
  –Sexual accessories (e.g., dildos)

aim mainly at reducing anxiety and are not motivated by thrill seeking. Another problem lies in the definition of "excessive." Frequency-based measures of hypersexuality, such as Alfred Kinsey's total sexual outlet score, originally defined as the number of orgasms per week, fail to capture the essence of the diagnosis because no clear boundaries of normative behavior have been established (Bradford, 2001; Kinsey, Pomeroy, & Martin, 1948; Kinsey, Pomeroy, Martin, & Gebhard, 1953). Perhaps a more sensible way to define "excessive" or "compulsive" is by the behavior's effects on the individual: the distress it causes in relationships, work, or school or, as suggested by Quadland (1985), by whether the behavior is accompanied by a sense of lack of control.

The addiction model has also been used to understand nonparaphilic sexual disorders (Goodman, 1993). Like DSM-IV–defined "substance dependence," nonparaphilic sexual disorders cause significant distress and dysfunction and are marked by: engaging in the activity more frequently and for longer periods of time than intended; failed attempts to cut back; preoccupation with the behavior or with preparation for it; continuation of the behavior despite awareness of its adverse consequences; and the presence of withdrawal symptoms when the behavior is stopped. Also similar to substance dependence are the mood-enhancing properties of the behavior and the temporary escape it can provide from inner discomfort and tension.

A third conceptual framework that bears parallels to nonparaphilic sexual disorders is the impulse control disorder model. Like impulse control disorders such as kleptomania, trichotillomania, and pathological gambling, nonparaphilic sexual disorders are characterized by a surge in anxiety and an accompanying desire to perform a behavior that is pleasurable and anxiety-relieving in the moment but that causes significant guilt and negative consequences in the long term. The relatively high comorbidity rate with impulse control disorders seen in some studies (16–38% range among studies) may lend some further credence to this hypothesis (Kafka & Hennen, 2002; Kafka & Prentky, 1998; Raymond, Coleman, & Miner, 2003). Also, based on a small comparison study, lower response rates to selective serotonin reuptake inhibitors (SSRIs) among participants with nonparaphilic sexual disorders compared with those with OCD, led the study authors to conclude that nonparaphilic sexual disorders may be closer to the impulsive end of the compulsivity/impulsivity phenomenologic and neurobiological spectrum (Stein et al., 1992).

Given the similarity to several diagnostic categories, the silence of DSM-IV on the subject, and the absence of a clear understanding of the etiology of these conditions, the term "nonparaphilic sexual disorders" seems appropriate. In the current DSM-IV nosology, these conditions would best be subsumed under the sexual disorder not otherwise specified category.

Diagnosis and Epidemiology

Little is known definitively about the epidemiology of nonparaphilic sexual disorders; the few published studies often lack established, validated diagnostic criteria, have small sample size, and group together paraphilic and nonparaphilic conditions. A reasonable diagnostic definition for nonparaphilic sexual disorders has been proposed by Raymond et al. (2003), inspired by Coleman's (1991, 1992) work. This definition stresses recurrent sexual fantasies, urges, or behaviors that last over a period of at least six months, are accompanied by distress or impairment in important spheres of functioning, and cannot be better explained by alternative diagnoses or etiologies. The detailed suggested criteria are shown in Table 17.3.

Published prevalence estimates for nonparaphilic sexual disorders range from 3 to 5 percent (Coleman, 1992; Goodman, 1993; Quadland, 1985). More men than women present for treatment, and more men appear to be affected, although this may result from bias toward a male-based definition of sexuality (Coleman, 1992) and more societal tolerance of sexual nonconformity by men, which may make it easier for them to admit to these behaviors and to seek help.

Table 17.3. *Proposed Diagnostic Definition for Nonparaphilic Sexual Disorders*

A. Over a period of at least six months, recurrent intense sexually arousing fantasies, urges, or behaviors, involving one or more of the following:
   - Compulsive cruising for sex and multiple sex partners
   - Compulsive fixation on an unobtainable partner
   - Compulsive masturbation
   - Multiple love relationships
   - Compulsive sexuality in relationship
B. The fantasies, urges, or behaviors cause clinically significant distress or impairment in social, occupational, or other important areas of functioning.
C. The symptoms are not due to a medical condition or to substance abuse or another Axis I or II diagnosis.
D. The diagnosis takes into account generally accepted sociocultural norms and sexual orientation.

Source: Data from Raymond, Coleman, and Miner (2003).

Comorbidity data show high rates for both anxiety and affective conditions. In Raymond and colleagues' (2003) study of 25 individuals with nonparaphilic sexual disorders (23 men and 2 women), 96 percent had a lifetime diagnosis of an anxiety disorder, most commonly social phobia, and 71 percent had a lifetime diagnosis of a mood disorder, most commonly major depressive disorder. Comorbidity with substance abuse and impulse control disorders was 71 percent and 38 percent, respectively. Among the personality disorders, cluster C conditions were the most prevalent at 39 percent.

Kafka and Hennen (2002) reported on 88 males with paraphilic disorders (PA) and 32 males with "paraphilia-related disorders" (PRD). The latter group manifested symptoms and behaviors matching nonparaphilic sexual disorders. Among the PRD individuals, the lifetime prevalence of mood disorders was 71.8 percent (most commonly dysthymia) and anxiety conditions, 37.5 percent (most commonly social phobia). Comorbidity for substance abuse and impulse control disorders were 25 percent and 15.6 percent, respectively. In comparing the PA and PRD groups, only childhood attention deficit and hyperactivity disorder was significantly more strongly associated with having PA as opposed to PRD (Kafka & Hennen, 2002). This replicated the finding of an earlier study, based on a smaller sample, in which PA and PRD were compared (Kafka & Prentky, 1998). In the 2002 study, the PA group was also more likely to report a history of physical, nonsexual abuse; lower educational achievement; greater school and job impairment; more psychiatric and substance-related hospitalizations; and more legal troubles. The typical person with PRD was a 37-year-old college graduate, employed, and earning a middle-class income.

Case Vignette

A 29-year-old married heterosexual graduate student with two children presented to our impulse control disorders clinic following separation from his wife for help with his "sex addiction." The patient described a history of "fascination with the female body" that he dates back to age 7 when his baby-sitter undressed before him. No sexual contact occurred at that time that the patient could recall. Since then, the patient describes a "sex addiction" that started out with intrusive, frequent thoughts about the female body, which, after the onset of puberty, were accompanied by compulsive masturbation (on average five times daily) and an "obsession" with acquiring and collecting pornographic magazines and videotapes. With the advent of the Internet, the patient started spending more time online, watching pornographic Web sites and masturbating to them and eventually posting sex ads online that he feels "exponentially" increased the ease of meeting partners for casual sex.

His marriage, which occurred four years before presenting to the clinic, had temporarily decreased his symptoms, but they returned after the birth, two years later, of his first child. At first, the patient succeeded at hiding his behavior from his wife, but eventually she found out when she discovered pornographic material stored on the family computer. At that point, the patient admitted his behavior to his wife, who promptly moved out with the two children, precipitating a depressive episode, which a community psychiatrist successfully treated with fluoxetine (20 mg/day) before he was referred to our clinic four months later for management of the nonparaphilic sexual disorder.

Other than the contact with the community psychiatrist and the fluoxetine trial, the patient had had no other psychopharmacologic or psychotherapeutic treatment. His history was significant for alcohol dependence but was negative for other substances or for any psychotic, anxiety process, or any medical condition, including sexually transmitted diseases. His psychosocial history was remarkable because his parents divorced when the patient was eight months old; the patient and his older brother were raised by a hard-working mother with minimal contact with the father. There was no evidence of physical or sexual abuse except for the possible one-time exhibitionistic behavior by the baby-sitter.

Marital therapy was recommended to the patient but was vetoed by the patient's wife. The fluoxetine dose, which had helped the depression, was increased to 40 mg/day. Cognitive-behavioral treatment was also undertaken; the patient was asked to keep a log of his online and other sex-related activities and to record any triggers as well as accompanying and subsequent emotions. He was asked to time himself while online and to reduce by 25 percent weekly the amount of time spent online. He was also instructed to resume swimming at least three times a week. The patient did not wish to revisit early childhood experiences, including possible exhibitionism by his baby-sitter, so little time was spent delving into his childhood and formative years. His alcohol intake was also monitored.

No specific triggers except "free time" were identified after six weeks of once to twice-weekly, one-hour therapy sessions. "Release" and anxiety reduction were common emotions accompanying the sexual act and "shame" and "guilt" were the most frequent emotional consequences of this behavior. The patient's alcohol consumption continued but without any episodes of intoxication or withdrawal noted during this period. After six weeks with treatment involving the combination of fluoxetine and cognitive-behavioral therapy, the patient's behavior had decreased by about 75 percent.

Treatment

Pharmacotherapy

No well-controlled trials of medications or psychotherapy are available to inform the treatment of nonparaphilic sexual disorders. However, expert opinion and case reports exist that can help guide treatment decisions. For example, Goodman (1993) suggested that if a comorbid condition is present—especially substance abuse, a mood disorder, or an anxiety condition—treating this comorbid disorder appears to be crucial in helping to reduce symptoms of the sexual disorder.

Small, open-label trials suggest the utility of SSRIs in the pharmacologic management of nonparaphilic sexual disorders. A 12-week, open-label trial of fluoxetine, 20 to 60 mg/day, in 10 male participants with nonparaphilic sexual disorders showed positive results in all seven study completers (Kafka & Prentky, 1992). However, all study participants had a depressive disorder (major depression or dysthymia) at baseline, and an unknown number received concomitant psychotherapy. A measurable improvement was seen by week 4, and participants were able to maintain conventional sexual interest and behavior.

A second open-label study tested sertraline, mean dose 99 ± 62 mg/day, in 12 male participants (Kafka, 1994). Mean treatment duration was 18 weeks. Of the 11 participants who completed the study, six were "much" or "very much" improved, whereas one participant's symptoms worsened, as rated on the Clinical Global Impressions Scale.

The existing research has not fully addressed whether response to SSRIs is a result of action on an underlying pathophysiologic dysfunction or merely a sexual side effect from a class of medications well known to cause them. The answer to this question awaits large, well-controlled trials that would also attempt to define carefully what constitutes normal sexual practice, both in range and frequency of behavior, and measure response against this criterion.

Some non-SSRI medications that are not thought to have significant sexual side effects have shown early promise in the treatment of nonparaphilic sexual disorders. A limited retrospective chart review of 14 men treated with nefazodone, mean dose 200 mg/day, showed that, of the 11 that continued on nefazodone long term, 6 participants reported a decrease in intrusive sexual thoughts and 5 reported complete remission (Coleman, Gratzer, Nesvacil, & Raymond, 2000).

The opiate antagonist naltrexone, which has been shown to be effective in impulse-control disorders such as pathological gambling and kleptomania, may also help treat nonparaphilic sexual disorders. Raymond and colleagues presented two cases, a 42-year-old woman and a 61-year-old man, with unwanted promiscuous sexual behavior, who responded after 50 mg/day of naltrexone was added to their SSRI regimen (Raymond, Grant, Kim, & Coleman, 2002). Similarly, topiramate, an anticonvulsant with anti-impulsivity properties in some studies, was helpful, at 200 mg/day, in treating a nonparaphilic sexual disorder in a 32-year-old male (Fong, de la Garza, & Newton, 2005).

A controversial pharmacologic approach—tested in paraphilias, especially pedophilia and sexual sadism, and in sex offenders—involves manipulating the hypothalamic-pituitary-testicular hormonal axis to achieve a state of hypotestosteronemia analogous to surgical castration. Such an approach lacks strong evidence for use in nonparaphilic sexual disorders, raises significant ethical questions, and can be associated with serious side effects. It might be considered in severely treatment-resistant cases or those with comorbid paraphilic conditions and should be adopted only with the patient's clear informed consent. For a description of the medication options, including dosing, side-effect profiles, and baseline medical workup recommendations, see reviews by Bradford (2001) and Saleh and Guidry (2003).

Psychological Treatment

Various psychotherapeutic approaches have been applied to the treatment of nonparaphilic sexual disorders. Like pharmacotherapeutic strategies, however, large, controlled studies are needed to separate opinion from fact.

In psychodynamic approaches, the therapist focuses on helping the patient identify and resolve inner conflicts and early losses that may be manifesting in hypersexuality. However, whatever the psychotherapeutic approach, certain defense mechanisms defined by the psychoanalytic literature will often be at play and should be recognized and confronted. Denial (minimizing the magnitude and consequences of a problem) and rationalization (searching for excuses to "explain" the behavior) are particularly common (Pincu, 1989).

Cognitive-behavioral therapy for nonparaphilic sexual disorders begins with a functional assessment of the undesirable behavior. This includes identifying the antecedents (triggers, e.g., free time), the specific aspects of the behavior itself (e.g., use of the Internet), and the consequences (e.g., sexual release, guilt). Motivational interviewing techniques might be used to help the patient generate strong arguments for change. Next, the patient is taught to identify "high-risk" situations and employ alternate behaviors instead of the sexual behavior at these times (e.g., habit reversal). At the same time, stimulus-control procedures might be used to minimize encounters with strong triggers (e.g., discarding pornography and making access to pornographic Web sites more difficult). In addition, the patient is helped to understand the differences between lapses (temporary slips) and relapse (a return to baseline functioning); lapses are reframed as opportunities to work harder on managing symptoms, rather than as occasions for self-punishment (Goodman, 1993; Koran, 1999).

Although desensitization techniques are not currently considered first-line behavioral interventions for compulsive sexual behavior, an older randomized trial found that imaginal desensitization (ID) was superior to covert desensitization (CD) in patients with either a paraphilia ($n = 15$) or compulsive sexual behavior ($n = 5$; McConaghy, Armstrong, & Blaszczynski, 1985). In ID, the patient imagines, while relaxed, situations that lead to unwanted sexual behavior but ends the scene without performing the behavior. In CD, the patient imagines an aversive event in which the unwanted behavior is blocked (e.g., being discovered in the act by a relative). Patients were treated with 14 sessions during a one-week inpatient stay and then followed for one year. ID patients had an 89 percent reduction in anomalous sexual urges compared with 55 percent in the CD group.

Carnes (1989) offered a group psychotherapy model that adapted the 12-step methods of Alcoholics Anonymous (AA), with a healthy sexual life substituting for the AA goal of abstinence from alcohol. Goodman (1993) proposed that a group therapy approach could be especially helpful for patients with fears of closeness, low self-esteem, shame, and isolation. A strong Internet presence for groups like Sex Addicts Anonymous suggests relatively easy access to group help resources in various locales across the United States. However, the lack of empirical data to support their efficacy, and the lack of quality control from locale to locale, makes recommending them dependent on the individual clinician's familiarity with the particular programs.

Regardless of the particular approach to psychological treatment, empathy and a nonjudgmental stance toward patients are crucial to promoting safety and trust and to helping the patient feel comfortable enough to reveal what often are heavily defended, guilt-ridden secrets. Strict confidentiality, which is also crucial, requires even more explicit statement and restatement. The therapist should appear interested in helping patients with the distress and impairment associated with their sexual behavior and not as moral arbiters of what constitutes acceptable or normative sexual practice. Patients are often aware of the historical mistakes committed by the psychiatric profession when it attempted to define normal sexuality—for example, the historical inclusion of homosexuality in DSM-I and DSM-II and its later removal as society evolved and mores changed—and this can add to patients' suspiciousness of the therapist and the profession as a whole.

As with medication treatment, any comorbid conditions should be explored. If there is a history of childhood physical or sexual abuse, this should be appropriately addressed, and its effects on the patient's sexual life understood. Input from a spouse or partner might be elicited, ideally on an ongoing basis through couple therapy, to understand more fully the impact on the family unit and explore reasons behind any sexual dissatisfaction or incompatibility.

Conclusion

Nonparaphilic sexual disorders pose many serious and unique difficulties to patients who have them and to clinicians treating them. The challenges include the lack of definitive research into their epidemiology, phenomenology, and treatment; the stigma that permeates them; and the sometimes shifting cultural definition of normative sexual behavior. Nonetheless, these disorders are common, distressing, and often highly debilitating. More research is needed to better understand and treat them, as well as a nonsensational, meaningful debate about their importance and cost.

REFERENCES

American Psychiatric Association. (1994). *Diagnostic and Statistical Manual of Mental Disorders* (4th ed.). Washington, DC: Author.

Blumer, D., & Walker, E. (1967). Sexual behavior in temporal lobe epilepsy. *Archives of Neurology, 16*, 37–43.

Bradford, J. M. (2001). The neurobiology, neuropharmacology, and pharmacological treatment of the paraphilias and compulsive sexual behavior. *Canadian Journal of Psychiatry, 46,* 26–34.

Carnes, P. (1989). *Contrary to love.* Minnesota, MN: CompCare Publishers.

Coleman, E. (1991). Compulsive sexual behavior: New concepts and treatments. *Journal of Psychology and Human Sexuality, 4,* 37–52.

Coleman, E. (1992). Is your patient suffering from compulsive sexual behavior? *Psychiatric Annals, 22,* 320–325.

Coleman E., Gratzer T., Nesvacil L., & Raymond N. C. (2000). Nefazodone and the treatment of nonparaphilic compulsive sexual behavior: A retrospective study. *Journal of Clinical Psychiatry, 61,* 282–284.

Colfax, G., Coates, T. J., Husnik, M. J., Huang, Y., Buchbinder, S., Koblin, B., et al. (2005). Longitudinal patterns of methamphetamine, popper (amyl nitrite), and cocaine use and high-risk sexual behavior among a cohort of San Francisco men who have sex with men. *Journal of Urban Health, 82* (Suppl. 1), i62–i70.

Cooper, A., & Scherer, C. (1999). Overcoming methodological concerns in the investigation of online sexual activities. *Cyberpsychology and Behavior, 4,* 437–447.

Elliott, M. L., & Biever, L. S. (1996). Head injury and sexual dysfunction. *Brain Injury, 10,* 703–717.

Fong, T. W., De la Garza, R., & Newton, T. F. (2005). A case report of topiramate in the treatment of nonparaphilic sexual addiction. *Journal of Clinical Psychopharmacology, 25,* 512–514.

Goodman, A. (1993). Diagnosis and treatment of sexual addiction. *Journal of Sex and Marital Therapy, 19,* 225–251.

Gorman, D. G., & Cummings, J. L. (1992). Hypersexuality following septal injury. *Archives of Neurology, 49,* 308–310.

Goscinski, I., Kwiatkowski, S., Polak, J., Orlowiejska, M. J., & Partyk, A. (1997). The Kluver Bucy syndrome. *Journal of Neurological Science, 41,* 269–272.

Johnson, T. J., & Stahl, C. (2004). Sexual experiences associated with participation in drinking games. *Journal of Genetic Psychology, 131,* 304–320.

Kafka, M. P. (1994). Sertraline pharmacotherapy for paraphilias and paraphilia-related disorders: An open trial. *Annals of Clinical Psychiatry, 6,* 189–195.

Kafka, M. P., & Hennen, J. (2002). A DSM-IV Axis I comorbidity study of males with paraphilias and paraphilia-related disorders. *Sexual Abuse, 14,* 349–366.

Kafka, M. P., & Prentky, R. A. (1992). Fluoxetine treatment of nonparaphilic sexual addictions and paraphilias in men. *Journal of Clinical Psychiatry, 53,* 351–358.

Kafka, M. P., & Prentky, R. A. (1997). Compulsive sexual behavior characteristics. (Letter.) *American Journal of Psychiatry, 154,* 1632.

Kafka, M. P., & Prentky, R. A. (1998). Attention-deficit/hyperactivity disorder in males with paraphilias and paraphilia-related disorders: A comorbidity study. *Journal of Clinical Psychiatry, 59,* 388–396.

Kinsey, A. C., Pomeroy, W. B., & Martin, C. E. (1948). *Sexual behavior in the human male.* Philadelphia: W. B. Saunders.

Kinsey, A. C., Pomeroy, W. B., Martin, C. E., & Gebhard, P. H. (1953). *Sexual behavior in the human female.* Philadelphia: W. B. Saunders.

Koran, L. M. (1999). *Obsessive compulsive and related disorders in adults.* Cambridge: Cambridge University Press.

Kuhn, D. R., Greiner, D., & Arseneau, L. (1998). Addressing hypersexuality in Alzheimer's disease. *Journal of Gerontological Nursing, 24,* 44–50.

McConaghy, N., Armstrong, M. S., & Blaszczynski, A. (1985). Expectancy, covert sensitization, and imaginal desensitization in compulsive sexuality. *Acta Psychiatrica Scandinavica, 72,* 176–187.

Monga, T. N., Monga, M., Raina, M. S., & Hardjasudarma, M. (1986). Hypersexuality in stroke. *Archives of Physical Medicine and Rehabilitation, 6,* 415–417.

Pincu, L. (1989). Sexual compulsivity in gay men: Controversy and treatment. *Journal of Counseling and Development, 68,* 63–68.

Quadland, M. C. (1985). Compulsive sexual behavior: Definition of a problem and an approach to treatment. *Journal of Sex and Marital Therapy, 11,* 121–132.

Raymond, N. C., Coleman, E., & Miner, M. H. (2003). Psychiatric comorbidity and compulsive/impulsive traits in compulsive sexual behavior. *Comprehensive Psychiatry, 44,* 370–380.

Raymond, N. C., Grant, J. E., Kim, S. W., & Coleman, E. (2002). Treatment of compulsive sexual behaviour with naltrexone and serotonin reuptake inhibitors: Two case studies. *International Clinical Psychopharmacology, 17,* 201–205.

Saleh, F. M., & Guidry, L. L. (2003). Psychosocial and biological treatment considerations for the paraphilic and nonparaphilic sex offender. *Journal of the American Academy of Psychiatry and Law, 31,* 486–493.

Savard, R., & Walker, E. (1965). Changes in social functioning after surgical treatment for temporal lobe epilepsy. *Social Work, 10,* 87–95.

Stein, D. J., Hollander, E., Antony, D. T., Schneier, F. R., Fallon, B. A., Liebowitz, M. R., et al. (1992). Serotonergic medications for sexual obsessions, sexual addictions, and paraphilias. *Journal of Clinical Psychiatry, 53,* 267–271.

Uitti, R. J., Ranner, C. M., Rajput, A. H., Goetz, C. G., Klawans, H. L., & Thiessen, B. (1989). Hypersexuality with antiparkinsonian therapy. *Clinical Neuropharmacology, 12,* 275–83.

Varela, M., Nogue, S., Oros, M., & Miro, O. (2004). Gamma hydroxybutirate use for sexual assault. *Emergency Medicine Journal, 21,* 255–256.

CHAPTER EIGHTEEN

Tourette Syndrome and Chronic Tic Disorders

Kieron P. O'Connor, Ph.D., and Julie Leclerc

Clinical Presentation

Diagnostic Features

In the *Diagnostic and Statistical Manual of Mental Disorders* (DSM-IV-TR; American Psychiatric Association, 2000), tics are defined as nonrhythmic series of movements of a nonvoluntary nature in one or several muscle groups. The first clinical report of tic disorder was from Itard (1825) and later Gilles de la Tourette (1885), who reported a case series of nine people presenting with multiple tics, all including phonic (vocal) tics. These early reports concerned severe cases and did not recognize the existence of more moderate cases of tics. The diagnostic category of Tourette syndrome has retained Gilles de la Tourette's name and is now a feature of both DSM-IV and ICD-X (Organisation mondiale de la santé, 1996) nosology (Table 18.1).

In both diagnostic manuals, tics are divided into transitory tics, chronic tic disorder (TD), and Gilles de la Tourette syndrome (TS; see Table 18.1). The diagnosis is categorical, not dimensional, and to have TS, one must have phonic tics. There is controversy over the categorical nature of diagnosis; some clini-

Table 18.1. Classification of Tics by ICD and DSM-IV-R

Tic		ICD		DSM-IV-TR
Transient tic disorder	F95.0	Single or multiple motor or vocal tic(s) or both, that occur over a period of at least 4 weeks to 12 months or less	307.21	Presence of single or multiple motor tics and/or vocal tics for at least 4 weeks, but for no longer than 12 consecutive months
Chronic motor or vocal tic disorder	F95.1	Motor or vocal tics, but not both, that occur over a period of at least 12 months with no period of remission more than 2 months	307.22	Presence of either motor tics or vocal tics, but not both, for more than 1 year
Tourette syndrome	F95.2	Combined multiple motor tics and one or more vocal and tics disorder	307.23	Presence of multiple motor tics and 1 or more vocal tics, for more than 1 year, and onset before age 18 years
Other tic disorders	F95.8	Spasmodic syndrome		
Tic disorder unspecified	F95.9	A nonrecommended residual for a disorder that fulfills the general criteria for a tic disorder but in which the specific subcategory is not specified	307.20	Characterized by tics that do not meet criteria for a specific tic disorder or with an onset after age 18 years

cians hold that TS and tic disorder are on a continuum (e.g., Spencer et al., 1998), and it is not clear that a phonic tic indicates greater symptom severity. In fact, it is possible to have a mild vocal tic (e.g., throat clearing) and some mild motor tics (e.g., eye blinks) and be classified as TS, while someone with multiple severe motor tics but no phonic tic would be classified as chronic TD. In addition, there seems no indication that chronic TD responds differentially to treatment than does TS (O'Connor, 2001).

Tic Subtypes

Tics are usually divided into simple and complex, within sensory, motor, phonic, and cognitive modalities. Tics need to be differentiated from simple habits, stereotypies, spasms, habit disorders, and compulsive rituals as observed in obsessive-compulsive disorder (OCD) (Table 18.2). Important features of the tic—its reflex-like nature, its rhythmicity, its link to behavioral activity, and lack of awareness—are all discriminating features.

Simple tics usually involve one muscle group such as the cheeks or shoulders. Complex tics usually occur in sequences and can appear as bizarre mannerisms, for example, a hand and shoulder movement leading to head turning or neck cracking. A phonic (vocal) tic may range from throat clearing to more complex phrases or noises. The most notorious vocal tic, coprolalia (swearing), is very rare, occurring in not more than 8 percent of TS cases, and it is observed most often in adolescence, with its incidence declining as a function of age (Kurlan, 1992).

Sensory tics are more controversial because some authors view them as precursors to motor tics. Conversely, not all motor tics are preceded by premonitory urges, and people do independently report sensations such as tingling, warming, or localized irritations that could be classified as sensory tics. Cognitive or mental tics are perhaps the least known tics. First noted by Cath, Roos, and van de Wetering (1992), and subsequently elaborated on by O'Connor (2005), mental tics take the form of repeated phrases, tunes, or scenes of an almost playful nature and are easily confused with obsessions or mental neutralizations as observed in OCD. This differential diagnosis is essential because treatment for mental tics and obsessions is quite distinct. For example, whereas exposure and response prevention is highly effective in reducing obsessions, this form of treatment does not reduce mental tics.

Table 18.2. Tic Subtypes and Other Unrelated Problems Important in Differential Diagnosis

Simple Tics				Complex Tics			
Motor	Sensory	Vocal	Mental	Motor	Sensory	Vocal	Mental
One muscle group	Focused sensation	Simple noise or sound	Image or idea or work turned over in head	Several muscle on groups	Traveling on variable sensation	Complex phrase	Complex mental operation

Differential Diagnosis

| Neurologic spasms, stereotypy | Somatoform disorders | Speech, voice problems | Obsessional intrusions | Habit disorders, rituals, stereotypies | Hypochondria, hysteria | Antisocial behavior | Mental rituals, neutralization |

Covariation, Comorbidity, and Associated Behavioral Problems

Individuals with tic disorders often evidence other types of stereotypical behaviors. For example, individuals with TS frequently have multiple tics and often evidence habit disorders (nail biting, hair pulling, skin scratching, skin picking; Knell & Comings, 1993). In a recent sample of 25 consecutively referred cases of TS in our research clinic, 28 percent had a comorbid habit disorder, and 20 percent of those diagnosed principally with habit disorder ($n = 15$) had had tics. Studies of adults with TS have reported levels of comorbidity with OCD, ranging from 24 percent to 63 percent. However, other Axis I and Axis II disorders do not show such elevated rates of comorbidity with TS or TDs in adults (O'Connor, 2001).

In contrast, up to 50 percent of children with TS evidence comorbid psychiatric diagnoses (Budman & Feirman, 2001; Coffey & Park, 1997). Attention deficit hyperactivity disorder (ADHD) is the most common comorbidity in children with TS, with estimates of comorbidity, ranging widely from 21 percent to 90 percent (Budman & Feirman, 2001; Freeman et al., 2000). When symptoms such as impulsivity and oppositional behavior occur in the presence of tics, it frequently leads to difficulties in psychosocial adaptation (Sukhodolsky et al., 2003). OCD is less likely to occur in children with TS than in adults with TS (Budman & Feirman, 2001; Comings, 1990), and children with both TS and OCD have a poorer prognosis than do those with only TS (Eapen & Robertson, 2000).

Kurlan et al. (2002) reported that up to 29 percent of 339 children with TS had a comorbid anxiety disorder other than OCD. Coffey and colleagues (2000) also showed that other anxiety disorders, including panic disorder (23%), agoraphobia (39%), separation anxiety disorder (51%), and overanxious disorder (46%), were significantly overrepresented among youths with severe TD. Tics may be exacerbated by a factor of 3.5 in anxious situations that increase stress reactivity, embarrassment, and disruption in daily life activities (Budman & Feirman, 2001; Coffey et al., 2000). However, major depression and bipolar disorder are the best predictors of the need for psychiatric hospitalization in young people with TS (Coffey et al., 2000; Wodrich, Benjamin, & Lachar, 1997). Other associated symptoms include sleep disorders (insomnia, somnambulism, and nightmare) and aggressive and oppositional behavior (Hickey & Wilson, 2000).

Aggressive behaviors, including sudden and explosive tantrums, occur in approximately 42 to 66 percent of children with TS (Alsobrook & Pauls, 2002), and such symptoms are more frequently reported in children (35% to 70%) than in adults (8%) (Budman, Bruun, Park, Lesser, & Olson, 2000; Sukhodolsky et al., 2003). Out of all the comorbidities and associated features of TS, tantrums and rage attacks are the most disruptive to familial, educational, and social aspects of the child (Budman, Rockmore, Stokes, & Sossin, 2003). One-third of children with TS have learning difficulties because of impairment in memorizing, visuospatial perception, and attention deficit (Wodrich et al., 1997). Rejection by peers, lack of self-esteem, and loneliness, often experienced by children with TS, may help to reduce school and social adaptation.

Natural History and Prevalence of Tic Disorders

Tics usually develop in a rostal-caudal manner (from head to toes). The majority of tics occur in the upper body. Simple tics develop before complex tics, and vocal tics usually develop subsequent to motor and sensory tics, with complex vocal tics developing usually in adolescence (Comings, 1990; Shapiro, Shapiro, Young, & Feinberg, 1988). Although tics have been reported in newborns, the age of onset of tics is typically around 7 years (Freeman et al., 2000). At this age, around 15 percent of all children present with transitory tics (perhaps related to myogenic development), which, in 80 percent of cases, spontaneously remit. However, for those whose tics persist, the symptoms can become more intense, generalize to other parts of the body, and become more complex. Vocal tics usually appear between 8 and 9 years, and more complex tics, around 12 years. Tics can, however, develop for the first time at any age of adulthood (Leckman et al., 1998).

Accurate estimates of the prevalence of TDs and TS are difficult to obtain for a number of reasons, an important reason being difficulty distinguishing tics from other problem behaviors and movements. Nevertheless, once considered rare, TS is now estimated to occur in 1 in 100 boys and 1 in 800 girls. Other types of tics are estimated to occur in 4 percent to 12 percent of the population (Comings & Comings, 1990).

Case Vignette

The following case illustrates the typical evolution of tics and associated behaviors in an individual with TS:

Kevin had first presented with problems with inattention, distractibility, and hyperactivity at age 5. Despite pharmacotherapy (methylphenidate and imipramine), he continued to display these symptoms, which led to poor academic performance. Parent and teacher observations reported that Kevin, age 7, displayed mouth and eye tics. These took the form of repetitive winks, mostly present when the child was excited. During the next winter when Kevin had a cold, a throat clearing habit developed. Moreover, Kevin began to show complex tics, such as sudden arm movements that made him knock things over (e.g., beverages he was drinking). A phonic tic also emerged, which involved growls that could be accompanied by a chest spasm if the child restrained himself for a long period. At age 11, Kevin presented for a second medical opinion for his symptoms and also for adjustment problems. In particular, he was having difficulty with peer relationships and school performance. There were conflicts at home over completion of homework, chores, and his daily hygiene. Most of these led to oppositional behavior, explosive outbursts, and aggression. Kevin showed poor organizational skills, a high level of impulsivity, and frequent mood swings. At this time, he received a diagnosis of TS. Kevin learned, with counseling, to cope with TS symptoms, including managing the embarrassment that his motor and phonic tics caused him in social situations. At age 18, Kevin continued to exhibit the same tics, but by learning to better control his body movements, he was able to camouflage these symptoms to a great degree, which saves him some embarrassment.

Theoretical Models

There are currently three principal theoretical approaches to TD and TS: (1) neurobiological models, (2) a learning model, and (3) a sensorimotor regulation model. Each of these approaches points to discrete interventions.

Neurobiological Approach

The prevailing consensus is that TS and TD are essentially neurobiological problems (American Psychiatric Association, 2000; Comings, 1990). The specific locus of the deficit remains unclear, although most hypotheses propose that, like other movement disorders such as Huntington's, Sydenham's, and Parkinson's disease, TS and TD involve the basal ganglia (e.g., Rappoport, 1990). There is supportive evidence from brain-imaging studies; however, such findings are inconsistent and could easily be due to tic suppression or other compensatory strategies (Peterson et al., 2003). Neuropsychological findings have provided only inconsistent evidence of deficits in executive functioning, yet there are some signs of impaired visuomotor performance.

When brain functioning is examined through electrophysiologic means, it appears that certain kinds of cognitive processes are abnormal among individuals with TS. In particular, there is a tendency to overprepare and overinvest attentional resources, which could lead to wider cortical activating, impaired resource allocation, and distractions (Duggal & Haque Nizamie, 2002; Johannes et al., 2002). In addition, reported problems with response inhibition to automated tasks could be explained by overactive sensorimotor activation, which could also account for faster go responses and less discerning response selection (O'Connor et al., 2005).

Learning Model

Azrin and Nunn (1973) were the first to suggest that tics may develop as conditioned responses, particularly as adapted startle reflexes, which are then maintained by reinforcing factors such as social and attentional operants. Lack of awareness also helps perpetuate the tic because the person may repeat the tic under different contingencies without being aware and autoreinforce its appearance. However, the literature supporting tics as conditioned startle responses is inconclusive, and tics are often observed to wax and wane and to generalize to other body parts. Although case studies have highlighted social and situational reinforces that could conceivably maintain tics, there is no convincing evidence that counterconditioning procedures such as massed practice or extinction protocols can alleviate tics, even though environmental contingencies can certainly exacerbate tics (O'Connor, 2005).

Sensorimotor Regulation Model

The sensorimotor regulation model, unlike other approaches, views tics as serving a tension reduction function. Evers and van de Wetering (1994) were among the first to suggest that tics are performed as a response to elevated muscle tension and hence serve the purpose of short-term relief from chronic tension, while also sustaining the tension-release cycle in the long run. In a similar vein, Hoogduin, Verdellen, and Cath (1997) suggested that tics were a response to heightened internal sensations, which the tic neutralizes temporarily but reinforces over time.

Clinical implications of the two sensorimotor models are distinct. Evers and van de Wetering (1994) recommend tension reduction or stress management as a way of regulating the tic, whereas Hoogduin et al. (1997) recommend exposure to promote habituation to the heightened internal sensations. Single case studies have described the successful use of each approach, yet a larger controlled crossover trial comparing exposure with habit reversal produced inconclusive results (Verdellen, Keijsers, Cath, & Hoogduin, 2004).

An elaboration of the functional role of tics in sensorimotor regulation is found in O'Connor's (2002) cognitive psychophysiologic model. In this model, the notion of sensorimotor activation is expanded to include a number of behavioral, cognitive, and psychophysiologic inputs to overactivation other than muscle tension or sensory arousal. The theory places sensorimotor activation within a motor psychophysiology process, whereby overactive and overpreparatory styles of action driven in turn by perfectionist beliefs about personal organization lead the person to adopt behaviors that lead to chronic tension and overactivation. This overactivation forms the background for the tic appearance as a means of temporarily alleviating the activation but paradoxically stimulating higher activation in the long term.

Treatment

Three approaches to treatment for TDs are pharmacotherapy, behavioral therapy, and cognitive-behavioral treatment. Treatment aims to alleviate the most disruptive symptoms. Depending on comorbidities and dominant symptoms, a combination of approaches is often the best way to obtain positive results (Anderson, Vu, Derby, Goris, & McLaughlin, 2002; O'Connor, 2002; Peterson & Cohen, 1998).

Pharmacotherapy

The effectiveness of medication varies widely from individual to individual and sometimes even within patients, depending on the period of use (Peterson & Cohen, 1998; Robertson, 2000). There is no medication to *cure* TS, and tics rarely disappear with medication. The most successful agents are typical neuroleptics (dopamine antagonists), such as haloperidol and pimozide, or atypical neuroleptics, such as risperidone, clozapine, and olanzapine (Carter et al., 1998; Onofrj, Paci, D'Andreamatteo, & Toma, 2000). Clonidine appears to be the most prescribed medication in children with TS, ADHD, and OCD (Freeman et al., 2000; Gaffney et al., 2002; Robertson, 2000). Although published open-trial case studies give the impression that pharmacologic treatments consistently control tics, controlled trials paint a more sobering picture, suggesting that reduction rates of only 20 percent to 50 percent are the norm (Budman & Feirman, 2001; Robertson, 2000). In addition, almost 80 percent of patients abandon treatment due to undesirable side effects (Peterson, Campise, & Azrin, 1994).

Habit Reversal

Habit-reversal treatment programs typically include five steps: (1) awareness training, (2) relaxation training, (3) competing response practice, (4) habit control motivation, and (5) generalization training (Azrin & Nunn, 1977; Azrin & Peterson, 1988). Clinical case studies using habit reversal have shown decreased tic frequency between 75 and 100 percent (Peterson & Azrin, 1992, 1993; Woods, Twohig, Flessner, & Roloff, 2003). However, controlled trials show more conservative results with high rates of relapse (Wilhelm et al., 2003).

The aim of awareness training is to help the patient arrive at a clear recognition and detailed description of the form and appearance of the tic. The goal is to be able to detect tic onset as rapidly as possible. The incompatible response is a socially acceptable, convenient, and preferably invisible action, which is antagonistic to the tic. It can take several forms: a softer response, a slower response, a relaxation response, or a muscle contraction in the opposite direction to the tic contraction. So, for example, a head tic to the left could be counteracted by an antagonist contraction to the right, incompatible with the original tic. A hand or arm tic may be prevented by placing the hand firmly in contact with a flat surface.

Carr (1995) detailed a number of incompatible responses for different parts of the body, and Woods and Miltenberger (2001) give helpful instructions on its complementation. Typically, the incompatible response is practiced in and out of high-risk tic situations and within an appropriate positive reinforcement schedule with social support. The incompatible response can also be implemented within a larger behavioral context where approach behavior can replace avoidant behavior as an incompatible competing response. For example, direct eye contact antagonistic to blinking can replace gaze avoidance and repetitive blinking (O'Connor et al., 2001).

Researchers have evaluated the outcome of various combinations of habit reversal program components to elucidate the essential ingredients of this therapy (Jones, Swearer, & Friman, 1997; Miltenberger, Fuqua, & Woods, 1998;

Woods et al., 2003). Results of these dismantling studies suggest that awareness training and competing response practice plus social support are the most effective components of habit reversal for decreasing tic frequency and intensity.

The Cognitive-Psychophysiologic Model

The aim of therapy within the cognitive-psychophysiologic model is to prevent tic occurrence by addressing all inputs maintaining chronic tension and sensorimotor activation, and by encouraging, through cognitive-behavioral restructuring, a different (and less tension-producing) approach to high-risk situations. The model has been empirically validated, but like the habit-reversal package, it is a multicomponent treatment and the relative contribution of the various elements remains unclear (O'Connor, 2005). This treatment approach follows a 10-stage program over 14 weeks with one month of home practice. The program begins with awareness training using a daily diary, video, and monitoring by self and others. Psychophysiologic training includes education in muscle training, muscle discrimination, muscle isolation, and normalization of use of tic-affected muscles followed by progressive relaxation.

The next stages address hypervigilance to sensations, reattribution of interpretations of sensation, and exposure to aid habituation to any premonitory urge. At the same time, behavioral inputs to the tension-producing style of action typical in TS/TD are addressed by reducing overactivity and overpreparation in everyday styles of planning. Cognitive restructuring addresses perfectionist beliefs and other core beliefs and appraisals, which may be driving frustration and impatience associated with high-risk tic situations. Finally, alternative tension-reducing strategies are employed to restructure behavior and thinking in high-risk tic situations. These cognitive-behavioral restructuring strategies are generalized to other tics through home practice.

Case Vignettes

John was a 45-year-old engineer. His most disruptive complex tic affected breathing: an abdomen spasm that made him expire noisily and groan occurring at a frequency of 30 to 50 times per day. John also shrugged his shoulders up and down, bit his cheeks involuntary, and repeatedly cleared his throat. He also often put his hand on his genitals. Fifteen years previously, at the age of 30, he was given a diagnosis of TS with comorbid trichotillomania (repetitive hair pulling). John's motor tics began at age 10 and his vocal tics at age 30. The symptoms of trichotillomania began when he was about 15 years old. Subsequently, John consulted a neurologist and took medications (Orap, Topamax, Rivotril) to treat these problems. Before treatment, he was able to suppress his tics for 15 to 30 minutes at a time. The tic severity impaired his social, occupational, and family life.

The tic chosen as a treatment target was the most frequent and annoying, namely, his abdominal tic. High-risk tic situations included driving in the car, playing sports, and watching television—situations in which he was likely to become impatient or tense. Conversely, low-risk activities included reading a newspaper, cooking, and working on his computer—activities where he was attentively engaged. He showed a style involving overplanning in advance and investing too much effort, particularly when speaking to others or giving talks. He also attempted to do too much every day and realized he felt a self-imposed pressure to appear efficient and perfectly organized at all times. The cognitive-behavioral restructuring addressed perfectionist beliefs about the need to overprepare for tasks and overperform and modified focus during task performance away from the pressure to perform and the negative anticipations about performance to his ability to accomplish the task in a nonstressful natural manner. After 14 weeks of treatment, John's Tourette Syndrome Global Scale score (TSGS) had reduced from 33.7 to 10.0, and the daily tic diary frequency had reduced by 88 percent (Figure 18.1), showing a significant linear reduction over time.

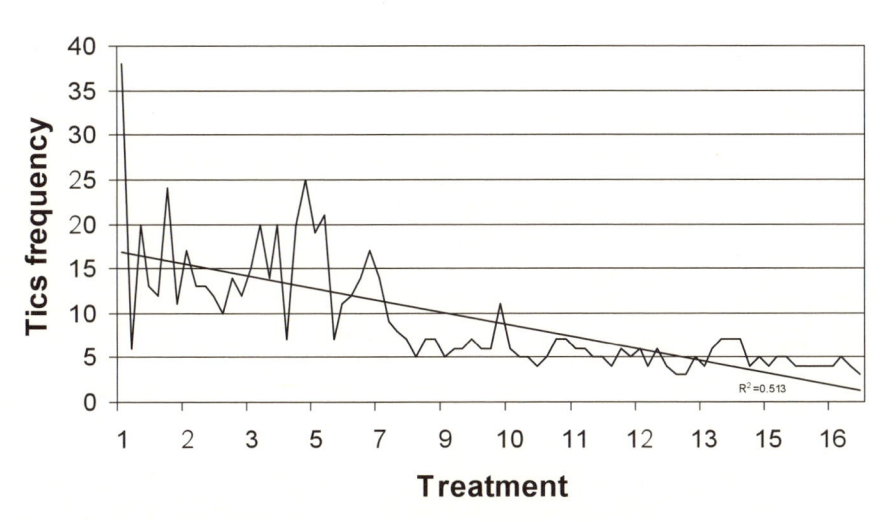

Figure 18.1. Daily tic frequency over treatment sessions for John.

Martin was a 38-year-old restaurant owner. He presented with excessive blinking that led to eye pain and difficulty making eye contact with others. His tics began at age 7, but the pain became noticeable at age 15. Before treatment, he blinked involuntarily at a frequency of 40 times per minute. He was unable to control the blinking and this impaired his interpersonal relationships. He had previously tried hypnosis and acupuncture to no avail but had never taken medication. Martin's high-risk situations included being at work, greeting people, and serving in his restaurant. The cognitive-behavioral restructuring addressed dysfunctional beliefs about the negative judgment of others, and ideas about how he must always be "on the go" and never waste time. These beliefs were assumed to lead to frustration. Martin began interacting more calmly, making eye contact when speaking to others, and not investing tension in maintaining false smiles or postures. He began relaxing when driving, listening to music, and driving more slowly. After 14 weeks of treatment, his TSGS score reduced from 26.75 to 2.50. The daily tic diary frequency reduced by 95 percent and showed a significant linear decrease over sessions (Figure 18.2).

Troubleshooting

The main obstacle to successful treatment of tics is often compliance with behavioral exercises. In both treatments, consistent application of new behaviors is essential for success, and reinforcement could involve planning a reward

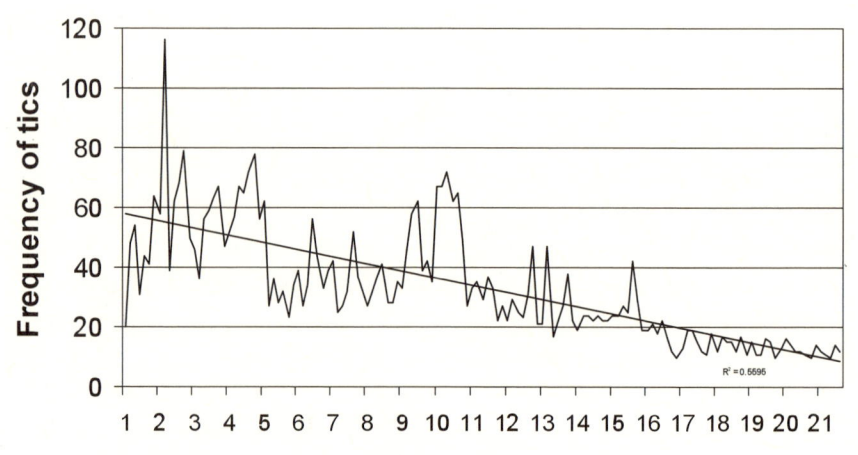

Figure 18.2. Daily tic frequency over treatment sessions for Martin.

schedule with the patient contingent on practice. After some initial improvement, patients may feel satisfied, and thus abandon treatment; but they must be encouraged to arrive at complete tic elimination for the sake of relapse prevention. Patients also need to be encouraged to maintain exercises post-treatment to avoid relapse. Ways of coping positively and realistically with slips, minor lapses, and unforeseen high-risk situations can be planned with the patient. Although there is some generalization to other tics, once one tic is controlled, the program may need to be applied independently across separate tic units.

Are TS and Tic Disorders Part of an OCD Spectrum?

The notion of a spectrum of disorders representing manifestations of the same neurogenetic dysfunction was popularized by Hollander (1993) who proposed that TS, OCD and other disorders shared similar repetitive characteristics and might involve similar neurotransmitter systems.

The focus in the spectrum debate has traditionally been on neurobiological and medical similarities between OCD disorders rather on the myriad behavioural and psychosocial differences. The original proposition put forward by Hollander et al. (1990) essentially tied the spectrum dimension with hyperhypofunctionality of the frontal lobes, but brain imaging pictures of regional activity show a much more complex pattern. Brain activity as recorded electrophysiologically shows a topographically distinct pattern of activity between OCD and TS. In OCD electrocortical characteristics are linked to attentional and evaluation components, while in TS, the affected electrocortical components are more related to motor processing (Duggal & Haque Nizamie, 2002; Johannes et al., 2002). A similar distinction is found within neuropsychological findings where visuomotor performance is exclusively affected in TS (Schultz et al., 1999). It is also unclear that impulsivity and compulsivity represent a natural dimension linking, respectively, stimulation and harm avoidance, and in any case, people with tics do not show other impulsive traits (Summerfeldt et al., 2004).

Behavioral and psychological aspects of both TS and OCD highlight distinctions between the two problems. OCD is triggered by intrusive thoughts and accompanied by anxiety, whereas tics in TS are triggered by tension and accompanied by frustration rather than anxiety. Treatment approaches in both cases are distinct: Awareness training and relaxation, while successful with tics, do not work with OCD. Similar maladaptive coping strategies may help to maintain OCD and tics, but the similarities are better explained through basic behavioral principles of reinforcement, which can occur in any psychological problem. The apparent high comorbidity of TS with OCD seemingly supports a link between the two disorders, yet may prove to be accounted for by the vagueness of differential diagnosis between mental tics and obsessions and between complex tics and compulsions (Shapiro & Shapiro, 1986). Finally, Cath et al. (2001) suggest distinct pharmacologic interventions for TS that point to a separate TS spectrum.

Conclusion

The application of cognitive-behavioral treatment to tic and habit disorders is still in its infancy. Clinicians need to be educated regarding these approaches, which can be difficult in a milieu in which the treatment models are overwhelmingly driven by hypothetical neurobiological models. Within this context, psychological interventions are sometimes greeted with skepticism and even disdain. Both habit reversal and exposure and response prevention have shown successful outcome. Although learning models may explain reinforcing and maintaining factors, in our opinion, a sensorimotor regulation model accounts best for the functional role of tics. If tics alleviate chronic sensorimotor activation, then addressing the cognitive, behavioral, and sensory inputs producing overactivation may prevent tic onset. The success of this model encourages an approach that genuinely views psychosocial and physiologic factors as two-way and interactive. More work needs to clarify the active components of cognitive-behavioral treatment, streamline matching to different tic subtypes, and implant the program effectively in clinic settings. After showing that these treatment strategies are efficient in treating tics in TD and TS, the field needs to address the issue of how best to make it effectively available.

REFERENCES

Alsobrook, J. P., II, & Pauls, D. L. (2002). A factor analysis of tic symptoms in Gilles de la Tourette's syndrome. *American Journal of Psychiatry, 159,* 291–296.
American Psychiatric Association. (2000). *Diagnostic and Statistical Manual of Mental Disorders* (4th ed., text revised). Washington, DC: Author.
Anderson, M. T., Vu, C., Derby, K. M., Goris, M., & McLaughlin, T. F. (2002). Using

functional analysis procedures to monitor medication effects in an outpatient and school setting. *Psychology in the Schools, 39,* 73–76.

Azrin, N. H., & Nunn, R. G. (1973). Habit-reversal: A method of eliminating nervous habits and tics. *Behaviour Research and Therapy, 11,* 619–628.

Azrin, N. H., & Nunn, R. G. (1977). *Habit control in a day.* New York: Simon & Schuster.

Azrin, N. H., & Peterson, A. L. (1988). Habit reversal for the treatment of Tourette syndrome. *Behaviour Research and Therapy, 26,* 347–351.

Budman, C. L., & Feirman, L. (2001). The relationship of Tourette's syndrome with its psychiatric comorbidities: Is there an overlap? *Psychiatric Annals, 31,* 541–548.

Budman, C. L., Rockmore, L., Stokes, J., & Sossin, M. (2003). Clinical phenomenology of episodic rage in children with Tourette syndrome. *Journal of Psychosomatic Research, 55,* 59–65.

Budman, C. L., Bruun, R. D., Park, K. S., Lesser, M., & Olson, M. (2000). Explosive outbursts in children with Tourette's disorder. *Journal of the American Academy of Child and Adolescent Psychiatry, 39,* 1270–1276.

Carr, J. E. (1995). Competing responses for the treatment of Tourette syndrome and tic disorders. *Behaviour Research and Therapy, 33,* 455–456.

Carter, A. S., Fredine, N. J., Findley, D., Scahill, L., Zimmerman, L., & Sparrow, S. S. (1998). Pharmacological and other somatic approaches to treatment. J. F. Leckman & D. J. Cohen (Eds.), *Tourette's syndrome, tics, obsessions, compulsions. Developmental psychopathology and clinical care* (pp. 370–398). New York: Wiley.

Cath, D., Roos, R., & Van de Wetering, B. (1992). Mental play in Gilles de la Tourette's syndrome and obsessive-compulsive disorder. *British Journal of Psychiatry, 161,* 542–545.

Cath, D., Spinhoven, T., van Woerkom, T., Hoogduin, C., Landman, A., Roos, R., Rooijmans, H. (2001). Gilles de la Tourette's Syndrome with and without Obsessive-Compulsive Disorder Compared with Obsessive-Compulsive Disorder without Tics: Which Symptoms Discriminate? *Journal of Nervous and Mental Disease, 189,* 219–228.

Coffey, B. J., & Park, K. S. (1997). Behavioral and emotional aspects of Tourette syndrome. *Neurologic Clinics, 15,* 277–289.

Coffey, B. J., Biederman, J., Smoller, J. W., Geller, D. A., Sarin, P., Schwartz, S., et al. (2000). Anxiety disorders and tic severity in juveniles with Tourette's disorder. *Journal of American Academy of Child and Adolescent Psychiatry, 39,* 562–568.

Comings, D. E. (1990). *Tourette syndrome and human behavior.* Duarte, CA: Hope Press.

Comings, D. E., & Comings, B. G. (1990). A controlled family history study of Tourette's syndrome: I. Attention-deficit hyperactivity disorder and learning disorders. *Journal of Clinical Psychiatry, 51*(7), 275–280.

Duggal, H. S., & Haque Nizamie, S. (2002). Bereitschaftspotential in tic disorders: A preliminary observation. *Neurology India, 50,* 487–489.

Eapen, V., & Robertson, M. M. (2000). Comorbid obsessive-compulsive disorder and Tourette syndrome, therapeutic interventions. *CNS Drugs, 13*(3), 173–183.

Evers, R. A. F., & van de Wetering, B. J. M. (1994). A treatment model for motor tics based on a specific tension-reduction technique. *Journal of Behavior Therapy and Experimental Psychiatry, 25,* 255–260.

Freeman, R., Fast, D., Burd, L., Kerbeshian, J., Robertson, M., & Sandor, P. (2000). An international perspective on Tourette syndrome: Selected findings from 3500 cases in 22 countries. *Developmental Medicine and Child Neurology, 42,* 436–447.

Gaffney, G. R., Perry, P. J., Lund, B. C., Bever-Stille, K. A., Arndt, S., & Kuperman, S. (2002). Risperidone versus clonidine in the treatment of children and adolescents with Tourette's syndrome. *Journal of the American Academy of Child and Adolescent Psychiatry, 41,* 330–336.

Gilles de la Tourette, G. (1885) Etude sur une affection nerveuse caractérisée par l'inco-ordination motrice accompagnée d'écholalie et de coprolalie. *Archives de Neurologie (Paris), 9:* 19–42.

Hickey, T., & Wilson, L. (2000). Tourette syndrome: Symptom severity, anxiety, depression, stress, social support, and ways of coping. *Irish Journal of Psychology, 21,* 78–87.

Hoogduin, K., Verdellen, C., & Cath, D. (1997). Exposure and response prevention in the treatment of Gilles de la Tourette's syndrome: Four case studies. *Clinical Psychology and Psychotherapy, 4*(2), 125–135.

Itard, J. M. G. (1825). Mémoire sur quelques fonctions involontaires des appareils de la locomtion, de la préhension et de la voix. *Archives de Géneral Médicin, 8,* 385–407.

Johannes, S., Wieringa, B. M., Nager, W., Muller-Vahl, K. R., Dengler, R., & Munte, T. F. (2002). Excessive action monitoring treatment of Tourette syndrome. *Journal of Neurology, 249*(8), 961–966.

Jones, K. M., Swearer, S. M., & Friman, P.C. (1997). Relax and try this instead: Abbreviated habit reversal for maladaptive self-biting. *Journal of Applied Behavior Analysis, 30*(4), 697–699.

Knell, E. R., & Comings, D. E. (1993). Tourette's syndrome and attention-deficit hyperactivity disorder: Evidence for a genetic relationship. *Journal of Clinical Psychiatry, 54*(9), 331–337.

Kurlan, R. (1992). Tourette syndrome in a special education population. Hypotheses. *Advances in Neurology, 58,* 75–81.

Kurlan, R., Como, P. G., Miller, B., Palumbo, D., Deeley, C., Andresen, E. M., Eapen, S., & McDermott, M. P. (2002). The behavioral spectrum of tic disorders: a community-based study. *Neurology, 59*(3), 414–420.

Leckman, J. F., Zhang, H., Vitale, A., Lahnikn, F., Lynch, K., Bondi, C., et al. (1998). Course of tic severity in Tourette syndrome: The first two decades. *Pediatrics, 102,* 14–19.

Miltenberger, R. G., Fuqua, R. W., & Woods, D. W. (1998). Applying behavior analysis to clinical problems: Review and analysis of habit reversal. *Journal of Applied Behavior Analysis, 31*(3), 447–469.

O'Connor, K. P. (2001). Clinical and psychological features distinguishing obsessive-compulsive and chronic tic disorders. *Clinical Psychology Review, 21,* 631–660.

O'Connor, K. P. (2002). A cognitive-behavioral / psychological model of tic disorders. *Behaviour Research and Therapy, 40,* 1113–1142.

O'Connor, K, P. (2005). *Cognitive-behavioral management of tic disorders.* New York: John Wiley & Sons.

O'Connor, K. P., Brault, M., Loiselle, J., Robillard, S., Borgeat, F., & Stip, E. (2001). Evaluation of a cognitive-behavioral program for the management of chronic tic and habit disorders. *Behavior Research and Therapy, 39,* 667–681.

O'Connor, K. P., Lavoie, M., Robert, M., Dubord, J., Stip, E., & Borgeat, F. (2005). Brain-behavior relations during motor processing in chronic tic and habit disorder. *Cognitive and Behavioral Neurology, 18*(2), 79–88.

Onofrj, M., Paci, C., D'Andreamatteo, G., & Toma, L. (2000). Olanzapine in severe Gilles dela Tourette syndrome: A 52–week double-blind cross-over study vs. low-dose pimozide. *Journal of Neurology, 247,* 443–446.

Organisation mondiale de la santé. (1996). Classification statistique internationale des maladies et des problèmes de santé connexes-CIM 10, 10ᵉ révision. Geneva: MS.

Peterson, A. L., & Azrin, N. H. (1992). An evaluation of behavioural treatments for Tourette syndrome. *Behaviour Research and Therapy, 30,* 167–174.

Peterson, A. L., & Azrin, N. H. (1993). Behavioral and pharmacological treatments for Tourette syndrome. *Applied and Preventive Psychology, 2,* 231–242.

Peterson, A. L., Campise, R. L., & Azrin, N. H. (1994). Behavioral and pharmacological treatments for tic and habit disorders: A review. *Developmental and behavioural pediatrics, 15*(6), 430–441.

Peterson, B. S., & Cohen, D. J. (1998). The treatment of Tourette's syndrome : Multimodal, developmental intervention. *Journal of Clinical Psychiatry, 59,* 62–72.

Peterson, B. S., Thomas, P., Kane, M. J., Scahill, L., Zhang, H., Bronen, R., et al. (2003). Basal ganglia volumes in patients with Gilles de la Tourette syndrome. *Archives of General Psychiatry, 60*(4), 415–424.

Rappoport, J. L. (1990). Obsessive compulsive disorder and basal ganglia dysfunction. *Psychological Medicine, 20,* 465–469.

Robertson, M. M. (2000). Tourette syndrome, associated conditions and complexities of treatment. *Brain, 123,* 425–462.

Shapiro, E., & Shapiro, A. K. (1986). Semiology, nosology, and criteria for tic disorders. *Review of Neurology, 142,* 824–832.

Shapiro, A. K., Shapiro, E. S., Young, J. G., & Feinberg, T. E. (1988). *Gilles de la Tourette syndrome.* New York: Raven Press.

Spencer, T., Biederman, J., Harding, M., O'Donnell, D., Wilens, T., Faraone, S., et al. (1998). Disentangling the overlap between Tourette's disorder and ADHD. *Journal of Child Psychology and Psychiatry, 39*(7), 1037–1044.

Sukhodolsky, D. G., Scahill, L., Zhang, H., Peterson, B. S., King, R. A., Lombroso, P. J., et al. (2003). Disruptive behavior in children with Tourette syndrome: Association with ADHD comorbidity, tic severity, and functional impairment. *Journal of the American Academy of Child and Adolescent Psychiatry, 42,* 98–105.

Verdellen, C. W. J., Keijsers, G. P. J., Cath, D. C., & Hoogduin, C. A. L. (2004). Exposure with response prevention versus habit reversal in Tourette's syndrome: A controlled study. *Behaviour Research and Therapy, 42,* 501–511.

Wilhelm, S., Deckersbach, T., Coffey, B. J., Bohne, A., Peterson, A. L., & Baer, L. (2003). Habit reversal versus supportive psychotherapy for Tourette's disorder: A randomized controlled trial. *American Journal of Psychiatry, 160,* 1175–1177.

Wodrich, D. L., Benjamin, E., & Lachar, D. (1997). Tourette's syndrome and psychopathology in a child psychiatric setting. *Journal of the American Academy of Child and Adolescent Psychiatry, 36,* 1618–1624.

Woods, D. W., & Miltenberger, R. G. (2001). *Tic disorders, trichotillomania, and other repetitive behaviour disorders: Behavioural approaches to analysis and treatment.* Boston: Kluwer Academic.

Woods, D. W., Twohig, M. P., Flessner, C. A., & Roloff, T. J. (2003). Treatment of vocal tics in children with Tourette syndrome: Investigating the efficacy of habit reversal. *Journal of Applied Behavior Analysis, 36,* 109–112.

CHAPTER NINETEEN

Body Dysmorphic Disorder

David H. Gleaves, Ph.D., and Suman Ambwani, M.A.

Case Vignette

To the outside observer, Sarah was a petite, attractive blonde woman in her late twenties. To herself, she was unimaginably ugly, flat chested, big bottomed, with a receding hairline (making her look as if she were in her fifties), a huge, bulbous nose, and prominent acne scars. Insofar as she could, Sarah avoided going out in public, opting to work from home instead. To leave home required that she engage in a lengthy preparation process: She carefully applied makeup, selected clothing to mask her body, and wore a large hat and oversized sunglasses to conceal her thinning hair and her face. After almost six agonizing hours of preparation, involving constant mirror checking, picking at her acne scars, and a great deal of frustration, Sarah would feel no better. Greatly distressed, she would eventually make a phone call and cancel her appointment, believing that she was too repulsive to unleash herself onto the world.

Description of the Disorder

Although most people are concerned to some degree about their appearance, concerns similar to those experienced by Sarah may reflect body dysmorphic disorder (BDD). In the scientific literature for more than 100 years, and previously referred to by such terms as "dysmorphophobia" and "obsession with the shame of the body" (see Jerome, 2001), BDD is defined in the current *Diagnostic and Statistical Manual of Mental Disorders* (DSM-IV-TR; American Psychiatric Association, 2000) as "the preoccupation with an imagined or exaggerated defect in physical appearance" (p. 485). This preoccupation with appearance causes significant impairment in functioning or marked distress, is typically pervasive, unrelenting, and leads to continued efforts to remedy the imagined or exaggerated defect. Exclusionary criteria specify that the preoccupation cannot be a function of another psychological disorder (e.g., the body-image concerns of an eating disorder). However, persons with delusional beliefs may be diagnosed with BDD and a comorbid delusional disorder (somatic type).

Although the DSM definition focuses on the idea of an exaggerated or imagined defect, it seems that individuals with BDD also have high standards for attractiveness. Thus, they feel particularly ugly in reference to their idealized self-image rather than in reference to general population standards (Neziroglu & Khemlani-Patel, 2003). It may be that for persons with BDD, as for those with eating disorders, a distorted view of their current body combines with a very difficult-to-obtain ideal body, thus yielding a high level of body dissatisfaction (Gleaves et al., 1995).

To the degree that it has been studied, BDD seems to occur in different cultures around the world. Thus, appearance-based preoccupations are global phenomena, even though the *foci* of the preoccupations vary by culture (Gleaves & Ambwani, 2005). Fairly recently, a possible subtype of BDD was described and termed *muscle dysmorphia*. Olivardia (2001) described this problem as an individual's preoccupation that he or she is not lean and muscular enough. Typically, individuals with muscle dysmorphia avoid activities that interfere with their workout schedules or that require them to expose their bodies. A variety of techniques may be used to enhance muscularity, including, anabolic steroid use (Cafri et al., 2005), despite awareness of (and experience with) negative aftereffects.

For various reasons, including the patient's reduced insight, feelings of shame, or lack of explicit questioning by the service provider, BDD typically remains underrecognized by general practitioners, cosmetic surgeons (Gorbis, 2004), and in other clinical settings (Perugi & Frare, 2005). For instance, Veale (2000) described multiple patients with BDD who underwent 46 cosmetic procedures before being diagnosed as having BDD. Phillips (2001) further described two studies of general outpatients and depressed individuals in which BDD was overlooked by the clinician every time. Despite the under-recognition of this disorder, BDD prevalence estimates suggest that the disorder is somewhat common in certain settings. In the general population, BDD estimates range from 0.7 percent (Faravelli et al., 1997; Otto, Wilhelm, Cohen, & Harlow, 2001) to 1.1 percent (Phillips, 2001), and 2–13 percent among non-clinical student samples (Phillips, 2001). Among those seeking dermatologic or cosmetic treatment, rates of BDD are predictably higher (e.g., 12%; Phillips, Dufresne, Wilkel, & Vittorio, 2000). Finally, data suggest that BDD occurs in about 13 percent of clinical inpatient samples (Phillips, Menard, Fay, & Weisberg, 2005).

Adolescence appears to be the typical age of onset for BDD (Phillips, Menard, Fay, & Weisberg, 2005), however, clients are often not diagnosed until 10–15 years later, and the mean age of clients is usually in the early-to-mid thirties (Phillips & Diaz, 1997). Whereas the largest published series on BDD suggests that it occurs about equally in men and women (i.e., 51% men; Phillips & Diaz), others have suggested either that it occurs more frequently in men (Hollander, Cohen, & Simeon, 1997) or women (Phillips Menard, Fay, & Weisberg, 2005; Veale et al., 1996). These differences may be due to inconsistencies in inclusion/exclusion criteria, referral bias, and acuteness of symptoms.

Recent research has highlighted the high incidence of substance use disorders among individuals with BDD. Phillips Menard, Fay, and Weisberg (2005) reported rates as high as 50 percent and 43.9 percent for BDD comorbid (lifetime) substance use disorders (SUDs). Grant, Menard, Pagano, Fay and Phillips (2005) noted that 48.9 percent of BDD clients had a lifetime SUD, and 35.8 percent had a lifetime substance dependence disorder, usually for alcohol or marijuana use. Moreover, 68 percent of the individuals with a lifetime SUD reported that their BDD had contributed in some way to their SUD. Further, individuals with lifetime SUDs tended to have a higher rate of suicide attempts. Among those with and without a current SUD, there were no differences between groups on various clinical correlates, including, delusionality, social anxiety, functioning, BDD severity, depression, or rates of comorbidity with other disorders (Grant et al., 2005). Overall, BDD, particularly when severe, is associated with a strikingly poor quality of life and functioning (Phillips, Menard, Fay, & Pagano, 2005).

BDD as an Obsessive-Compulsive Spectrum Disorder

Within the DSM system, BDD is classified as a somatoform disorder. Although BDD does clearly involve the *soma* (i.e., body) and bears some resemblance to hypochondriasis (another somatoform disorder) in that persons with both conditions have a preoccupation that is generally unresponsive to reassurance, there is ample reason to question this placement within the system. It seems clear that BDD does not even meet the category's basic definition (i.e., "the presence of physical symptoms that suggest a medical condition"; APA, 2000, p. 485). Moreover, many researchers have suggested that it may be better conceptualized as an obsessive-compulsive (OC) spectrum disorder (Hadley, Newcorn, & Hollander, 2002; Neziroglu & Khemlani-Patel, 2003; Phillips & Diaz, 1997; Phillips, McElroy, Hudson, & Pope, 1995).

The connection with the OC spectrum dates back to the original work of Morselli who described the obsessions and *impulsions* of the disorder (Jerome, 2001). Indeed, the appearance-preoccupation seen among BDD patients is currently conceptualized as "obsessive" in nature, although there is some variation in the degree of insight into the disorder. If one considers insight on a continuum, BDD symptoms likely range from milder, obsessive preoccupations, to overvalued ideation, to more severe, clearly delusional thoughts in some cases. Moreover, these symptoms resemble obsessions in their persistence, recurrence, and ability to cause distress and anxiety (Phillips, Kim, & Hudson, 1995).

As with obsessive-compulsive disorder (OCD), persons with BDD appear to have "compulsions," or at least tend to engage in ritualized behaviors designed to reduce anxiety. More specifically, these behaviors are performed with the intention of examining, hiding, correcting, or looking for reassurance about one's concerns. For instance, some individuals with BDD check their appearance for prolonged periods of time—looking in mirrors, glasses, store windows, and so forth—whereas others focus their energies in avoiding all reflective surfaces. Other compulsive behaviors might include dieting, comparing oneself to others, skin picking, reading all relevant information, measuring the "flawed" body part, and seeking a cure (e.g., dental, dermatologic, cosmetic) for the perceived defect (Perugi & Frare, 2005).

Similar response to treatment is another piece of evidence that BDD is an OC spectrum disorder. Here we are mainly referring to the response to serotonin reuptake inhibitors (see below) which may suggest the presence of similar biological mechanisms. It is also now known that BDD and OCD respond to similar psychological interventions (e.g., exposure and response prevention). Of course, it is a logical fallacy to infer etiology from response to treatment. However such findings are at least consistent with the position that BDD is linked to OCD and other disorders in the spectrum.

The comorbidity of BDD with OCD further suggests that both disorders may occur on an obsessive-compulsive continuum. Estimates for OCD among individuals with BDD tend to be fairly high (e.g., 21.2% to 38.8%; Phillips Menard, Fay, & Weisberg, 2005). Both disorders tend to have a similar gender distribution, adolescent age of onset, and a chronic course (Neziroglu & Khemlani-Patel, 2003). Finally, as reviewed by Cororve and Gleaves (2001), persons with OCD and BDD respond similarly on measures of depression, anxiety, obsessionality, and personality.

Etiologic Models

The vast majority of the literature on the etiology of BDD has focused on biological or cognitive and behavioral factors. This does not exclude that possibility that other factors might play an etiologic role; rather that such factors have not been addressed or studied.

Neurobiological Factors

Abnormal serotonergic functioning has been posited as the most likely biological factor associated with BDD, although abnormalities in dopaminergic circuits have also been proposed (Hadley et al., 2002). The conclusions regarding serotonin are generally based on findings of treatment response or neurochemical challenge studies. That is, persons with BDD appear to respond, at least partially, to serotonin reuptake inhibitors and to experience increased symptomatology in response to serotonin agonists (Hollander & Wong, 1995) or following tryptophan depletion (Barr, Goodman, & Price, 1992). Studies of neuropsychological factors in BDD suggest possible underlying abnormalities of the frontal-striatal and temporoparieto-occipital systems (Perugi & Frare, 2005). Authors have also hypothesized that BDD may involve a dysfunction of the orbitofrontal or the orbitofrontal-amygdalar axis, or a dysfunction in the temporal, parietal, or occipital lobes (Snaith, 1992). However, these latter possibilities are largely speculative and based on what is known about body-image correlates of neurologic disorders.

Psychodynamic/Psychoanalytic Factors

Psychoanalytic theories suggest that BDD develops from the individual's unconscious displacement of sexual or emotional conflict, guilty feelings, or low self-image, and that the perceived bodily defect symbolizes another part of the body (Phillips, 1991). Others psychoanalysts have also suggested that BDD is a representation of core, *deeper,* personality problems (Oosthuizen & Castle, 1998). However, these views have not yet been supported by empirical evidence.

Behavioral/Learning Factors

Neziroglu, Roberts, and Yaryura-Tobias (2004) described a largely behavioral model for BDD based on Mowrer's (1960) two-factor theory of learning. According to their model, persons with a genetic predisposition to an anxiety-related disorder who may have also had previous adverse environmental experiences (such as sexual or emotional abuse) are initially reinforced for their physical appearance as children or adolescents. Classical conditioning then occurs when, usually around the time of puberty (as numerous body changes occur), an individual is teased or otherwise socially traumatized in some way related to his or her body. The shame, disgust, or other emotions associated with the events become classically associated with particular body parts. Negative reinforcement then occurs when persons engage in avoidance or other types of rituals that temporarily reduce anxiety but do not allow for unlearning of the initial emotional reaction, thereby strengthening the avoidance behavior. This model has clear implications for treatment and generally leads to the use of exposure-based interventions.

Cognitive Factors

Cognitive factors also seem to play a role in the etiology and maintenance of BDD (for a recent review, see Buhlmann & Wilhelm, 2004). Neuropsychological data suggest that such individuals tend to focus on small details and features, rather than on global figures. This finding may explain why persons with BDD tend to focus on specific details of their appearance while ignoring global features. In other cognitive research (Buhlman, McNally, Wilhelm, & Florin, 2002), persons with BDD appear to attend to selective emotional

BDD-related stimuli (both positive and negative); thus, they are concerned about both beauty and their own perceived ugliness. Studies of cognitive inhibition suggest that although persons with BDD experience distressing, intrusive thoughts about their appearance, they generally do not try to suppress them because they are perceived as valid (Wilhelm, Buhlmann, & McNally, 2003). Interpretive biases also occur, in which persons with BDD may interpret ambiguous situations as threatening (as with social anxiety disorder). Recognizing others' emotional expression is also a problem for persons with BDD in that they may misinterpret others' facial expression as negative. Interestingly, they have a tendency to rate attractive facial photographs of others as more attractive than do persons without BDD. Thus, in general, such persons may be more sensitive to beauty and aesthetics. Interestingly, several researchers have noted that persons with BDD are often educated in, or work in, art-related fields (Phillips & Menard, 2004).

Cognitive-Behavioral Models

Cognitive-behavioral models of BDD incorporate and expand on most of what was previously described. According to Veale's (2004) cognitive-behavioral model, the chain of events begins with an "external representation" of the individual's appearance—such as seeing one's reflection—which triggers a defective mental image. Through selective attention, the individual experiences heightened awareness of specific characteristics within the image, which then offer the individual information on how he or she appears to others, or, an observer perspective. This imagery is then associated with greater self-focused attention, to the extent that, in more severe cases of BDD, the individuals' entire attentional capacity is focused on the distorted image and the poor evaluation. Next, the individual engages in negative appraisal of his or her appearance, turning toward his or her existing values and assumptions about the importance of physical appearance. The individual may make assumptions such as, "If I am unattractive, then life is not worth living" (Veale, p. 117). Core beliefs regarding feelings of inadequacy, worthlessness, abnormality, and rejection are activated. The individual then engages in rumination, comparing his or her "defective" features with the ideal. A variety of emotions follow, ranging from feelings of self-disgust, anticipatory social anxiety, to depression, anger at oneself, and guilt at one's self-destructive (e.g., skin picking) tendencies. The individual then engages in various "safety behaviors," such as avoidance or active escape and camouflage, to prevent feared outcomes and reduce distress. Although these safety behaviors may temporarily alleviate distress, and are thus negatively reinforced, in the long run they increase self-consciousness, preoccupation with the imagined defect, and negative appraisal of oneself. In sum, Veale's model incorporates a unique integration of cognitive and behavioral perspectives for other disorders, such as depression and body-image disturbance, to create a comprehensive etiologic perspective on BDD that is supported by some research and has implications for treatment.

Treatment

Virtually all of the outcome literature for BDD has focused on either pharmacotherapy or some variant of behavioral or cognitive therapy. Very little is known about the combined use of pharmacologic and psychological interventions, although this approach is commonly used in clinical practice. Next, we discuss these various approaches after mentioning what may be the most common treatment strategy chosen by persons with BDD.

Cosmetic Surgery

Although not officially viewed as a treatment of BDD per se, it is established that a large percentage of persons with BDD (48% to 76% according to Crerand et al., 2004) seek out cosmetic surgery. Although the idea that correcting the perceived physical defect will eliminate the BDD problem is intuitively appealing, the available data suggest otherwise. That is, the majority of individuals with BDD who receive cosmetic surgery do not benefit from it in terms of BDD severity, and may even be more likely to become violent or litigious in response to the procedure (Crerand et al., 2004). Thus, cosmetic surgery should not be considered a treatment for BDD, and the condition may even be considered a contraindication for the procedure.

Pharmacotherapy

Various pharmacologic interventions have been tried with BDD (for a recent discussion, see Phillips, 2001). Available data most consistently suggest that serotonin reuptake inhibitors (most often clomipramine and to a lesser degree fluoxetine) are associated with a reduction in the intensity of appearance concerns and time spent being preoccupied with the perceived defect and performing compulsive rituals. These medications may also be associated with reduced distress and improved insight. Much of this research is not controlled, but there are now double-blind controlled studies of both clomiprimane (Hollander et al., 1999) and fluoxetine (Phillips, Albertini, & Rasmussen, 2002), with reported response rates of 65 percent and 53 percent, respectively. However, many people do not respond or respond only partially to psychopharmacologic interventions. For this reason, and the fact that many persons with BDD evidence delusional thinking, researchers have tried to augment serotonin reuptake inhibitors with antipsychotic medication. However, in one controlled study, results did not support the use of pimozide augmentation of fluoxetine (Phillips, 2005).

Psychological Treatment

These treatments focus on the patterns of thoughts and behaviors that maintain the disorder and are based on the corresponding models previously described. They are also somewhat derived from treatments for OCD. As with treatment for OCD, strictly behavioral (i.e., exposure with response prevention; McKay, Todaro, Neziroglu, & Campisi, 1997) and cognitive treatments (Geremia & Neziroglu, 2001) as well as those integrating the two components (Rosen, Reiter, & Orosan, 1995) have been developed and studied. Most treatments seem to also include a psychoeducational component in which patients are presented with the model on which the therapy is based and educated about the psychological nature of BDD.

Although we are not aware of any comprehensive meta-analyses of the BDD treatment literature, Cororve and Gleaves (2001) examined effect sizes across published outcome research and concluded that the effect sizes found for BDD are similar to those that have been reported in meta-analyses of bulimia nervosa (Lewandowski, Gebing, Anthony, & O'Brien, 1997), OCD (Abramowitz, 1996), and the associated features of depression and anxiety in patients with OCD (Abramowitz, 1996). Although still preliminary, this is impressive, given that BDD is often viewed as a more severe disorder than OCD (and perhaps bulimia nervosa). We are not aware of any studies that directly compared strictly cognitive with strictly behavioural programs (as has been done with other disorders).

The comprehensive cognitive-behavioral treatments generally incorporate psychoeducation, self-monitoring, exposure with response prevention, cognitive restructuring, and relapse prevention (Sarwer, Gibbons, & Crerand, 2004; Veale, 2002). The exposure component requires that the patient systematically face situations and stimuli that provoke appearance-related anxiety and preoccupation (both in therapy sessions and in their daily life) while resisting the urge to perform rituals (i.e., compulsions) and other safety behaviors. The cognitive component involves targeting patients' dysfunctional thought patterns relating to their appearance, including their faulty beliefs about self-worth and appearance. As with cognitive therapy for other disorders, behavioral experiments may be used to test beliefs. These treatments can be administered in both individual and group format. As with CBT for other problems, group format may have some advantages as it allows individuals to collect evidence from other group members and to get feedback from persons other than the therapist. The social interactions may at times be quite striking and therapeutic (Sarwer et al., 2004) and simply being observed in a group represents a form of exposure.

Case Vignette

Sarah was 27, Caucasian, and single when she presented for treatment. Her eventual decision to seek therapy was not due to her body image concerns but because of a deepening depression, social isolation, and thoughts of suicide. Furthermore, it was only at the urging of her family physician that she considered psychological treatment. Although the physician had not recognized the presence of BDD per se, he had noticed the highly irrational nature of Sarah's appearance concerns, which prompted him to recommend referral to a psychologist. A trial of fluoxetine (prescribed by him) had given only slight relief and more so for her mood than her appearance preoccupation. At intake, it became clear that her negative cognitions regarding her appearance went beyond what might be explained by depression. The psychologist used the Body Dysmorphic Disorder Exam (BDDE; Rosen and Reiter, 1996) to assess further the problem. This measure was chosen because it not only assists in the diagnostic process for BDD but also provides a detailed assessment of typical symptoms that could be targets for treatment. BDDE items assess various aspects of preoccupation with appearance including self-consciousness and embarrassment, excessive importance given to appearance in self-evaluation, avoidance of activities, body camouflaging, and body checking. In addition, several items help determine the extent of conviction that the defect truly exists or is significant.

Sarah clearly met the diagnostic criteria for BDD but also for social anxiety disorder and major depression. Although her BDD was moderately severe, her level of conviction was not delusional. Her depression was also moderately severe, but she reported that her appearance concerns existed even when she was not feeling depressed. The depression seemed to have worsened only lately in response to her social isolation and anxiety, which was largely the result of her BDD. Thus, the psychologist viewed the BDD as the core problem and the focus of treatment. However, he was concerned about her depressed and suicidal state and chose to initially use cognitive (targeting her depressive cognitions) and behavioral (increasing her activity level without requiring social confrontation) interventions for depression before challenging her to do exposure-based behavioral work for BDD. The first goal was to give her hope that her condition would improve and to pull her out of her depression. After her mood had lifted somewhat, and she started to become adept at challenging her own thinking, her BDD-related cognitions became the target of treatment. Furthermore, graduated exposure to feared stimuli was instituted based on a hierarchy of situations that she and her therapist had agreed on together. This work occurred both in the therapy setting and in Sarah's natural environment, requiring her to engage in increased social exposure and mirror confrontations, while wearing less makeup and without being able to engage in her regular grooming ritual.

After Sarah had made some improvement in individual therapy, she started also attending a group treatment for persons with social anxiety disorder. Although a group for persons with BDD may have been more ideal, one was not available at the time. Furthermore, the social anxiety group fit well because Sarah also experienced social anxiety, and many persons in the group had concerns about physical appearance. The group was particularly helpful because it (a) increased her level of social contact, (b) allowed her to test many of her cognitions related to appearance and the reactions of others, and (c) served as an opportunity for exposure. Her cognitive reactions to the events that occurred in the group were also addressed in individual therapy.

As Sarah's condition improved, she was able to return to college to pursue an undergraduate program in art history. Although on occasion she continued to struggle with social anxiety and concerns about her appearance, her depression and suicidality were greatly improved and her social avoidance and time spent grooming were in the relatively normal range. She began to date again for the first time since dropping out of college at age 19.

Troubleshooting

For the many reasons, BDD can be a challenging disorder to treat. Further, there are several unique clinical issues that may arise in working with individuals with BDD, thus exacerbating the difficulty in treatment.

The current diagnostic scheme allows persons with delusional beliefs to be diagnosed as having BDD (in addition to the delusional disorder). Although the data do not clearly indicate that such individuals respond more poorly to treatment, it is the opinion of many researchers and clinicians (e.g., Neziroglu & Khemlani-Patel, 2003) that the delusional subgroup is more difficult to treat. Cognitive and pharmacologic treatments may be necessary in such cases before implementation of exposure-based therapies. The time spent in treatment may also be longer for such cases, and therapists should have realistic goals regarding the amount of change that can occur.

BDD is generally defined as involving imagined or grossly distorted physical imperfection. The clinical picture becomes much more complicated when an individual has genuine disfigurement. In such cases, clients' fears are obviously more reality based and their perceptions of the reactions of others may be more accurate. Veale (2002) argued that there is no theoretical reason that persons with actual (mild) disfigurement would not respond to cognitive-behavior therapy for BDD; however, this possibility has not been empirically tested.

Following the development of BDD symptoms, clients often lead lives that are very socially isolated. They are frequently unmarried and unemployed, resulting in poor financial resources and poor social support.

In addition to missing the diagnosis of BDD, clinicians may have a tendency to trivialize it. However, as Phillips (2000) noted, BDD may be conceptualized as "a more depressed, socially phobic, and psychotic relative of OCD" (p. 22), and OCD is already viewed as a severe condition. Thus, clinicians should be reminded of the severity and level of debilitation associated with the disorder but need also not be overwhelmed. As described by Malatesta (1995) (in the context of complicated cases of OCD), in such cases there is a strong need for an adequate case formulation rather than relying on a simplistic "technological" approach.

Suicidality is common among BDD, again illustrating the severity and the need to avoid trivializing the disorder. For persons who are highly suicidal, this problem needs to be targeted before directly addressing the BDD. Clinicians need to be aware that exposure therapies can temporarily destabilize and are thus risky with highly suicidal clients. Patient safety should be the primary goal of treatment in such instances.

Conclusion

BDD is a relatively common, challenging, but potentially treatable OCD spectrum disorder that may be frequently overlooked. When accurately recognized and diagnosed, persons with the disorder appear to respond to cognitive-behavioral therapy and serotonin reuptake inhibitors. However, more research is clearly needed, particularly controlled outcome studies comparing various psychological treatments or comparing those treatments with pharmacologic interventions.

REFERENCES

Abramowitz, J. S. (1996). Variants of exposure and response prevention in the treatment of obsessive-compulsive disorder: A meta-analysis. *Behavior Therapy, 27,* 583–600.

American Psychiatric Association. (2000). *Diagnostic and statistical manual of mental disorders* (4th ed., text revision). Washington, DC: American Psychiatric Association.

Barr, L. C., Goodman, W. K., & Price, L. H. (1992). Acute exacerbation of body dysmorphic disorder during tryptophan depletion. *American Journal of Psychiatry, 149,* 1406–1407.

Buhlmann, U., McNally, R. J., Wilhelm, S., & Florin, I. (2002). Selective processing of emotional information in body dysmorphic disorder. *Journal of Anxiety Disorders, 16,* 289–298.

Buhlmann, U., & Wilhelm, S. (2004). Cognitive factors in body dysmorphic disorder. *Psychiatric Annals, 34,* 922–926.

Cafri, G., Thompson, J. K., Ricciardelli, L., McCabe, M., Smolak, L., & Yesalis, C. (2005). Pursuit of the muscular ideal: Physical and psychological consequences and putative risk factors. *Clinical Psychology Review, 25,* 215–239.

Cororve, M. B., & Gleaves, D. H. (2001). Body dysmorphic disorder: A review of conceptualizations, assessment, and treatment strategies. *Clinical Psychology Review, 21,* 949–970.

Crerand, C. E., Sarwer, D. B., Magee, L., Gibbons, L. M., Lowe, M. R., Bartlett, S. P., et al. (2004). Rate of body dysmorphic disorder among patients seeking facial plastic surgery. *Psychiatric Annals, 34,* 958–965.

Faravelli, C., Salvatori, S., Galassi, F., Aiazzi, L., Drei, C., & Cabras, P. (1997). Epidemiology of somatoform disorders: A community survey in Florence. *Social Psychiatry and Psychiatric Epidemiology, 32*, 24–29.

Geremia, G. M., & Neziroglu, F. (2001). Cognitive therapy in the treatment of body dysmorphic disorder. *Clinical Psychology and Psychotherapy, 8*, 243–251.

Gleaves, D. H., & Ambwani, S. (2005). Is BDD a culturally determined expression of a body image disorder? In M. Maj, H. S. Akiskal, J. E. Mezzich, and A. Okasha (Eds.), *Evidence and experience in psychiatry* (Vol. 9, pp. 231–232). Chichester: Wiley.

Gleaves, D. H., Williamson, D. A., Eberenz, K. P., Sebastian, S. B., & Barker, S. E. (1995). Clarifying body image disturbance: Testing a multidimensional model using structural modeling. *Journal of Personality Assessment, 64*, 478–493.

Gorbis, E. (2004). Crooked mirrors: The externalization of self-image in body dysmorphic disorder. *Behavior Therapist, 27*, 74–76.

Grant, J. E., Menard, W., Pagano, M. E., Fay, C., & Phillips, K. A. (2005). Substance use disorders in individuals with body dysmorphic disorder. *Journal of Clinical Psychiatry, 66*, 309–316.

Hadley, S. J., Newcorn, J. H., & Hollander, E. (2002). The neurobiology and psychopharmacology of body dysmorphic disorder. In D. J. Castle & K. A. Phillips (Eds.), *Disorders of body image* (pp. 139–155). Petersfield, England: Wrightson Biomedical Publishing.

Hollander, E., Allen, A., Kwon, J., Aronowitz, B., Schmeidler, J., Wong, C., et al. (1999). Clomipramine vs. desipramine crossover trial in body dysmorphic disorder: Selective efficacy of a serotonin reuptake inhibitor in imagined ugliness. *Archives of General Psychiatry, 56*, 1033–1039.

Hollander, E., Cohen, L. J., & Simeon, D. (1993). Body dysmorphic disorder. *Psychiatry Annals, 23*, 359–364.

Hollander, E., & Wong, C. (1995). Introduction: Obsessive-compulsive spectrum disorders. *Journal of Clinical Psychiatry, 56*(Suppl. 4), 3–6.

Jerome, L. (2001). Dysmporphophobia and taphephobia: Two hitherto undescribed forms of insanity with fixed ideas. *History of Psychiatry, 12*, 103–114.

Lewandowski, L. M., Gebing, T. A., Anthony, J. L., & O'Brien, W. H. (1997). Meta-analysis of cognitive-behavioral treatment studies for bulimia. *Clinical Psychology Review, 17*, 703–718.

Malatesta, V. J. (1995). "Technological" behavior therapy for obsessive compulsive disorder: The need for adequate case formulation. *Behavior Therapist, 18*, 88–89.

McKay, D., Todaro, J., Neziroglu, F., & Campisi, T. (1997). Body dysmorphic disorder: A preliminary evaluation of treatment and maintenance using exposure with response prevention. *Behaviour Research and Therapy, 35*, 67–70.

Mowrer, O. H. (1960). *Learning theory and behavior.* New York: John Wiley.

Neziroglu, F., & Khemlani-Patel, S. (2003). Therapeutic approaches to body dysmorphic disorder. *Brief Treatment and Crisis Interventions, 3*, 307–322.

Neziroglu, F., Roberts, M., & Yaryura-Tobias, J. A. (2004). A behavioral model for body dysmorphic disorder. *Psychiatric Annals, 34*, 915–920.

Olivardia, R. (2001). Mirror, mirror, on the wall, who's the largest of them all? The features and phenomenology of muscle dysmorphia. *Harvard Review of Psychiatry, 9*, 254–259.

Oosthuizen, P. P., & Castle, D. (1998). Body dysmorphic disorder—a distinct entity? *South African Medical Journal, 88,* 766–769.

Otto, M. W., Wilhelm, S., Cohen, L. S., & Harlow, B. (2001). Prevalence of body dysmorphic disorder in a community sample of women. *American Journal of Psychiatry, 158,* 2061–2063.

Perugi, G., & Frare, F. (2005). Body dysmorphic disorder. In M. Maj, H. S. Akiskal, J. E. Mezzich, and A. Okasha (Eds.), *Evidence and experience in psychiatry* (Vol. 9, pp. 191–221). Chichester: Wiley.

Phillips, K. A. (1991). Body dysmorphic disorder: The distress of imagined ugliness. *American Journal of Psychiatry, 148,* 1138–1149.

Phillips, K. A. (2000). Body dysmorphic disorder: Diagnostic controversies and treatment challenges. *Bulletin of the Menninger Clinic, 64,* 18–35.

Phillips, K. A. (2001). Body dysmorphic disorder. In K. A. Phillips (Ed.), *Review of Psychiatry Series: Somatoform and factitious disorders* (pp. 67–94). Washington, DC: American Psychiatric Publishing.

Phillips, K.A. (2005). Placebo-controlled study of pimozide augmentation of fluoxetine in body dysmorphic disorder. *American Journal of Psychiatry, 162,* 377–379.

Phillips, K. A., Albertini, R. S., & Rasmussen, S. A. (2002). A randomized placebo-controlled trial of fluoxetine in body dysmorphic disorder. *Archives of General Psychiatry, 59,* 381–388.

Phillips, K. A., & Diaz, S. F. (1997). Gender differences in body dysmorphic disorder. *Journal of Nervous and Mental Diseases, 185,* 570–577.

Phillips, K. A., Dufresne R. G., Jr., Wilkel, C. S., & Vittorio, C. C. (2000). Rate of body dysmorphic disorder in dermatology patients. *Journal of the American Academy of Dermatology, 42,* 436–441.

Phillips, K. A., Kim, J. M., & Hudson, J. I. (1995). Body image disturbance in body dysmorphic disorder and eating disorders. *The Psychiatric Clinics of North America, 18,* 317–334.

Phillips, K. A., McElroy, S. L., Hudson, J. I., & Pope, H. G., Jr. (1995). Body dysmorphic disorder: An obsessive-compulsive spectrum disorder, a form of affective spectrum disorder, or both? *Journal of Clinical Psychiatry, 56,* 41–51.

Phillips, K. A., & Menard, W. (2004). Body dysmorphic disorder and art background. *American Journal of Psychiatry, 161,* 927–928.

Phillips, K. A., Menard, W., Fay, C., & Pagano, M. E. (2005). Psychosocial functioning and quality of life in body dysmorphic disorder. *Comprehensive Psychiatry, 46,* 254–260.

Phillips, K. A., Menard, W., Fay, C., & Weisberg, R. (2005). Demographic characteristics, phenomenology, morbidity, and family history in 200 individuals with body dysmorphic disorder. *Psychosomatics, 46,* 317–325.

Rosen, J. C., & Reiter, J. (1996). Development of the body dysmorphic disorder Examination. *Behaviour Research and Therapy, 34,* 755–766.

Rosen, J. C., Reiter, J., & Orosan, P. (1995). Cognitive-behavioural body image therapy for body dysmorphic disorder. *Journal of Consulting and Clinical Psychology, 63,* 263–269.

Sarwer, D. B., Gibbons, L. M., & Crerand, C. E. (2004). Treating body dysmorphic disorder with cognitive-behavioral therapy. *Psychiatric Annals, 34,* 934–941.

Snaith, P. (1992). Body image disorders. *Psychotherapy and Psychosomatics, 58,* 119–124.
Veale, D. (2000). Outcome of cosmetic surgery and DIY surgery in patients with body dysmorphic disorder. *Psychiatric Bulletin, 24,* 218–220.
Veale, D. (2002). Cognitive behaviour therapy for body dysmorphic disorder. In D. J. Castle, & K. A. Phillips (Eds.), *Disorders of body image* (pp. 121–138). Petersfield, England: Wrightson Biomedical Publishing.
Veale, D. (2004). Advances in a cognitive behavioral model of body dysmorphic disorder. *Body Image, 1,* 113–125.
Veale, D., Boocock, A., Gournay, K., Dryden, W., Shah, F., Willson, R., et al. (1996). Body dysmorphic disorder: A survey of fifty cases. *British Journal of Psychiatry, 169,* 196–201.
Wilhelm, S., Buhlmann, U., & McNally, R. J. (2003). Negative priming for threatening versus nonthreatening information in body dysmorphic disorder. Acta Neuropsychiatrica, 1, 180–183.

CHAPTER TWENTY

Hypochondriasis

Steven Taylor, Ph.D., and Gordon J. G. Asmundson, Ph.D.

Alexander P., a 32-year-old architect, was referred by his primary care physician for psychological assessment and treatment because of Alexander's persistent fear that recent headaches, associated episodes of dizziness, and general clumsiness meant that he was going to have a stroke. A comprehensive medical evaluation, including a neurologic investigation, revealed no evidence of a general medical condition that might account for his problems.

We will meet Alexander several times throughout this chapter as we discuss the diagnosis, assessment, and treatment of hypochondriasis. Further details on his assessment and treatment are discussed in our clinician's guide to treating hypochondriasis (Taylor & Asmundson, 2004).

Hypochondriasis is characterized by preoccupation with fears and beliefs about having a serious disease, based on misinterpretations of bodily sensations (American Psychiatric Association [APA], 2000). To receive a diagnosis of hypochondriasis, the preoccupations must persist for at least six months, despite appropriate medical evaluation and reassurance. People with hypochondriasis have either excessive fear that they currently have a serious disease or excessive fear that they are at high risk for contracting one in the future. The fear that one *currently* has a serious disease is the more common of these fears in hypochondriasis.

Undue fear of having a disease is associated with (a) excessive seeking of reassurance from primary care physicians and from family members that one's health is good, (b) frequent checking of one's body (e.g., frequent testicular self-examinations for cancerous lumps), (c) repetitively checking other sources of information on the dreaded disease (e.g., checking medical textbooks or the Internet), and (d) persistently exploring various kinds of remedies such as herbal preparations (Taylor & Asmundson, 2004). Fear of contracting a disease is typically associated with phobic avoidance. The activities associated with these hypochondriacal fears are known as *safety behaviors*, which the person performs in an effort to protect their health.

> *Alexander developed a number of safety behaviors that he thought would reduce his risk of stroke. He abstained from many formerly enjoyable activities, including hiking, biking, and playing with his children, for fear that physical exertion might strain his blood vessels. He also spent increasing amounts of time surfing the Internet for information about stroke and other medical conditions that might account for his symptoms. He purchased a portable blood pressure monitor that he carried with him, in order to check whether he was having a "hypertensive crisis" that would warrant immediate medical attention. Alexander also repeatedly visited a local pharmacy to check his blood pressure on a "more accurate" device.*

People with hypochondriasis typically object to the idea that they have a mental disorder. They tend to misinterpret the seriousness of harmless, naturally occurring bodily fluctuations, such as those that might arise during times of stress or other changes in daily routine and to overestimate the seriousness of symptoms of general medical conditions.

> *Alexander was told on many occasions by various doctors that his troubling bodily sensations were "not physical" and that he had nothing to worry about. Alexander was not satisfied with the explanations because they didn't tell him what was causing his problems. He worried that the doctors weren't taking him seriously, and that they thought his problems were "all in his head." Alexander firmly believed that his symptoms were real, not imaginary.*

Persistent complaining about personal health and well-being is another common characteristic of people with hypochondriasis. They make a point of trying to discuss their concerns at length with anyone who will listen. This can lead to strained relationships with their family, friends, and physicians. Frustration and anger on the part of physician and patient are not uncommon (APA, 2000). "Doctor shopping"—visiting many different physicians in the hope of finding help—is often the result. Seeing many different physicians puts some people with hypochondriasis at risk for unnecessary and repeated medical or surgical interventions, some of which can produce troubling side effects or treatment complications (e.g., scarring, pain). Thus, hypochondriasis can be worsened by iatrogenic (physician-induced) factors.

Estimates of the lifetime prevalence of hypochondriasis in the general population range from 1 to 5 percent (APA, 2000). The disorder can arise at any age, although it most commonly develops in early adulthood (APA, 2000). It typically arises, or is exacerbated, when the person is under stress, seriously ill or recovering from a serious illness, or has suffered the loss of a family member (Barsky & Klerman, 1983). Most studies have found that hypochondriasis is equally common in women and men (Asmundson, Taylor, & Cox, 2001). The course of hypochondriasis is often chronic, persisting for years in most cases (Robbins & Kirmayer, 1996).

Preliminary behavioral-genetic (twin) research and retrospective studies of patient's early (e.g., childhood) experiences suggests that hypochondriasis is not strongly heritable and that learning experiences probably play an important role in the development of the disorder (Taylor & Asmundson, 2004). Learning experiences such as the following appear to be important in leading the person to misinterpret benign bodily sensations and to view themselves as sickly:

- *Parental modeling* experiences where the child observes that their parents are excused from home responsibilities or receive special attention when they are ill.
- *Parental overprotection*, in which parents treat the child as frail and vulnerable, thereby leading the child to believe that he or she is at risk for succumbing to illness.
- *Parental reinforcement* of illness behaviors, which occurs when a child often receives toys, food treats, attention, sympathy, or special care or is excused from school or home chores when ill.

Cultural factors, such as societally transmitted values and expectations, can also influence how a person interprets bodily changes and sensations and whether treatment seeking is initiated. There appear to be cross-cultural differences in which bodily changes and sensations tend to be feared the most (Escobar et al., 2001). People in the United States and Canada, for example, appear to be particularly highly concerned about immunologically based symptoms, such as those related to viruses, "sick building syndrome," and "multiple chemical sensitivity" (Escobar et al., 2001).

Is Hypochondriasis an Obsessive-Compulsive Spectrum Disorder?

Classification systems serve several functions, one of which is to organize phenomena and thereby facilitate research into underlying mechanisms. The DSM-IV-TR classification system defines and diagnoses hypochondriasis on purely descriptive features. Hypochondriasis is classified as a somatoform disorder because of the prominence of bodily complaints. Yet, hypochondriasis shares many symptom similarities with other disorders, including mood disorders, and particularly panic disorder, generalized anxiety disorder, and obsessive-compulsive disorder (OCD; Taylor & Asmundson, 2004). Some theorists therefore consider hypochondriasis to be a mood disorder (Lesse, 1980), while others suggest that it may be an obsessive-compulsive spectrum disorder (Hollander, 1993). This suggests that classification on the basis of descriptive features is of limited value in understanding whether hypochondriasis should be grouped with somatoform disorders or with other disorders.

One can look to biology for an alternative classificatory system. The most widely used system for classifying organisms is based on cladistics (Kitching, Forey, Humphries, & Williams, 1998), which emphasizes the process of evolution. The merits of this approach for classifying psychopathology in general, and hypochondriasis in particular, remain to be investigated. One aspect of the cladistic approach that can be used is the emphasis on theory; that is, the theory of evolution. Cladistics is the dominant school of biological classification, which suggests that classification of psychopathology might benefit from a similar approach in which hypochondriasis and other disorders are classified according to similar methods (theory and etiology) rather than simply in terms of descriptive features (Taylor & Asmundson, 2005).

A classificatory model of hypochondriasis (and related disorders) based on a diathesis-stress formulation is consistent with the theory-driven emphasis of cladistics. According to a diathesis-stress approach to classification, disorders would be grouped on the basis of the similarity of their diatheses. Two classes of diathesis are widely recognized in understanding psychopathology; genetic factors and environmental factors. The latter include learning experiences that may give rise to dysfunctional beliefs that several theorists have implicated in hypochondriasis (Taylor & Asmundson, 2004). Ideally, disorders would be grouped together on the basis of the similarities of their diatheses; for example, the similarity of their molecular genetic profile and the similarity of disorder-promoting environmental events (e.g., learning experiences). Unfortunately, this information is currently lacking, and so it is currently unclear whether hypochondriasis should be regarded as falling within the obsessive-compulsive spectrum or some other spectrum.

Assessment

General Considerations

A medical evaluation is needed to rule out general medical conditions that might account for the patient's presenting concerns. By the time hypochondriasis is diagnosed, the patient typically has had numerous medical evaluations, with the results failing to find a general medical condition that could account for their concerns. Sometimes a general medical condition may be diagnosed. In these cases, a diagnosis of hypochondriasis is made if the diagnosed medical condition does not fully account for the person's concerns about disease or for their bodily changes or sensations (APA, 2000).

Patients with hypochondriasis often request extensive medical evaluations. Some doctors try to placate the patient by providing these medically unnecessary assessments. Such tests are not helpful and may perpetuate hypochondriasis because repeated testing can have iatrogenic effects and can reinforce the patient's mistaken belief that she or he has a serious disease (e.g., "I must have something seriously wrong with me because the doctor has agreed to conduct more tests.").

A thorough psychological assessment of hypochondriasis can be completed following general medical evaluation and should include an assessment of current DSM-IV-TR Axes I and II diagnoses (to assess for comorbid disorders), an evaluation of the patient's personal history, current living circumstances, specific features of hypochondriasis, and his or her reasons for seeking treatment for hypochondriasis. Some patients present for treatment because they have been pressured to do so by their doctor or family members. It is important to identify and address such issues because they can interfere with treatment adherence.

The patient's personal history should be assessed to identify the learning experiences that may have contributed to the development of hypochondriasis. Research suggests that environmental factors such as learning experiences with illness may play an important role in hypochondriasis (Taylor & Asmundson, 2004).

> *Alexander had been worried about having a stroke for several years. These concerns began after his father, now 65, had a stroke (10 years earlier). His father blamed his doctor for not giving him proper treatment. At the time, his father went to his doctor complaining of headache, lightheadedness, and feeling unsteady. His doctor said the symptoms would probably pass and that the father should go home to rest. However, the symptoms became progressively worse, to the point that his father collapsed and was rushed to the hospital. Fortunately, the father was successfully treated and was left with only minor residual problems. This near-tragic experience led Alexander to worry about the competence of medical practitioners in looking after his own health. His worry worsened three years ago when a 33-year-old neighbor died suddenly and unexpectedly from a ruptured cerebral aneurysm. Alexander worried that he too might one day have a brain hemorrhage. As a result, he made repeated visits to hospital emergency departments. All evaluations found no evidence of medical abnormalities that might account for his concerns.*

The patient's living circumstances should also be assessed to identify stressors, which may contribute to tension or anxiety-related bodily sensations that may be misinterpreted as indications of disease and to assess the patient's relationship with her or his significant others (e.g., do family and friends provide excessive reassurance or take on many of the patient's responsibilities?).

> *Alexander had major problems at work. He worked in a large architectural firm that was in dire financial straights. There were rumors that staff would be laid off, and so Alexander felt pressured to excel at his work, to convince the senior partners that he was indispensable. He worked long hours and made sure that each of his projects were completed on schedule. To keep up his performance, he consumed a lot of coVee throughout the long days at the offce.*

Structured Interviews and Self-Report Measures

The Structured Clinical Interview for DSM-IV (SCID-IV; First, Spitzer, Gibbon, Williams, & Lorna, 1994) provides a comprehensive assessment of the more common disorders, along with an assessment of hypochondriasis. The Health Anxiety Interview (Taylor & Asmundson, 2004), a supplement to the SCID-IV, can be used to gather more detailed information in complicated cases. There are numerous self-report measures of hypochondriasis, the most widely used of which appear in an appendix in Taylor and Asmundson (2004). The questionnaires differ in several ways, including breadth of assessment, time required for administration and scoring, availability of norms, and the amount of research on their reliability and validity. The choice of scale depends partly on the purpose of the assessment. If the clinician requires a quick assessment of health anxiety, then the Whiteley Index (Pilowsky, 1967) is a particularly good choice because, unlike other brief measures, norms and screening cutoff scores are available. The Whiteley Index is short enough for periodic readministration throughout treatment to monitor progress. If a more detailed assessment of the various facets of health anxiety are desired, then the Illness Attitude Scales (Kellner, 1987) is a good choice, particularly because it is easy to score, there are a good deal of data on its reliability and validity, and norms are available.

Treatment

A meta-analysis examined 25 treatment trials of clinically severe or subclinical hypochondriasis (Taylor et al., 2005). Although there were not a large number of studies for inclusion, the meta-analytic findings provided some suggestive results, which were consistent with the results of individual studies that compared two or more interventions, and with the results of narrative reviews (Asmundson et al., 2001); and with research appearing after the meta-analysis had been completed (Barsky & Ahern, 2004).

The medications included in the meta-analysis were various types of selective serotonin reuptake inhibitors (SSRIs; e.g., paroxetine, fluvoxamine, fluoxetine) and the most commonly examined psychosocial interventions were cognitive-behavioral interventions, which included psychoeducation about the causes and treatment of health anxiety, exposure and response prevention, cognitive therapy, cognitive-behavior therapy, and behavioral stress management. Behavioral stress management involved teaching patients that their unwelcome bodily "symptoms" (sensations) are largely due to stress and then showing the patients ways of reducing harmless but unpleasant stress-related bodily sensations (e.g., using time-management techniques or relaxation training).

The meta-analyses suggested that effect sizes were larger for all psychosocial interventions and SSRI interventions than for waitlists. Combining cognitive and behavioral interventions may be more effective than either intervention alone, with treatment gains maintained, on average, at the six-month follow-up. The most promising medication was fluoxetine. These results are illustrated in Table 20.1.

Little is currently known about the long-term efficacy of medications for treating hypochondriasis, or about the relapse rates once the medications are discontinued. No information is currently available about the efficacy of combining cognitive-behavioral interventions with psychotropic medications.

The meta-analysis further indicated that for mild (subclinical) hypochondriasis, psychoeducation alone is an effective intervention, compared with no-treatment controls (see Table 20.1). Psychoeducation involves the provision of information about the roles of dysfunctional beliefs and maladaptive behaviors, such as checking and reassurance seeking, in the maintenance of hypochondriasis. Patients receiving psychoeducation are given information about methods that they can use to challenge dysfunctional beliefs and eliminate maladaptive behaviors (for an example of a self-help book, see Asmundson & Taylor, 2005).

Cognitive-behavioral interventions typically begin with psychoeducation. The "noisy body" analogy is a useful psychoeducational tool for introducing patients to a cognitive-behavioral approach. Here, troubling sensations are relabeled as harmless "bodily noise" rather than indications of physical dysfunction. A short period of prospective monitoring of "symptoms" is valuable in psychoeducation.

After completing his initial assessment, Alexander completed a diary for the purpose of monitoring uncomfortable bodily sensations for two weeks and then returned for his first treatment session. He found the diary to be useful because it helped him realize the extent to which health anxiety was a problem for him; "The diary helped me realize that I freak out every time I have a headache, thinking 'This time for sure it's a stroke.' I'm starting to think that I might be worrying way too much about my health."

Cognitive restructuring of dysfunctional beliefs (e.g., "healthy people do not experience bodily sensations") and exposure exercises (e.g., taking an aerobics class to prove to oneself that you will not collapse and die) are also highly effective interventions (Taylor, 2004; Taylor & Asmundson, 2004).

Table 20.1. Treatment Studies of Hypochondriasis: Summary of Meta-analytic Findings

Treatment Condition (n of trials)	Mean % Size Dropout	Mean Pre-post Effect (duration = 12 weeks)	Mean Pre-follow-up (follow-up duration = 6 months)
Studies of patients with hypochondriasis			
Control conditions			
Waitlist control (n = 3)	0	0.29	—
Pill placebo (n = 1)	25	—	—
Psychosocial treatments			
Psychoeducation (n = 1)	22	1.05	1.27
Cognitive therapy (n = 1)	11	0.83	0.96
Exposure and response prevention (n = 2)	14	1.00	1.19
Cognitive-behavior therapy (n = 4)	10	2.05	1.74
Behavioral stress management (n = 1)	4	1.59	1.25
Drug treatments			
Paroxetine (n = 1)	18	1.34	—
Fluoxetine (n = 2)	15	1.92	—
Fluvoxamine	21	—	—
Nefazodone (n = 1)	18	1.07	—
Studies of mixed samples, full and abridged hypochondriasis			
Waitlist control (n = 1)	0	0.19	0.18
Optimized medical care (n = 1)	0	0.20	0.30
Psychoeducation (n = 2)	2	0.74	0.87
Cognitive-behavior therapy (n = 1)	13	0.51	0.61

Source: Adapted from Taylor et al. (2005).

Note: Larger effect sizes indicate greater reductions in hypochondriacal symptoms. A dash indicates that data are unavailable. Optimized medical care consisted of routine medical care administered by primary care physician who received extra training to identify psychiatric disorders.

Cognitive-behavioral interventions for Alexander included the following: (a) Formal tracking of his pattern of headaches and other symptoms to see if they were associated with stress. (b) Reducing his caffeine consumption on some days, and increasing it on others, to test the idea that some of his troubling bodily sensations are caffeine related. (c) Conducting "behavioral experiments" to determine whether the "clumsiness" symptom is more likely to occur on days when he focused versus distracted himself from bodily sensations. (d) Gradually increasing his level of physical activity to challenge his belief that he is at risk for a stroke. (e) Reducing his frequency of reassurance-seeking in some weeks, and increasing it in others, to test the idea that excessive reassurance-seeking perpetuates his health preoccupation. (f) Enlisting the support of his wife and primary care physician (e.g., in refraining from offering unnecessary medical reassurance).

Once Alexander's hypochondriacal concerns were reduced, he was also provided with stress management skills (e.g., relaxation training, time management, conflict negotiation skills). These provided him with further evidence that his troubling bodily concerns were due to stress and helped him better cope with his job demands.

There is little evidence that specific characteristics of hypochondriasis indicate that specific treatments should be used. Patients with a strong preference for one type of treatment (e.g., cognitive-behavior therapy) may have a worse prognosis if offered some other type of treatment (e.g., medications) because the odds of dropping out may be higher if they receive a nonpreferred treatment. Otherwise, the bulk of useful prognostic factors appear to predict outcome for a range of treatments, including medications and psychosocial interventions. Good prognostic signs, as identified by various sources, are hypochondriasis that is mild, short-lived, and not associated with complicating factors such as personality disorders, comorbid general medical conditions, or contingencies ("secondary gains") that reinforce health anxiety or sick-role behavior (Taylor & Asmundson, 2004).

Conclusion

Research has shown that effective methods for treating hypochondriasis are available. For mild or short-lived forms of this disorder, psychoeducation may be sufficient, delivered either by the primary care physician or in the form of educational courses. If that proves ineffective, or if the patient has full-blown hypochondriasis, then more intensive interventions could be considered. Among the most promising psychosocial interventions is cognitive-behavior therapy. For patients preferring medications, evidence suggests that fluoxetine is promising. However, it is unclear whether the gains from medications are maintained in the long term, when the drugs are discontinued. The gains from psychosocial treatments tend to be maintained at the six-month follow-up visit or longer.

Despite the availability of effective treatments, it remains to be determined whether the majority of people with hypochondriasis are willing to accept such interventions. People with hypochondriasis typically resist the idea that they have a psychological disorder. What proportion of hypochondriasis patients are willing to accept treatment for health anxiety? If most are *unwilling* to accept such treatment, then the results from the treatment studies of hypochondriasis would apply to only a small proportion of patients. Thus, the question remains as to whether the encouraging results from treatment studies can be generalized to the majority of people with hypochondriasis. This is one of the most important issues for further investigation in the treatment of this chronic, disabling disorder.

REFERENCES

American Psychiatric Association. (2000). *Diagnostic and statistical manual of mental disorders* (4th ed., text revision). Washington, DC: Author.

Asmundson, G. J. G., & Taylor, S. (2005). *It's not all in your head: How worrying about your health could be making you sick—and what you can do about it.* New York: Guilford Press.

Asmundson, G. J. G., Taylor, S., & Cox, B. J. (2001). *Health anxiety: Clinical and research perspectives on hypochondriasis and related disorders.* New York: Wiley.

Barsky, A. J., & Ahern, D. K. (2004). Cognitive behavior therapy for hypochondriasis: A randomized controlled trial. *Journal of the American Medical Association, 291*, 1464–1470.

Barsky, A. J., & Klerman, G. L. (1983). Overview: Hypochondriasis, bodily complaints, and somatic styles. *American Journal of Psychiatry, 140*, 273–283.

Escobar, J. I., Allen, L. A., Hoyos Nervi, C., & Gara, M. A. (2001). General and cross-cultural considerations in a medical setting for patients presenting with medically unexplained symptoms. In G. J. G. Asmundson, S. Taylor, & B. J. Cox (Eds.), *Health anxiety: Clinical and research perspectives on hypochondriasis and related conditions* (pp. 220–245). New York: Wiley.

First, M. B., Spitzer, R. L., Gibbon, M., Williams, J. B. W., & Lorna, B. (1994). *Structured Clinical Interview for DSM-IV Axis II Personality Disorders (SCID-II).* Version 2.0. New York: Biometrics Research Department, New York State Psychiatric Institute.

Hollander, E. (1993). *Obsessive-compulsive related disorders.* Washington, DC: American Psychiatric Press.

Kellner, R. (1987). *Abridged manual of the Illness Attitudes Scale.* Unpublished manual. Department of Psychiatry, School of Medicine, University of New Mexico, Albuquerque.

Kitching, I. J., Forey, P. L., Humphries, C. J., & Williams, D. M. (1998). *Cladistics: The theory and practice of parsimony analysis.* 2nd ed. Oxford: Oxford University Press.

Lesse, S. (1980). Masked depression—the ubiquitous but unappreciated syndrome. *Psychiatric Journal of the University of Ottawa, 5,* 268–273.

Pilowsky, I. (1967). Dimensions of hypochondriasis. *British Journal of Psychiatry, 113,* 89–93.

Robbins, J. M., & Kirmayer, L. J. (1996). Transient and persistent hypochondriacal worry in primary care. *Psychological Medicine, 26,* 575–589.

Taylor, S. (2004). Understanding and treating health anxiety: A cognitive-behavioural approach. *Cognitive and Behavioral Practice, 11,* 112–123.

Taylor, S., & Asmundson, G. J. G. (2004). *Treating health anxiety: A cognitive-behavioral approach.* New York: Guilford.

Taylor, S., & Asmundson, G. J. G. (2005). Hypochondriasis: Future directions in classification and etiology research. In M. Maj (Ed.), *Evidence and experience in psychiatry: Somatoform disorders.* Vol. 9. New York: Wiley.

Taylor, S., Asmundson, G. J. G., & Coons, M. J. (2005). Current directions in the treatment of hypochondriasis. *Journal of Cognitive Psychotherapy.*

CHAPTER TWENTY ONE

Obsessive-Compulsive Personality Disorder

Jane L. Eisen, M.D., Maria C. Mancebo, Ph.D., Kimberley L. Chiappone, M.D., Anthony Pinto, Ph.D., and Steven A. Rasmussen, M.D.

Clinical Presentation

Description of Obsessive-Compulsive Personality Disorder

Obsessive-compulsive personality disorder (OCPD) is a chronic maladaptive pattern of excessive perfectionism and need for control over one's environment that affects all domains of an individual's life. Individuals with this disorder are characterized by rigidity, preoccupation with detail, order, rules and schedules, and being overly controlling. They might find it difficult to relax, feel obligated to plan out their activities to the minute, and find unstructured time intolerable. They are often inflexible when it comes to morality, ethics, societal rules, and their own personal beliefs. As it is currently conceptualized by the *Diagnostic and Statistical Manual of Mental Disorders* (4th ed.; DSM-IV), OCPD is defined by the presence of at least four of the following eight criteria: (1) preoccupation with details, (2) perfectionism, (3) excessive devotion to work, (4) hypermorality, (5) inability to discard worn or useless items, (6) inability to delegate tasks, (7) miserliness, and (8) rigidity (American Psychiatric Association, 1994). The most common age of onset is considered to be in early adulthood, but most individuals with this difficulty describe having at least some of these characteristics since childhood.

More than 100 years ago, Pierre Janet, who wrote a classic description of the symptoms of obsessive compulsive disorder (OCD), described aspects of the current conceptualization of OCPD, using the term "psychasthenic state" (Janet, 1904). This phase of illness, which Janet believed preceded the onset of actual obsessions and compulsions, was characterized by feelings of inadequacy, and the inability to achieve a feeling of satisfaction or perfection: "Psychasthenics are continually tormented by an inner sense of imperfection" (Janet, 1904). In addition to describing the need for perfection, Janet also reported the presence of indecisiveness and emotional aloofness. Of Janet's original traits, only perfectionism remains as a diagnostic criterion for OCPD in DSM-IV (American Psychiatric Association, 1994).

OCPD was first included in DSM-II (American Psychiatric Association, 1968), largely based on Freud's concept of the obsessive personality or analerotic character style characterized by orderliness, parsimony, and obstinacy (Freud, 1908/1963). The diagnostic criteria for OCPD have undergone substantial changes with each DSM revision (see Table 21.1). For example, DSM-IV (American Psychiatric Association, 1994) dropped two criteria present in DSM-III-R (American Psychiatric Association, 1987): (a) restricted expression of affect and (b) indecisiveness, largely based on reviews of the empirical literature that found these traits lacked internal consistency (Pfohl, 1996). Despite changes in the criteria for OCPD over time, it continues to be essentially based on the impairment in functioning due to excessive and chronic perfectionism, work devotion, and rigidity.

Prevalence

DSM-IV estimates OCPD prevalence rates to be about 1 percent in community samples and 3–10 percent in clinical settings (American Psychiatric Association, 1994). Using data from the Epidemiologic Catchment Area (ECA) survey, it was estimated that 1.7 percent of individuals met DSM-III criteria for OCPD (Nestadt et al., 1991). Another study (Torgersen, Kringlen, & Cramer, 2001), using DSM-III-R criteria, found a prevalence rate of 2.0 percent in a large community sample ($N = 2,053$) and noted consistency with a median prevalence rate of 2.1 percent for the disorder based on a pooled sample of 3,786 individuals in 10 previous community studies of personality disorders. The only community study based on DSM-IV criteria found a much higher

Table 21.1. Changes over Time in DSM Criteria for Obsessive-Compulsive Personality Disorder

Criteria	DSM-III	DSM-III-R	DSM-IV
Preoccupation with details	+	+	
Perfectionism	+	+	+
Excessive devotion to work	+	+	+
Overconscientiousness regarding ethics (hypermorality)	+	+	
Inability to discard worthless objects	+	+	
Inability to delegate tasks[a]	+		
Lack of generosity (miserliness)	+	+	
Rigidity	+	+	+
Indecisiveness	+	+	
Restricted expression of affection	+	+	
Number of criteria for diagnosis	4 of 5 (80%)	5 of 9 (56%)	4 of 8 (50%)

Note: DSM, *Diagnostic and Statistical Manual of Mental Disorders*; III, third edition; III-R, third edition, revised; IV, fourth edition.
[a]New criterion added in DSM-IV.

rate of 7.8 percent (Grant et al., 2004). This unusually elevated rate may be related to the particular instrument used to collect personality disorder data in this study, the NIAAA Alcohol Use Disorder and Associated Disabilities Interview Schedule-DSM-IV Version (AUDADIS-IV). The study also reported (Grant et al., 2004) higher prevalence rates for several other personality disorders, including avoidant and paranoid personality disorder, compared with rates described in DSM-IV. In contrast, rates of histrionic and antisocial personality disorders were similar to those described in DSM-IV. The cause of the markedly elevated rate of OCPD in this large ($N = 43,093$) U.S. community sample is not clear, and further research to assess community prevalence of personality disorders is warranted. Based on the literature to date, a conservative estimate of OCPD prevalence in the community is 1–2 percent.

Ethnic minorities in the United States seem to be underrepresented in clinical settings, but epidemiologic studies of the general population have found similar prevalence rates of OCPD cross-culturally (Karno, Golding, Sorenson, & Burnam, 1988). The Collaborative Longitudinal Study of Personality Disorders (CLPS) found that ethnic minorities recruited from multiple clinical settings were evenly distributed among the four personality disorders studied, including OCPD, and that they were not over- or underrepresented in any particular disorder (Chavira et al., 2003). However, a more recent study looking at prevalence rates of personality disorders in the general U.S. population found that OCPD was significantly less common in Asians and Hispanics relative to Caucasians and African Americans (Grant et al. 2004).

Studies of OCPD have reported mixed results regarding gender distribution. Although there were no gender differences in one community sample (Grant et al., 2004), another large community study found OCPD to be twice as common in men than women (Torgersen, Kringlen, & Cramer, 2001). Findings regarding gender distribution in clinical samples have been inconsistent as well. Some clinical samples to date report a higher frequency in men (Albert, Maina, Forner, & Bogetto, 2004), while others do not (Chavira et. al. 2003; Mancebo, Eisen, & Rasmussen, 2004).

Although there is controversy about whether personality disorders should be diagnosed in childhood, several researchers have examined the prevalence of OCPD traits in children. One study using a structured interview found that 13.5 percent of children ages 9–19 ($N = 733$) met criteria for OCPD, making it the most frequent disorder in this large community sample of children (Bernstein et al., 1993). This study found that OCPD, like the other personality disorders studied, was associated with a greater risk of Axis I psychopathology, depressive symptoms, and social impairment. However, unlike other personality disorders, children with OCPD were not at risk for academic impairment. Another study, using the Personality Disorder Examination (PDE) to assess personality disorders in an adolescent community sample ($N = 299$), did not find any adolescents who met DSM-III-R criteria for OCPD. Of note, this study found very low rates of the other personality disorders as well (Lewinsohn, Rohde, Seeley, & Klein, 1997).

Course

Clinical wisdom suggests that persons with OCPD have a chronic and stable pattern of rigidity, orderliness, and being overly controlling that persists throughout adulthood. However, there has been little systematic study to date regarding the course of this disorder. The studies that have addressed this have assessed the stability of the diagnosis of OCPD over time and the stability of each criterion over time. In one follow-up study of adolescents with personality disorders, only a third of the adolescents initially diagnosed with OCPD met criteria for OCPD at a follow-up interview two years later (Bernstein et al., 1993). Odds ratios indicated that children were four times as likely to receive an OCPD diagnosis at the two-year follow-up if they had been initially diagnosed with moderate levels of OCPD and 15 times more likely to continue to have an OCPD diagnosis if they initially had severe symptoms (27% persisted). In a longitudinal study of personality disorders, only half the participants with OCPD at baseline continued to have it after two years (Grilo et al., 2004). In this study, three of the eight DSM-IV OCPD criteria, "preoccupied with details," "rigid and stubborn," and "reluctant to delegate" were the strongest predictors of a continued OCPD diagnosis after two years.

Differential Diagnosis

Despite the similarities between some of the symptoms of OCPD and the obsessions and compulsions found in OCD, such as list making and hoarding, there are distinct qualitative differences between these disorders. In OCD, obsessions are intrusive and distressing. They are sometimes referred to as *egodystonic* because they seem so foreign and abhorrent to the individual experiencing them. In contrast, the symptoms of OCPD are considered *ego-syntonic* as individuals with the disorder view their behaviors and attitudes as appropriate and correct. In the example of excessive list making, a patient with OCD feels driven to write down all her daily activities and present the list to her husband each night to ensure that none of her activities could lead to possible contamination even though she knows this is excessive and unrealistic. In contrast, a person with OCPD will justify making overly detailed lists of daily activities as a reasonable use of time, as this behavior prevents overlooking necessary tasks. Another instance of overlapping symptoms between the two disorders is hoarding. Typically, in OCD, useless objects are saved because the individual is afraid that they may discard something important by accident. The individual may realize that his or her home is excessively cluttered but the worry about inadvertently discarding an important document dominates the concern or embarrassment about living in disarray. Individuals with OCPD may have enormous collections of obsolete materials such as documents or bills, but they believe that their system is logical and necessary.

OCPD and OCD also differ in terms of what leads patients to seek treatment. Typically, individuals with OCPD seek treatment because of the family turmoil resulting from the need to have others conform to their way of doing household tasks. While the person believes that he or she is doing these tasks "correctly," the insistence that others follow suit frequently leads to family or marital discord, which may result in the patient seeking treatment. In contrast, individuals with OCD who are preoccupied with orderliness, exactness, and symmetry experience considerable distress about the time-consuming and interfering nature of these obsessions/compulsions and seek treatment to better manage their symptoms. Although useful, these guidelines are not absolute, and sometimes, clinical presentations defy simple categorization. Some patients, for example, spend hours each day engaged in ego-syntonic behaviors, such as repetitive and excessive cleaning, and may seek treatment not because they are disturbed by their behaviors, but because of problems in functioning or family friction caused by these behaviors. It may be helpful with such patients to determine whether they have other obsessions and compulsions in addition to their excessive cleaning that would support a diagnosis of OCD.

Clinical Vignettes

Mrs. A came in for treatment at the request of her family because she was "driving them crazy" and they were concerned about her. Mrs. A described a history of excessive house cleaning, organizing, and arranging throughout her entire adult life. She had a system for cleaning her house, which involved particular activities each day of the week. These cleaning activities required at least four hours daily. She refused to leave the house until these tasks were completed. In her view, while she understood that others considered her a "neat freak," she thought this was the proper way to clean, and it was disgusting to live any other way. She also described herself as worrying excessively about the health and well being of her adult children. She required them to check in with her multiple times daily regardless of their activities, including if they were on vacation in distant places. Mrs. A was willing to take a serotonin reuptake inhibitor to determine whether it would help decrease her distress about her children's health and safety. She was not interested in changing her cleaning behaviors, although she admitted to being exhausted because of them. She refused to participate in cognitive-behavioral treatment.

Mrs. B. came for an initial outpatient evaluation with a psychiatrist, mostly prompted by the urgings of her husband. She was a 30-year-old schoolteacher without previous treatment. She reported friction between herself and her husband over her exactness and rigidity. She described having an extensive book collection that she dusted daily and would not let anyone else, including her husband, touch. She insisted that her husband get into bed at night before her so that she could make sure that nothing in the house had been moved after she went to bed. If they were late for an engagement, she was unable to modify her routine of getting ready. Both at work and at home, she refused to allow others to do any tasks that might be helpful to her, as she felt that only she could perform these tasks correctly. When leaving the house, she insisted on driving or walking a predetermined route despite any obstacles, such as traffic, that presented themselves along the way. She was critical and outspoken about "shortcuts" that she thought other teachers took in their work. These patterns of behavior and attitudes caused major marital conflict and conflict with other teachers. She was unwilling to pursue any kind of therapy, including cognitive behavioral therapy or marital therapy. She agreed initially to a trial of a serotonin reuptake inhibitor but stopped taking the medication after several weeks and was unwilling to return to treatment. Although she was aware that her "style" was causing problems in her life, she essentially considered others too sloppy and thought her behavior was reasonable, for the most part.

Is OCPD an OCD Spectrum Disorder?

Domains of inquiry relevant to this question include the degree to which OCD and OCPD overlap both in terms of clinical characteristics and comorbidity and whether there is a relationship between the two disorders in terms of family history and longitudinal course. To date, both descriptive and systematic research has explored the differences and similarities between OCD and OCPD in these areas. Other important domains such as underlying etiologic similarities have not been adequately addressed to date. There is also a striking paucity of data regarding OCPD treatment so that similarities in treatment response between the two disorders cannot be assessed at present.

Overlap between Clinical Presentation of OCD and OCPD

In clinical practice, differentiating between OCD and OCPD may be difficult because of some similarities in phenomenology. For example, excessive list making can be viewed as a compulsion if it is repetitive, time consuming, and distressing; it is included in the Yale-Brown Obsessive Compulsive Scale (YBOCS) checklist, an instrument widely used to identify obsessions and compulsions (Goodman et al., 1989). Excessive list making can also be viewed as a preoccupation with details and is included in the DSM-IV description of OCPD. Similarly, perfectionism is an OCPD criterion and a symptom of OCD if it involves the need for order, symmetry, and arranging. Hoarding is also considered both a compulsion (found in OCD) and a criterion for OCPD in DSM-IV. In fact, the DSM-IV states that if hoarding is extreme in a patient with OCPD, an additional diagnosis of OCD should be given. As these examples demonstrate, although OCPD and OCD are conceptualized as two separate disorders, there is overlap in their symptom presentations.

The Relationship of OCPD Criteria to OCD

There has been interest in examining whether specific OCPD criteria are particularly associated with OCD. In one study, the majority of 114 OCD patients were found to have perfectionism and indecisiveness (82% and 70%, respectively). In contrast, other OCPD traits such as restricted affect, excessive devotion to work, and rigidity were seen infrequently (Eisen & Rasmussen, 1991). In a more recent study of personality disorders, three of the eight OCPD criteria (hoarding, perfectionism, and preoccupation with details) were significantly more frequent in patients with comorbid OCD ($n = 89$) than in those without OCD ($n = 540$) (Eisen et al., 2006). The relationship between OCD and these three criteria remained significant after controlling for the presence of other anxiety disorders and major depressive disorder, showing unique associations with odds ratios ranging from 2.71 to 2.99. This finding suggests that only certain OCPD criteria are associated with OCD.

The Relationship of OCD Symptom Factors to OCPD

Another approach to studying the relationship between OCPD and OCD is to examine whether OCPD has a unique relationship with any of the symptom factors of OCD. Factor-analytical methods have reliably identified a subtype of OCD characterized by symmetry and ordering (Baer, 1994; Denys, de Geus, van Megen, & Westenberg, 2004; Leckman et al., 1997; Summerfeldt, Richter, Antony, & Swinson, 1999), and there are data to suggest that OCPD is associated with the symmetry factor. Baer (1994) derived a grouping of OCPD symptoms that accounted for the majority of variance in OCPD symptoms. This primary OCPD factor was composed of preoccupation with details, perfectionism, and hoarding. Baer's primary OCPD symptom factor was most strongly correlated with the OCD symptom factor characterized by symmetry and hoarding and was not significantly correlated with checking compulsions.

Comorbidity with OCD

Comorbidity between OCPD and OCD has been reported in numerous studies, most of which have assessed the frequency of OCPD in clinical samples of OCD (Mancebo, Eisen, Grant, & Rasmussen, 2005). Studies using DSM-III and DSM-III-R criteria for OCPD have shown marked variability in prevalence rates of the disorder in subjects with OCD. These earlier studies found OCPD comorbidity rates of 0–31 percent, with slightly higher rates found using the more lenient DSM-III-R definition of OCPD (Baer et al., 1990; Black, Noyes, Pfohl, Goldstein, & Blum, 1993; Black, Yates, Noyes, Pfohl, & Kelley, 1989; Eisen & Rasmussen, 1991; Joffe, Swinson, & Regan, 1988). More recently, studies using the DSM-IV criteria have consistently found prevalence rates of OCPD, ranging from 23 percent to 32 percent (Albert et al., 2004; Mancebo et al., 2004; Samuels et al., 2000a). Although it does not appear that OCPD is the most common personality disorder in patients with OCD, based on the literature to date, these studies do suggest that individuals with OCD who have a personality disorder are most likely to have one from Cluster C (i.e., OCPD, avoidant, dependent).

To test the specificity of the diagnosis of OCPD in individuals with OCD, some studies have looked at groups of patients with other anxiety disorders, as well as healthy controls. OCPD rates are consistently higher in individuals with OCD than in healthy community controls using DSM-III-R criteria (Albert, Maina, Forner, & Bogetto, 2004) as well as DSM-IV criteria (Samuels et al., 2000b). However, rates of OCPD in individuals with other anxiety disorders have been found to be similar to those with OCD in some studies (Albert et al., 2004), though significantly less in others (Crino & Andrews, 1996; Diaferia et al., 1997). The Collaborative Longitudinal Personality Disorders Study (CLPS; Gunderson et al., 2000) investigated the link between the two disorders in a large sample of individuals with personality disorders. In that study, McGlashan and colleagues (2000) reported that 20.9 percent of their patients with DSM-IV OCPD also met criteria for OCD; this was not higher than the rates of OCD in the other personality disorders evaluated in the study.

In summary, although results have been varied, particularly with earlier versions of DSM, studies using DSM-IV criteria have found that a fourth to a third of patients with OCD also meet criteria for OCPD. However, the majority of individuals with OCD do *not* have OCPD, which does not support theories of OCPD as a developmental precondition for OCD. However, individuals with OCD and other anxiety disorders are much more likely to have OCPD than individuals who do not have psychiatric disorders. Results from personality disorder samples show that individuals with OCPD are not more likely to develop OCD than other Axis I disorders. Future research focusing on prospective studies of individuals with OCPD personality criteria could help shed light on whether and on which of these criteria represent psychological vulnerabilities to anxiety disorders.

Family History

The question of a genetic link between OCD and OCPD has yet to be answered conclusively although there are indications that there may be a familial relationship between these disorders. An older study reported that 11 percent of the parents of 46 children and adolescents with OCD had OCPD, based on DSM-III criteria, although this diagnosis was made without the use of a structured instrument (Lenane et al., 1990). In a study assessing OCPD traits in the family members of twins with OCD, 17 percent of parents and 13 percent of siblings were found to have "obsessional features" (Carey, 1981). Again, a structured instrument to assess OCPD traits was not used. In a more recent study using the Revised Structured Instrument for the Diagnosis of Personality Disorders (SIDP-R), Samuels and colleagues (2000b) found a significantly greater frequency of OCPD in first degree relatives of OCD probands compared with relatives of control probands (11.6% vs. 5.8%, $p = .02$). A familial relationship between OCPD and OCD was not supported in a study, which assessed the frequency of OCD in first degree family members of probands with both OCD and OCPD. In that study, the presence of comorbid OCPD in the probands did not increase the likelihood of having OCD in the family members. More genetics research needs to be conducted to address more clearly the genetic/familial link between these two disorders.

The Course of OCD with Comorbid OCPD

The relationship between OCPD and OCD has also been investigated by examining the longitudinal course of these disorders. Rasmussen and Eisen (1998) retrospectively assessed childhood traits in 90 adults with OCD. Results showed that a substantial proportion of the OCD patients endorsed having perfectionism, hypermorality, ambivalence, and excessive devotion to work before the onset of their OCD. This constellation of traits, similar to those described by Janet, may be the precursor of adult-onset OCD. Two studies have evaluated individuals treated for OCD in childhood and used the Structured Clinical Interview for DSM-IV Axis II Personality Disorders (SCID-II) to assess the presence of OCPD in adulthood. The first study assessed children who had been hospitalized for OCD and those who had been hospitalized for other psychiatric problems (Thomsen & Mikkelsen, 1993). Both groups had similar rates of personality disorders in general (68% vs. 61%) as well as OCPD in particular (17% vs. 10%, $p > .05$). OCPD was more common in those subjects whose OCD persisted into adulthood compared with the patients who no longer had OCD at follow-up. The second study (Swedo et al., 1989) had a different finding. Those whose OCD symptoms had remitted were just as likely to have OCPD as those with persistent OCD. Clearly, the longitudinal association between OCD and OCPD is an understudied area, which would shed light on the relationship between these two disorders.

In summary, several lines of evidence suggest a link between OCPD and OCD. Numerous studies have now documented the frequency of comorbid OCPD in patients with OCD compared with community samples. There is also data regarding the familial link between these two disorders. Further light on this question will be shed by systematic investigation of treatment response and course of OCPD.

Theoretical Models

Early psychoanalysts were the first to give significant attention to factors that contribute to the development of OCPD (Abraham, 1921/1953; Freud, 1908/1963). Conflicts stemming from issues of control at the anal stage due to inappropriate toilet training were considered to be developmentally related to the onset of OCPD (Kline, 1968). Both OCD and OCPD were viewed as stemming from defense mechanisms warding off feelings of unconscious guilt, shame, and insecurity (Gunderson & Gabbard, 2000). Defense mechanisms, such as regression, reaction formation, isolation, and undoing, were thought to be instrumental in both disorders. Later, family environments characterized by anger and hostility as well as inconsistent parenting were linked to OCPD (Angyal, 1965; Sullivan, 1956). Salzman (1973), who wrote extensively on OCPD, thought that individuals with this disorder were preoccupied with control over themselves and their environment as a reaction to an inner sense of helplessness. In one early study, obsessional children's parents were noted to be overly controlling and conforming, with low empathy and negative responses to spontaneous affect (Adams, 1973). Although these models remain intriguing, they have little empirical support.

An alternative to psychoanalytic theory is a dimensional view of normal personality traits. According to this model, individuals with personality disorders represent extremes in a range of normal personality traits. The five-factor model (FFM) is one of the most widely used dimensional classification systems and encompasses five basic personality traits: neuroticism, extraversion, openness to experience, agreeableness, and conscientiousness (Costa & McCrae, 1992). Under this model, people who carry the diagnosis of OCPD would likely be classified as having excessive conscientiousness, characterized by dutifulness, order, competence, self-discipline, and deliberation (Costa & McCrae, 1992; Lynam & Widiger, 2001; Zanarini, Ruser, Frankenberg, Hennen, & Gunderson, 2000). One study, which supports this conceptual view of OCPD, demonstrated that OCPD was associated with high scores on all domains or facets of conscientiousness (Lynam & Widiger, 2001).

Little has been written on OCPD from a behavioral perspective. Millon (1981; Millon & Everly, 1985) postulated that OCPD is related to having overly controlling parents with negative consequences to the child who demonstrates any degree of independence. This interaction was thought to lead to the development of the need to conform to strict standards. A number of cognitive theorists have written about OCPD. Shapiro (1981) described people with OCPD as being overly focused, rigid in their thinking (considering what they *should* do as opposed to what they *would like* to do), and lacking certainty about their preferences and decisions. Guidano and Liotti (1983) hypothesized that both OCD and OCPD are fueled by beliefs about perfectionism and the notion that there is one correct response to any given situation. These beliefs, in turn, fuel symptoms/traits of indecisiveness, procrastination, and excessive doubt. Beck and Freeman (1990), in their book on cognitive therapy for personality disorders, described automatic thoughts based on assumptions, such as a narrow range of acceptable feelings and actions, and the critical importance of both not making a mistake and completely controlling one's environment. They postulated additional cognitive distortions with a predominant pattern of seeing things "in strictly black-and-white terms." This way of thinking leads to rigidity, procrastination, and perfectionism. To date, no studies have been conducted that support the use of cognitive therapy for OCPD.

There is some evidence to suggest a familial/genetic relationship between

OCPD and OCD (Lenane et al., 1990). Genetic models have investigated a link between OCPD and OCD and comorbid disorders such as Tourette disorder (Pauls et al., 1986).

Treatment

There is a striking paucity of data on the efficacy of psychological and pharmacologic treatments for OCPD. Cognitive and cognitive-behavioral approaches for this disorder have been described (Bailey, 1998; Beck, 1997; Beck & Freeman, 1990). Therapy can involve challenging cognitive distortions such as "all-or-nothing" thinking and overestimating the importance of making mistakes (catastrophizing). Because individuals with OCPD tend to show rigid thinking patterns and downplay the importance of emotional connections, establishing rapport can be difficult. Using a systematic and problem-based approach to identify and then address underlying core schema such as the need to be perfect may be particularly helpful. To date, there is no outcome data on the effectiveness of these approaches. Psychodynamic treatment has also been described as useful for OCPD (Gabbard, 2005; Gabbard & Newman, 2005). In one small study, supportive-expressive psychodynamic therapy was found to be effective for 14 patients who were treated for one year (Barber et al., 1997). There is no empirical evidence for pharmacologic interventions for OCPD (Koenigsberg, Woo-Ming, & Siever, 2002), although selective serotonin reuptake inhibitors are often used to treat Axis I symptoms that may be present (Stein et al., 1996).

The impact of OCPD on treatment response for OCD is not clear. Some studies have found a negative impact on response to pharmacologic treatment (Cavedini, Erzegovesi, Ronchi, & Bellodi, 1997), but others have not found significant differences (Baer et al., 1992).

The ego-syntonic nature of symptoms and a lack of occupational impairment often contribute to a lack of motivation to seek treatment in individuals with OCPD. However, many will pursue treatment for disorders and problems that are secondary to, or are comorbid with, OCPD, including anxiety disorders, health problems (e.g., cardiovascular disorders), and relational problems (martial, familial, occupational). Treatment may be complicated by a patient's inability to appreciate the contribution of his or her personality to these problems (Stone, 1993).

Conclusion

OCPD is characterized by profound rigidity, stubbornness, and perfectionism. Many theories regarding the etiology of OCPD range from a psychoanalytic model involving regression to the anal-erotic stage of development to cognitive and behavioral models. Most recently, investigators have postulated that OCPD may represent a genetic vulnerability to the development of OCD. Individuals with OCPD generally feel comfortable with their behaviors, which so trouble those around them. Because of this, treatment is often not sought; and when it is, it is generally because of the interpersonal or occupational problems that invariably arise. There are no empirically based treatments for this disorder although the literature describes the utility of both cognitive and psychoanalytically based approaches. Clearly, more systematic research is needed to investigate further the treatment options for OCPD.

Despite longstanding interest in the psychiatric community, the relationship between OCD and OCPD currently remains unclear. Patients with OCD have higher rates of OCPD than the general population. Patients who have comorbid OCD and OCPD tend to have specific OCPD criteria in common. Whether OCD with comorbid OCPD is a specific subtype of OCD characterized by certain OCD symptoms such as symmetry has yet to be investigated. The constructs of ego-syntonicity versus ego-dystonicity have been used to help differentiate OCPD and OCD. However, in clinical practice, differentiating the two can be difficult.

REFERENCES

Abraham, K. (1921/1953). Contributions to the theory of the anal character. In D. Bryan & A. T. Strachey (Eds.), *Selected papers of Karl Abraham*. London: Hogarth Press.

Adams, P. (1973). *Obsessive children: A sociopsychiatric study*. New York: Brunner/Mazel.

Albert, U., Maina, G., Forner, F., & Bogetto, F. (2004). DSM-IV obsessive-compulsive personality disorder: Prevalence in patients with anxiety disorders and in healthy comparison subjects. *Comprehensive Psychiatry, 45*(5), 325–332.

American Psychiatric Association. (1968). *Diagnostic and statistical manual of mental disorders* (2nd ed.). Washington, DC: Author.

American Psychiatric Association. (1987). *Diagnostic and statistical manual of mental disorders.* (3rd ed., revised). Washington, DC: Author.

American Psychiatric Association. (1994). *Diagnostic and statistical manual of mental disorders* (4th ed.). Washington, DC: American Psychiatric Association.

Angyal, A. (1965). *Neurosis and treatment: a holistic theory.* New York: Viking Press.

Baer, L. (1994). Factor analysis of symptom subtypes of obsessive compulsive disorder and their relation to personality and tic disorders. *Journal of Clinical Psychiatry, 55* (Suppl.), 18–23.

Baer, L., Jenike, M. A., Black, D. W., Treece, C., Rosenfeld, R., & Greist, J. (1992). Effect of Axis II diagnoses on treatment outcome with clomipramine in 55 patients with obsessive compulsive disorder. *Archives of General Psychiatry, 49,* 862–866.

Baer, L., Jenike, M. A., Ricciardi, J. N., Holland, A. D., Seymour, R. S., Minichiello, W. E., & et al. (1990). Standardized assessment of personality disorders in obsessive-compulsive disorder. *Archives of General Psychiatry, 47,* 826–830.

Bailey, G. R., Jr. (1998). Cognitive-behavioral treatment of obsessive-compulsive personality disorder. *Journal of Psychological Practice, 4*(1), 51–59.

Barber, J. P., Morse, J. Q., Krakauer, I., Chittams, J., & Crits-Christoph, K. (1997). Change in obsessive-compulsive and avoidant personality disorders following time-limited supportive-expressive therapy. *Psychotherapy, 34,* 133–143.

Beck, A. T., & Freeman, A. (1990). *Cognitive therapy of personality disorders.* New York: Guilford Press.

Beck, J. S. (1997). Cognitive approaches to personality disorders. In J. H. W. M. E. Thase (Ed.), *Cognitive therapy review of psychotherapy.* Washington, DC: American Psychiatric Press.

Bernstein, D. P., Cohen, P., Velez, C. N., Schwab-Stone, M., Siever, L. J., & Shinsato, L. (1993). Prevalence and stability of the DSM-III-R personality disorders in a community-based survey of adolescents. *American Journal of Psychiatry, 150*(8), 1237–1243.

Black, D. W., Noyes, R., Jr., Pfohl, B., Goldstein, R. B., & Blum, N. (1993). Personality disorder in obsessive-compulsive volunteers, well comparison subjects, and their first-degree relatives. *American Journal of Psychiatry, 150*(8), 1226–1232.

Black, D. W., Yates, W. R., Noyes, R., Pfohl, B., & Kelley, M. (1989). DSM-III personality disorder in obsessive-compulsive study volunteers: a controlled study. *Journal of Personality Disorders, 3*(1), 58–62.

Carey, G. G., II. (1981). Twin and family studies of anxiety, phobic, and obsessive disorders. In D. F. K. J. Rabkin (Ed.), *New research and changing concepts* (pp. 117–136). New York: Raven Press.

Cavedini, P., Erzegovesi, S., Ronchi, P., & Bellodi, L. (1997). Predictive value of obsessive-compulsive personality disorder in antiobsessional pharmacological treatment. *Eur Neuropsychopharmacol, 7*(1), 45–49.

Chavira, D. A., Grilo, C. M., Shea, M. T., Yen, S., Gunderson, J. G., Morey, L. C., et al. (2003). Ethnicity and four personality disorders. *Comprehensive Psychiatry, 44*(6), 483–491.

Costa, P. T., Jr., & McCrae, R. R. (1992). The five-factor model of personality and its relevance to personality disorders. *Journal of Personality Disorders, 6,* 343–359.

Crino, R. D., & Andrews, G. (1996). Personality disorder in obsessive compulsive disorder: A controlled study. *Journal of Psychiatric Research, 30*(1), 29–38.

Denys, D., de Geus, F., van Megen, H. J., & Westenberg, H. G. (2004). Symptom dimensions in obsessive-compulsive disorder: Factor analysis on a clinician-rated scale and a self-report measure. *Psychopathology, 37*(4), 181–189.

Diaferia, G., Bianchi, I., Bianchi, M. L., Cavedini, P., Erzegovesi, S., & Bellodi, L. (1997). Relationship between obsessive-compulsive personality disorder and obsessive-compulsive disorder. *Comprehensive Psychiatry, 38*(1), 38–42.

Eisen, J. L., Coles, M. E., Shea, M. T., Pagano, M. E., Stout, R. L., Yen, S., et al. (in press). Clarifying the convergence between obsessive compulsive personality disorder criteria and obsessive compulsive disorder. *Journal of Personality Disorders, 20*, 394–405.

Eisen, J. L., & Rasmussen, S. A. (1991). *OCD and compulsive traits: Phenomenology and outcome.* Paper presented at the American Psychiatric Association 144th annual meeting, New Orleans, LA.

Freud, S. (1908/1963). Character and anal eroticism. In P. Reiff (Ed.), *Collected papers of Sigmund Freud* (Vol. 10). New York: Collier.

Gabbard, G. O. (2005). *Psychodynamic psychotherapy in clinical practice.* (4th ed.). Washington DC: American Psychiatric Publishing.

Gabbard, G. O., & Newman, C. F. (2005). Psychotherapy of obsessive compulsive personality disorder. In J. B. G.O. Gabbard & J. A. Holmes (Ed.), *Oxford textbook of psychotherapy.* Oxford: Oxford University Press.

Goodman, W. K., Price, L. H., Rasmussen, S. A., Mazure, C., Fleischman, R. L., Hill, C. L., et al. (1989). The Yale-Brown obsessive-compulsive scale: I. Development, use and reliability. *Archives of General Psychiatry, 46,* 1006–1011.

Grant, B. F., Hasin, D. S., Stinson, F. S., Dawson, D. A., Chou, S. P., Ruan, W. J., et al. (2004). Prevalence, correlates, and disability of personality disorders in the United States: Results from the national epidemiologic survey on alcohol and related conditions. *Journal of Clinical Psychiatry, 65*(7), 948–958.

Grilo, C. M., Skodol, A. E., Gunderson, J. G., Sanislow, C. A., Stout, R. L., Shea, M. T., et al. (2004). Longitudinal diagnostic efficiency of DSM-IV criteria for obsessive-compulsive personality disorder: A 2-year prospective study. *Acta Psychiatrica Scandinavica, 110,* 64–68.

Guidano, V. F., & Liotti, G. (1983). *Cognitive processes and emotional disorders.* New York: Guilford Press.

Gunderson, J. G., & Gabbard, G. O. (eds.) (2000). *Psychotherapy for personality disorders.* Philadelphia: Brunner/Mazel.

Gunderson, J. G., Shea, M. T., Skodol, A. E., McGlashan, T. H., Morey, L. C., Stout, R. L., et al. (2000). The Collaborative Longitudinal Personality Disorders Study: Development, aims, design, and sample characteristics. *Journal of Personality Disorders, 14*(4), 300–315.

Janet, P. (1904). *Les obsessions et al psychasthenie* (2nd ed.). Paris: Bailliere.

Joffe, R. T., Swinson, R. P., & Regan, J. J. (1988). Personality features of obsessive-compulsive disorder. *American Journal of Psychiatry, 145*(9), 1127–1129.

Karno, M., Golding, I., Sorenson, S., & Burnam, M. (1988). The epidemiology of obsessive-compulsive disorder in five US communities. *Archives of General Psychiatry, 45,* 1094–1099.

Kline, P. (1968). Obsessional traits, obsessional symptoms, and anal eroticism. *British Journal of Medical Psychology, 41,* 299–305.

Koenigsberg, H. W., Woo-Ming, A. M., & Siever, L. J. (2002). Pharmacological treatments for personality disorders. In P. E. Nathan & J. M. Gorman (Eds.), *A guide to treatments that work* (2nd ed., pp. 625–641). New York: Oxford University Press.

Leckman, J., Grice, D. E., Boardman, J., Zhang, H., Vitale, A., Bondi, C., et al. (1997). Symptoms of obsessive-compulsive disorder. *American Journal of Psychiatry, 154*, 911–917.

Lenane, M., Swedo, S. E., Leonard, H. L., Pauls, D. L., Sceery, W., & Rapoport, J. L. (1990). Psychiatric disorders in first degree relatives of children and adolescents with obsessive-compulsive disorder. *Journal of the American Academy of Child and Adolescent Psychiatry, 29*, 407–412.

Lewinsohn, P. M., Rohde, P., Seeley, J. R., & Klein, D. N. (1997). Axis II psychopathology as a function of Axis I disorders in childhood and adolescence. *Journal of the American Academy of Child and Adolescent Psychiatry, 36*(12), 1752–1759.

Lynam, D. R., & Widiger, T. A. (2001). Using the five-factor model to represent the DSM-IV personality disorders: An expert consensus approach. *Journal of Abnormal Psychology, 110*(3), 401–412.

Mancebo, M. C., Eisen, J. L., Grant, J. E., & Rasmussen, S. A. (2005). Obsessive compulsive personality disorder and obsessive compulsive disorder: Clinical characteristics, diagnostic difficulties, and treatment. *Annals of Clinical Psychiatry, 17*(4), 197–204.

Mancebo, M. C., Eisen, J. L., & Rasmussen, S. A. (2004). *Axis I comorbidity in Obsessive Compulsive Disorder: Preliminary results from a naturalistic follow-up study of OCD.* Paper presented at the Association for Advancement of Behavior Therapy (AABT), New Orleans, LA.

McGlashan, T. H., Grilo, C. M., Skodol, A. E., Gunderson, J. G., Shea, M. T., Morey, L. C., et al. (2000). The Collaborative Longitudinal Personality Disorders Study: Baseline Axis I/II and II/II diagnostic co-occurrence. *Acta Psychiatrica Scandinavica, 102*(4), 256–264.

Millon, T. (1981). *Disorders of personality: DSM-III, Axis II*. New York: Wiley.

Millon, T., & Everly, G. (1985). *Personality and its disorders*. New York: Wiley.

Nestadt, G., Romanoski, A. J., Brown, C. H., Chahal, R., Merchant, A., Folstein, M. F., et al. (1991). DSM-III compulsive personality disorder: An epidemiological survey. *Psychological Medicine, 21*(2), 461–471.

Pauls, D. L., Towbin, K. E., Leckman, J. F., Zahner, G. E., & Cohen, D. J. (1986). Gilles de la Tourette's syndrome and obsessive-compulsive disorder: Evidence supporting a genetic relationship. *Archives of General Psychiatry, 43*(12), 1180–1182.

Pfohl, B. (1996). Obsessive-compulsive personality disorder. In T. A. Widiger, H. A. Pincus, R. Ross, M. First, & W. Wakefield (Eds.), *DSM-IV Sourcebook* (Vol. 2, pp. 777–789). Washington, DC: American Psychiatric Association.

Rasmussen, S., & Eisen, J. (1998). The epidemiology and clinical features of obsessive compulsive disorder. In M. A. Jenike, L. Baer, & W. E. Minichiello (Eds.), *Obsessive Compulsive Disorders: Pratical Management* (3rd ed.). Boston: Mosby.

Salzman, L. (1973). *The obsessive personality*. New York: Jason Aronson.

Samuels, J., Nestadt, G., Bienvenu, O. J., Costa, P. T., Jr., Riddle, M. A., Liang, K. Y., et al. (2000a). Personality disorders and normal personality dimensions in obsessive-compulsive disorder. *British Journal of Psychiatry, 177*, 457–462.

Samuels, J., Nestadt, G., Bienvenu, O. J., Costa, P. T., Jr., Riddle, M. A., Liang, K. Y., et al. (2000b). Personality disorders and normal personality dimensions in obsessive-compulsive disorder. *British Journal of Psychiatry, 177,* 457–462.

Shapiro, D. (1981). *Autonomy and rigid character.* New York: Basic Books.

Stein, D. J., Trestman, R. L., Mitropoulou, V., Coccaro, E. F., Hollander, E., & Siever, L. J. (1996). Impulsivity and serotonergic function in compulsive personality disorder. *Journal of Neuropsychiatry and Clinical Neuroscience, 8*(4), 393–398.

Stone, M. H. (1993). Long-term outcome in personality disorders. *British Journal of Psychiatry, 162,* 299–313.

Sullivan, H. S. (1956). *Clinical studies in psychiatry.* New York: Norton.

Summerfeldt, L. J., Richter, M. A., Antony, M. M., & Swinson, R. P. (1999). Symptom structure in obsessive-compulsive disorder: A confirmatory factor-analytic study. *Behaviour Research and Therapy, 37*(4), 297–311.

Swedo, S. E., Rapoport, J. L., Leonard, H. L., Lenane, M. C., & Cheslow, D. (1989). Obsessive compulsive disorder in children and adolescents: Clinical and phenomenology of 70 consecutive cases. *Archives of General Psychiatry, 46,* 335–341.

Thomsen, P. H., & Mikkelsen, H. U. (1993). Development of personality disorders in children and adolescents with obsessive-compulsive disorder: A 6-to 22-year follow-up study. *Acta Psychiatrica Scandinavica, 87*(6), 456–462.

Torgersen, S., Kringlen, E., & Cramer, V. (2001). The prevalence of personality disorders in a community sample. *Archives of General Psychiatry, 58*(6), 590–596.

Zanarini, M. C., Ruser, T. F., Frankenburg, F. R., Hennen, J., & Gunderson, J. G. (2000). Risk factors associated with the dissociative experiences of borderline patients. *Journal of Nervous and Mental Disease, 188*(1), 26–30.

Index

Page references followed by *f* and *t* refer to figures and tables, respectively.

abbreviation therapy, 56–57
ABGAs. *See* antibasal ganglia antibodies
acceptance and commitment therapy (ACT), 214, 216–17
acral lick dermatitis, 209
ACT. *See* acceptance and commitment therapy
aggressive OCDs: classification of, 10–11; comorbidities, 127, 142–44, 143*t*, 160; treatment, 66–67, 69. *See also* unacceptable obsessional thoughts
amoxicillin, for PANDAS, 99, 103
AN. *See* anorexia nervosa
ANAs. *See* antineuronal antibodies
animal reminder disgust, 20
anorexia nervosa (AN): behavioral and cognitive features, 189; case vignettes, 190–91; ego-syntonicity of, 189, 193; models and etiology, 195; as OCD, 192; treatment, 196–98, 199. *See also* eating disorders
antibasal ganglia antibodies (ABGAs), and PANDAS, 100–103
antibiotics, for PANDAS, 103–4, 105
antidepressants, 196, 229–30
antineuronal antibodies (ANAs), and PANDAS, 100–103
antipsychotics, 117, 120, 131, 209, 296
antistreptococcal antibodies, PANDAS and, 99, 105
antistreptolysin O (ASO), PANDAS and, 99, 105
anxiety disorders, comorbidities, 201, 262, 274, 328
Anxiety Disorders Association of America, 152
arginine vasopressin, in PDDs, 244

ASO (antistreptolysin), PANDAS and, 99, 105
Asperger disorder: behavioral and cognitive features, 238–39, 240; case vignette, 240–41, 250; treatment, 247, 249–50. *See also* pervasive developmental disorders
Association for Behavioral and Cognitive Therapies, 152
attention deficit hyperactivity disorder (ADHD), comorbidities, 274
atypical antipsychotics: for OCD with poor insight, 117, 120, 122; for OCD with schizotypy/schizophrenia, 131; for PANDAS, 100; for PDDs, 248–49, 250; for tic disorders, 278; for trichotillomania, 215
audio-tape habituation, 69
autism: behavioral and cognitive features, 238–40; models and etiology, 241–43; treatment, 245–50. *See also* pervasive developmental disorders
autoimmune neuropsychiatric disorders. *See* PANDAS
autoimmunity, and PDDs, 245
aversion therapy, 232
avoidance: in body dysmorphic disorder, 294–95; in checking compulsions, 34, 37–40; in contamination obsessions, 19, 21–22, 24, 26–27; in health obsessions, 114; in hypochondriasis, 305; in ordering and arranging compulsions, 45–46, 50; in postpartum OCD, 140*t*, 141, 143, 143*t*, 144, 145; in scrupulosity, 159, 167, 170; in unacceptable obsessional thoughts, 62–63, 64
awareness training, 212–13, 279

basal ganglia, PANDAS and, 100–103, 106
BDD. *See* body dysmorphic disorder
binge-eating disorder (BED), 188
biological stressors, and OCD, 2. *See also* PANDAS; postpartum OCD
bipolar disorders, comorbidities, 259
BN. *See* bulimia nervosa
body dysmorphic disorder (BDD): behavioral and cognitive features, 288–90, 291; case vignettes, 288, 297–98; classification of, 291; comorbidities, 290, 297–98; definition of, 289; models and etiology, 292–95; neurobiological correlates, 292–93; and poor insight, 113, 114; prevalence, 290; as spectrum disorder, xi, 179, 291–92; treatment, 291–92, 295–98; underrecognition of, 289–90, 299
bulimia nervosa (BN), 188, 189, 192, 198–99, 199. *See also* eating disorders
buying compulsions. *See* shopping compulsions

castration, pharmacological, 265
CBT. *See* cognitive-behavior therapy
cephalexin (Keflex), 99–100
cephalosporin, 103
certainty subtype, 10
checking compulsions: behavioral and cognitive features, 30–36; case vignettes, 32–33, 37–40; classification of, 10, 14; comorbidities, 19, 62, 96, 114; demographic data, 33; models and etiology, 34–35; neurobiological correlates, 13; as subtype, 33–34; treatment, 36–41
childhood-onset OCDs, vs. PANDAS, 96–97, 103
chorea: in PANDAS, 98; Sydenham (SC), 95, 96, 98, 100, 101
chunking of motor action, neurobiological correlates, 182–84
citalopram, 209, 215, 248
cladistic approach to classification, 307–8
classification of disorders, 6–7. *See also* subtype(s)
cleaning obsessions. *See* washing and cleaning obsessions
clomipramine: for body dysmorphic disorder, 295–96; for childhood-onset OCDs, 97; for OCD with schizotypy/schizophrenia, 128; for pervasive developmental disorders, 246; for scrupulosity, 159; for trichotillomania, 215, 216
clonazepam (Rivotril), 281
clonidine, 278
CLPS. *See* Collaborative Longitudinal Personality Disorders Study
cognitive behavioral models: of BDD, 294–95; of eating disorders, 194–96; history of, 177–78; of hoarding OCDs, 83; of incompleteness obsessions, 46–48; of postpartum OCD, 145–46; of tic disorders, 280
cognitive behavioral self-help, for eating disorders, 198
cognitive-behavior therapy (CBT): for BDD, 296–97, 299; for checking compulsions, 36–37; for disgust in contamination obsessions, 21, 25–26, 27f; for eating disorders, 196–99; for hypochondriasis, 310–11, 312t, 313, 314; for impulse-control disorders, 231–32, 232; for nonparaphilic sexual disorders, 265–66; for OCPD, 328; for PANDAS, 105; for PDDs, 249–50; for poor insight, 119, 120; for trichotillomania, 211–14, 215–16, 217; for unacceptable thoughts, 12. *See also* exposure and response prevention
cognitive restructuring: for BDD, 296–97; for eating disorders, 199; for hypochondriasis, 312; for OCPD, 328; for postpartum OCD, 147; for trichotillomania, 214; for unacceptable obsessional thoughts, 67–68
cognitive therapy: for eating disorders, 199; for hypochondriasis, 310–11, 312t; for incompleteness obsessions, 49; for OCD with schizotypy/schizophrenia, 129; for OCPD, 328
Collaborative Longitudinal Personality Disorders Study (CLPS), 318, 324
collaborative model building, for hoarding OCDs, 86
competing response (CR) training, 212–13
compulsion(s): common, xi; definition of, 1, 5, 31
concealment: in impulse-control disorders, 233; in kleptomania, 223–24; in postpartum OCD, 146, 149; in trichotillomania, 218. *See also entries under* covert

contamination obsessions: behavioral and cognitive features, 19, 21–23; case vignettes, 24–26, 27f; classification of, 9–12, 14; comorbidities, 96, 98, 140–41, 140t, 190–91, 192; disgust in, 20–21; nature of fear in, 18–21; neurobiological correlates, 13; treatment, 23–27. *See also* washing and cleaning obsessions
control-loss fears, 64, 69–74, 85
coprolalia, 272
core disgust, 20
cortical-striatal-thalmic-cortical (CSTC) circuits, in OCD, 179–85
counting compulsions, 22, 44, 127
covert avoidance, in unacceptable obsessional thoughts, 64
covert desensitization, for nonparaphilic sexual disorders, 266
covert neutralization, 19, 69
creative attentional bias, in hoarding OCDs, 81–82
CR training. *See* competing response (CR) training
CSTC (cortical-striatal-thalmic-cortical) circuits, in OCD, 179–85

Danger Ideation Reduction Therapy (DIRT), 24
decision-making difficulties, in hoarding OCDs, 77, 82
deficit model, of incompleteness obsessions, 48
depression: comorbidities, 142, 146, 159, 201, 262, 263, 297–98; impact on treatment, 40; and insight, 112, 113, 121
desensitization therapy, for nonparaphilic sexual disorders, 266
desipramine, 215, 246
Diagnostic and Statistical Manual of Mental Disorders: DSM-I, 266; DSM-II, 173–74, 266, 317; DSM-III, 109, 173–74, 258, 318t, 324; DSM-IV, xi, 5, 109, 173–74, 188, 222, 258, 260–61, 270, 289, 291, 307, 316, 317, 318t, 324; DSM-V, xii–xiii
DIRT. *See* Danger Ideation Reduction Therapy
disgust: animal reminder disgust, 20; in contamination obsessions, 20–21, 25–26; core disgust, 20; neurobiological correlates, 15; treatment, 21, 24–26
DNAse B, and PANDAS, 99, 105

dopamine antagonists, 178, 244, 278
dopaminergic system: and body dysmorphic disorder, 292; and ICDs, 227–28, 230; and nonparaphilic sexual disorders, 259; and OCDs, 179, 184; and reward processing, 181; and trichotillomania, 209
downward arrow technique, 86, 90, 91

eating disorders: as action chunking disorders, 183; behavioral and cognitive features, 189–91; case vignettes, 190–91; comorbidities, 191–92, 201; in DSM-IV, 188; ego-syntonicity of, 189, 193, 200; medical complications, 200; models and etiology, 193–96, 197f; prevalence, 190; as spectrum disorder, 191–93, 201; treatment, 193, 196–201
ERP. *See* exposure and response prevention
escitalopram, 248
estrogen levels, and postpartum OCD, 144
exposure and response prevention (ERP): for BDD, 296–97; for checking compulsions, 36–40; for contamination obsessions, 23–24; depression and, 40; disadvantages of, 152; for eating disorders, 199–200; for hypochondriasis, 310–11, 312, 312t, 313; for incompleteness obsessions, 48–55, 56; for OCD with schizotypy/schizophrenia, 127–28, 128–29, 130f, 131, 133–35; for ordering and arranging compulsions, 48–55; poor insight and, 117–19, 120; for postpartum OCD, 146, 147–48, 150–51, 151t, 152; for scrupulosity, 163–64, 166–68, 167t, 169; for unacceptable obsessional thoughts, 67, 68–74

FDA. *See* Food and Drug Administration
feather-picking disorder, 209
five-factor model (FFM), 327
fluoxetine: for BDD, 295–96, 297; for eating disorders, 196; for hypochondriasis, 310, 311, 312t, 314; for nonparaphilic sexual disorders, 263, 264; for PDDs, 247; for trichotillomania, 208, 215, 216
fluvoxamine: for contamination obsessions, 23; for hypochondriasis, 310, 312t; for impulse-control disorders, 229; and insight, 116; for OCD with schizotypy/schizophrenia, 131; for PDDs, 246–47; for trichotillomania, 215

Food and Drug Administration (FDA), Pediatric Advisors Subcommittee, 153
freezing (protective ritual), 19

GABA, and PDDs, 244
GABHS pharyngitis, and PANDAS, 99–100
Gamblers Anonymous (GA), 231
gambling. *See* pathological gambling
GAS (group A streptococcus) infection, 103–5. *See also* PANDAS
GAS pharyngitis, 103–4
genetic factors: in impulse-control disorders, 227; in OCDs, 178, 179, 184; in OCPD, 324, 327–28; in PDDs, 241–43; in trichotillomania, 209
glutamate: and PDDs, 244; and reward processing disorders, 182
group A streptococcus (GAS) infection, 103–5. *See also* PANDAS

habit-reversal training (HRT), 212–14, 215–16, 216–17, 279–80
habituation therapy: audio-tape, 69; for disgust in contamination obsessions, 24–26; imaginal desensitization therapy, 24, 232, 266; for nonparaphilic sexual disorders, 266. *See also* exposure and response prevention (ERP)
haloperidol, 117, 246, 278
handwriting deterioration, in PANDAS, 98
harming OCDs, 10–12, 14. *See also* aggressive OCDs
hoarding OCDs: behavioral and cognitive features, 76–79, 81–85; case vignettes, 78–79, 89–91; classification of, 9–12, 14; comorbidities, 80, 224, 320, 323; ego-syntonicity of, 76, 78–79, 80, 84–85, 86, 89–90; models and etiology, 81–85; neurobiological correlates, 80–81, 82; patient motivation to change, 86, 91; as subtype, 1, 79–81; treatment, 12, 23, 85–91
homovanillic acid (HVA), and PDDs, 244
HRT. *See* habit-reversal training
hypersexual disorder, as reward processing disorder, 181–82
hypochondriasis: assessment, 308–10; behavioral and cognitive features, 304–6; case vignettes, 304, 305–6, 309, 311–13; models and etiology, 306–7, 309; and poor insight, 113, 114; prevalence, 306; as spectrum disorder, 180, 307–8; treatment, 310–14, 312*t*

ICDs. *See* impulse-control disorders
ICD-X, 270
imaginal desensitization therapy, 24, 232, 266
imipramine, 276
impulse-control disorders (ICDs): as action chunking disorders, 183; behavioral and cognitive features, 223–25; case vignette, 224–25, 232; comorbidities, 225–26, 262; disorders included in, 222; models and etiology, 227–29; neurobiological correlates, 226–27; patient motivation in, 233; as spectrum disorder, 218, 225–27, 233; treatment, 228, 229–33
incompleteness obsessions: age of onset, 54–55; association with symmetry obsessions, 44; behavioral and cognitive features, 44–46; case vignettes, 45–46, 50–54; ego-syntonicity of, 54–56; models and etiology, 46–48; neurobiological correlates, 48; treatment, 48–58. *See also* ordering and arranging compulsions
information-processing deficits: in hoarding OCDs, 81–82; in OCD with schizotypy/schizophrenia, 129–31, 133–35
informed consent, and effectiveness of treatment, 40, 67. *See also* psychoeducation
insight. *See* poor insight
intermittent explosive disorder: as action chunking disorders, 183; as impulse-control disorder, 222
Internet compulsions, as impulse-control disorder, 222
interpersonal therapy, for eating disorders, 198
intravenous immunoglobulin (IVIG), for PANDAS, 101–2, 105
intrusive thoughts, as normal, 149, 161, 169
IVIG. *See* intravenous immunoglobulin

Janet, Pierre, 45, 317

Keflex (cephalexin), for PANDAS, 99–100
Kinsey, Alfred, 260

kleptomania: as action chunking disorder, 183; behavioral and cognitive features, 223–24; case vignette, 224–25; comorbidities, 227; as impulse-control disorder, 222; models and etiology, 228; treatment, 231, 232. *See also* impulse-control disorders

lithium, for impulse-control disorders, 230

magical thinking, 44. *See also* sympathetic magic
maladaptive cognition, in checking compulsions, 35
MBP (myelin basic protein), 244
memory confidence, lack of, in hoarding OCDs, 82, 84
memory deficits, in OCD with schizotypy/schizophrenia, 129, 130
mental pollution, in contamination obsessions, 22
methylphenidate, 250, 275–76
molecular mimicry, in PANDAS and SC, 100–102
mood disorders: comorbidities, 262; as reward processing disorder, 181
mood stabilizers, for impulse-control disorders, 230
moral-action fusion, 30–33
motivational interviewing, 86
motor action chunking, neurobiological correlates, 182–84
movement disorders, autoimmune antibodies and, 101
M protein, and streptococcal molecular mimicry, 100–102
muscle dysmorphia, 289
myelin basic protein (MBP), and PDDs, 245

nalmefene, 230
naltrexone, 228, 230, 232
National Institute for Health and Clinical Excellence (NICE), 120
nefazodone, 264–65, 312*t*
neurobiological correlates, 13–14, 179–85; BDD, 292–93; checking compulsions, 13; chunking of motor actions, 182–84; contamination obsessions, 13; disgust, 15; hoarding, 80–81, 82; impulse-control disorders, 226–27; incompleteness obsessions, 48; nonparaphilic sexual disorders, 259; ordering and arranging disorders, 48; reward processing disorders, 180–82, 184; scrupulosity, 160–61; spectrum disorders, 179–85; symmetry and ordering OCDs, 13; tic disorders, 276–77; trichotillomania, 209
neuroleptics, 100
NICE. *See* National Institute for Health and Clinical Excellence
nonparaphilic sexual disorders: behavioral and cognitive features, 258–59, 259*t*, 261, 261*t*; case vignette, 262–64; comorbidities, 262; as impulse-control disorder, 222; lack of research on, 257–58; models and etiology, 259–61; neurobiological correlates, 259; prevalence, 261; as spectrum disorder, 259–60; treatment, 264–67
nutritional deprivation, and obsession, 195

obsession(s): common, xi, 5; definition of, 1, 5; nutritional deprivation and, 195
obsessionals, as subtype, 10
obsessive-compulsive disorder. *See* OCD
Obsessive-Compulsive Foundation, 57, 68, 152
obsessive-compulsive personality disorder (OCPD): age of onset, 316–17; behavioral and cognitive features, 316–17, 318*t*, 320–21, 322–23; case vignettes, 321–22; comorbidities, 319, 324–25, 325–26, 328, 329; course, 319–20, 325–26; ego-syntonicity of, 320, 328, 329; models and etiology, 324, 326–28; prevalence, 317–19; as spectrum disorder, 322–26; treatment, 321, 322, 328–29
OCD (obsessive-compulsive disorder): comorbidity with OCPD, 324–25, 325–26, 329; comorbidity with tic disorders, 274; definition of, xi, 109–10, 126; models and etiology, 177–79; vs. PANDAS, 96–97; vs. psychosis, 109–10, 121; related disorders (*see* spectrum disorders)
OCD with schizotypy/schizophrenia: definition of schizotypy, 126–27; information-processing deficits in, 129–31; schizophrenia, 128–29; schizotypy, 126–28; as subtype, 127; treatment, 127, 128–29, 130*f*, 131–35

OCPD. *See* obsessive-compulsive personality disorder
olanzapine, 117, 131, 215
opioid antagonists, 228, 230, 265
ordering and arranging compulsions: age of onset, 54–55; association with symmetry obsessions, 44; behavioral and cognitive features, 44–46; case vignette, 45–46, 50–54; comorbidities, 96, 193; ego-syntonicity of, 54–56; models and etiology, 46–48; neurobiological correlates, 48; treatment, 48–58. *See also* symmetry and ordering OCDs
overestimation of threat: in contamination obsessions, 22, 23*t*; in unacceptable obsessional thoughts, 64, 67
overvalued ideas (OVI). *See* poor insight
oxytocin, 144, 244, 249

PANDAS: age of onset, 96, 97–98, 104; behavioral and cognitive features, 96–100, 97*t*, 98; case vignettes, 99–100; vs. childhood-onset OCD, 96–97, 103; models and etiology, 100–103, 103–5, 106; and OCD onset, 2; treatment, 102–3, 103–5
paraphilias, 258, 258*t*
paroxetine, 215, 229, 310, 312*t*
pathological gambling (PG): behavioral and cognitive features, 223; case vignettes, 224–25; comorbidities, 226, 227, 228; as impulse-control disorder, 222; models and etiology, 227–28; as reward processing disorder, 181–82; treatment, 228–29, 230, 231–32, 233. *See also* impulse-control disorders
patient expectations, impact on treatment, 40
PDDs. *See* pervasive developmental disorders
Pediatric Advisors Subcommittee (FDA), 153
pediatric autoimmune neuropsychiatric disorder associated with streptococcal infection. *See* PANDAS
penicillin, for PANDAS, 103–4, 105
perfectionism: in contamination obsessions, 22, 23*t*; in hoarding OCDs, 77, 91
perinatal depression, and OCD, 154
personality disorders: as action chunking disorders, 183; comorbidity with nonparaphilic sexual disorders, 262; and insight, 112–13; schizotypal personality disorder, 127
pervasive developmental disorders (PDDs): as action chunking disorders, 183; behavioral and cognitive features, 238–41; case vignettes, 240–41, 250; models and etiology, 241–45; as spectrum disorder, 239–40, 251; subtypes, 238; treatment, 244, 245–50
PG. *See* pathological gambling
pharmacotherapy: advantages and disadvantages of, 152–53; for BDD, 295–96; for checking compulsions, 36; for contamination obsessions, 23; for eating disorders, 196, 198; for hypochondriasis, 310–11, 312*t*, 314; for impulse-control disorders, 226, 229–30; for incompleteness obsessions, 49; for nonparaphilic sexual disorders, 264–65; for OCD with schizotypy/schizophrenia, 128; for OCPD, 321, 328; for PDDs, 245–49, 250; poor insight and, 116–17, 122; for postpartum OCD, 147, 152–53; predictability of effectiveness, 12; for tic disorders, 278–79; for trichotillomania, 211, 215
pharyngitis, and PANDAS, 99–100, 103–4
phenelzine, 12
pimozide (Orap), 278, 281, 296
plasma exchange, for PANDAS, 101–2, 105
poor insight: assessment, 110–11; case vignettes, 114; congruence of intellectual and emotional insight in, 122; correlates of, 111–15; definition of, 109; and OCDs vs. psychoses, 109–10, 121; in OCD with schizotypy/schizophrenia, 132–35; and patient motivation, 120; as subtype, 121, 122; and treatment efficacy, 2, 40, 115–21, 122
postpartum depression, postpartum OCD and, 142, 146
postpartum OCD (ppOCD): behavioral and cognitive features, 140–44, 140*t*, 143*t*; case vignette, 143–44, 148–51; ego-dystonicity of, 142–43, 143*t*; models and etiology, 144–46; and postpartum depression, 142, 146; vs. postpartum psychosis, 142–43, 143*t*; treatment, 2, 146–53
postpartum psychosis, vs. postpartum OCD, 142–43, 143*t*

ppOCD. *See* postpartum OCD
progesterone levels, and postpartum OCD, 144
protective rituals: in contamination obsessions, 19; covert, 61–62, 63–64, 114, 141; etiology, 145–46, 161–62; in hypochondriasis, 305; in scrupulosity, 159–60; subtype identification and, 11–12; in unacceptable obsessional thoughts, 61–62, 63–64. *See also* exposure and response prevention (ERP)
psychodynamic therapy, 265, 328
psychoeducation: for body dysmorphic disorder, 296; for checking compulsions, 38; for eating disorders, 198, 200; for hypochondriasis, 310–11, 312t, 313–14; for incompleteness obsession, 55; for nonparaphilic sexual disorders, 266; for OCD with poor insight, 120; for OCD with schizotypy/schizophrenia, 129; for postpartum OCD, 147, 149; for scrupulosity, 163–64; for unacceptable obsessional thoughts, 67
psychogenic excoriation (skin picking), 222, 226, 288, 291
psychosis, vs. OCD, 109–10, 121
pure obsessions, as subtype, 10, 14, 63
pyromania, as impulse-control disorder, 222

relabeling and reattribution, 55
relaxation training, for trichotillomania, 214
religion: benefits of, 156; vs. pathological practices, 164, 168
religious OCDs. *See* scrupulosity
repugnant obsessions. *See* unacceptable obsessional thoughts
responsibility overestimation, 22, 23t, 64, 84–85, 113, 114
reward processing disorders, OCDs and spectrum disorders as, 180–82, 184
risperidol, 117
risperidone, 120, 131, 248–49, 250, 278
ritual(s). *See* protective rituals
ritual interference, 57

safety behaviors, in hypochondriasis, 305
SC. *See* Sydenham chorea
schizoeffective disorder, comorbidities, 259

schizophrenia: relation to schizotypy, 127. *See also* OCD with schizotypy/schizophrenia
schizotypal personality disorder (SPD), 127
schizotypy: definition of, 126–27; measures of, 127; vs. schizophrenia, 127. *See also* OCD with schizotypy/schizophrenia
scrupulosity (religious OCDs): behavioral and cognitive features, 157–59, 169; case vignettes, 158–59, 165–68; classification of, 10, 14; models and etiology, 160–63; neurobiological correlates, 160–61; vs. normal religious practice, 68, 164, 168; and poor insight, 113; prevalence among OCD patients, 160; schizotypy comorbidity, 127; self-reporting instruments, 157; as subtype, 159–60; treatment, 12, 68, 163–70; unique challenges of, 2
selective serotonin reuptake inhibitors (SSRIs): for childhood-onset OCDs, 97; for hypochondriasis, 310–11; for nonparaphilic sexual disorders, 260, 264–65; for OCPD, 328; for PANDAS, 100, 105; for PDDs, 246–48, 250; for trichotillomania, 209, 211, 215
self-injury disorders, as action chunking disorders, 183
self-monitoring: in body dysmorphic disorder, 296; in hypochondriasis, 311–12; in incompleteness obsession, 51–52, 55–56; in unacceptable obsessional thoughts, 12, 66–74, 71
sense of imperfection, 9. *See also* incompleteness obsessions
serotonergic medications, 12, 146, 163
serotonergic system: and impulse control disorders, 183; and OCDs, 144, 160–61, 179, 182–84, 183, 185; and PDDs, 242–44; and trichotillomania, 209
serotonin reuptake inhibitors (SRIs): for BDD, 180, 291–92, 292, 295–96; for contamination obsessions, 23; discontinuation of, 148; for eating disorders, 198; for impulse-control disorders, 226, 229; for incompleteness obsessions, 49; insight and, 116, 120; for OCD with schizotypy/schizophrenia, 131; for OCPD, 321; for PDDs, 245; and perinatal syndromes, 153; for postpartum OCD, 148; for trichotillomania, 207. *See also* selective serotonin reuptake inhibitors

sertraline, 116, 163, 247, 250, 264
sex addiction. *See* nonparaphilic sexual disorders
Sex Addicts Anonymous, 266
sexual OCDs: classification of, 10, 14; comorbidities, 160; treatment, 12, 66–67. *See also* nonparaphilic sexual disorders; unacceptable obsessional thoughts
Shopaholics Anonymous, 231
Shoplifters Anonymous, 231
shopping compulsions: as action chunking disorders, 183; behavioral and cognitive features, 224; case vignette, 224–25; comorbidities, 226, 227; as impulse-control disorder, 222; models, 228; treatment, 228, 229, 231, 232. *See also* impulse-control disorders
similarity component of sympathetic magic, 19–20
skin picking. *See* psychogenic excoriation
social support, 152, 213–14
somatic obsessions, 113, 114, 160
SPD. *See* schizotypal personality disorder
spectrum disorders: as action chunking disorders, 182–84; empirical basis for, 177–85; neurobiological correlates and, 179–85; as reward processing disorders, 180–82, 184; vs. subtypes, xii; usefulness of concept, xi, 173–75. *See also specific disorders*
SSRIs. *See* selective serotonin reuptake inhibitors
stereotypic disorders, as reward processing disorder, 181–82
stimulus control, for trichotillomania, 211–12, 216–17, 217
Streptococcus pyogenes, 95–96. *See also* PANDAS
stress, and OCDs, 184, 311, 312*t*, 313
striatum, in OCDs and spectrum disorders, 181–85
substance abuse disorders: comorbidities, 201, 227, 259, 262, 290; as reward processing disorder, 181
subtype(s): definition issues, xiii; identification of, 6–12, 14; neurobiological correlates, 13–14; overview of, 1; vs. spectrum disorders, xii; usefullness of concept, xi, 1–2, 3, 6, 12, 33–34, 49
suicidal ideation, in body dysmorphic disorder, 297–98, 299–300
support groups, 57
Sydenham chorea (SC), 95, 96, 98, 100, 101
symmetry and ordering OCDs: classification of,

9–12, 14; in eating disorders, 193; neurobiological correlates, 13; treatment, 12. *See also* ordering and arranging compulsions
sympathetic magic, 19–20

taxonomy: history of, 177–79; overview of, 173–75
thought-action fusion: in Christian tradition, 162–63; in contamination obsessions, 22, 23*t*, 26; in eating disorders, 195; treatment, 149–50; in unacceptable obsessional thoughts, 64, 68, 69
thought-shape fusion, 195, 199
thought suppression, 71
tic disorders: association with PANDAS, 96–97, 97*t*, 103–6; case vignettes, 275–76, 280–82, 281*f*, 282*f*; comorbidities, 274–75; definition of, 270; models and etiology, 100–101, 276–78; natural history and prevalence, 275; neurobiological correlates, 276–77; as spectrum disorder, 283–84; treatment, 102, 272, 275–76, 278–82, 281–82, 281*f*, 282*f*; types and subtypes, 270–72, 271*t*, 273*t*. *See also* Tourette syndrome
topiramate (Topamax), 265, 281
Tourette syndrome: association with PANDAS, 96, 99–100; behavioral and cognitive features, 270–72, 271*t*; case vignettes, 280–81, 281*f*; comorbidities, 274–75, 280–81, 328; coprolalia in, 272; as reward processing disorder, 181; as spectrum disorder, xi, 9, 32, 178, 283–84; treatment, 275–76, 278–79. *See also* tic disorders
transparency, and efficacy of treatment, 40, 67
trauma, and OCDs, 184
treatment. *See* pharmacotherapy; *specific disorders*
treatment planning, subtypes and, 1–2, 3, 12, 33–34, 49
trichotillomania (TTM): behavioral and cognitive features, 205–7; case vignettes, 208, 216–17, 280–81, 281*f*; comorbidities, 217, 226, 280–81; focused, 210–11, 217; as impulse-control disorder, 222; medical complications, 206; models and etiology, 208–11; neurobiological correlates, 209; nonfocused (automatic), 210, 217; prevalence, 205–6; as reward processing disorder, 181–82; as spectrum disorder, xi, 9, 32, 205, 207; treatment, 207, 208, 209, 211–18, 228
tricyclic antidepressants, 100, 211, 215, 246
TTM. *See* trichotillomania
twelve-step programs, for sexual disorders, 266

unacceptable obsessional thoughts: behavioral and cognitive features, 61–63, 64–66; case vignette, 62–63, 70–74; models and etiology, 63–64; in postpartum OCD, 140–41, 148–51; as subtype, 11–12, 63; treatment, 12, 66–74
uncertainty intolerance, 23*t*, 64, 72–73
undoing (protective ritual), 19
urinary hygiene rituals, in PANDAS, 98

ventral cortical-striatal-thalmic-cortical (CSTC) circuits, in OCD, 179–85
ventral striatum, and reward processing, 181

washing and cleaning obsessions: characteristics of, 22; comorbidities, 96, 98, 114, 131–35, 140–41, 140*t*, 160, 191, 192; purpose of, 18–19; treatment, 23–24. *See also* contamination obsessions